After Caliban

THE VISUAL ARTS OF AFRICA AND ITS DIASPORAS

A SERIES EDITED BY KELLIE JONES & STEVEN NELSON

ERICA MOIAH JAMES

After Caliban

Caribbean Art in a Global Imaginary

DUKE UNIVERSITY PRESS

Durham and London

2025

Printed in the United States of America on acid-free paper ∞
Project Editor: Liz Smith
Designed by Matthew Tauch
Typeset in Garamond Premier Pro and Real Head Pro
by Westchester Publishing Services

Library of Congress Cataloging-in-Publication Data
Names: James, Erica Moiah, author.
Title: After Caliban : Caribbean art in a global imaginary / Erica Moiah James.
Description: Durham : Duke University Press, 2025. | Series: The visual arts of Africa and its diasporas | Includes bibliographical references and index.
Identifiers: LCCN 2025004838 (print)
LCCN 2025004839 (ebook)
ISBN 9781478032137 (paperback)
ISBN 9781478028871 (hardcover)
ISBN 9781478061069 (ebook)
Subjects: LCSH: Arts, Caribbean—20th century. | Arts, Caribbean—21st century. | Postcolonialism and the arts—Caribbean Area. | Arts and globalization—Caribbean Area.
Classification: LCC NX523 .J36 2025 (print) | LCC NX523 (ebook) | DDC 709.729—dc23/eng/20250220
LC record available at https://lccn.loc.gov/2025004838
LC ebook record available at https://lccn.loc.gov/2025004839

Cover art: Janine Antoni, *Lick and Lather*, 1993 (detail). One licked-chocolate self-portrait bust on pedestal. © Janine Antoni. Courtesy of the artist and Luhring Augustine, New York. Photo by the author.

For my grandfather

EDDINGTON BURROWS

CONTENTS

ix *Acknowledgments*

1 INTRODUCTION "Wat Wrong wit Dis Place?"

37 CHAPTER ONE From Behind God's Back: Janine Antoni's Embodied Histories

77 CHAPTER TWO Meeting in the Upper Room: Belkis Ayón's *La cena*, 1988–1993

121 CHAPTER THREE Historical Drag: Genre, Violence, and History in Edouard Duval-Carrié's *Mardigras at Fort Dimanche*, 1992

163 CHAPTER FOUR The Caribbean Does Not Exist: Maurizio Cattelan's 6th Caribbean Biennial, 1999

205 CONCLUSION "Wrong Way" Lenny, Tempests, and Other Détournements

223 *Notes*

259 *Bibliography*

281 *Index*

ACKNOWLEDGMENTS

....

I GIVE THANKS,

To the artists, academics, writers, curators, and collectors whose work, conversations, and critiques were important in the formation and development of this project over the many years it took shape: Christopher Cozier, Edouard Duval Carrié, Marc Latamie, Janine Antoni, Joy Gregory, Joscelyn Gardner, Nari Ward, Tavares Strachan, Tomas Esson, Blue Curry, Ricardo Brey, Ebony G. Patterson, Graham Fagen, Mira Schor, the late John Beadle, Antonius Roberts, Tyrone Ferguson, Maxwell Taylor, the late Brent Malone, Dave Smith, Kendal Hanna, Allan Wallace, Ian Gregory Strachan, Eric Williams, Didier William, Jolyon Smith, Clive Stuart, Dawn Davies, the late Jackson Burnside, and the late Belkis Ayón.

I GIVE THANKS,

To the many institutions, private and public archives, and individual researchers and collectors who provided access and worked with me to realize this text: The National Archives of The Bahamas, National Gallery Jamaica, National Library of Jamaica, Institute of Jamaica, Minneapolis Institute of Art, Racine Art Museum, Bass Art Museum, Archives of the *Jamaica Gleaner*, Institute of Contemporary Art Miami, Beinecke Library–Yale University, Humanities Center at the University of Miami, Cuban Heritage Collection at the University of Miami, the Oakley Center for the Humanities and Social Sciences at Williams College, the Clark Art Institute, Visual Identities Art and Design at the University of Johannesburg, the late Alex and Carole Rosenberg, the estate of Belkis Ayón, the estate of Ronald Moody, Colin McGeehan, Adam King and Signe Prøis, Lilianne Lugo Herrera, Yolanda Martinez San Miguel and Lisa Rivero, and Penelope Nottage.

To my editor Rachel Rosekind, who loves words as much as I do but is far better at marshaling that love.

I GIVE THANKS,

To my doctoral mentor, Richard J. Powell, and C. T. Woods-Powell—honorable, brilliant, and kind people. I work every day to earn the faith they have in me.

To the founding board and staff of the National Art Gallery of The Bahamas, especially the late Dr. Gail Saunders and the late Dr. Petrine Archer-Straw, for trusting me with the establishment of that institution and supporting my vision for it and the work. And to Ms. Louanne Morris, who was there from the beginning and protected me from more things than I will ever know or need to know.

I GIVE THANKS,

To my mentors, teachers, colleagues, graduate students, and friends at Vassar College, the University of Chicago, Duke University, the John Hope Franklin Center at Duke, Washington University in St. Louis, Yale University, University of The Bahamas, ICA (Institute of Contemporary Art) Miami, Museum of Contemporary Art North Miami, Dean Leonidas Bachas and my colleagues in the School of Arts and Sciences and Department of Art and Art History at the University of Miami.

To the Small Axe Project Team: David Scott, Wayne Modest, Jerry Philogene, Juliet Ali, and Vanessa Perez.

I GIVE THANKS.

I often say that I have the very best friends in the world. Some I have known my entire life, and others are more recent. But in their own way, each has given me so much. I took so long to finish this book that a few of my older friends are no longer here, but I feel their joy in this moment. Thank you to Suzette Knowles Parker, Dionne Benjamin-Smith, Bernadette Butler, Dionne Joseph-Scott, Don Ashford Stubbs, Virginia Hopson, Mora Beauchamp-Byrd, Patricia J. Saunders, Paul Rodgers, Christian Campbell, Anthony Jervis, Thomas Mtumwa Cleare, Richard Gray, Lawrence Bascom, and the late Gloria Wilson and Robert Eliot Johnson.

I GIVE THANKS,

To my small but mighty "Hanna, Heastie, Tynes" clan and James and King families, my aunts, uncles, and cousins and my precious sisters Evadnie and Keshia, and their children, my nephews Rohan, Myles, Noah, and August.

To my late father, Carmi Beriah "C.B." James, who helped me to understand the value of laughter, forgiveness, and joy in others.

To my beautiful mother—Elverna Burrows-James. Mummy is a woman who values life more than anyone I know and is a fierce mama bear with her love. As an octogenarian, she would still enter a fistfight to defend me, and no one trusts me more. Who can ever fully articulate the hope of a mother for her children? My joy, my achievements, all belong to my mother.

I GIVE THANKS.

Through the years I have lived with an amazing group of dachshunds and one cocker spaniel, the indomitable Winnie. Where would I be without the late Wallace "Wally" Thurman, Winnie and Laila, Biggie Smalls, and Georgia? They greeted me each day with such gusto that it always felt I must have done something good to deserve their joy. Many evenings they kept me company and protected me as I wrote or gardened away my stress deep into the night. On those beautiful evenings they never left my side.

I GIVE THANKS.

To my neighborhood. A thousand lives. A million stories. An Epic. Seventh Street. The "Black" Grove.

To Ken Wissoker, Kate Mullen, Liz Smith, Steven Baker, the awesome series editors Kellie Jones and Steven Nelson, and the entire Duke University Press team for their patience, precision, and care.

And finally, to the good Lord, I give thanks.

This book is dedicated to my grandfather, Eddington "Eddie" Burrows, the best person I have ever known.

INTRODUCTION

"Wat Wrong wit Dis Place?"

JOHN LAHR: Most people of color who come to America [from the Caribbean] and encounter it, especially in the '50s, didn't have an opportunity to tell their stories to too many people, necessarily, or to many people that were listening. And the thing that is so extraordinary to me is that somehow you made that transition almost *effortlessly*.

GEOFFREY HOLDER: I walk through doors.

JOHN LAHR: Now, why, what do you attribute that to?

GEOFFREY HOLDER: I walk through doors.

If I am not wanted in a place. There is somethin' wrong with de place, not me.

GEOFFREY L. HOLDER IN CONVERSATION WITH JOHN LAHR

Several years ago, I was invited to speak on a panel accompanying an exhibition of new work by the Martinican-born artist Marc Latamie. In the months leading up to the event, I had several discussions with the organizers about my contribution. Familiar with Latamie's oeuvre and fascinated, yet deeply troubled, by the ways the trope of Shakespeare's Caliban had been historically applied to the Caribbean, I insisted that the conversation neither begin with nor be framed by this discursive boundary and relational construct.[1]

These aspirations may well have been logistically and conceptually unachievable in the setting.[2] Martinican poet, writer, and politician Aimé Césaire's final play, *A Tempest* (1969), attempts to decolonize Shakespeare's Caliban and, through a retelling of his story as allegory, the Caribbean itself. Both the exhibition and my contribution centered on a Martinican artist whose oeuvre portrays and promotes similar decolonizing aspirations. The connection seemed intuitive and obvious.

However, at the time, Césaire's *A Tempest* was not widely known or discussed beyond the academy. Although, as I will argue, it is a seminal intervention in the decolonial process, I did not think it would provide the most generative framing for Latamie's work in a public setting, without substantial buttressing. More than four hundred years after Caliban's first appearance in Shakespeare's *The Tempest* (1611), it was his relationship to Prospero in the 1611 text that still dominated popular characterizations of the enduring colonizer-colonized connection in the Caribbean—now borne by Caliban's so-called children. This anachronistic and infantilizing graft endures as allegory despite its patent failure to account for the complexities of the contemporary landscape. As conceptual and discursive architecture, it seals the Caribbean within a neocolonial cul-de-sac, rendering a public conversation focused on Latamie's decolonizing artwork nearly impossible.[3]

Despite my request, when the panel convened that early summer evening, the moderator opened by declaring Latamie a "child of Caliban." A quick read of the room suggested that the reference, regardless of its source, did not resonate with those gathered. As the night wore on, I became more certain of the need to reorient the Caribbean contemporary art conversation away from this trope. When my turn came, I set aside Caliban and instead asked the audience to consider Latamie's installation in relation to the practices of other contemporary global Caribbean artists. I cited Ebony G. Patterson, whose art, rooted in the Jamaican experience, confidently affirms her subject's humanity amid postcolonial challenges. I discussed Magdalena Campos Pons, who, like Latamie, centers local and personal memories as history through performance, sculpture, and installation. Finally, I positioned Latamie's work in conversation with Blue Curry's playful yet trenchant interventions in Caribbean consumerism, tourism, and iconography. I hoped that my approach would open new horizons to explore Latamie's art and its relational webs and influence. Instead it became clear that once Caliban entered the room, the dimensions of Latamie's production, its engagement with contemporary practices, the signifying possibilities of absinthe and the story of Lumina Sophie—fundamental elements of the exhibition that initiated the gathering and contextualized its decolonizing work—would be largely subsumed by the weight of this fictional-historical trope. It remains one of the most frustrating public panels I have ever participated in.

Long before the exhibition opened, Marc Latamie's work had departed from and exceeded the metaphorical limits of Shakespeare's Caliban. The panel affirmed that the critical discourse around it had not kept pace. The event encouraged me to rethink Latamie's position as a *global Caribbean artist* and his oeuvre's relationship with Césaire's reimagination of this figure. By "global Caribbean artist," I refer to artists that may or may not have been born in the Caribbean or be of Caribbean descent, and who engage the Caribbean as a conceptual point of departure or constitutive idea in their work. These artists practice around the world, including the Caribbean. Their work is not wholly directed to the Caribbean but is prismatic in character, meaning that its critical capacity permits participation in multiple conversations simultaneously. Latamie's work embodies this dynamic. Yet, if a conceptual connection between him and Césaire, channeled through a revision of Shakespeare's Caliban, existed, why had no one teased out the linkages beyond their common place of birth? If both were engaged in ongoing intergenerational decolonial action in the aesthetic realm, what was the shared character of their intervention? Might it be possible to see Césaire's *A Tempest* as precedent for the work of global Caribbean artists like Latamie in the 1990s? And, if so, how might one render the contours of an emergent global Caribbean art history through this work?

This book considers these questions and offers a response. It positions Césaire's *A Tempest* as a decolonizing work of art in concept, form, and content; a work that heralds the decolonial labor of global Caribbean art in the 1990s. Like many artists of his generation, Latamie reimagines history to enact a Derridean différance in relation to the theoretical arrangements of Césaire's Caliban and the colonial theater in which he is cast. My employment of différance in this context aligns with that of Stuart Hall, who describes it as "a marker which sets up a disturbance in our settled understanding or translation of the word/concept [or work of art, setting it] in motion to new meanings without erasing the *trace* of its other meanings."[4] While Latamie's art accounts for Caliban's discursive trace in ways aligned with Césaire's Caliban, I argue that it also breaks free of its confines through the language of contemporary art to become what Césaire's decolonial imagination conjured.

Akin to Geoffrey Holder's declaration in this introduction's epigraph, this book posits that these global artists rejected the geographical and conceptual marginalization of their work, but doing so was by no means an effortless enterprise. The 1990s marked an abyss for critical approaches to Caribbean art. The work of artists tied to places outside metropoles was ensnared in temporally delimited and delimiting colonial models intended to elide and obfuscate its critical heft. Approaches to art from these so-called margins presented a cognitive and discursive feedback loop that reinforced and reinscribed paradigms of power tied to notions of authenticity and nation that were predicated by the colonialist project, even as the authority of art history's disciplinary narrative was increasingly called into question.

This book reimagines this work's critical valence in relation to the transformative landscape of global art histories and curatorial practices in the 1990s. It uncovers its decolonizing work and uplifts global Caribbean artists' assertion of their right to occupy, exist, and move freely within the art world during this period. Their work points toward a critical rethinking, a political and aesthetic *dechoukaj*,[5] of this atrophied order; a reworlding of the art worlds they chose to occupy.

To repurpose a metaphor exceptionally deployed by Peter Linebaugh and Marcus Rediker toward decidedly different ends, colonialism does not have a single face.[6] As the consort of early capitalism, it too is a "many-headed hydra" set loose on the world with a unified goal of extraction, power, and control. In prioritizing the work of artists emerging in this decade, this book pointedly examines the colonialist underpinnings of the discipline of art history and explores how Caribbean artists, intimate with its apparatus, unmoored its multivalent foundations. All artists discussed in this book confront history and historicization in their work differently. They employ multiple mediums and approaches and draw on and in various sociopolitical conditions, both inside and outside the geographic Caribbean as subject. Following Césaire, they practice what I describe as *autohistoriography*, the process by which formerly colonized people reengage and reauthor official history rendered from a colonial perspective. In rewriting and reimagining these narratives, they become "historical actors," agents of decolonization within postcoloniality, or what David

Scott terms the "political-theoretical" project centrally concerned with the "decolonization of representation; the decolonization of the West's theory of the non-West."[7] In this critical arena, there are no masters or margins. Like Césaire, like Holder, global Caribbean artists who emerged in the 1990s recognized thresholds, then pushed past and stepped beyond them toward new horizons.

After Caliban: Caribbean Art in the Global Imaginary thus argues that in *A Tempest* Aimé Césaire breaks apart the certainty of colonial relationships entombed in Shakespeare's play through the practice of autohistoriography and the reimagination of form. In the process he models the work of Caribbean artists wherever they are in the world in taking similar control over narratives, histories, and conditions that seek to delimit their creative imagination and work. The book posits that this generation of artists, whether consciously aware of it or not, did just that, in ways specific to their practices. Through the work of Marc Latamie, Janine Antoni, Belkis Ayón, Edouard Duval-Carrié, Christopher Cozier, and the Italian-born Maurizio Cattelan, it offers an expansive reading of what *Caribbean* and specifically what being an artist in the "global Caribbean" came to mean, revealing ways these and countless artists like them navigated various problem spaces to avoid and/or overcome the marginalization of their work as "Caribbean" at the time.

In 1999 Cattelan declared that the Caribbean did not exist in the art world. This book pushes against that claim to write a new art history of this period; one that narrates beyond the limits of the discourse on this work during the time it was created. It offers a dense critical reengagement with this art and maps how, through their oeuvres, and where possible by exercising control over the discourse around their work, these artists and many others like them created art that engaged multiple histories simultaneously to craft decolonial autohistoriographies through aesthetics. In process the art that grounds this book refuses the lens of marginalization; it navigates difficult critical terrains, crafts new forms in order to make transformative demands of local and global art histories, to rise to the upper echelons of regard in contemporary art in ways Césaire would recognize and applaud.

This introduction maps this archive and argument first by carefully assessing Aimé Césaire's work and positioning it within the social and political terrain in which *A Tempest* emerged, to illuminate the critical strategies his reimagination of Caliban in *A Tempest* performs. It then returns to the work of Latamie, using Césaire's approach as a model. This methodology repeats in each chapter of the book, architecting a text, which like *A Tempest*, becomes decolonial in process and form.

DECOLONIZING CALIBAN

What do I mean when I propose that as a work of art Césaire's *A Tempest* performs the decolonization of the West's theory of the non-West, and then claim that contemporary artists reenact this process through their work again and again?

Peter Hulme has described Shakespeare's Caliban as "a compromised formation," a character that "can exist only within discourse."[8] Conceptually confined and "resistant to visualization," Caliban has served as a perennially versatile metaphor for extending the language of Caribbean abjection.[9] He is human-like but not human—the colonizers' foil—and is a summation of their "dishonest equation" whereby self-proclaimed altruism defined their artillery and ideology in the battle of civilization against savagery.[10]

Exactly thirty years after his long-form poem *Cahier d'un Retour au Pays Natal: Return to My Native Land* (1939), Césaire published his revision of Shakespeare's *The Tempest*, the drama *A Tempest*. His shift in genre was intentional. In a series of conversations with Françoise Vergès toward the end of his life, Césaire expressed his persistent desire to reach people through his work.[11] He initially turned to poetry, believing it most amenable to public discourse. But, beginning in the 1940s, he redirected his public voice first to historical biography (*Toussaint Louverture*, 1960) then to the theater. In his dramatic works, Césaire grappled with the possibilities of postcolonial nationhood and the prospect of freedom. In the process, he publicly exhibited an increasingly rare intellectual vulnerability and transparency. This important trajectory adds both dimension and clarity to his decolonization of Caliban, contextualizing *A Tempest* as decolonial act and artwork within the movements of its time and intertwining with the ways Caribbean art and art history move beyond political boundaries toward a philosophy of ideas grounded in history.

By the time *A Tempest* was published in 1969, Césaire's position on sovereignty in the postcolonial world was far more nuanced than when he began serving as mayor of Fort-de-France and a member of the French Assembly, drafting legislation favoring department status for all French colonies (1946). Although some view his opposition to independence as a misfire by an otherwise brilliant mind, to me, it represents a courageous *détournement*. When theory converged with reality, Césaire met the moment by changing course, in contravention to the global Pan-African momentum for independence. As Vergès noted, Césaire's decision has often been framed around the binary of assimilation (department status) versus autonomy (independence). But I posit that this reductive scaffolding effaces the complexities of Césaire's cognition and the contemporary political landscape. In conversation with Vergès, Césaire reflected on his decision to decouple political independence and autonomy and challenge the equation of independence with freedom: "On one end you have assimilation; on the other, independence. If you bring them together, you go beyond both to reach another position, which is broader, more humane, and more in line with our goals. I am against assimilation. . . . I'm for independence. . . . My own position is neither pro-independence nor pro-assimilation, but pro-autonomy, which means preserving our uniqueness, our own institutional practices, our own ideals, all while belonging to a greater whole."[12] Sixty years on, the ongoing opposition to his stance still baffled him.[13] He firmly believed that given the full context, he had made the right, albeit imperfect, decision. Further, while Césaire led the action and shaped its rationale, it's worth remembering that a majority in the French Caribbean Islands agreed to proceed alongside him.

In retrospect, Césaire's support of department status amid the global Pan-African independence movement reflected core beliefs and observations that inform *A Tempest* and, through it, this book. He was largely unmoved by rhetoric, ideology, or romantic notions of liberation. A pragmatic Marxist with an ongoing disdain for *békés* and the Black petit bourgeois, whom he saw as békés' foot soldiers,[14] Césaire sought a path forward toward freedom. He did not associate that path with independence. His research and experiences had revealed the limits of that connection in ways that deeply impacted his thinking.

Césaire studied the period's liberation movements and carefully tracked the social, cultural, economic, and political trajectories of former colonial nations. He was particularly interested in Black postindependence leadership and its dynamics in Haiti and the Congo, as exemplified in the historical biography *Toussaint Louverture*; the plays *La Tragédie du Roi Christophe* (The Tragedy of King Christophe, 1963) and *Une Saison au Congo* (A Season in the Congo, 1966); and later *A Tempest*. His position toward Haiti and Haitian leadership after the revolution gained nuance during an extended stay there in the 1940s.

Suzanne and Aimé Césaire arrived in Haiti in May 1944.[15] Although Suzanne returned to Martinique in October to care for their children, Aimé stayed through December of that year. It was a troubling visit for someone who had long admired, studied, and sought to understand the Haitian Revolution. In a letter to the French anthropologist Henry Seyrig while there, Césaire expressed profound disappointment, lamenting that he "suffered from his interactions with 'la petite bourgeoisie de couleur (the lower-middle class mulattoes),'" whom he found "mediocre and subject to prejudice." Césaire had long grappled with how to bridge the divide between the intelligentsia and everyday citizens and viewed ordinary Haitians as a "good and unfortunate people."[16] He observed that the Haitian Revolution's success had hinged on the mulatto class's unification with enslaved Africans under Louverture's leadership, representing a quintessential illustration of what is possible when oppressed people, regardless of color and class, coalesce under the banner of a shared vision. Césaire refused to criticize Louverture for walking into his betrayal or to dismiss Henri Christophe as a mimic of French royalty, as was and still is common. Rather, he leapfrogged over superficial and expedient misreadings to recognize Louverture's tactical genius and Christophe as "a deep thinker who suffered real anguish."[17]

Césaire's time in Haiti made clear to him that Toussaint, Jean-Jacques Dessalines, and Christophe had confronted overwhelming obstacles; and that the revolutionary alliance that delivered success did not and could not last, since the problems of Haiti before revolution—divisions based on race and class—did not magically disappear after it ended. The mulatto class eventually took power and "never ceded" it. While he greatly admired the achievements of its revolution, Haiti exemplified for Césaire the difficulties of building nations in formerly colonized spaces. Years later, he reflected: "In Haiti I saw above all else what shouldn't be done! A country that had supposedly won freedom, won independence, and which I saw more miserable than Martinique, a French colony!" In Haiti, intellectuals cut themselves off from the people. "It was tragic, and Martinique could have gone in the same direction."[18]

Césaire's disappointment was palpable. The cautionary tale of Haiti, coupled with the power of Martinique's békés, whom he regarded in the same vein as Haiti's wealthy white and mulatto class, clearly influenced his support for departmental status. His decision was likewise informed by a lifelong allegiance to Marxism, if not communism. To choose independence from France in 1946 meant that nothing would stand in the way of the economically dominant béké class gaining even more power on the island, leaving the Black majority defenseless against their exploitation. For Césaire, such a predicament was untenable.

Césaire's research and creative focus on formerly colonized, predominantly Black and mixed-race societies in the wake of revolution or independence are notable. I am not convinced he believed a true postcolonial condition had been realized by the late 1960s. Rather, his execution of *A Tempest* frames up a door for a new generation to open on the path to such an achievement. Césaire understood colonialism and the need to decolonize, but in his purview, independence initiated neocolonial forces rather than a postcolonial condition; neocolonialism was, he declared, not "the abolition of the colonial world, . . . only its reorganization."[19] Independence was neither a utopia nor an entrée to a postcolonial future; at best it was measured freedom, if such a thing existed. For Césaire, freedom encompassed the totality of what it means to be human—the political, economic, social, historical, and cultural. It could not be apportioned. This fullness of vision registers in his reimagination of Caliban as both human and historical actor within neocolonial contexts.

Césaire's position toward sovereignty and postcolonial nationhood was also influenced by pragmatic and moral factors. He did not regard existing local institutions in colonialized places like Martinique as robust enough to hold békés and those bound to them accountable. Békés controlled the plantation economy and would continue to do so. Only France had legal structures in place to delimit the békés and protect the working class. Raising six children with his wife on an island with no major resources or industry, Césaire was also no doubt sensitive to the practical needs of Martinicans. Department status meant that they would be French, and to be French meant that they were entitled to the same benefits as French citizens—equal pay for work, equal benefits.[20] Though entitlement was no guarantee, theoretically, the position conferred value.

Césaire's decision also stemmed from his position on slavery and the prospect of reparations, which has been viewed with increasing scrutiny given the current reparations movement in the Caribbean, led in part by Sir Hilary Beckles. Césaire deemed slavery "irreparable." In response, Vergès asked him whether it was possible in a capitalist society to pay one's way out of genocide and dehumanizing violence and whether one can quantify the "innumerable consequences [of slavery] into a tidy sum." Césaire did not waver in his response:

> For me no act can put an end to it. It's irreparable. It's done. It's history. I can't do anything about it. . . . I know the Western world too well: "All right dear friend, how much? I'll give you half of that to pay off the slave trade. Okay? It's a deal!" Then it's over: they repaired the matter. But for me it's utterly irreparable. I don't really like the term "reparation." It implies that repairing the matter is possible. The West has to do something, it has to provide aid to countries as they develop, help them thrive. It owes us this aid, but I don't believe a simple check can pay for reparations. It's a question of aid, not a contract. It's purely moral.[21]

These important considerations informed Césaire's political and creative articulations. And as Jackqueline Frost and Jorge E. Lefevre Tavárez propose, Césaire's dramatic work explores answers to these questions of "revolutionary social transformation" in postindependent Black societies not as "tales of tragically flawed leaders and destined defeats" but as "elaborations of a notion of the tragic [in] . . . the long struggle for sovereignty [in the Caribbean]."[22] He wanted political independence but not without genuine autonomy. Within the system of colonialism and neocolonialism he observed, independence was doomed to severe compromise, if not failure; it could not sufficiently address the decolonization of economies, class, culture, and histories.

In Shakespeare's *The Tempest*, the colonizers eventually leave the island. Caliban's future is rendered uncertain, though presumably he and his people regain control. But in Césaire's redux the possibility of sovereignty and freedom through a postcolonial nation-state is foreclosed. Drawing on Yarimar Bonilla's work on sovereignty in the context of the French Caribbean and Gary Wilder's exploration of the relationship between Négritude and decolonization, or what Wilder describes as the possibility of a "transcontinental political association" over state sovereignty,[23] I argue that the concluding scenes of *A Tempest* reflect Césaire's belief that postcolonial sovereignty within the container of the nation-state was possible but improbable in the Caribbean. Like Wilder, I posit that through his careful study of Black liberation struggles in the wake of the Pan-Africanist independence movement—made evident in the first two of his three plays—Césaire "recognized that colonial emancipation posed a genuine problem whose institutional solution was not self-evident."[24] Following Frost and Tavárez, I do not see this as a tragic position in the literal sense but instead recognize its "potential instead of implausibility."[25] In my view—and pace Wilder—for Césaire "a national state was only one of *many possible* frameworks within which self-determination could be exercised. He saw no necessary relationship between colonial emancipation and national liberation."[26] In other words, statehood, a perceived portal into postcoloniality within the Pan-African movement, was not a precondition of freedom. *A Tempest* suggests that Césaire disaggregated nationhood and freedom, choosing to fight for the latter on the individual and collective level of psychology and in the realm of art and culture.

Césaire's use of the theatrical arts as a decolonizing tool was not his alone; it is vital that we understand the ways it is tethered to the work and ethos of his wife, Suzanne. Kara M. Rabbitt's work has been illuminating in this regard. I propose that Suzanne's "almost revolutionary" decision to rewrite and produce Lafcadio Hearn's novel *Youma: The Story of a West Indian Slave* as the play *Aurore de la Liberté* (*The Dawn of Liberty*) in a "popular" rather than "professional" production in 1952 more than likely influenced her husband's transition from poetry and prose to plays, providing a template for his Shakespearean recasting seventeen years later.[27] The public discursive intention of Suzanne and Aimé Césaire's work is notable. Art had to reach people. This intentionality surfaces in the work of global Caribbean artists in significant ways.

Although a full transcript of the play is now lost, it is known that *The Dawn of Liberty* focused on the May 22 and 23, 1848, slave uprising in Martinique and was written and produced a few years after the event's centennial. In Hearn's novel, Youma, a slave raised in a white household, sacrifices her life as an act of preternatural loyalty to her enslavers on the very night Martinicans rise to claim their freedom, unaware that slavery has already been abolished in France. Although the work's details cannot be assessed, the title Suzanne Césaire chose for her reinterpretation suggests that she shifted narrative positions from Youma's personal story to a community narrative that subsumed the individual within collectively articulated Black liberation efforts. As Rabbit observes, at the time of her rewrite, the events of May 1848 were not officially recognized: "What was present until [1998 as official history] was French legacy rather than Martinican agency." Suzanne Césaire's decision to rewrite Hearn's novel as a play and perform it in the wake of the French government's decision to commemorate the hundredth anniversary of the April 1848 emancipation proclamation, instead of the May 1848 uprising, despite the fact that emancipation was not formally announced on the island until June of that year, evidenced her navigation of "contemporary questions of self-determina[tion]" through the "historic events the play referenced" and revised.[28]

Furthermore, and this is extremely important in the context of this book, Suzanne Césaire's usurpation of a seminal event in Black Martinican history that had been narratively colonized spoke "to the individual acts and collective refusals of men and women overturning the official story to create their own histories."[29] By appropriating and transforming Hearn's text, Suzanne Césaire engaged in autohistoriography, decolonizing "the West's theory of the non-West" by setting aside French perspectives of 1848 and centering Black Martinican accounts of their liberation. In the process, the play models how art can mobilize new political visions and activate political agency. Her recharacterization of Youma prefigures Aimé's approach to Caliban. It is art doing decolonial work.

RECASTING *A TEMPEST*

A Tempest is the most conceptual of Césaire's three plays. Written ten years after his oft-cited speech turned essay "L'homme de culture et ses responsabilités" (The Man of Culture and His Responsibilities), it represents a cognitive plateau—a pragmatic acceptance of what is and what must come. While writing it, Césaire returned to ideas introduced in the earlier essay for a speech delivered at the Havana Cultural Congress of 1968. By then he had come to believe that the work of Louverture, Dessalines, Christophe, Patrice Lumumba, and other Black revolutionaries belonged to the future, a world that did not yet exist.[30] The futurist aspect of Black liberation he cites is a key element in Césaire's thinking in the 1960s and presages the work of the generational visual artists featured in this text. It also suggests an appreciation for the uniquely nonlinear character of Caribbean modernism.

Adlai Murdoch's illumination of the potential impact of France's 1931 Colonial Exposition on Césaire's 1946 decision yields insight as to what I see as his historically based liberatory futurism. Murdoch proposes that, when Césaire, Léopold Senghor, and Léon Damas developed Négritude in the 1930s, it was seen as "an agent of challenge and change. . . . [It] articulated a black consciousness aimed at rehabilitating, constructing and valorizing identity on the individual and communal levels."[31] As an emancipatory discourse, Négritude struck at the heart of colonial othering. By centering and valuing Blackness, Murdoch posits, the movement exposed the "hypocrisy that had long undergirded western claims to a superiority of humanism and reason even as the most egregious colonial depredations and exploitations took place" and, in this way, "inscribe[d] a new modernity for blackness."[32]

Caribbean modernism and the practices that constitute it manifest as ways of being that are atemporal, spatially boundless, and ongoing. What Murdoch describes is a process of dissembling, reimagining, and remaking—a reworlding that sows fertile ground for Black things and Black life. This humanist modernism necessarily takes shape as refusal of Black and colonial abjection, stasis, and marginalization in service to a world yet to come. It is an ethos that centers art's decolonizing work, as encapsulated in *The Dawn of Liberty*, *A Tempest*, and Marc Latamie's oeuvre.

A Tempest arrived in the wake of World War II, ongoing revolutions, and independence movements and at the point of the formation and continued growth of regional and transcontinental cultural events and organizations. In 1950 the West Indian Cricket Team defeated Britain in a powerful display of the colony David defeating the colonizer Goliath that reverberated across the empire. Two years later, in 1952, the first Caribbean Festival of the Arts took place in San Juan, Puerto Rico; Aimé Césaire's former student Frantz Fanon published his first major text, *Black Skin, White Masks*; and Suzanne Césaire's *The Dawn of Liberty* was staged. That same year, riots erupted during a sugar workers' strike in Guadeloupe against French rule and economic stagnation. Several people were killed when French police fired on the crowd of striking workers.

Four years later Césaire resigned from the French Communist party in a scathing letter addressed to Maurice Thorez, party chair, denouncing its racism. Later that year he delivered the speech "Culture et colonisation" at the First International Conference of Black Writers and Artists in Paris. The talk was included in the inaugural issue of Alioune Diop's groundbreaking publication *Présence Africaine* the following year. The year 1957 marked Haiti's election of François Duvalier and the inauguration of the Caribbean Festival of Arts, CARIFESTA (1957–67). In 1958 the Parti Progressiste Martiniquais formed, triggering protests on the streets of Fort-de-France demanding independence. That same year, the first Institute of Caribbean Studies was established at the University of Puerto Rico, Rio Piedras, just as the West Indian Federation coalesced. The following year saw the irruption of the Cuban Revolution, and Césaire attended the International Congress of Black Artists and Writers in Rome, where he delivered the speech "The Man of Culture and His Responsibilities."

Meanwhile, in Paris, a young Martinican poet named Édouard Glissant was forming the Front Antillo-Guyanais, a group calling for Martinique's independence and its integration into the Caribbean.

For Césaire and the wider Caribbean, the 1960s were filled with tragedy and triumph. The decade opened with the publication of George Lamming's *The Pleasures of Exile*, which includes a reading of *The Tempest* and a critical engagement with Caliban, guided by a luminous invocation of Césaire's poetry. Fanon's *Wretched of the Earth* was also published at this time. The book's opening chapter, "On National Culture," vocalizes many of Césaire's concerns about neocolonial sovereignty and the role of the békés and petit bourgeois in fostering Black oppression in postindependent colonial states. Fanon died soon after the book was released.

In 1962 the West Indian Federation, a grand experiment in regional collective governance, dissolved, as Trinidad and Jamaica claimed independence from Britain and the Cuban Missile Crisis unfolded. The following year Césaire published *La Tragédie du Roi Christophe*, and he and Suzanne divorced after twenty-five years of marriage. Notably, C. L. R. James's *The Black Jacobins* (originally published in 1939) was reissued that year with a new appendix, and the March on Washington took place in the United States. The year ended with John F. Kennedy's shocking assassination, the first in a series of successive high-profile murders that included Malcolm X (1965), Martin Luther King Jr. (1968), and Robert F. Kennedy (1968).

In April 1966 the First World Festival of the Arts was held in Senegal, where *La Tragédie du Roi Christophe* was performed by a France-based troupe led by Guadeloupean-French filmmaker Sarah Maldoror and Haitian actor and singer Toto Bissainthe. The Caribbean Artist Movement formed in London, and Césaire published the play *Une Saison au Congo*, based on the rise and fall of Patrice Lumumba. Barbados also gained independence from Britain. Tragically, Suzanne Césaire died on May 16 in Yvelines, France, of a brain tumor.

More labor riots erupted in Guadeloupe in 1967, and in December of that year, Césaire arrived in Havana to participate in the 1968 Havana Cultural Congress.

I cite this history to make clear that Aimé Césaire played a central role in most, if not all, major Pan-Caribbean and Pan-African gatherings across the Black Atlantic in the 1950s and '60s. His presence and voice were highly regarded, and he was granted honored roles in key assemblies that positioned arts and letters as a critical component in the struggle for political liberation. In this expansive context, *A Tempest* resides as a future-driven text, a theoretical form in which Césaire staked out generative visions and pathways in a landscape he may have known best.

If the Prospero-Caliban relationship in Shakespeare's *The Tempest* prefigures that between colonizer and colonized, Césaire's recasting warns that postcoloniality's deliverance of political sovereignty and personal freedom, whether secured through independence or through revolution, was theoretically plausible but limited in its ability to clear a path to freedom.[33] In Césaire's *A Tempest*, Prospero, the colonizer, never changes and never leaves the island. It is Caliban who is recast as the transformed and transformative figure.

For Césaire, colonialism established differences between colonizers and colonized based on a willful misrecognition of the colonized as approximations of human beings (Caliban figures). This was affirmed by who possessed economic, political, and territorial control and power, and who didn't. In this way, postcolonialism was configured as a psychic state; art had the capacity to unveil and unmask the colonizer's imposed binary and usher in freedom.[34] This position is transmuted through Caliban. At the end of the play, Prospero expresses a desire to live peaceably with Caliban. Rejecting his desires, Caliban replies that he isn't interested in peace but in freedom. Unable to accept his wishes being ignored, Prospero continues to press Caliban to affirm them. Tired of Prospero's refusal to listen, Caliban delivers a response that serves as the apex of the play:

> For years I bowed my head
> for years I took it, all of it—
> your insults, your ingratitude . . .
> and worst of all, more degrading than all the rest,
> your condescension.
> But now it's over! . . .
> Prospero you're a great magician:
> you're an old hand at deception.
> And you lied to me so much,
> about the world, about myself,
> that you ended up by imposing on me
> an image of myself:
> underdeveloped, in your words, undercompetent
> that's how you made me see myself!
> And I hate that image . . . and it's false!

But now I know you, you old cancer,
And I also know myself!
And I know that one day
my bare fist, just that
will be enough to crush your world!
The old world is crumbling down![35]

In this remarkably sure-footed declaration, Caliban speaks himself into an emancipatory existence. In so doing, he calls on the Yoruba god Shango and thereby reorients to the foundations of his African past. Shango is the god of lightning and thunder, the god of protection, justice, male virility, and vengeance.[36] What is most important, he is the son of the creator god Obatala. No longer Hulme's "compromised formation," Caliban has (re)created himself as fully human. While Prospero continues to seek absolution and grows infuriated by Caliban's disregard, Caliban ends the conversation. And his evocation of Shango marks his last word on the matter. In Césaire's retelling, Caliban does not produce offspring. There are no children. As an emancipatory figure, he represents the close of one chapter and the start of another.

CARIBBEAN STYLE

In his letters to Henri Seyrig in the 1940s, Césaire affirmed the presence of a "Caribbean genius, a Caribbean style" in arts and culture. This book follows in his footsteps to explore a unifying ethos in 1990s Caribbean art that not only deeply aligns with Césaire's view on the decolonizing impact of autohistoriography and the arts but also models it. As Wilder observes, "Decolonization, for Césaire, was as much about reworking time as it was about reworking space. It meant, on the one hand, interrupting the apparent historical destiny of colonized peoples by transforming Antilleans into history-making actors."[37] If, as Césaire observed, colonialism "ruptured" when "imperialism divided history" and "'balkanized' time," hope lay in decolonizing history and in creating "new forms of temporal, as well as spatial, solidarity" in the arts.[38]

This book occupies that space of hope and possibility. It explores the ways Caribbean artists in global spaces became "history-making actors" by challenging old forms, creating new ones, and affirming their artistic vision outside and beyond institutional spaces. If these artists were not wanted in a museum, gallery, exhibition, discipline—if their work was not considered worthy of regard or valued—then, as Caliban and Holder declared, something was wrong with *that* place, space, or discourse, because there was absolutely nothing wrong with them.

Considering the foregoing now, when thinking back to the Latamie panel, I think this is what I should have said: Like many Caribbean artists entering major global exhibition spaces in the 1990s, Marc Latamie produces speculative, often multisensory aesthetic arrangements in quiet, powerful sculptures and installations that reconfigure dominant notions of history across space and time. In this way, he performs the decolonial work his countryman the late writer and politician Aimé Césaire had hoped to see uplifted by future generations of artists and writers. Latamie's work is typical of the art that emerged in the global Caribbean imaginary during this era, which sought to transform our way of seeing in real time. This is plainly evident in the installation *Caldera* (1994) (figure I.1), where a volcano-shaped mound of refined white sugar evocative of Martinique's Mount Pelée, its land/*terre*, is encircled at three points by the words *sky*, *mer*, and *indigo* written in blue-white neon tubing. *Caldera* demands a discourse that can account for how its aesthetics converse with extended space-time relationships, economies, and global histories. *Terre*/land that produced sugar, "sky," "mer," and "indigo" were integral and interconnected components of the regional slave economy, components that have since been rebranded for mass tourism's neocolonial marketing apparatus. Today's tourism industry is overseen by the same békés who controlled the island's production during slavery. Césaire would have recognized this continuum instantly.

For his 2012 Americas Society exhibition, Latamie arranged a three-part installation in the galleries, using another signifying commodity, absinthe, as conceptual anchor. Absinthe is a 100 proof, anise-flavored alcoholic beverage known for its mind-altering capabilities. Referred to colloquially as the green fairy, it is closely associated with late nineteenth-century French modernism and memorialized in depictions of French café society such as Edouard Manet's *The Absinthe Drinker* (1859) and Edgar Degas's *In a Café (The Absinthe Drinker)* (1875–76). Latamie's exhibition extended this association beyond France to the Caribbean. Although the liquor was banned in France in 1914, absinthe's manufacture and consumption in Martinique never ceased after its introduction in the 1840s. Its production was primarily a domestic and personal enterprise, mostly undertaken in local kitchens rather than formal factories.

In the central gallery space of the Americas Society exhibition, Latamie installed an absinthe distillery comprising a small wooden shack in

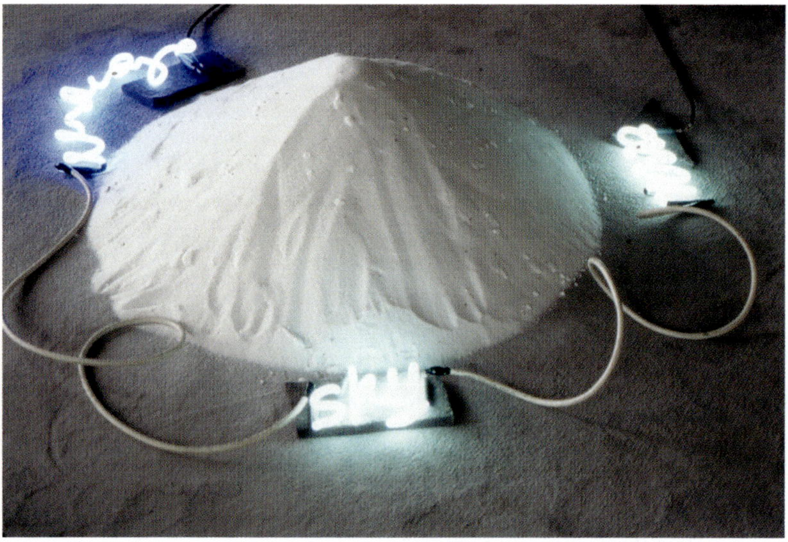

I.1 Marc Latamie, *Caldera*, 1994. Sugar, neon light tubing. Courtesy of the artist. © Marc Latamie.

a simple post-and-beam, pitched-roof style found in Martinican homes (figure I.2). The structure, pierced with copper rays reminiscent of Gian Bernini's *The Ecstasy of St. Theresa* (1647–52), marked this as an alchemic space. The shack's interior, visible through a small oculus embedded in its wall, held a miniaturized version of the wormwood tree whose leaves are used to produce absinthe, spinning magically like a ballerina on point (figure I.3). Centrally positioned in the main gallery, the shack was surrounded by a series of metal sculptures ranging in height from four to nine feet. Fabricated of sheet metal, their large, abstracted forms were drawn from discrete mechanical elements found in Martinican absinthe home distilleries.

Latamie has described his approach to art-making as "the minimum of demonstration and the maximum of thinking."[39] The installation's arrangement encapsulates this mantra. He traces the work's conceptual beginnings to his encounter with Robert Rauschenberg's *Oracle* (1962–65) many years prior at the Pompidou Centre in Paris. For him, *Oracle*, already in conversation with the centralization of process as art epitomized by Marcel Duchamp's *Large Glass* (1915–23), became a conceptual wormhole, a point of catalysis that expanded Latamie's thinking and, subsequently, his process. As he spent time with *Oracle*, he became particularly attentive to Rauschenberg's use of deconstructed aesthetic forms and theatricality to commu-

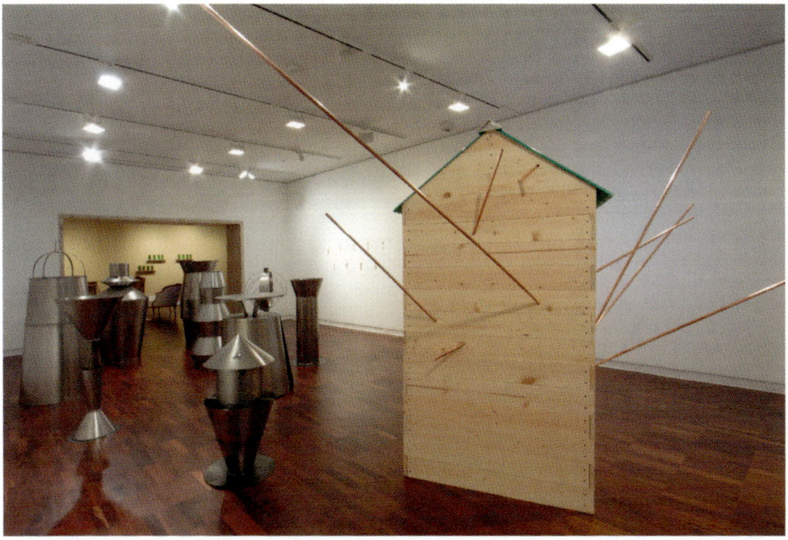

I.2 Marc Latamie, Central Gallery Space, Americas Society, New York, 2012. Courtesy of the artist. © Marc Latamie.

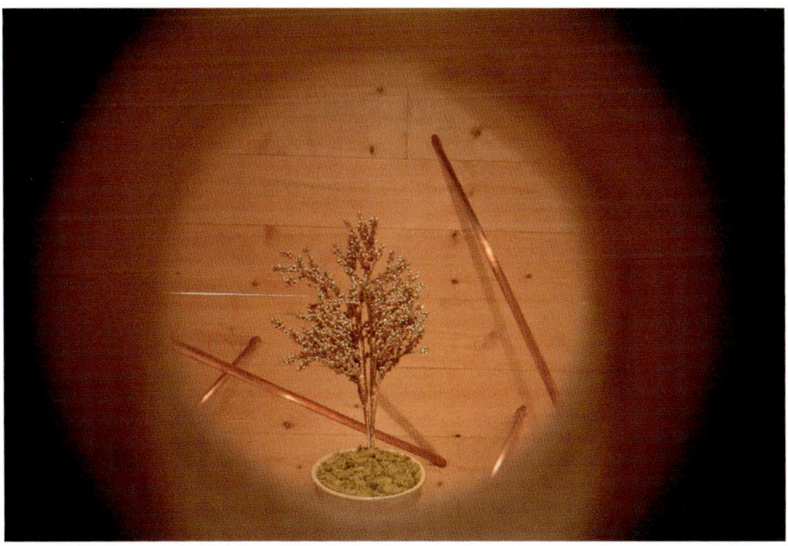

I.3 Marc Latamie, Oculus, Central Gallery Space, Americas Society, New York, 2012. Film Still. Courtesy of the artist. © Marc Latamie.

nicate the effects of mechanization. In his much larger sculptures, or what he calls malic molds, Latamie echoed this stylistic approach by drawing on mechanized elements as form and deploying the defamiliarizing effects of monumental, three-dimensional abstraction. His technique achieved two conjoined ends: He was able to center absinthe without physically articulating it and enable spectators to literally enter the work. And, through the latter, he insisted on the audience's complete attention, time, mobility, and cognition to fully experience the work and its signifying implications.

Just beyond the sculptures, a short film by Myrtha Richards Marie Joseph, entitled *L'Absinthe de Monsieur Gentil* (Mr. Gentil's Absinthe), was screened on a loop (figure I.4). It documents a Black Martinican man in the process of making the liquor. His name, Mr. Gentil, simultaneously evokes tenderness, refinement, and, in its similarity to the word *gentile*, a kind of otherness. The film's intimacy and intentional view into Mr. Gentil's home distillery transformed the aesthetic experience and Latamie's practice into an important rhizomatic affair that was, in every sense of the word, Caribbean. Here, absinthe, Mr. Gentil, a home distillery, and Rauschenberg come together in the exhibition form, interweaving subjects and traces.

In the adjoining gallery, the work shifted. Painted in a deep-green jewel tone, the space displayed a collection of prints, photographs, drawings, and paintings by canonical French modern artists, including Paul Gauguin, André Masson, Raoul Dufy, Henri Matisse, and Man Ray. All exhibited works were portrait reproductions of Martinican or Guadeloupean women, except one. A small wall plaque noted that the artist had dedicated the room to the life of a Black Martinican woman named Marie-Philomena Roptus, also known as Lumina Sophie or Surprise, whom Latamie had learned about through tales passed down by generations of Black Martinicans, including his family.

Lumina Sophie's story was a source of immense pride: She was lionized for her leadership in the fight against the continuing oppression of the island's Black plantation workers in the late nineteenth century. Yet despite her centrality to (Black) Martinican history, her story is not referenced in the island's historical curriculum, nor is her life nationally celebrated. On one hand, her absence from official state narratives may call into question the legitimacy of Black islanders' oral lore. On the other, the narrative's persistence over time suggests the existence of a vibrant discourse *outside* the realm of state-sanctioned authorship. Latamie learned that despite her omission from the official historical narrative, Sophie's life *is* recorded in Martinican state archives, which document her arrest, trial, and sentencing

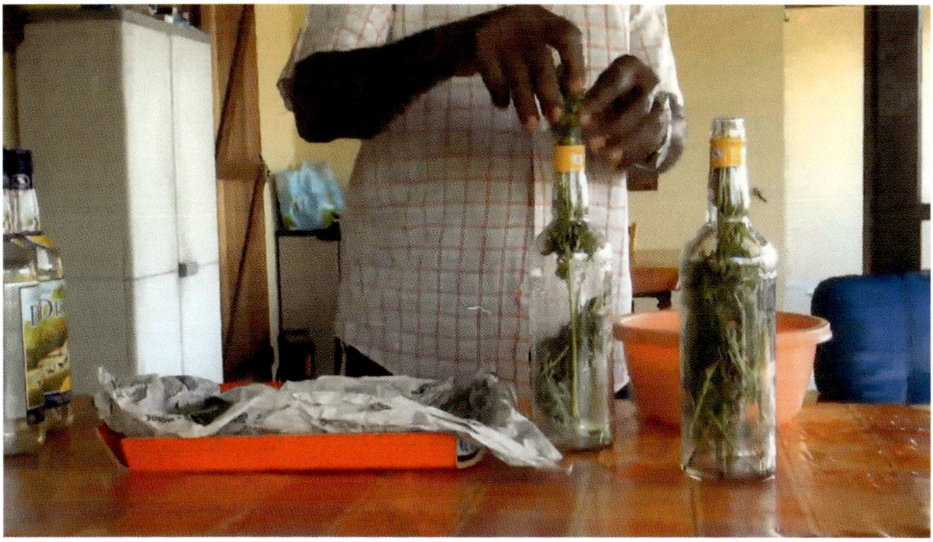

I.4 Marc Latamie and Myrtha Richards Marie Joseph, Mr. Gentil making absinthe in his kitchen, 2012. Film still. Courtesy of the artist. © Marc Latamie.

following her command of the 1870 rebellions that pitted Blacks against local whites. Charged with committing "blasphemy," "subversion," and "male domination" by inciting men to riot and burn plantations to the ground, Sophie was convicted and sent to the prison of Saint Laurent du Maroni in French Guiana, where she died in December 1879 at the age of thirty-one.[40] A criminal in one story, subject to historical erasure; a hero in another, celebrated and kept alive through oral tradition despite limited access to material evidence of her existence.

Many of the names of women in the portraits displayed in the gallery remain unknown. But among them, Latamie includes a fabricated portrait of Lumina Sophie (figure I.5).[41] In this gallery, the spatial curation enacts an art-making process designed to reconfigure official narratives that perpetrate historical erasure. Drawing on situational aesthetics, Lumina's inclusion in the gallery finds meaning in its relational différance to the other women.[42] Her presence affirms an organic Martinican autohistoriography, an active decolonizing element Césaire believed could be found and activated in the creative arts. In this exhibition, Latamie, like Suzanne Césaire before him, revealed the dimensions of historical erasure by recentering and rendering what and who has been devalued, disregarded, and dismissed in official Martinican historical narratives and representations.

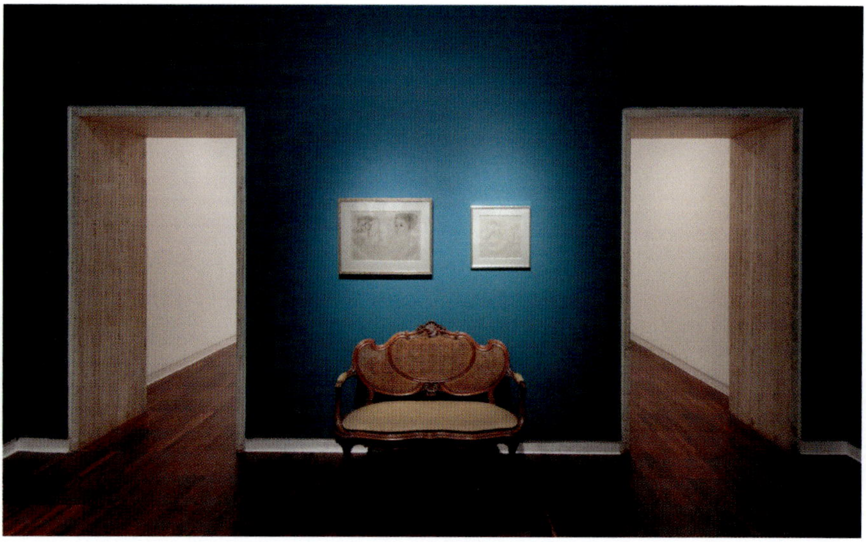

I.5 Marc Latamie, installation, Americas Society, New York, 2012. On the left is Raoul Dufy's etching *Deux Antillaises*. Latamie's drawing of Lumina Sophie is on the right. Courtesy of the artist. © Marc Latamie.

Latamie repeated this act of authorship through aesthetics in every gallery. The Lumina Sophie room mirrored the final gallery, whose green walls transferred to the containers of absinthe being offered to guests in what appeared to be a nineteenth-century-era French salon where visitors might sit and enjoy a glass of absinthe. The presumed intent was that imbibement would literalize the mind-altering experience the artist operationalized through the exhibition. His work to render Martinique's place in the history and production of absinthe, as well as the story of Lumina Sophie in contemporary space and time, echoes the output of global Caribbean art and artists in the 1990s vis-à-vis the Western art world—not as children of Caliban awaiting regard but as Césaire envisioned, artists capable of reshaping the very world that occludes them.

CRITICAL METHODS FOR PROBLEM SPACES

As an art historian who teaches courses on the discipline's critical methodologies and history, I understand the pedagogical import of tracing a line from Shakespeare's Caliban to Césaire to Latamie. But to leave it there positions art-making as conceptual evidence rather than generative, often disruptive theoretical form. My scholarly intervention departs from this premise to enact methodology that recenters artistic production and attends to the theoretical and historical (re)positions embedded in works of art. It examines the ways Latamie and his cohort align with Suzanne and Aimé Césaire's decolonial intentions in enacting through their work what Walter Mignolo calls "epistemic reconstitution,"[43] producing art that demanded new methodologies and a decolonized art history for sites mapped outside what has historically been understood as "the West."

This book seeks to render Césaire's vision of the arts as a decolonial force capable of creating postcolonial futures. As *A Tempest*'s conclusion suggests, and the work of Édouard Glissant subsequently makes clear, the possibility of return to a precolonial state or future situated prior to Prospero's arrival presented a theoretical and pragmatic lacuna. In *Discourse on Colonialism*, Césaire articulated this predicament: "For us, the problem is not to make a utopian and sterile attempt to repeat the past, but to go beyond. It is not a dead society that we want to revive. . . . It is a new society that we must create."[44] For the formerly colonized (Caliban), an emancipated, sovereign state or a culturally distinct island operating within a transcontinental economy where the békés no longer held sway were impossibilities. Both Prospero and Caliban had been transformed through contact with each other, a nexus that precluded return and *occluded* certain future visions. The silence, or dead calm, shared between the two figures during their final scenes ossifies a hermeneutic of disappointment *and* acceptance, evidencing Césaire's recognition of the need for new models, new approaches, new art, and new imaginaries that emergent generations would be tasked with creating.[45]

A Tempest underscores the internal crossroads that people of the diaspora, colonized people, navigate repeatedly. Glissant marked the initiating moment of this encounter as the Middle Passage, the space between the known and the unknown.[46] In conversations with Manthia Diawara on board the *Queen Mary* in 2009, he opined about confronting and navigating this crisis state. To him, the collective memory and survival of slavery and colonialism offered Caribbean peoples the revelation of a quiet truth—that their humanity exceeded any attempt to physically or ideologically contain it. He believed that creolization, a process fundamental to the multifarious character of Caribbeanness, moved its people beyond the role of "historical avatars."[47] Drawing on this conceptual lens, I see Caliban as a historical avatar who clears a path to lead his people to the promised land but, like Moses, is unable to cross into it with them. Therefore, to continue to designate Caliban as an embodiment of the "Caribbean" reinforces an internal estrangement between history and the present, trapping the region in a perpetually reduced state of Other in a colonial-defined hierarchical system of values. *A Tempest* thus renders a critical silence in the "postcolonial record," intimating what few dare say—that in 1969, and arguably today, postcoloniality as a lived reality has yet to arrive.

This book hopes for, illuminates, and anticipates the aesthetic visions of contemporary artists in the global Caribbean. The cohort featured in this text understood the generative power of creolization and forged practices that reconfigured local and global Caribbean histories and imaginaries with speculative tools and languages that transcended the critical capacity of Caliban's literal and metaphorical island. Their work thus demands different methodologies and critical approaches—in museums and galleries and on the page. Guided by the expansiveness and diversity of their visions, my examination is modeled differently in each chapter, while the work of the work, echoing Césaire, remains the same: decolonization.

In recent years the contemporary art world has expressed significant interest in Glissantian thinking, particularly his concept of the rhizome and deployment of the term *creolization*. I, too, have turned to his work many times in order to think through a philosophical or ethical quandary and locate the conceptual architecture needed to break the mirror of colonialism systemically embedded in dueling neo- and postcolonial visions of the Caribbean. Glissant certainly merits this level of engagement. But when his theory is detached from a robust consideration of the artwork in question, it misses the point, veering into ahistorical waters. For both Glissant and Césaire, art was critical to the reformations and recastings they envisioned. In this text, I retrieve Glissant from the romance of apolitical universalism by reconsidering Caribbean art in the global imaginary.

According to Glissant, *creolization* is a generative process that makes space for individualized artistry forged in the catalysis of ongoing contact. Caribbean people live "in" creolization, wherein one "can change, you can be with the Other, you can change with the Other while being yourself, you are not one, you are multiple, and you are yourself. You are not lost because you are multiple. You are not broken apart because you are multiple."[48] This poetic, political, and anticolonial statement echoes Césaire's notion of freedom and verifies the extreme heterogeneity historically used to dismiss the region and its claims to modernity.[49] Here I must pause and repeat: Unmoored from the specificities of the Caribbean, the poetics of

Glissantian relation may appear romantic, forgetful of histories and the realities of violence embedded in and inflicted on the region. To be clear, this is not the rhizome of Gilles Deleuze and Félix Guattari, who, in *A Thousand Plateaus*, describe the concept in ways familiar to those of us who grew up growing or eating cassava and yams, as a "subterranean stem . . . absolutely different from roots and radicles."[50] For them, this fundamental food system was the perfect metaphor for mechanisms of human activity and social machines, because "any point of a rhizome can be connected to anything. . . . A rhizome ceaselessly establishes connections between semiotic chains, organizations of power, and circumstances relative to the arts, sciences, and social struggles. A semiotic chain is like a tuber agglomerating very diverse acts, not only linguistic, but also perceptive, mimetic, gestural, and cognitive."[51] These relational principles were instantly recognizable in my world. And though I found Deleuze and Guattari's framing beautiful, provocative, and affirming, it was at the same time troublingly ahistorical and spatially and culturally unmoored. It perpetuated a feedback loop—shorthand for a feature of Caribbean life that I had always known but without reference to the brutal conditions and violent forces that underpinned it.

Glissant's central concept of the rhizome must be situated in relation to the historical, cultural, and political dross of colonialism, indigeneity, transatlantic slavery, and East and South Asian influences within the space and character of Caribbean-ness. Without context, the notion of rhizomatic, creolizing systems of relation can easily devolve into dehistoricized universality, divorced from the particularities of world-shattering forces like slavery, colonialism, imperialism, and neoliberalism. In this process, the ethics of creolization are severed from its aesthetics, and the concept is transformed into a romance for global art cosmopolitans' appropriation and consumption. In the spirit of Sylvia Wynter, the work produced by this book's featured generation of artists signals a *praxis of humanness* that seeks to embrace and lift the entire expanse of Caribbean peoples—past, present, and future.[52]

As I engaged Glissant more intentionally to render the post-Caliban world Césaire had envisioned, I looked to Antonio Benítez-Rojo, who helped explain my ambivalence and ultimate discomfort with the contemporary adoption of the Glissantian paradigm. He argued that "the specifications of their [Deleuze and Guattari's] model are clear and final: [But] here [the Caribbean] is a flow machine" of multiple dimensions. He continued: "The Caribbean machine . . . is something more; it is a technological-poetic machine, or, if you like, a metamachine of differences whose poetic mechanism cannot be diagrammed in conventional dimensions, and whose user's manual is found dispersed in a state of plasma within the chaos of its own network of codes and subcodes . . . polyrhythm (rhythms cut through by other rhythms, which are cut by still other rhythms)."[53] Like Glissant, Benítez-Rojo believed that Deleuze and Guattari's approach flattened relations by rendering them in linear, mechanized, one-dimensional space and time and, in so doing, foreclosed imagination and the spectrum of potentialities embedded in the creolization process. Both Benítez-Rojo and Glissant retained the yam's polymorphic nature in their retheorization of the rhizome concept. A machine suggests relative certainty and uniformity; action in opposition to the machine induces panic. Even the shape of a yam is inconsistent; where it chooses to bulb cannot be predetermined, and if left wild, its root system cannot be mapped. And yet no matter the root's positionality and contours, it will always become a yam. In Glissantian terms, a yam represents a plateau catalyzed by the creolization process, in which to be "in creolization" admits no known or final destination and plans are at best speculative. In anticipation of Benítez-Rojo, Glissant moored rhizome theory as a Caribbean reality or, more specifically, conscience.

To situate the work in this text and avoid the romance of theory, I ask, following David Scott, What are the demands of art history and art criticism in the postcolonial present? How might we render a continuum of global Caribbean artists that is not beholden to traditional art historical rubrics such as shared styles, location, social communities, formal problems, materials, and aesthetic approaches, that trajects a common ethical approach to what Scott describes as the "problem spaces" these artists find themselves in? Scott observes that these problem spaces are "conceptual-ideological ensembles, discursive formations, or language games that are generative of objects, and therefore of questions," and are "necessarily historical inasmuch as they alter as their (epistemic-ideological) conditions of existence change."[54]

The Latamie panel evidenced the need for a deeper consideration of these problem spaces. It clarified that applying ill-defined tropes to contemporary Caribbean art was a fatigued and one-sided romance. And it showed that the retention of this relational model not only reinforced an epistemic blindness that the postcolonial, postindependence Caribbean project claimed to dematerialize and delegitimize,[55] but also imprisoned the Caribbean within an atemporal Other world whose place on the art world's margins had fossilized—in theory. Despite the hopes for a postcolonial Caribbean art history, in the art world, perhaps Massa day was still not done.[56]

GLOBAL CARIBBEAN ART HISTORY

In the Caribbean context, Glissant provides a point of departure for a rhizomatic, decolonizing, global Caribbean art history in service to transformative practices, or to Césaire's imagined future. This book envisions the Caribbean as a mutable and migratory problem space, a historically configured archipelago that is without a geographically or psychically defined boundary or center. It seeks to contribute to the field of global Caribbean art history, in which memory and re-memory are significant and history is part of a continuing present.[57] It interpolates multiple histories and creolizes to author new ones.

This book reflects that belief that works of art participate in multiple discourses and engage many processes and sites. It resists Western-centered hierarchies of value that privilege (white) men as creators, define innovation through a narrow avant-garde lens, and essentialize geopolitical spaces and relations between place, race, culture, and ethnicity. It rejects notions of value that depend on defining the Other in binary terms and prioritizes the art object as both primary material and theoretical form.[58] It is issued in the spirit of an art history that resists the foreclosure of the single frame, the single story. It claims opacity as a right even as it develops prismatic methodologies that aspire to clear-eyed vision.

In other words, global Caribbean art history demands a nonhegemonic practice beyond modern binaries. It does not cohere temporally, formally, or theoretically within the traditional frames of the art history discipline. Yet it is resolutely contemporary. As an ethical practice, it generates a discourse on the art of Others as autohistoriography rather than as a shadow of the West. Here, those formerly known as subalterns not only speak but decenter the concept of the West and its systems of value.

Global Caribbean art history does not foreclose the possibility that its discursive subject can occupy and participate in multiple conversations simultaneously. It is a field fueled by intellectually rigorous, humanistic, and ethically grounded critical methodologies. Not anchored in a fixed institutional framework tied to immutable geographic boundaries, it embodies a fluid field able to code switch in order to attend to theoretical implications and varying points of departure presented in diverse works of art.

Latamie's oeuvre and that of his contemporaries demand a rhizomatic art historical approach to render the problem spaces that their art engages and occupies. Regrettably, a disconnect exists between the work of Caribbean artists emerging in the 1990s and the critical discourse around it—if one can describe it as such. The conversation between Lahr and Holder that opens this chapter maps this project's political domain and vocalizes the imperative to challenge the critical canon's vacuousness and the frameworks that have sought to delimit the art it misapprehended. This text aims to walk with the artists it engages through the disciplinary doors of art history. And beyond them.

The critical literature on Caribbean artists in the global imaginary during the 1990s is extraordinarily ordinary, particularly given the level of exhibition and market renown some of these artists achieved. Either the literature is severely limited in quantity, or one finds the same story repeated over and over again—as if the art under discussion occupies a fixed point. In this critical discourse, the work is typically reduced to the exotic or fantastic, especially if it engages spirituality or critiques tourism and other neocolonial enterprises. At the same time, the Caribbean is often positioned as a shadow, a place where attachment was tenuous for native artists now based elsewhere.

Rather than outline the reasons and anxieties that animate these practices, this text provides a studied reengagement of the work of several Caribbean artists who emerged in the global imaginary during the 1990s, using public discourse as its archive. Echoing Holder, I show that the archival thinness and superficial engagement did not reflect the work's critical, aesthetic, or historical heft but rather the values of the discipline, the critical environment, or the art world it encountered. I advance a rhizomatic, decolonial methodology that broaches a more complex conceptual plane. Through critical methods and approaches modeled by these artists, this text illuminates how they challenged the art historical status quo to initiate an epistemic reformation that decolonizes and expands the art historical archive in vital and invigorating ways.

Like Césaire's, Holder's approach to his 1950s-era milieu presaged that of the Caribbean artists under review. In many ways, not much changed in the intervening four decades, and some may argue that, despite optics, things remain much the same today. In the 1990s, the discipline of art history was initially consumed by the concept of multiculturalism, a current it quickly cast aside in a slow push toward global art histories. But how can this field of study be defined if Western art history only sees "the global" vis-à-vis its reflections in its Others? Global art history is discursively and practically possible only if the discipline suspends the narrative and teleological authority of Western art history to see the world horizontally and relationally, not as a mechanized vertical hierarchy.

The global art history conversation captures this project's ethical contours to imagine what becomes visible beyond the blinders of historical avatars like Caliban. This book argues that Latamie's generation of artists affected a field reformation in global (Caribbean) art during the 1990s and, moreover, that their work provided the architecture for a rhizomatic art history = Caribbean art history = global art history. This feat was aided in no small part by the remarkable convergence of an equally remarkable set of factors and events in the United States, this text's primary landscape outside the Caribbean. These artists were part of and beneficiaries of the simultaneous rise of multiculturalism, an ongoing institutional critique by Black artists, AIDS and Gay Rights activism, and art's political engagement in these movements. Much of this work was foregrounded by the efforts of feminist—specifically Black feminist—artists and became entangled with the culture wars, which stimulated pivotal social, political, artistic, and institutional fissures in a righteous battle among artists committed to deeply personal and political work, the seemingly all-powerful "Art World," and the US federal government, with the support of the political far right. The establishment of institutions such as the Studio Museum in Harlem, the New Museum, and the Museum of Contemporary Hispanic Art orchestrated new arrangements by collaborating on transformative statement exhibitions such as *The Decade Show*, exemplifying how curatorial innovation reset the landscape of American and global art during the 1990s.

In the 1990s, New York was the capital of the art world. Challenges generated by smaller, innovative institutions created tentative entry points for the migrant Caribbean artist to stake their claim and engage Glissant's "state of multiplicity." The world they engaged and would go on to shape was far different than Wifredo Lam's Paris in the 1920s and '30s; Ronald Moody's Paris or later London in the 1920s, '30s, and '40s; Frank Bowling's, Althea McNish's, and Aubrey Williams's London in the 1950s and '60s; and Mavis Pusey's and Geoffrey Holder's New York in the 1950s and '60s.

In the 1990s, the presence of Caribbean artists and their work in the so-called metropoles was felt more palpably due to the sheer number who came to the art world's fore and simultaneously rose to its greatest heights.[59] The numbers are remarkable, and, while I explore this history in greater depth elsewhere,[60] this text focuses on the art of Marc Latamie, Janine

Antoni, Belkis Ayón, Edouard Duval-Carrié, and Christopher Cozier in conversation with Maurizio Cattelan's 6th Caribbean Biennial. I could have made a similar argument with any number of artists and artworks, but I am particularly interested in the ways *these* artists tread the path cleared by Césaire's Caliban to confidently deploy the conceptual capacity of Caribbean history and culture in a global arena inclusive of the Caribbean. Their willingness to confront erasure in the then-dominant American art world *as well as* in the Caribbean is extraordinary. And wide-ranging. Their oeuvres' diversity in media, production, location, and historicity embodies the need to do decolonizing work in multiple arenas, multiple problem spaces, simultaneously.[61]

These artists came of age in the wake of colonialism, revolution, and independence. They are part of a transformative generation that may never have learned the words to hymns and anthems of empire such as "Rule Britannia," "God Save the Queen," or "La Marseillaise," or have long since forgotten them. They made their way to places beyond the geographically defined region to forge critically human, multilingual art practices resonant in varied sites, histories, and formal languages participating in global conversations.

In the opening chapters, I focus on Janine Antoni, Belkis Ayón, and Edouard Duval-Carrié, all of whom cultivated artistic practices that enunciated deeply personal aesthetic visions rooted in Caribbean imaginaries and global art histories, and performed the decolonial work of Césaire's imagined future in three very different problem spaces. Chapter 4, on Cattelan's 6th Caribbean Biennial, further illuminates the discursive environment these artists consciously engaged and the impact of their work in reshaping the critical landscape.

While this text walks through disciplinary doors in service to an enlarged and ongoing generative vision of art history, I am not advocating for a Western-styled school or "movement" in which artists or "communities" are consciously linked through stylistic affinity or aesthetic concerns. My project does not promote the existence of a unifying aesthetic or medium or support critical field formation organized around a singular unifying narrative, aesthetic, innovation, or medium. It does not attempt to answer an overarching formal problem held in common, nor does it reflect a single collectivity expressed by politicized aesthetic imperatives (though there are sites of convergence).

For the most part, the artists featured in this text did not live in close proximity to one another, though in multiple instances their work was jointly exhibited. Instead, I think of this period and its artists as constitutive of a globally situated meta-archipelago whose articulation point and place of recognition required both linkages to the region and spatial and temporal distance from it. Albeit grounded in a particular Caribbean experience, the content of their art is not limited to a single national history or nation-space. In fact, the period under consideration was pointedly critical of national narratives, revealing disappointment in the independence project and reflecting the rise of global Caribbean art as a distinctly postnational phenomenon. Despite this attribute, the idea of nation remains a subject of interrogation.

This text illuminates how artists cultivated practices and created work that quietly but resolutely moved against the art world's colonial and colonizing assumptions, which regarded the Caribbean as a place where "Art" could not be philosophically imagined, institutionally supported, or epistemologically rendered.[62] Reaching back to Césaire, their art and aesthetics emerged as transgeographic, transtemporal, and transideological, cumulatively situating the linear narrative of the West in an anachronistic relation to the present. Neither linear nor strictly nonlinear, their work shaped a prismatic field that enabled an ethical, multidimensional discourse attendant to the rich life of art objects and ideas as allegory and metaphor, from wherever and whomever they emerge.[63]

The final decade of the twentieth century saw profound change within the art world, change that arguably shaped the global turn in ways still not fully rendered. Spatial and narrative boundaries interrogated by Césaire were now being challenged by global travel, international exhibitions, and biennials' geographic expansion beyond self-proclaimed artistic capitals. This era was also marked by pointed and at times scathing critiques of the failures of independence and the limits of national identity. Nonetheless, my project neither assumes nor subsumes cultural and historical specifications of various sites within the Caribbean. Cuba, Haiti, Jamaica, Trinidad, Martinique, Curaçao, The Bahamas, and other Caribbean places—all are both local and relational sites. They meet at various plateaus, of which the Caribbean is but one nexus, and bear their own prismatic histories.

I am also not concerned with anxieties regarding perceived hierarchies between artists living and working in the geopolitical Caribbean and those working and living abroad, those born in the region and those born outside it. Likewise, I do not marshal signifiers of African, European, and Asian descent to mark authenticity or delineate claims to Caribbeanness. *All* Caribbean people are from somewhere else, and all are differentially marked by the unequal violence of genocide, slavery, indentureship, colonialism, and capitalism. Thus, I am not interested in labeling authenticity or inauthenticity, generally or specifically, as it relates to rootedness, land, and race-based affiliations. Following debates in African art history around myths of authenticity, such binaries fuel a problematic essentialism, rooted in colonialism.[64] Demands for "authenticity" sustain a narrow frame of reference based on colonial determinations of purity that has rarely, if ever, been applied to those who once defined the terms of colonial Otherness. As a pervasive "truth," authenticity has never existed beyond the ideological objectives of hegemony, colonialism, and domination.

On the other hand, I *am* deeply interested in the ways artists in the emerging global Caribbean of the 1990s dismantled such binaries. In their work, one finally sees the promise of postcolonial rupture and futurity that Césaire had envisioned, moving us beyond closed temporal, spatial, theoretical, national, and formal assumptions of the contours and possibilities of Caribbean art to see our world anew.

The seeds of this book germinated many years ago during a quest to understand the Caribbean's absence from contemporaneous critical discourses even as these artists entered global exhibition spaces. In case after case, the region was noted as a site of birth and family history but summarily dismissed thereafter. My hope is that my archive and argument will shed light on this absence and fill this critical void.

Each chapter attends to the ways the artists' work was translated for the public through critical texts and exhibitions. A consideration of cultural documents, artist writings, exhibition records, and public discourse, alongside artist and collector interviews and formal engagement with the work, reveals that histories, ethnographies, and aesthetic and performance practices in the Caribbean were often ignored or superficially glossed once the work entered so-called globalized spaces. More important, my inquiry unmasks the epistemological blindness affected through methodologies and frameworks that occluded nuances and multivalences and thereby reinforced the boundaries of the art world and the discipline of art history. As a response to this omission, I show how artists strategically wielded both silence and self-curation as a weapon, often permitting facile critical discussions, sometimes even assisting in reproducing them, to ward off more troubling alternatives and diffuse and dismantle the structures built to exclude them.

I do not speculate on the utility of considering multiple modernisms or cosmopolitanisms in relation to the Caribbean. I find the inclination to debate these terms in places outside Europe and the United States troubling and myopic, serving to fix these *movements* within spatial and temporal vectors that reinscribe value to the West's project by affirming difference under the guise of criticality. This text refuses that point of departure and instead renders the Caribbean in the world from the perspective of the Caribbean.

In this book, the compression of time in the global Caribbean is a sign of anticolonial futurity rather than evidence of belatedness on the part of the formerly colonized. Rather, "belatedness" typifies the position of Western art history in relation to the rest of the world.[65] In the spirit of *Black Martinik* and drawing on Roshini Kempadoo's work on creolizing the archive, this text sets aside the authority of the Western conception of archive to see what has been occluded or disappeared in service to official colonial history and its concept of time.[66] The archives that inform this text include oral, performative, and aesthetically based, self-critical Caribbean autohistoriographies that emerge from local strategies and practices in the face of oppression.

Chapter 1 focuses on the work of Bahamian-born artist Janine Antoni and her subtle, often deliberate, and sometimes humorous evocation of and claim to American feminist art histories as decolonial work. A doyen of American feminist art and breakout star of the nineties, Antoni deployed personal Caribbean ethnographies in ways completely ignored in the surrounding critical discourse. This absence can be seen as evidence of the incapacity of national or disciplinary histories to account for the complexity of intersectional work by Caribbean women artists. It also highlights Antoni's Césairean Caliban-like awareness of the power of narrative historicization to both concretize and erase and her subsequent attempt to control the narrative on her work. I argue that Antoni's seeming cultivation of a critical distance from "Caribbeanness" and "Caribbean art" is both grounded in and situated beyond what José Muñoz eloquently theorized as "disidentification";[67] it may even be seen as an extreme deployment of Glissant's claim regarding Caribbean people's right to opacity. Antoni's resolve to define the terms of engagement for her work *and her identity* is Césairean in its assumption and execution of authority and authorship. The success of her discursive authorship remains not only unprecedented during her time but reflective of her greatest work.

Chapter 2 centers on the late artist Belkis Ayón's master print *La cena* (1991) in historical relation to filmmaker Tomás Gutiérrez Alea's film *La última cena* (1976). Unlike Antoni, Ayón spent her entire career in the Caribbean, specifically Cuba. As an artist, she was able to travel freely, and her work was exhibited and collected globally. While Antoni's discursive plane is pointedly outside the region in ways that speak to C. L. R. James's notions of Caribbean art in *Beyond a Boundary*,[68] Ayón's work is deeply rooted in Cuban history and culture and conceptually echoed in global discourses. Born in the wake of the Cuban revolution, Ayón presents a formidable critique of its consistent alignment with hegemonic racial positions—specifically Blackness—and gendered power relations through her brilliant redeployment of the founding myths of the all-male Abakuá secret society. The intergenerational discourse between her work, Alea's, and Roberto Fernández Retamar's reconceptualization of Caliban typifies how art practices of the decade link and delink with artistic forebears. Following Césaire's decolonial vision, Ayón's art elucidates how pivotal events like revolution and independence did not magically yield the egalitarian promises they envisioned. Instead, they offered a chance to begin again and recognized the continuing need to decolonize histories and attendant values.

Chapter 3 considers the weight of history and criticality embedded in the decolonial work of Edouard Duval-Carrié's contemporary history painting. It focuses on a single painting, *Mardigras at Fort Dimanche* (1992), to explore Duval-Carrié's engagement of a postmodern baroque style to reimagine the presentation and perception of history through a contemporary lens. Rather than produce paintings that re-present events of the past, Duval-Carrié projects the entire container of history into the aesthetic arena for debate. His art critically fabulates in order to ask its audience to self-reflexively interrogate accepted historical narratives and the mechanisms of power, privilege, violence, and visuality that crafted them.

It is notable that Duval-Carrié and Ayón both drew on African Caribbean traditions that formed in the context of the transatlantic slave trade. Often dismissed as primitive and outside the contemporary frame, Abakuá and Haitian Vodoun, engaged by Ayón and Carrié, respectively, represent contemporized conceptual fulcrums that regard modernism as a generative condition, a creolization process that creates out of what Wilson Harris masterfully describes as "states of cramp," referencing the contortions of bodies in the bowels of slave ships and their reemergence from those hulls in the Americas.[69]

The art of Latamie, Antoni, Ayón, and Duval-Carrié foregrounds this book's fourth chapter, which centers on the American-based Italian artist Maurizio Cattelan's 6th Caribbean Biennial. This chapter's presence, placement, and content may seem odd at first; Cattelan is not a "Caribbean" artist per se, but his insertion in this text is purposeful. Produced in 1999, after the work discussed in the first three chapters, Cattelan's biennial represented an important signpost in global Caribbean art history that merits closer scrutiny. By highlighting Cattelan's theatrical "counterbiennial," alongside attempts to historicize the decolonizing process in the Caribbean through the public discourse that arose in the 1960s around colonial monuments, I hope to illuminate how the art world attempted to reaffirm the status quo even as its frameworks were dissolving around and within it.

Produced by Cattelan and curator Jens Hoffmann, the 6th Caribbean Biennial drew heavily on the presumptions and orchestrations of colonial power that shaped Western modernism, tourism, and the museum.[70] Devoid of substantive artistic exhibition, it was instead an "artist exhibition"; the event consisted solely of celebrated artists who had been invited to take a vacation from art. After the event, Cattelan declared that he was able to fool the art world into believing the biennial was real because the Caribbean "did not exist." Cattelan's performance concretized the perspective of the art world in relation to its perceived Others, inadvertently evidencing its critical blindness to the global outside narcissistic projections.

In *The Pleasures of Exile*, Lamming posits that "Caliban is never accorded the power *to see*. . . . Caliban is the excluded, that which is eternally below possibility. . . . He is seen as an occasion, a state of existence which can be appropriated and exploited for the purposes of another's own development."[71] This is the eerie premise and conclusion of Cattelan's colonial performance. For him, the Caribbean was a place without art and a site where the production of art was impossible.

Advertised exclusively within major global art magazines as a biennial event and slated to occur at a resort on St. Kitts, the project went seemingly unnoticed in the Caribbean. Since the region's population was completely ignored as a potential audience, the "show" was not advertised locally. I argue that the Caribbean's disregard for an event not marketed to them verified neither the disengagement nor the marginal status of the Caribbean or Caribbean art. Cattelan's exhibition was not about the contemporary Caribbean at all; instead, it was a final push to validate the supremacy of Western discursive power in art history. Rather than put the Caribbean on the map, the biennial revealed how deeply rooted "Art World" anxieties pulsed around the loosening of the Western grip on the art historical narrative and its commingled markets. The performance was unmasked as a problematic bully pulpit and performative anachronism, dependent on colonial models for articulation. Its critical failure suggests that the epistemic breaks and reconstitution that catalyzes and coheres the decolonial art produced by artists like Latamie, Antoni, Ayón, and Duval-Carrié were bearing fruit. Whether the West chose to see it or not, the borders of the world had shifted long before Cattelan and his "tourists" mounted their stage set. In art history, Massa day was done.

CHAPTER ONE

From Behind God's Back

Janine Antoni's Embodied Histories

> Janine, you should go out and see the world,
> Because the place you come from is behind God's back.
> LYNETTE ANTONI

NATURE, NURTURE, AND THE ART OF SELF-MAKING

In July 1973, Mierle Laderman Ukeles performed *Washing Tracks, Maintenance: Maintenance Art Activity III* in the galleries at the Wadsworth Atheneum in Hartford, Connecticut. Positioned on her hands and knees, she repeatedly hand-washed the Athenaeum's highly trafficked areas, as patrons filed in and soiled the areas, until closing time. The used rags were piled into a heap in the cleaned sections and amassed into a material archive, reliquary, and sculpture. Laderman Ukeles demarcated the area with a "Maintenance Art" stamp, claiming authorship of the performance space and documenting her labor as creative act.[1] With this double gesture, she centered and materialized the invisibility of women's work in public and domestic settings and of women's art in institutions and archives, advancing a significant and unique political position in the contemporary feminist art scene.

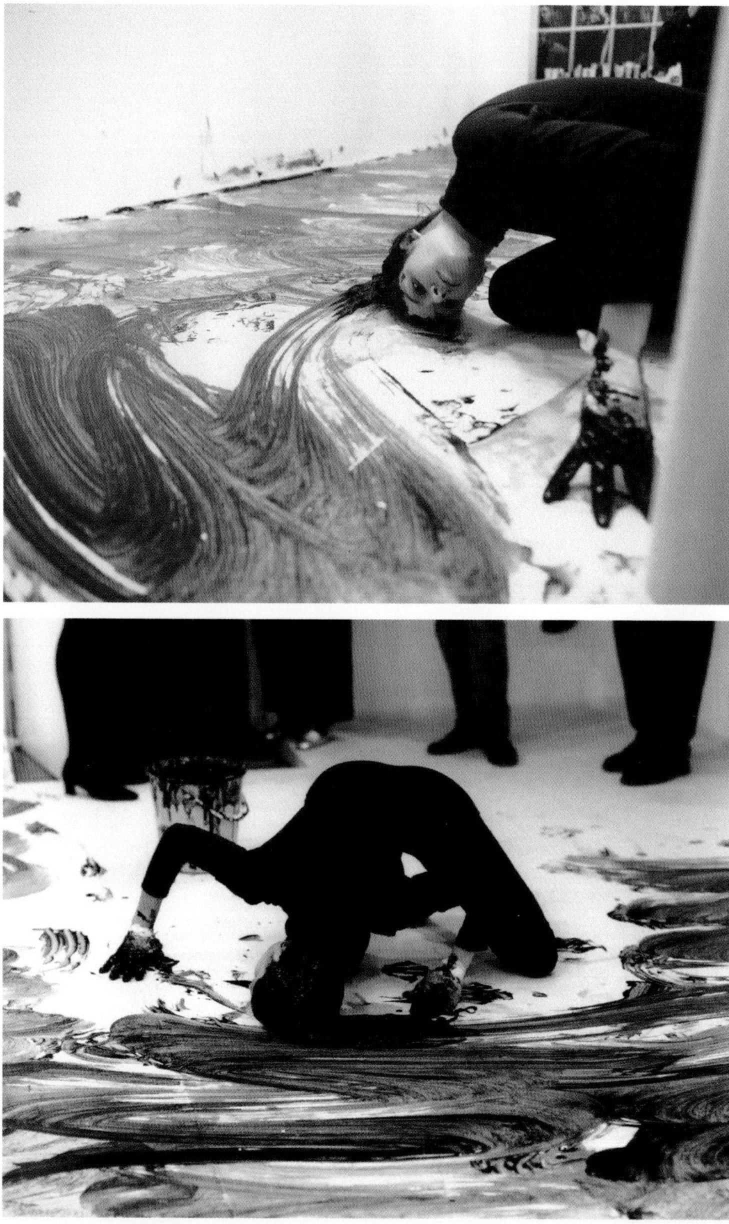

1.1 Janine Antoni, *Loving Care*, 1993. Performance with Loving Care hair dye "Natural Black." Dimensions variable. Photographed by Prudence Cuming Associates at Anthony d'Offay Gallery, London, 1993.

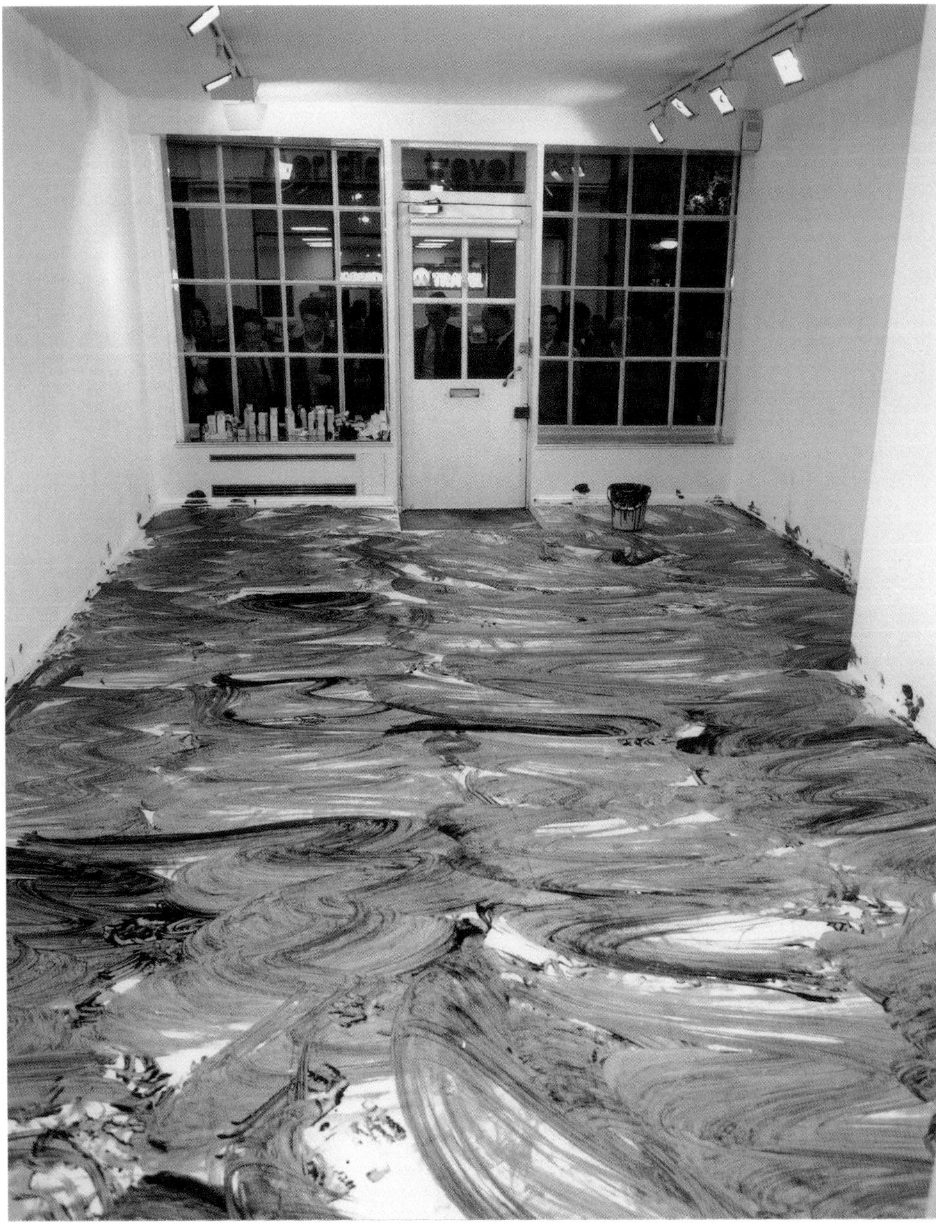

As Laderman Ukeles was hand-washing the Athenaeum's floors, nine-year-old Janine Antoni watched the country of her birth celebrate its independence from Britain.[2] Twenty years later, Antoni performed *Loving Care* in the very same gallery Laderman Ukeles had occupied. Dressed in a black leotard, she dipped her hair in Loving Care natural black dye and proceeded to paint the floors, using her hair and body as brush. Her body flowed like a dancer's as she swirled dye across the floor. In the process, the audience was forced to give way and was eventually pushed out of the gallery space entirely (figure 1.1).

Antoni's rejection of traditional matrices like canvas to the floor broadcast an atonal historical echo and rhizomatic performance that intersected multiple narratives across time and space. Like Laderman Ukeles, in making the Athenaeum's floors her matrix, Antoni laid claim to institutional space and its attendant histories to insert herself simultaneously into the currents of American feminist, global Caribbean, and contemporary art.

The full signification of Antoni's performance and the oeuvre she produced in the 1990s has never been engaged from a Caribbean postcolonial feminist perspective as decolonial work. At first glance, this may seem understandable, since her oeuvre, in contradistinction to Marc Latamie's, does not overtly draw on Caribbean histories and imaginaries. But, in the context of the prevailing center-margin construct that dominated artistic discourse in the 1990s, I argue that Antoni's authorial strategies and production illuminate the contemporaneous global Caribbean movement through a singularly intriguing and deeply personal post(trans)national feminist perspective. Like Latamie, Antoni embodies and exposes the formal range of global Caribbean art. Her work "plays mas" with histories and canons in the problem space of the United States in order to navigate theoretical, institutional, and critical architectures designed to exclude non-Western, globally circulating artists.[3]

MANGROVE, BEACH, PINE FOREST, METROPOLE

Raised on the island of Grand Bahama, a small and insignificant place that the artist's mother describes as lying "behind God's back," Janine Antoni received a formal Catholic education replete with appeals to piety, purity, and deference to the feminine ideal embodied by the Virgin Mary. After high school, Antoni attended Sarah Lawrence College and subsequently decided to apply to a master of fine arts program. By the time she received her bachelor's degree, however, she had not yet compiled a portfolio that evidenced clarity of focus and creative confidence. Unsure of her artistic direction, Antoni's parents convinced their daughter to travel to Japan to mentor with a family friend and develop a portfolio. With few options, she did as she was told. It did not take long for her to realize she'd made a huge mistake. The family friend had no idea what to do with her and made it clear that he did not want her there. She returned home.

Back in Freeport, Antoni immersed herself in the landscape she had come to love as a child. Focusing on three aspects of the local environment—the pine forest, beach, and mangrove—she produced intimate, ephemeral sculptures and installations and documented her creative process through photography. This suite of photographs became Antoni's portfolio and the basis of her applications to art school.

Although Antoni did not receive any outright acceptances, she was wait-listed at the Rhode Island School of Design (RISD) and subsequently enrolled there when another admitted student decided to go elsewhere. She began the MFA program in 1987. Six years later, her work was shown at both the Whitney and the Venice Biennales. Since then, she has exhibited all over the world, from South Africa to South Korea, Sweden to Australia. While working and living primarily in New York City, she became known as a global artist—an identity that seemed to disappear both her Caribbean origins and any historical referents present in the work. Antoni was fully aware of this suppression. In fact, it represented a tactical engagement: She used this vacuum to demarcate visibility for her work and to surface the process of erasure inherent in the colonial playbook. She manipulated the art world's power and presumptions to quite literally, as David Scott suggests, "make demands of criticism in the postcolonial present."[4]

COMMUNION FOR THE BODY

In 1992 Antoni held her first solo exhibition at the Sandra Gering Gallery in New York City, which earned her near-instantaneous international recognition. Reflecting on this early work, she noted her interest in "everyday body rituals and converting the most basic sort of activities—eating, bathing, mopping—into sculptural processes. Even in doing this, I imitate basic fine art rituals such as chiseling (with my teeth), painting (with my hair and eyelashes), modeling and molding (with my own body). In terms of material, I use . . . soap, lard, chocolate, and hair dye, [which] all come in intimate contact with the body and redefine or locate the body within our culture. These materials also have a specific relationship to women in our society. The gender of the viewer informs their reading of my work."[5] Antoni's seemingly unorthodox approach echoed the feminist art practices Laderman Ukeles had employed in the 1960s, with a few twists.

One of the most important pieces included in the Gering exhibition was *Gnaw* (1992), a sculpture composed of two 600-pound cubes, one of chocolate and the other of lard (figure 1.2). Antoni said that the piece was born of her simple desire to chew on a huge chunk of chocolate. And, after having it cast, she proceeded to do just that, biting and then spitting out the chocolate. She repeated the same process with the cube of lard. With the expectorated pieces, Antoni manufactured new objects. She made tubes of lipstick from the lard and heart-shaped boxes with the chocolate. While researching the project, she learned that chocolate contains phenylethylamine. Known by the humorous acronym PEA, the chemical is produced naturally by the body during orgasm. In exhibition, Antoni placed these objects in a display case, with her name as the brand and the title "Phenylethylamine Display." Rather than foregrounding a literal reading of the materials, she highlighted their different significations by gesturing toward chocolate's intimacy and "sweetness" and lard's "oiliness," deepening our encounter with the objects by defamiliarizing our point of entry.

Antoni's production process was inseparable from the signification of her raw materials and their art historical and social references. It was also a poignant example of meaningful formalism in a critical space of Derridean différance that typifies the work of this period's global Caribbean artists. *Gnaw*'s materiality and fabrication configured Antoni's body as a creative, laborer, machine, and producer while calling up the complex commodity histories of chocolate and lard in the Caribbean and wider Americas. She appropriated, transformed, and disfigured the clean, minimalist cube with each bite she took. Although gallerygoers encountered a polished presentation, the repetition the work incarnated, its emphasis on the body as maker and tool, and the forensic capacity of her bite marks—in a period of essentialist identity politics—expanded the work's conceptual implications, experiential possibilities, and interventionist capabilities. The intensity of physical labor and endurance required to produce *Loving Care* and *Gnaw* (a month and a half of biting) dramatized Antoni's creative process and the invisibility of women's labor.

When she first arrived in the United States, Antoni was made painfully aware that her body language was "inappropriate." She touched people too

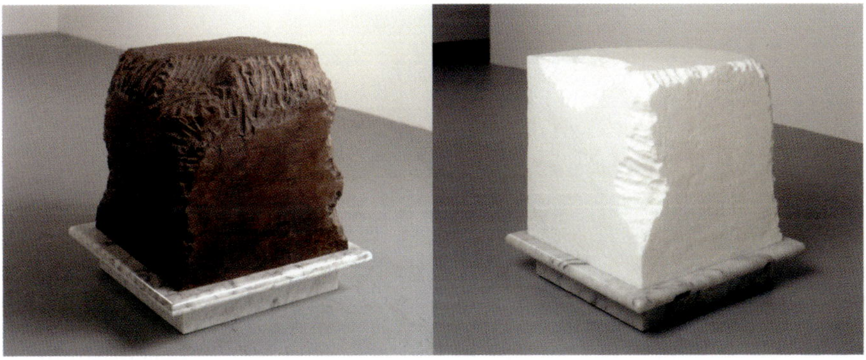

1.2 Janine Antoni, *Gnaw*, 1992. A 600-pound chocolate cube and a 600-pound lard cube gnawed by the artist: 45 heart-shaped packages of chocolate made from chewed chocolate removed from chocolate cube and 150 lipsticks made with pigment, beeswax, and chewed lard removed from lard cube. Each cube, 24 × 24 × 24 in. (60.96 × 60.96 × 60.96 cm).

much and didn't cross her legs properly. Perceived reactions to her body's offenses in this new space forced her to retrain it and, in the process, claim it as a site of knowledge. This became a fundamental concept in her practice, and she openly discussed the connection between body and knowledge in her work: "I put myself through these physical tasks to set up a situation where the viewer might empathize with the process. I want the viewer to imagine what it is like to do these things, to feel it through their body, to relate to the work in terms of body knowledge. They can consider their relationship to the object in terms of the process, as opposed to the normal way we approach these types of artworks by objectively decoding visual information."[6] What makes this empathy plausible or possible? How does communion with the artist's body catalyze meaning and audience connection? In *Beyond a Boundary*, Trinidadian writer and theorist C. L. R. James goes far afield from American feminism to consider how cricket, as practiced in the Caribbean, represents an art form that makes communion not only possible but necessary and intrinsic to its production. He insists that the people who watched cricket, *the audience*, were central to the process.[7] This concept extends art beyond artifact and the threshold of encounter to render it as experiential and relational, a phenomenon formed and reformed in Glissantian relation. James's paradigm is an instructive analog to Antoni's desired communication with audiences through *body knowledge* and participatory art- and meaning-making.

James recognized that the cricket player, while engaged in an individual battle with a bowler, also represented a social group.[8] Frantz Fanon had described, in *Black Skin, White Masks*, a similar experience of multiple identification when, in a moment of crisis, he perceived acute responsibility for his body, race, and ancestors.[9] Where Fanon and James differed was the potential for resolution. James suggested that the "fundamental relation of the One and the Many, Individual and Social, Individual and Universal, leader and followers, representative and ranks, the part and the whole" is reconciled by the call-and-response between cricket players and audience;[10] Fanon conjured the perennial psychosis of a divided self. In James's schema, the individual burden is cast off, and borne collectively through shared experience.

In James's spirit, Antoni establishes her relationship to audiences by forging commonalities and shared intimacies through her body and artwork. Everyone can relate to the physical act of biting she used to sculpt *Gnaw*. Universal and prelinguistic, it is a primary means through which we come to understand and acquire knowledge about the world around us and our place in it.[11] In *Loving Care*, Antoni invited her audience to share in the Jamesian framework of discursive formation through encounter and shared experience.

Both *Gnaw* and *Loving Care* resonated with audiences and received massive public attention, both inside and outside the art world. The establishment was intrigued by what it perceived as Antoni's evocation and reworking of canonical modernist practices, including Abstract Expressionism in *Loving Care* and Minimalism in *Gnaw*. Deliberate and wry, these references imbued the works with a critical feminist edge whose significance was often subdued in paean texts.

Gnaw was embraced by diverse audiences and spawned critical discussions that the artist neither foresaw nor intended but that developed organically around, for example, bulimia and other eating disorders. Antoni recognized such spontaneous interpretations as part and parcel of an artwork's passage from the studio into public space:

> The cube showed up in *Food Arts Magazine*, it was in health magazines, it was in fashion magazines. It was used in so many different ways. . . . My feeling about the work is that it was about eating. But the culture came back to me and said: "We have a disorder. That's what we're interested in." That reading of the work seems more about the culture's response to eating than my original intentions for the work. There is something very interesting

about that. I think success for an artist often has to do with becoming a way of illustrating ideas that people are thinking about at the time and need to verbalize. In effect, though, I had produced this somehow. I wanted to introduce a dialog.[12]

Though presented in and as body knowledge, the work finds meaning and takes unexpected shape through interaction that extends beyond both artistic intention and the audience's expectations.

After the Gering show, *Gnaw* appeared in the game-changing 1993 Whitney Biennial, curated by Thelma Golden. Although many critics praised the sculpture and cited its feminist redux of Minimalism, others derisively situated the work in the "Bulimic Art" category.[13] Antoni processed the latter response as another unanticipated discourse, wryly commenting that "bulimia seemed interesting as a metaphor for a society that ferociously gobbles everything up, and rather than digest [what they consume], they spit it up."[14]

The extensive process of consumption and regurgitation of manufactured products presented multiple points of entry and interpretation and touched on the cruel and extreme measures women adopted to attain an elusive standard of beauty. Antoni's material dialectic interrogated the billion-dollar cosmetics industry and its predominantly female market, probing its commodified promise of pleasure, perfection, transformation, and eternal youth. Her deployment of the beautification process and its attendant products exposed how women's efforts to maintain and "improve" their bodies could also destroy them. For example, although the amounts of phenylethylamine found in chocolate and generated during orgasm are minute, excessive ingestion has been associated with depression and paranoid schizophrenia. Through materials, process, performance, and exhibition, Antoni's art, and the Glissantian state of multiplicity it engenders, continues to produce and circulate meaning.

Loving Care reinscribed and expanded upon *Gnaw*'s ideas. After its debut, the curator Dan Cameron observed: "By scrambling the historically loaded image of scrubbing the floor on one's hands and knees with the equally over-determined notion of updating one's hair in order to ward off the effects of aging, Antoni seems to be forming a wry comment on the history of women's self-abnegation, in which menial labor is transformed into a metaphor for the straitjacket definition of beauty as a by-product of youth." From a decolonial perspective, this is where the piece's interpretive work begins. Both *Gnaw* and *Loving Care* probe the competing forces, pleasure, and repetition in rituals of labor. Cameron noted that, contrary to commonplace views that indulgent bodily pleasure has "no redeeming social value," Antoni felt "that in a society which attempts to dictate the terms by which pleasure is incorporated into one's life, the 'disputed' realm of the body offers both the opportunity to put up a symbolic resistance to this control, and the means to refer to other issues."[15] Reaching toward those other issues, Juli Carson, who first curated *Loving Care*, said that "for Antoni, ritual itself is the fetish played out through desire, specifically, the desire of repetition-compulsion as it relates to elusive notions of mastery over one's own subjectivity."[16] Although one could argue that these readings of bodily pleasure and aesthetics are more consistent with the American mainstream and thus antithetical to many "Caribbean" aesthetic ideals, this essentialist framing is challenged by Antoni's situatedness within an American problem space. Certainly, the manufacture and re-presentation of chocolate and lipstick gesture toward an "American" consumerist culture targeted mostly to women, but these items and ideals are also global in reach, and Antoni's sculptural processes—biting and mopping—are universal. Indeed, the commodities are marketed to the Caribbean and the rest of the world as normative or, more specifically, attainable. Geeta Kapur was right to suggest that in the universalist rhetoric deployed during this period, "what is being globalized is an American style capitalism and its implicit worldview."[17] Within this theoretical paradigm and its commodified circulation were ideas coding domestic labor (mopping) as feminine and increasingly foreign. Caribbean people were positioned as passive receptacles rather than active participants in defining their own standards of beauty. Although Antoni replicates the production of beauty products as art commodity, in the process she creates space for the audience's reflexive critique. Regardless of the encounter's cultural milieu, the emphasis pivots not toward the product per se but to one's personal relationship to its representational capacities and reach.

In this reflective interaction, a Caribbean postcolonial finds value in the signifying qualities of *Loving Care*. They may hear echoes of Peter Minshall's "Washerwoman," a central character in Minshall's seminal Trinidad carnival performance, *The River* (1983). In this street opera, the *blanchisseuse*, dressed in a simple white cotton gown representative of beauty, love, and nature, battles the antagonist ManCrab, who represents technological intervention and appears dancing in movements drawn from Kathakali. He confronts Washerwoman, who dismisses him; rebuffed, he eventually returns to destroy her.[18] In the gallery setting, Antoni offers a wry and knowing take on similar battles waged between technology and nature; colonial power and postcolonial aspirations; access and dispossession; history, archive, and authorship; presence and power. This time, however, the "Washerwoman"/Antoni prevails.

Loving Care also spoke to the complex histories of hair in the Caribbean, where texture is a signifier of non-Blackness, and its length, femininity. Antoni, who is from a multiracial background but presents as white, deploys her long hair to great effect. Its visibility and flow in relief conjures beyond art historical references. In plantation societies, enslaved Black and mixed-race women were not permitted to expose their hair and were forced to conceal it to shield against the elements and the slavers' desirous gaze and jealous wrath.[19] Moreover, cutting of the hair was commonly practiced as a form of degradation and punishment in the Americas. In *Loving Care*, Antoni defies concealment to demand and command specularization. She controls the gaze, a position of power unknown to most Caribbean women, even today. Capable of occupying multiple discourses simultaneously and generating content depth in ways that move across space and time, the work's mutable and multiple signifying character became a key feature of the artist's oeuvre in the early 1990s.

SILENCES, SINS, AND ABSOLUTIONS

In 1993 Antoni created *Lick and Lather* for the Venice Biennale. During the work's first phase, she cast fourteen classicized busts in her image—seven in chocolate and seven in soap. She then changed and expunged details through "licking" and "lathering." She licked the chocolate for weeks and lathered herself with the soap sculptures in the tub and shower, until her features and body parts were erased. In exhibition, the busts were placed on simple columns and arranged in two rows facing each other (figure 1.3).

When engaging this early work, critics called attention to Antoni's use of "her body as both the subject/object of her representation, but also the creative force behind the process of subject/object[ification]."[20] In her patently feminist conceptual actions, the artist—pace bell hooks—"rewrites her body." Reclaiming her narrative, Antoni becomes "author, authority" of the process; the speaking subject "is now the center of her talk."[21] Although Antoni's work clearly evidences a strategic and generative postcolonial feminist aesthetic practice, her rapid ascendancy was not without casualty, fabrication, and complication. To wit, it's notable that by this time,

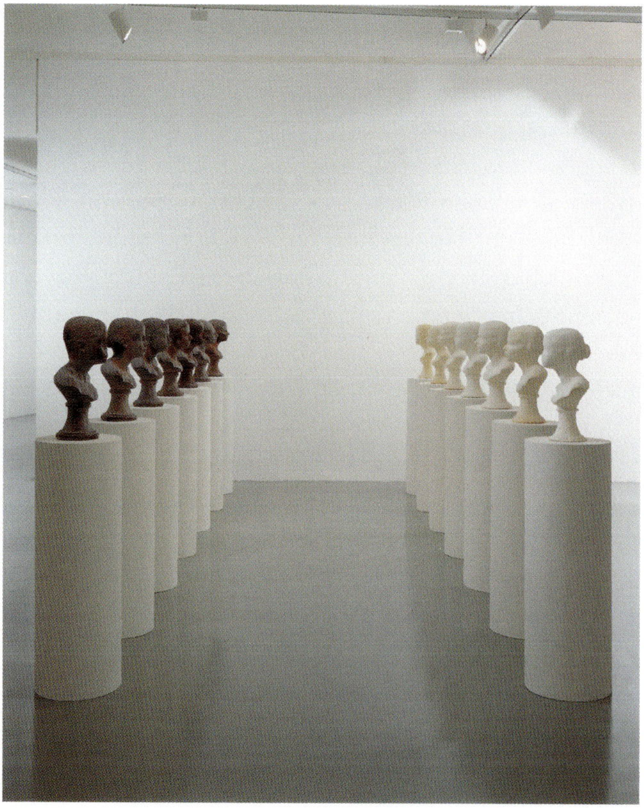

1.3 Janine Antoni, *Lick and Lather*, 1993. Seven licked-chocolate self-portrait busts and seven washed-soap self-portrait busts on fourteen pedestals. Bust: 24 × 16 × 13 in. (60.96 × 40.64 × 33.02 cm) (each, approximately). Pedestal: 45⅞ × 16 in. (116.01 × 40.64 cm) (each). Installation dimensions: variable. Photographed by Lee Stalsworth at the Hirshhorn Museum and Sculpture Garden, Washington, DC, 1999.

the Caribbean had already disappeared from the conversation—not as an identifier in the literal sense (Antoni never hid her place of birth) but as a contributor to her work's discursive positioning and material context.

Antoni's artistic maturation emerged from a growing awareness of her power to think through objects, a studied engagement with American feminist art history, and an apprehension of her capacity to shape it through her work. At RISD, Antoni met the artist Mira Schor, through whom she tapped into a feminist archive and lineage that validated and mobilized a desire for recognition and public voice or, put simply, her will to be an artist.[22] Schor came of age during the first wave of American feminist art and was nurtured by the Feminist Art Program at the California Institute of the Arts (CalArts) and her participation in seminal exhibitions at Womanhouse. There, she interacted with Judy Chicago and Miriam Schapiro. This was a time of groundbreaking transformation as well as generational knowledge exchange and field formation. The movement's sensibilities, processes, philosophies, and revolutionary potential crystallized at CalArts. As Chicago has asserted again and again, "Feminist art education is about making art which is authentic to one's lived experience. . . . It's about helping people find personal content, getting at that content, and then determining the most appropriate forms to express that content."[23] This pathway was extended through Chicago's and Schapiro's students, many of whom also went on to teach in the academy, Schor included.

Schor was Antoni's professor at RISD, and Antoni has cited her mentorship as a key midwife in her awakening to the history and labor of the American feminist art movement. Through Schor, Antoni was exposed to a living archival resource and introduced to the field's rich landscape of interventions and significations. At a momentous meeting, Antoni was struggling to contextualize and find the language to speak about the work she wanted to make. Schor sent her to the library with a list of women artists and documents to research. Antoni's visit yielded nothing; there were no books, catalogues, articles, or reference materials that recorded the existence of these artists or their work. When Antoni reported her findings, or lack thereof—lesson learned—Schor provided access to her personal library and trove of original documents. As Antoni devoured the archive, her thoughts fell into place, and her development as an artist was set into motion. Schor's archive and the portal it offered to the feminist art movement resonated with Antoni, providing her with an aesthetic language and lineage in which to ground and articulate her own practice.

Exchanges like this were probably common for Schor; she likely sent many of her female students to the library knowing exactly what they would, or wouldn't, find. Through this exercise, they could viscerally grasp what women's "absence" and historical erasure looked like on an institutional level and felt like on a personal one. In the essay "Liberation to Lack," Schor clarified her strategy: "Feminism has little institutional memory, there has been no collective absorption of early achievements and ideas, and therefore feminism cannot yet afford the luxury of storage. Teaching young women to paint, I have found that every young woman who feels in herself the inchoate desire to do something, say something about her life, must begin at the same beginning, or very close to it, that my sisters and I did seventeen years ago."[24] The encoding of history and memory is subject to power and patriarchy. For Schor, this fact manifested in the ongoing tendency for women theorists, critics, and artists to legitimate women's creative output by tracing its artistic descent to a named male father, such as Courbet, Duchamp, Beuys, Picasso, or even Vito Acconci. It's no coincidence that this practice mirrored the ways colonial power structures and binary narratives shaped the art historical epistemes and discursive positioning of Others. Life outside (Western art) history was as much a gendered condition as it was a colonial and Caribbean one.

Years after their teacher-student relationship ended, Schor reiterated the problem of gender and genealogy in American art narratives in the essay "Patrilineage," using Antoni's emergence as an example.[25] As she noted later, "*Most* art historians, including almost *all male* art historians, and an unfortunate number of women art historians, assign value to art work by women and also to work by men by giving them a patrilineage even when a matrilineage evidently exists for the work in question."[26] Writers had leapt to situate *Gnaw* in relation to Joseph Beuys (the lard) and Dieter Rot (the chocolate). While Schor acknowledged some degree of connection, particularly to Beuys, it troubled her that feminist artists were excised from Antoni's narrative. In effect, Antoni was remade into an artist who was fathered but not *mothered*. For Schor, art critics' and historians' failure (or refusal) to discuss Antoni's work in relation to that of Ann Hamilton and Maureen Connor, for example, severed her fundamental feminist aesthetic connections and erased the presence and production of the women artists whose work she had engaged as generative formal, performative, and conceptual references.

Schor recalls a performance by Ann Hamilton that took place at Louver New York, a Los Angeles–based gallery on Prince Street, some months before the *Gnaw* exhibition opened. The piece was entitled *Malediction*. Hamilton sat at a table, which was covered by white cloths soiled with red wine, and proceeded to bite into "lumps of dough, which she then spat out and placed in a basket for them to rise and decay."[27] For Schor, the work spoke to issues of "bulimia and waste," and the soiled cloths drew on Christian iconography.[28] In process, theme, and "biting" humor, this performance was echoed in *Gnaw*.

Antoni's work also resonates with Maureen Connor's *Ensemble for Three Female Voices*, which was featured at her exhibition *The Senses*, which opened at Germans Van Eck in New York on the same day Antoni's Gering show closed. Connor had been Antoni's sculpture professor at RISD prior to Schor and had exhibited *Ensemble* previously and widely. The piece consisted of "cast female larynxes in red lipstick" and embedded themes of anorexia and bulimia.[29] Yet the critical narrative on Antoni's emergence elided or expunged these connections. Schor was particularly troubled because Antoni had privately discussed both Hamilton's and Connor's work with her. This pointed omission prompted her to wonder whether Antoni was complicit in crafting a lineage narrative that excluded her teachers and interlocutors. Taking her to task, Schor questioned Antoni's commitment to the principles of feminism and feminist art: "Matrilineage can only begin when a woman artist risks foregoing validation via mega-fathers in favor of her own female teachers and contemporaries, or at least when she enriches the public's understanding of her work by a more balanced self-contextualization."[30] While the statement may reflect an unfortunate takedown, its cogency parallels the originary excision of the Caribbean from Antoni's artistic narrative and critical discussions of her work. Scholarship from the period persistently tethered Antoni's seminal works to Western artistic traditions. *Gnaw* was positioned as a descendant of Minimalism; *Loving Care* was articulated in relation to Yves Klein and, specifically, Jackson Pollock's version of Abstract Expressionism; and *Lick and Lather* was linked to Greek classicism.

Antoni's participation in this narrow framing could be construed as a strategic reinvention of a contrapuntal identity, or global Caribbean mas—the rendition of self as complex being and enactment of one's right to multiplicity, or mythology. That is, rather than turning her back on the cultural, aesthetic, and historical formations that anchored her work, Antoni was straining to go beyond them while simultaneously exposing the tenacity of their grip.

As an emerging postcolonial, global, Caribbean, feminist artist, Antoni was committed to feminist ideals and never concealed the formative connections that were contextualizing her work. She didn't hide her place of birth, the subject of her artistic interest, or the issues she grappled with. And while one does sense a pointed resistance to claiming these histories as singular sites or sources, a stronger current of self-invention evidences a strategy of illumination and opacity deployed by many global Caribbean artists during this period.

Antoni's awareness of the colonial terrain of art history is notable. She was remarkably cognizant of the fact that the art world's disengagement with her past and failure to make discursive connections to other feminist artists would, in time, expose the power relations and hierarchies it claimed to have transcended. In interviews, Antoni exploited her critics' prejudices and ignorance, seizing on their laziness, pretensions to connoisseurship, and predilection for scripted responses over studied engagement with the work. In spotlighting the art world's xenophobia, racism, and sexism, she was willing to pay the up-front costs of entering art history, even if it appeared that she was discarding the political, historical, and cultural formations that centered her practice. She was playing the long game. Feminist histories and critical aesthetics, alongside cultural references to the Caribbean, are self-evident in her work, as is her performative and conceptual reimagining of canonical Western art movements. Perhaps Antoni mused that someday art history would absolve her.[31]

The silences in the literature on Antoni's work speak to the critical terrain on which it emerged and the decolonial capacity of her practice. Recalling a salient point that Schor made: What is one to make of generations of women artists trained in feminist spaces who claim the politics of feminism as history rather than as central to their contemporary practice? How does one process the work of emerging women artists who do not feel responsibility to assume the weight of ongoing feminist struggle? Why did women artists risk exile from the communities that nurtured them? The answers to these questions are complex. I posit that Antoni and her generational peers didn't leave feminist histories behind but rather negotiated power differently, asserting a level of freedom and right to inclusion within white patriarchy in ways that would have been politically untenable for first-wave feminist artists.

While Antoni's gesturing toward feminist art practices from the late 1960s was remarkably obvious and yet rarely engaged, the resonance of her early work within a global Caribbean imaginary is literally nonexistent, even as it is threaded with various cultural narratives and practices tethered to the region. I argue that the raison d'être of Antoni's well-documented engagement of Minimalism, Abstract Expressionism, pop art, and Western classical forms is in fact rendered through a Caribbean, transnational, feminist lens.[32]

Gnaw engages Minimalism not only in form or as art historical validation but also, as Martha Buskirk proposes, as a challenge to early modern notions of authorship and authenticity.[33] In this vein, canonical Minimalists and their associates, like Donald Judd and Frank Stella, are well known for selling multiples and plans of works for collectors to execute at a later date, according to the artist's specifications. So is Antoni. The lard portion of *Gnaw* is not stable.[34] When the Museum of Modern Art purchased it, Antoni included the cast of a second original, with instructions to cast a new version each time the work was exhibited. The lard sculpture as artifact retains Antoni's touch only as shadow, invoking an unintended distancing between her body and the exhibited object that approximates Minimalism's production philosophy. Yet the deeper resonances between her signifying materials and processes and feminism and global Caribbean aesthetic practices undercut the tenacity of an intentional and integral connection with Minimalism.[35]

Antoni's selection of organic materials and creative process evoke medieval ideals of guild production. It values the haptic and handmade. They run counter to Minimalists' dependence on industrial precision and the elevation of indelibility through the use of stone, steel, and other metals. Moreover, Antoni's insistence on the body's durability and creative agency opposes any attempt to replace the artist's material presence with the aura of trace. In *Gnaw*, Antoni eats and regurgitates the perfect Minimalist cube. The bite marks erode and contest its exclusionary aesthetics by literally possessing and deconstructing its pretensions. As Buskirk observes, in Antoni's work, "the touch or mark is not simply a vehicle for creating an aesthetic effect; rather, recognition of the mark itself and its relation to the body of the artist is central to the message of the work . . . [as are] her exploration of endurance and the power of repetitive actions, her interest in gender, particularly as articulated through the female body, her use of materials with strong cultural associations, and her continued and varied assertion of the artist's presence in the work."[36] Buskirk's analysis tells us that the artist's formal language, the tenor of her critical process, owes much to histories and practices outside the male-dominated Western art canon. Returning to C. L. R. James, if Antoni represents both the individual and the collective(s), how can a more balanced historical contextualization of her practice within a feminist and Caribbean frame materialize when critics, curators, and scholars have persistently refused to engage it from these points of departure?

In the 1990s, Antoni intentionally crafted a practice in conversation with feminist and institutionally sanctioned histories of art. Through this strategy and the production that emerged from it, she expressed a desire to be seen as a complex being, free to draw from multiple art histories and traditions—mainstream, feminist, and Caribbean—without having to choose or prioritize among them. Antoni consumed feminist art so completely that her work resonates not as mere quotation but as formal and conceptual point and counterpoint to the process of historicization and the authority of the archive.

WEAN, WEANING, WEANED

Wean was the first work Antoni completed after graduate school (figure 1.4). The installation documents the voyage from nature to culture, from attachment to distance, rendered through a series of sculptural depressions embedded in the gallery wall. The first depression is a negative impression of Antoni's full breast, and the second an impression of her nipple. The third, fourth, and fifth depressions are a series of three latex nipples from a baby's bottle, and the sixth is an impression of a baby bottle with nipple. The series maps lines of continuity and an arc of absence, embedded in gallery walls where this body has been historically absented.

Antoni has noted that the installation was in some ways obvious, straightforward, and literal and "mapped out a certain territory" from which all her subsequent work followed. It certainly reflects her artistic maturation and the forces that had collectively and continuously nourished her, including the Caribbean and the American feminist movement.[37] Recalling Glissant, Antoni's simultaneous displacement and transmutation of materials shows that even as she created art with an eye to the future, her contemporary practice assumed and represented the weight of the unrendered past and made space for it to enter into the historical record.

Antoni's early work clearly engenders conversations with other seminal pieces of American feminist art from the period. *Wean* recalls the prosthetic breast forms protruding from the walls and ceiling in Susan Frazier and Vicki Hodgetts's collaborative work *Eggs to Breasts* (1972) and Robin Weltsch's *Nurturant Kitchen* (1972), both of which were exhibited at Womanhouse. Robin Schiff's *Nightmare Bathroom* (1972) can be seen as a formal positive to Antoni's *Eureka* (1993). *Loving Care* bears a conceptual echo of Laderman Ukeles's *Maintenance Art*, as well as *Scrubbing*, performed by Chris Rush at Womanhouse in 1972. One also sees traces of Faith Wilding's *Waiting* (1971, 1972) in the formal architecture of Antoni's table of contents for the catalogue

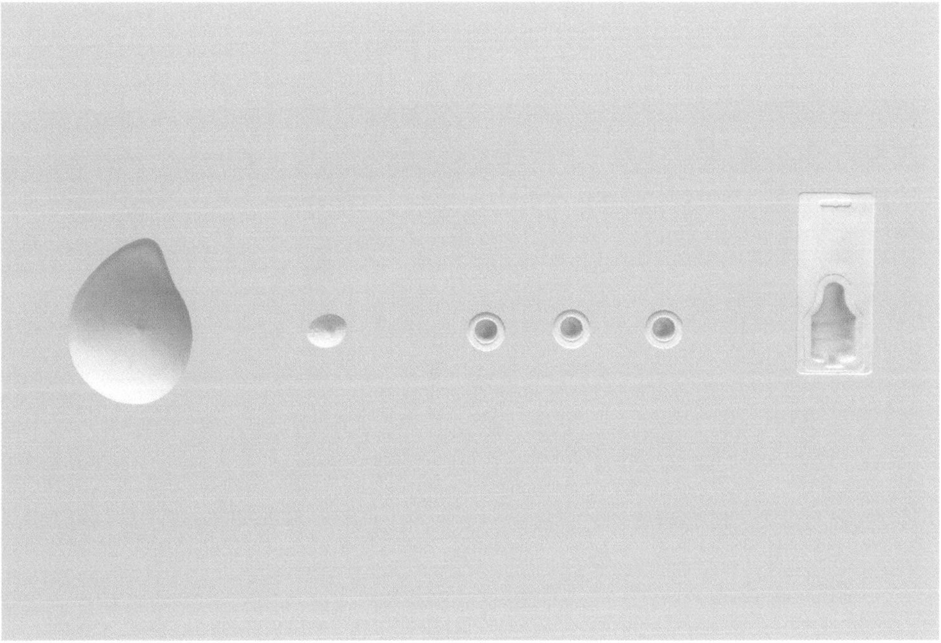

1.4 Janine Antoni, *Wean*, 1989–90. Plaster, sheet rock, 12 × 38 × 2 in. (30.48 × 96.52 × 5.08 cm). Photographed by John Bessler.

The Girl Made of Butter (2001). Finally, Antoni's *Ingrown* (1998) echoes Claire Prussian's *Prismacolor IV* (1976) (figures 1.5 and 1.6). These resonances and connections are not incidental, nor are they total. In Antoni's words, the linkages between her early work and this history were *obvious*, yet mainstream critics refused to see and register them, instead relying on and thereby simultaneously reinscribing the authority of a heroic history of modern and contemporary art dominated by white male artists.

When Chicago, Schapiro, and their students curated and produced the Womanhouse installation, they worked collaboratively, purposefully drawing on processes associated with uncompensated and repetitive tasks often described as "women's work," such as scrubbing, washing, painting, and sweeping. Antoni related to this conceptual turn—theoretically, formally, and personally—and this recognition registers in her artworks' gestural complexity. Regarding *Loving Care*, Antoni specified:

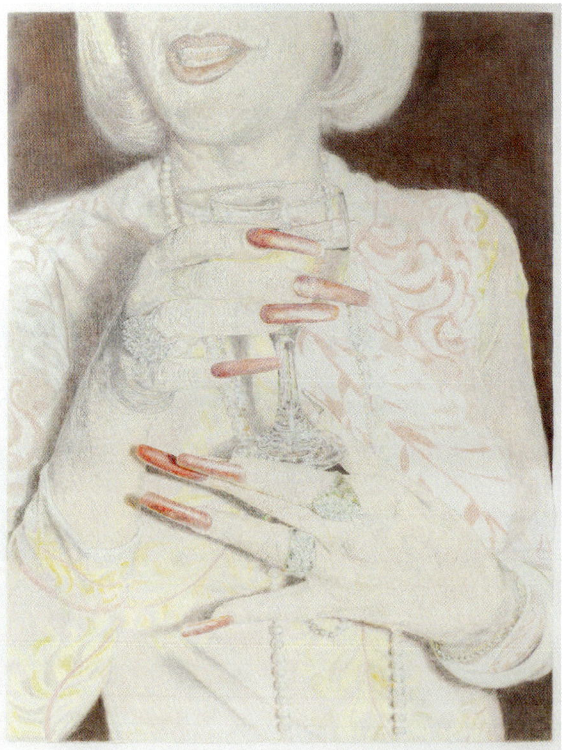

1.5 Claire Prussian, *Prismacolor IV*, 1976. Color pencil and graphite on paper, 56 × 43 in. Racine Art Museum, the Karen Johnson Boyd Collection. Photographed by Jarvis Lawson.

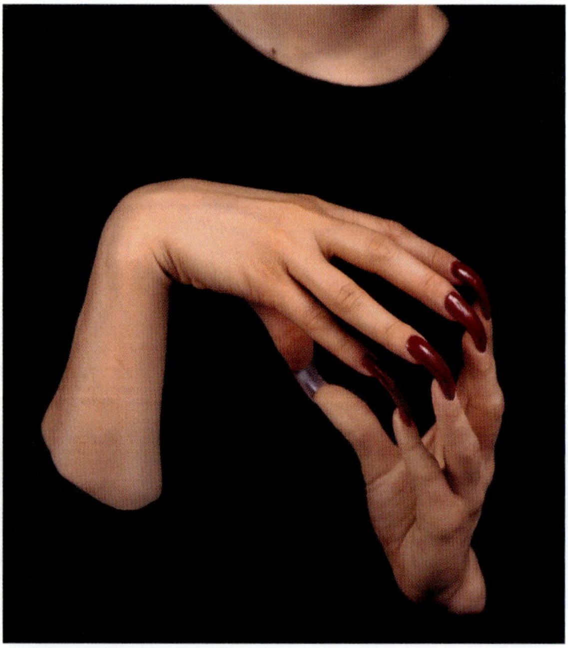

1.6 Janine Antoni, *Ingrown*, 1998. C-print, 18⅛ × 16³⁄₁₀ in. (46.04 × 41.4 cm). Framed: 21¾ × 19⅞ in. (55.25 × 49.85 cm). Photographer unknown.

> This idea of mopping people out of the room is important for you to know because for me to be there on my hands and knees was very vulnerable, but for me to claim the space at the museum or the gallery was very empowering. And I was really thinking about being a kid and my mom telling me, "OK, Janine, you have to go and play outside because I've just mopped the kitchen floor," . . . for that time, the kitchen becomes her space, and how could I do the same thing with the gallery or the museum?[38]

In the 1980s and '90s, these intentions aligned with the work of global feminist artists deeply committed to decolonizing art history and the art world. At the time, Gilane Tawadros compared the artist Lubaina Himid's appropriation and transformation of Picasso's *Two Women Running on the Beach* (1922) with the practice of postcolonial artists like Antoni who worked in global spaces and repurposed Western and feminist art histories for conceptual ends. Tawadros suggested that Himid's use in *Freedom and Change* (1984) of "preexisting art forms from the history of Western art can be seen to be a part of a coherent political and aesthetic strategy based on an interrogation of Western history *through* history." Antoni's aesthetic and political conversations with Minimalism, Abstract Expressionism, and feminist art arguably performed similar work, in turn affiliating with global contemporaries who deployed similar strategies, including Sutapa Biswas in *Housewives with Steak Knives* (1985), which according to Tawadros, also defied "the distinction drawn between the private and avowedly 'feminine' domestic sphere, in this case exemplified by the kitchen, and the public, allegedly 'masculine' domain of political action" and, we may insert here for Antoni, the gallery space.[39]

Coming from a small island tucked behind God's back, Antoni was encouraged by her mother to go out and see the world, to move beyond the limits of home. Although her work is deeply rooted in feminist discourse, her use of the body speaks to a relationship between history and subjectivity that includes the Caribbean in its conceptual reach. Antoni conjured the threads between her formal education and her positionality as follows:

> The work from the nineties, you can look at it as directly coming out of my education, you know, the classical—the art historical references in the work. With the early work it was about trying to locate myself in relation to that—whether it was the Minimalist view—the classical bust. This is what I knew of art history as a canon, and *feeling outside of that*. And feeling like I am going to take this and manipulate it to incorporate me. So I

> think there was that and there was the feminism which first came out in an unconscious way. [. . .] [T]hen when I got introduced to all of these women [I realized] it was where I was coming from. It was important to me, and then I started to locate myself in terms of women's art.[40]

These are incredible statements to make in a postcolonial Caribbean context. Like the Caribbean festivals carnival and Junkanoo,[41] the performance of *Loving Care* establishes authorship within a space of personal and historical exclusion. Antoni's positioning of the work in response to Yves Klein's *Anthropométries de l'époque bleue* (1960) marks a double claim, whereby she assumes the right of ownership not only to the space but to her body and the art historical narrative. Through this act of insertion and assertion, Othered audiences can *experience* "the conflict of wanting to be the model and the master at the same time."[42]

In this first decade of her professional career, Antoni tapped into the ongoing decolonial labor of those positioned outside history. Although she was not physically in the Caribbean making work, the mechanisms deployed to sideline her were eerily similar to colonial apparatuses of exclusion. So, what of the Caribbean? Antoni's play with history is definitively aligned with a Césairean vision for decolonizing space, time, and history itself. But if the work was conceived within global movements, how might it resonate and be recognized at the intersection of multiplicity in a postnational, decolonizing, feminist, global Caribbean imaginary?

ON PASSING

Antoni's interception in a new, yet historically freighted cultural domain presupposes a legitimate claim to belonging. Yet, as Edward Said noted of migration, "one can never go back to some earlier and perhaps more stable condition."[43] This was particularly true for Antoni and other global Caribbean artists during the 1990s. Besides the steady practice of citing her birthplace at the end of essays and in exhibition ephemera, any trace of cultural recognition prior to Antoni's freshman year became a floating signifier that was never interrogated and thus exiled her past and severed her connection to the Caribbean. Even the year she spent in The Bahamas developing her portfolio marked a blank space.

Some years ago, I presented on Antoni's work at the Bahamas Association of Cultural Studies (BACUS) conference held at the College of The

Bahamas (COB) (now University of The Bahamas). During the question-and-answer period, some audience members posited that Antoni, as a Caribbean person, should be making art that spoke to them and their experiences more directly.[44] They asserted that *because* Antoni had the attention of the art world, she had the *obligation* to represent them. It was a difficult exchange. While it was clear that the time had come to seriously examine Antoni's work in relation to the Caribbean, it was equally clear that such a discussion would likely succumb to an anachronistic consideration of the burden of representation, a thread as worn and fruitless as Shakespeare's Caliban. In this venue, the artist's body and perceived whiteness were seen as a wall, not a perforated screen, and her work "foreign" rather than conceptually grounded, despite her efforts to produce and embody art that functions as sites of exchange and knowledge transmission.[45]

Although this type of response was tempered in ensuing years, its manifestation at this time and in this place could not be ignored. It stumbled toward a necessary conversation that remains verboten in polite Caribbean circles—questions around race and economies of color that are distinct from those of majority-white societies like the United States. In the Caribbean, to be European white or Caribbean white is to be a minority, an identity that, more often than not, accrues economic power.[46]

Belinda Edmondson posits that although the white Caribbean Creole, such as Antoni, is subject to the same cultural shifts and frames registered by Caribbean theorists from Kamau Brathwaite and Hall to Glissant and Fanon, he or she "occupies an ambiguous space in West Indian society. . . . [S]he is the descendant of the colonizer: [and] by virtue of her color she is virtually guaranteed a position of relative power and privilege if she so chooses."[47] At the same time, white Caribbean creoles are cultural hybrids, descending from Black, Indian, Chinese, and other races and ethnicities, in a lineage that embodies both colonizer and colonized, both Prospero and Caliban.[48] As in Césaire's *A Tempest*, in the Caribbean, the vicissitudes of the colonial relationship are scripted onto postcolonial racial ontologies and are not relegated to a specific population. All postcolonial Caribbeans bear the ambivalence of transculturation achieved through the violence of the limbo gateway of the Middle Passage. Yet they bear it differently.

At the BACUS conference, there was a pervasive sense that Caribbean cultural workers and intellectuals working in the region should receive greater local, regional, and international recognition. As an organization, BACUS prioritized locality as the primary criterion for authenticity and bound it to what Kobena Mercer has described as the "social responsibility of the artist." For Mercer the catch-22 of these "prescriptive" demands that tether the artist "ever more closely to the burden of being representative,"[49] colluding with a populist modernism that precludes art's emergence within an expansive and reflexive theoretical framework. Rather than engender innovative practices, this quest for illusory authenticity destroys art's transformative potential by insisting on endless reflection, ensuring that the weight of representation remains a marginalizing, colonizing force.

In an American context, as a Caribbean woman artist, Antoni was in a double bind: Like all Caribbean artists at the time, she was also subject to the art world's ghettoization as Other. She needed to maneuver beyond it. Antoni centers art's communicative capacity to induce reflection rather than representation per se, producing an aesthetic experience that stresses who the work is speaking *to, with, and about*, not who the artist or work is speaking *for*. Following Glissant, Paul Gilroy, and Mercer, I contend that the most politically astute artists do not seek or anticipate "a single, uniform audience but a plurality of publics" and assert polyvalence as a principal characteristic.[50] If, as Mercer posits, "artists don't have the last word when it comes to the public circulation and dissemination of their work,"[51] then audiences must also cede the right to demand what an artist can or cannot do.

Coming from an island "behind God's back," Antoni was aware of the boundaries and limitations placed on her and her work inside and outside the Caribbean. She was privy to the narrow ways the region and those who called it home were stereotyped and ignored and aware of the possibility that the authenticity of her work might be challenged and dismissed as mimicry in global spaces and within the region itself.[52] When Antoni *passed* into the postnational, global imaginary in the early 1990s, she perceived the discursive stakes and determined the narrative around her work in unprecedented ways.[53] Because of her legitimate distrust of art world criticism, she refused to bear the costs of legibility that would result in her work's erasure. These were not abstract concerns in the 1990s, as reflected by the curatorial ethos of many of the era's major exhibitions. Nonetheless, Antoni's decision to control the critical discourse was multivalent: On one hand, it limited engagement by diverse publics; on the other, it powerfully repudiated the era's indexical assumptions of one-dimensional identity politics.

BY REPETITION AND ROTE: RENDERING THE SELF-AUTHORED POSTCOLONIAL ARTIST

> But Janine, they all say and write the same thing.
> LYNETTE ANTONI

When I surveyed critical writings on Antoni's work from the 1990s, several common interpretive themes surfaced: What was expressed in 1993 was rearticulated in 2003, almost verbatim.[54] Most texts that focused solely on Antoni's work were either written by Antoni or edited by her, and the literature seemed so tightly curated, so orchestrated, that there is little doubt that the artist had a heavy hand in crafting it. Moreover, its repetitive content and monocular perspective established Antoni as a universal artist, absent politics, race, class, nation, history, or roots. And while it's clear that gender is foregrounded in her early work and that her female body is an inescapable boundary, even then, as previously discussed, the full range of its significance is only cursorily engaged.

Did Antoni cultivate and court ambivalence as identity, a persona underwritten by her ontological whiteness? Was Antoni's approach to her art, career, and archive a practice of deliberate opacity? An assertion of the right to be unknowable, private, undefined, and unframed? Surely this was impossible. But if it *were* possible, the maintenance of almost absolute control over her narrative—by providing the same story over and over, foreclosing alternate interpretations, and bulletproofing the archive—can be seen as her greatest work.

The first time we met face to face, I asked Antoni:

EJ: I have always wondered how much of a role you play or control you have in crafting or writing the narrative on your own work.

JA: Complete.

EJ: Completely?

JA: Anything you read in anyone else's voice is probably coming from me.

EJ: You edit everything?

JA: I edit as much as I can. Of course, with the internet I can't but . . .

EJ: Why? Why did you think that was so important?

JA: One is I realized that a lot of writers . . . were happy to take my word. And really—control—that is the honest answer. It is rare that somebody has the time to think about their work as much as I have, so it's rare that somebody comes up with something that is . . . interesting. . . . That's what I am looking for and that rarely happens.[55]

Through repetition and rote, Antoni employed a degree of strategic mastery over her narrative that recalls the infamous Royal Readers, textbooks the British used to educate their colonial subjects well into the 1960s. Repetition imparts consensus and generates belief. Whether she consciously or unconsciously used colonial methods to decolonize and shape perception of her practice, I understand why she would choose to resist categorization within the nadir of "Third World artist" or the tropicalized label "Caribbean artist" and instead chose to cultivate an ambivalent identity at the time. However, Antoni affirms that she never personally edited anything out of these texts regarding her identity. She recognized the assumption that she was a white American and not Caribbean and that this misrecognition increased focus on the work. It is here where she emphasized narrative control. Writers were free to engage her Caribbean identity at will, but few were willing.[56]

Jennifer Fisher's essay "Interperformance: The Live Tableaux of Suzanne Lacy, Janine Antoni, and Marina Abramovic" is a period example of art criticism retaining patriarchal methods, values, and critical blind spots, even while promoting generative feminist aesthetics.[57] At first, the piece reads as a critique of the first-wave feminist movement's endorsement of Victorian ideals of womanhood; Fisher positions Lacy, Antoni, and Abramović as disrupting this paradigm through reworking the tableau vivant form. However, pace Schor's argument, the value of this critical intervention is compromised by its point of departure, namely, patriarchal ideals. Asserting the dominance of the male gaze reinforces the colonizing gaze's mirror, merely replacing "one system of exclusion with another."[58] If, in the Freudian structure, the son assumes control by slaying the father, must the same be true for daughters and mothers? Is there no alternative paradigm for empowerment that sustains connection rather than sacrificing it?

Although few writers took it up at the time, Antoni offered a means to interrogate and surpass the critical cul-de-sacs that reinscribed the canons and histories that had historically excluded women. Most of her sculptures are generated through performance, which by the nineties had become the aesthetic weapon of choice for nonwhite, women, feminist, queer, intersectionally identified artists marginalized by the American art mainstream; for example, Carolee Schneemann, James Luna, Ana Mendieta, Lorraine O'Grady, Adrian Piper, Annie Sprinkle, Sherman Fleming, and Chris Burden, all of whom drew on a Brechtian sensibility to dissolve the wall between artist and audience. The relationship cultivated between artist and audience in performance is more horizontal than hierarchical; immediate and personal than managed and distant. Antoni's exhibitions draw on these hallmarks to gesture toward relationships beyond the boundary of art history, place, and space, upending the essentialization of race, sex, gender, and class while centering them as subject. But what becomes visible in Antoni's oeuvre if one views it through Caribbean street performance, beyond histories of performance art? How might a perspectival shift to the Caribbean open new sight lines? If one considers Antoni's art within a richer, more historically and culturally expansive problem space than it has been given and allowed, how might the critical work of her art in this period unfold?

ANTONI'S CALLING CARD

Antoni's control over the literature on her work had a rhizomatic effect on its critical landscape and its terms of reception in the 1990s. Like Marc Latamie, Antoni placed a great deal of trust in her audience and the catalytic potential of encounter, inviting creative engagement that prioritized perception over preconception. At the same time, the curation and cultivation of a Glissantian opacity around Antoni's work succeeded in erasing a prismatic critical engagement, circumventing a deeper experience that might resist the totalizing effect she rejected. As Adrian Piper's *Calling Card* series (1986) demonstrates, indeterminacy and (in)direct address have the potential to not only create a space for political subversion but also generate reflection in areas where discourse might prove difficult but necessary.

Most critical texts published during the era of identity politics do not mention Antoni's Caribbeanness or consider how it might help parse the aesthetics and meaning of her work. Ewa Lajer-Burcharth's extensive 1998 essay "Antoni's Difference" is a notable exception. In reference to *Lick and Lather*, Lajer-Burcharth contends:

> The varying degree of defacement defamiliarize the self *as such*, defining it as unintelligible, as a site of oscillation between resemblance and disguise, between recognition and misrecognition. Both the contrast of colors, brown and white, and the meanings of the materials—the rewarding chocolate, an object of desire, versus the purifying soap, an instrument of purge—metaphorize alterity and play of difference *within* the self. Moreover, the contrasting materials articulate that play of difference in terms of racial identity, through the trope of "race" as skin color. (This is also an

issue of personal relevance for Antoni, who was born of parents of different color in the Bahamas, where she also grew up.)[59]

In this singular moment within critical discussions of Antoni's work at the time, Lajer-Burcharth courageously repositions her line of sight toward a Caribbean postcolonial feminist art. Yet one can sense Antoni navigating around or stopping short of thresholds that may offer critics an opportunity to collude in narratives whose terms they do not fully understand, much less control. Perhaps sensing this ambivalence, Lajer-Burcharth surmises that Antoni's work mobilizes the "psyche as an instrument of resistance to culture, an agency of productive self-redefinition."[60] Acknowledging this portal's fertile interpretive possibilities, she ultimately declines to pursue it, adhering to Antoni's unprecedented control over the narrative.

Following Lajer-Burcharth's tentative lead, what might a Caribbean postcolonial feminist reading of *Lick and Lather* reveal? The work was specifically created for the 1993 Venice Biennale; from the outset, Antoni intended to engage the city as interlocutor. She was particularly drawn to the manner in which its public sculptures had weathered and thus effaced the features of the original form. She consequently drew on these acts of historical and cultural erasure as conceptual approach and aesthetic practice.

One finds multiple critical discourses at play in the work. Beyond its ode to Venice, Antoni has described *Lick and Lather* as an exploration of society's obsession with surface appearances and a rumination on aging through a Freudian lens (figure 1.7). Freud linked castration anxiety to men's obsession with phallic objects, from fire hydrants to skyscrapers and sculptural plinths. In his lexicon, commingled fear and desire activated the fetish object, alleviating feelings of loss via castration and emasculation. The loss of the penis, positioned as the highest totem of desire, is dramatized in the Oedipal scenario for men and as penis envy in women. From this point of view, women compensate for their lack of a penis through pregnancy, motherhood, and narcissism. Antoni disrupts this hysterical analysis by removing men entirely from the equation of creation, pleasure, and arousal. In process and form, *Lick and Lather* exceeds Freudian limits of feminine power and desire. It not only cuts through his reductive readings but forces audiences to look elsewhere for meaning and signification,[61] suggesting that God may indeed be a woman.

We can now take another look at *Lick and Lather* by reconsidering the literal juxtapositions of chocolate and soap and situating Antoni's process (cast, lick, lather) in relation to what she describes as Freud's "cliché of nar-

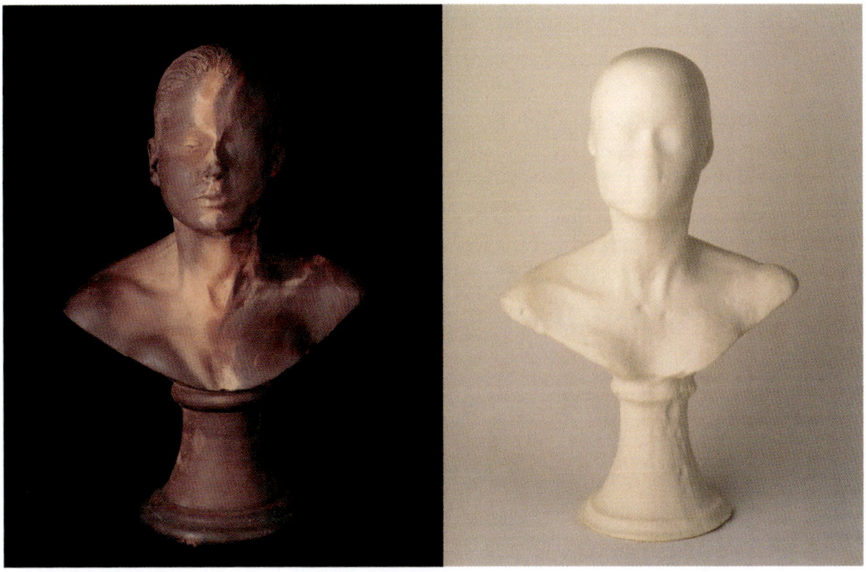

1.7 Janine Antoni, *Lick and Lather*, 1993. One licked-chocolate self-portrait bust and one washed-soap self-portrait bust on pedestals. Bust: 24 × 16 × 13 in. (60.96 × 40.64 × 33.02 cm) (each, approximately). Pedestal: 45 × 13 inches (114.3 × 33.02 cm) (each). Photographed by John Bessler.

cissism." How might one engage this work in situ, walking between the columns, exceeding the boundaries of love and desire? As Stephen Nichols argued, eating "combines the private, the intimate, and the gregarious in a manner that permits artists to maneuver between the various options, from ritual solemnity to the carnivalesque."[62]

The material, economic, and social histories of chocolate and soap, as explored by Stuart Hall and Anne McClintock, extend engagement beyond authorial intention into contingent circumstances open to multiple significations by different audiences. In "The Spectacle of the Other," Stuart Hall explained how imperial conquest was determined by a territory's capacity to supply raw materials for commodities and establish new markets.[63] While Hall foregrounded the commodification of race within the engine of imperial expansion, he believed that this commodification cut across all rubrics of difference, including gender, sexuality, and class. These linkages provide an additional lens through which to evaluate Antoni's early production through a global Caribbean postcolonial feminist framework.

Anne McClintock's groundbreaking research on the imbrication of Victorian consumption habits and imperial constructions of race, gender, class, and nation centered Hall's analysis. She focused on racialized advertisements distributed throughout the colonies that sought to enlist subjects in a normative vision of English domestic life and place the Victorian home and its construct of domesticity at the center of female desire.[64] Within and through this framing, the consumption of English domesticity and Victorian femininity became the standard by which *all* women in the colonial Caribbean were judged. Material acquisition represented the vehicle by which to attain these ideals.

The central commodity within this paradigm was soap. As Hall observed: "In its capacity to cleanse and purify, soap acquired, in the fantasy world of imperial advertising, the quality of a fetish object. It apparently had the power to wash black skin white as well as being capable of washing off the soot, grime and dirt of the industrial slums and their inhabitants—the unwashed poor . . . keeping the imperial body clean and pure in the racially polluted contact zones 'out there' in the Empire. In the process, however, the domestic labour of women was often silently erased."[65] Antoni's use of soap as sensual, menial, and sculptural was strategic. As a perfect medium for fracturing singular discourses, its deployment encourages a rhizomatic approach. Soap's material history, and its specific relationship to Antoni's historically and culturally determined body as a white Caribbean Creole, invites readings beyond the classical frame and notions of purity and cleanliness associated with the artist's Catholic upbringing. In the Caribbean, the concept of racial purity is multivalent. Antoni's seven generations of busts evoke the historical dimensions of the region's economics of skin and economies of color, the politics of blood and belonging, and the ways Caribbeans endeavored to pass or succeeded in passing from various browns to white—not necessarily as a form of self-loathing but in defiance of ontological limits imposed on their racialized bodies. In treating race as a construct, the enslaved rendered it an element subject to manipulation in service to freedom.

In manufacture, packaging, and marketing, soap, tea, chocolate, rum, sugar, cloth, and biscuits (all initially refined from raw materials generated by slave and indentured labor) were extracted, transported, refined, and cleansed in imperial factories and exported as finished or refined goods to the plantation system. This was, in essence, a feedback loop. Antoni's choice of materials is certainly notable for the histories embedded in them. However, if we take the artist at her word and consider her body as a conduit of experience, the work is also informed by the *relationship* to this history that she, as a white, mixed-race, Caribbean-born, global, woman artist, illuminates. Object and referent combine to render the commodification of Otherness itself.

Antoni's work exhibits a humorous, self-conscious manipulation of visible and invisible identity markers. Dan Cameron, one of the few critics who recognized the cultivation of pleasure in her art, described how it became "something other than the mere immersion of the self in sensation" so as to serve "as a way of transforming the body's subjectivity into a universal point of reference."[66] Whereas Cameron's point resists objectifying Antoni, other critics failed to temper their gaze, referring to her as the "long-haired, long limbed Antoni."[67] While she certainly embraced sexuality and eroticism in her practice, she also contested the voyeuristic pose by employing autoerotic modalities, such as licking, biting, and lathering.[68] In process and effect, her pleasure is self-contained, and the viewer's possession of her body foreclosed. Without the artist's consent, possession does not automatically follow desire. Antoni asserts power and manipulates her body to the point of disfigurement to catalyze the audience's transformative, self-reflexive experience.

This conceptual positioning echoes Black Atlantic performance traditions in which women can *play* their bodies to communicate economic control and inhabit and enact autonomy denied them during slavery and indentureship. In these scenarios, women determine the bounds of their bodies, with whom and when to share them, and the type and degree of their labor. They also decide whether to affirm sexual freedom. Performance becomes an expression of bodily sovereignty, of bodies free from historical inscription, violence, and control, if only temporarily.

Antoni's use of desire resonates in Caribbean-based performance cultures, in which "objectifying and constraining bodily identities are challenged."[69] In Haitian Rara, women's movements are characterized by recourse to "muscle memory," thereby reflecting the embeddedness of history *in and on* the body.[70] Following the work of Patricia Mohammed, Beth Fowkes Tobin, Mia Bagneris, and others, the classical aesthetics Antoni manipulates position her at the pinnacle of desire in the colonial Caribbean. In the late eighteenth-century paintings of Agostino Brunias, such as *The Linen Market* (1780), the mixed-race woman, who reads phenotypically as white, occupies the center of the frame, signifying her elevated societal position in contradistinction to visibly black women, who are literally positioned closer to the ground.[71]

These same standards and hierarchies persist over time, even when subject to interrogation and disruption. Carolyn Cooper's work on twenty-first-century Jamaican beauty contests has documented the revelatory and subversive mechanisms in Jamaican dancehall culture that probe the facile link between race, beauty, and desire.[72] In the 1990s and 2000s, the queen of the dancehall stage was Lady Saw.[73] A former free zone seamstress, Lady Saw would not be regarded as a beauty in the Brunias sense. But in dancehall culture, the seamstress can become queen. Lady Saw was the first female dancehall artist to win a Grammy, record a gold record, go triple-platinum, and headline shows outside Jamaica. Even her stage name suggests precision cuts in a way suggestive of her border crossing and razor-sharp, lyrical poetics. Like Antoni, Lady Saw shrewdly deployed the language of her discipline to create irreverent, politically astute, socially enlightening, overtly sexual work that focused on female pleasure and liberation. To watch her perform is to become aware of her intent to assert women's power to claim and enjoy their sexual identities.

Reclamation is a demystifying process for Caribbean women, whose sex has historically not belonged to them, whatever their class. In this context, Saw's voice is primarily directed to the economic descendants of Brunias's washerwomen in Jamaica and the broader Caribbean. But considering the geographic breadth of her performance, in a Césairean vein, Lady Saw's work registers and disseminates a transcontinental feminist desire for freedom of bodily expression, perception, and consumption. Saw's appeal was fueled by her lyricism, wit, boldness, humor, fearlessness, and facility with double entendre. Her fearlessness was potently embodied in her "back chat"—often in freestyle—aimed at male DJs who publicly sought to suppress her message and project a limiting vision of femininity on her.[74] In the dancehall space, notoriously dominated by men, when Saw chats, men listen and pause, and women catch the spirit. If an individual can embody a *pito mitan*, that person would be Lady Saw.

Cooper has described the dancehall as a domain that "privileges dance as a mode of theatrical self-disclosure in which the body speaks eloquently of its capacity to endure and transcend material deprivation."[75] In this space, Caribbean women assume tropes of commodity culture that befit their reality. Their style inverts Western binaries in the sense that "private" attire crosses into the public arena and hierarchies promoted in American bodily aesthetics are dethroned. For example, "tall hair" is desired, but natural and artificial hair are equally valued.[76]

It's notable that modes of undress are often misunderstood by religious and upper-class Jamaicans, Caribbeans, and cultural outsiders as markers of self-denigration. But Cooper tells us that within the dancehall space, the organizational principles of mainstream culture are dissembled and rearranged. What one sector might deem representative of debased self-esteem, the participating culture reads as confidence through style. What might be perceived by some as sexual deviance represents a woman's right to lay claim to her body and its desires. Skinny, fleshy, and fluffy women alike assert themselves in this visual play. The club's dim light hides imperfections, and the cameras capture moments when the activated, dancing body and the surface presentation commingle. "In the dancehall world of make-believe," Cooper perceptively notes, "old roles can be contested and new identities assumed. Indeed, the elaborate styling of both hair and clothes is a permissive expression of the pleasures of disguise. In the words of dancehall diva Sandra Lee: 'The extension add a movie look to us . . . is like a disguise. I want to look different tomorrow.'"[77]

Antoni has said that "packaging is a symbol of our times. It is a seduction—unwrapping is like undressing. The stuff around the object is often more signifying than the object it contains."[78] She could easily have been speaking about dancehall. To contemporary viewers, Antoni's command of the uptown gallery paralleled Lady Saw's domination of the downtown dancehall. Both women exhibited a profound knowledge of the patriarchal arena they navigated, and both claimed a startling degree of success in the 1990s. However, while the dancehall celebrates female sexual possession and expression, it also intersects with the wave of skin bleaching. This is an issue in all diasporas of color that converge in the Caribbean, where skin lightening is entangled with hierarchies of desire and the political economy of melanin. Yet these causal readings are complicated by dancehall stars like Vybz Kartel, who lightened his skin to yield greater contrast to showcase his tattoos.

The dancehall space is not merely celebratory, nor does it romanticize the very real social and economic exploitation that many women face when the lights come on.[79] But it *is* a space where the subject-object relationship is constantly rearranged by shifting power dynamics and the community values that sustain it. In this context, it would be difficult to view Antoni's work as an insular or singular conversation with Western classical aesthetics. As C. L. R. James proposes and Antoni enacts, the audience is fundamental to art-*making*; in the aesthetic encounter, metanarratives emerge and take shape as constitutive of the art's work.

Antoni approached the dialectic between subject, object, and audience differently in her 1994 work, *Tender Buttons* (figure 1.8). For this piece, she used a cast of her nipples to make twenty sets of twin brooches in solid gold, complete with velvet boxes and certificates of authenticity. She priced the disembodied simulacra at $2,500.00 a pair. The work's name is taken from Gertrude Stein's long-form poem *Tender Buttons* (1904), an ode to household items that can be considered fetish objects for castrated nipples. Antoni first appears to fetishize her own body (parts), indulging, but also denying, the fetishistic desires of her art world audience.[80] In the process, she performs the role of the trickster, whose character and exploits in Native American and African cultures evince an *ironic imagination*.[81] The simulacra of her Creole nipples is sold to those who can afford the dream of possession. A playful yet painful humor is embedded in these relational representations, which bore different significance for the artist in later years. In *Tender Buttons*, she created a critical space for the engagement of historically shifting identity markers, labor, and commodity culture, a conversation she had begun years earlier with *Gnaw*.

TAUGHT, TETHER, TEETER

In 1998, a little more than ten years after returning to The Bahamas to develop her portfolio, Antoni was awarded a MacArthur Foundation genius grant. The following year, she received the Larry Aldrich Award, and in 2001, she mounted an exhibition at the Aldrich Contemporary Art Museum, the art world's equivalent to ascending from beatification to canonization. Antoni's achievement marked a critical juncture in an already celebrated career. Aldrich championed promising young artists, and his museum's pedigree was impressive. The original trustees included luminaries Alfred Barr Jr., Vera List, Joseph Hirshhorn, and Philip Johnson.

Amid these professional triumphs, Antoni was battling breast cancer. In 1999 she underwent surgery and completed the first of a five-year cycle of cancer drugs. As her health improved, a new confidence entered her practice that coincided with a shift in her use of the body and the degree of its availability to the audience.

Antoni chose the title *The Girl Made of Butter* for her Aldrich exhibition, conjuring a fairytale theme. To enact its narrative framing, she attended to

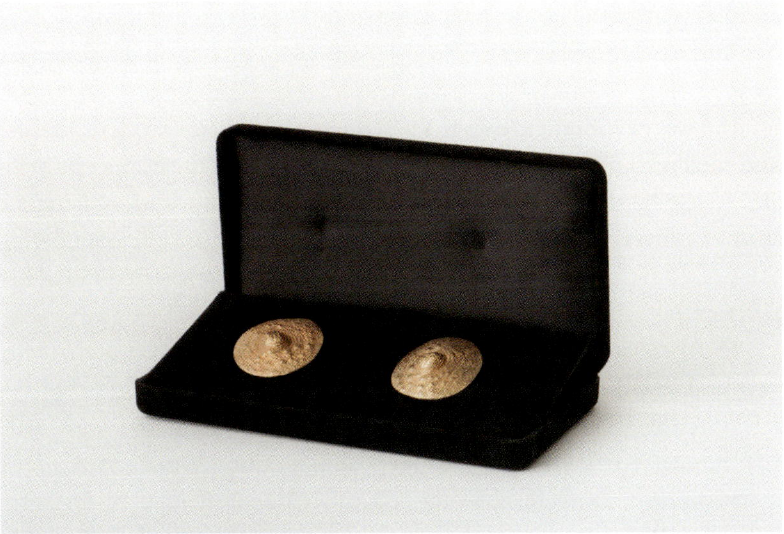

1.8 Janine Antoni, *Tender Buttons*, 1994. Two gold brooches cast in the form of the artist's nipples in velvet box. Brooches: 1¼ × 1¼ × ⅜ in. (3.3 × 3.3 × 0.9 cm) (each). Box: 6¼ × 3⅛ × ⅞ in. (15.88 × 7.9 × 2.2 cm). Published by Anders Tornberg, Lund. Photographed by Farzad Owrang.

the smallest of details, going so far as to paint the galleries "Snow White" and including a color swatch in the catalogue for good measure. As a "white" on yet another "white" square, Antoni's reference to Kazimir Malevich and Josef Albers was both humorous and pregnant with significations around racial ontologies. The exhibition affirmed Antoni's growing intentionality and control over her work's points of entry. It also, perhaps for the first time, represented a full reconciliation of her process of artistic *mothering*. The show's narrative quality and corresponding text foregrounded her love of language and literature, and her assembly of prose and poetic forms, though restrained, was conceptually powerful.

The exhibition text drew on at least five literary forms: Bahamian and Trinidadian folktales, Catholic prayers for the rosary, poetry in the style of Virginia Woolf, fairy tales, and cooking recipes. *Girl Made of Butter* is first and foremost a Bahamian folktale. It serves as the exhibition's title, and the story is printed in its entirety at the beginning of the exhibition catalogue. In the tale, a mother who has devoted her life to shielding her daughter from every challenge and misfortune she can think of is ultimately unable to protect her from her own desires. One day, while the mother is busy in another part of the house, men command the girl's attention and seduce her into leaving with them. The girl melts away, literally and figuratively disappearing.

The story's content speaks to rootedness and risk, the work of nurture and the limits of parental protection. It also catalogs the human propensity to foolhardiness, absolution, and forgiveness. In addition, it can be seen as a metaphor for the artist's own departure from the comforting arms of home and the art and cultural histories that hitherto guided her practice.

The ideas conjured in *Girl Made of Butter* crystallized the following year in Antoni's first full retrospective at SITE Santa Fe, *taught, tether, teeter*. A massive play on words, form, history, and meaning, the work's title pays homage to the feminist movement and, specifically, to Betty Friedan's demarcation of the woman's realm as "Kinder, Kuche, Kirche" in *The Feminine Mystique* (1963). The connection between Friedan's words and the title resonated not only historically and theoretically within the artist's oeuvre, but also in rhythm, meaning, and knowledge. It spoke to growth, learning, moving, cleaving, clinging, and connecting—the elemental features of the development processes that Antoni drew on to make the newer works on exhibition, *Moor* (2002) and *Touch* (2002). Both pieces demonstrate Antoni's rhizomatic ability to absorb and transform histories of feminist, Caribbean, postnational, modern, and contemporary art in her practice.

The film *Touch* documents Antoni walking a tightrope set in alignment with the horizon line on the beach of her childhood home in The Bahamas. According to Antoni, after receiving the SITE commission:

> I went home to The Bahamas, and I set up a tightrope on the beach in front of my house, and I walked back and forth on that rope, and when the wire actually bows, it lines up with the horizon, and for a second, I can balance in that place. The piece was inspired by the horizon because it's really probably the image I looked at the most in my life. And my mother used to say in this Trinidadian saying: "Janine, you should go out and see the world, because this place you come from is behind God's back," so I always had this idea that I came from this little island that not even God cared about, and I would look out at the horizon and imagine the world out there. And thinking about the horizon, I thought, "Well, that's weird," because it's not really a place, in the sense that it's just a visual illusion: the closer you get to the horizon, the more it recedes. So I liked the idea of thinking of the horizon as this kind of . . . you know, walking in the place of my imagination.[82]

Moor is a rope form made of objects of significant personal value to the artist's family and friends. It is also an externalized biography narrated through objects that retain the smell, touch, and trace of the people Antoni loves. Like the exhibition title, it too plays with words to engage the polysemic nature of linguistic and physical markers, drawing on the act and metaphor, previously seen in *Slumber* (1993), of mooring, weaving, and spinning. Antoni speaks frequently about imbuing objects with life. While *Moor* may seem on its surface to express a great deal of sentimentality, an almost verboten quality in contemporary art, there is something poignant in its ongoing vitality, expansion, and mutability, in the manner in which its form and process are tied directly to the artist's life. The SITE exhibition demonstrated that Antoni had been mothered, mentored, and matured *and* that she had come into her own as an artist. She confirmed this in conversation:

> I think that for myself, at the beginning of my career, I couldn't assume a voice, and I think part of locating myself was to locate myself in terms of art history, so I think the work was very consciously doing that. I think it was also very conscious of taking on a kind of topic related to women; and I think the reality of that has changed for me now, so I feel like I've established an identity, and so I tend to let that drop away to a certain extent, or I don't have to be so overt that people assume that it's there. [. . .] I think I am much less controlling than I used to be, but actually much less controlling in the work. [. . .] I guess I thought that the most generous position was to be as direct as possible. Now I am thinking that maybe it's more generous to leave some space for people to interpret the work. Maybe that's maturity, maybe that is having more confidence than I had. I think I had a real vision of how I wanted to be situated. And I figured if people were going to let me have control of that, why wouldn't I take it? (Laughter)[83]

A MATTER OF RECOGNITION

In 2016, Janine Antoni performed *The Paper Dance* at the Fabric Workshop in Philadelphia. The work, which resulted from collaboration with noted postmodern dancer Anna Halprin, harked back to the collective artmaking of early American feminist artists who resisted the narrative and discursive authority of the solitary male genius. In the open, intimate studio space, Antoni danced naked and alone before a small audience sitting on crates containing her signature works. During some performances, the crates were open, the works exposed. During others, they were closed.

Returning to *Gnaw*'s prelinguistic realm of communication, Antoni spoke through her nude body in performance. Many things tumbled out in this address. As she moved, she commanded her audience's gaze and controlled the elicited specularization to great effect. The exchange's directness encouraged those in attendance to note details: the body that signified and bore memory; the scars from her lumpectomy; the gray lines of her hair; and the softening folds of her flesh, facial expressions, and gentle smile.

In the Caribbean, movement is textual and intimately tied to speech; a simple gesture can assume the communicative heft of a paragraph or poem. *The Paper Dance* was performed on and as a rhizomatic plateau for Antoni's work. Like *Moor*, it exuded a distinctly literary sensibility. It was a text. It was also a retrospective, though without objects affixed to or within gallery walls. As with *Loving Care*, the audience and artist occupied the same space; this time, rather than shooing them out, Antoni invited everyone to stay. She danced in and around the audience with reams of craft paper as her partner, matrix, and burden. Stretched and crumpled by the end of her performance, the paper bore evidence of her sweat and labor and the medium's handling. It recalled Antoni's early desire to compel viewers to imagine "what it is like to . . . feel [the work] through their body, to relate to the work in terms of body knowledge."[84] Toward the end of the performance, Antoni assembled the paper she danced with into heaps, returning us to Laderman Ukeles's piles of rags and her exhibition's material documentation of labor.

Paper Dance inverted retrospective conventions by centering the artist's primary medium, her body, and, through it, immaterial aspects that have been central to her practice: vulnerability, courage, and vision. It highlighted the artist as the laborer-maker and creative force, and her body as the discursive text that had conceived, mobilized, and nurtured ideas over the past thirty years. The entire history of her practice was conceptually imagined as being held in her body, which she gave to the audience as art object and kept for herself as archive.

Janine Antoni has curated the narrative surrounding her work over the span of her entire career, at times rewriting history to do it.[85] Though at times seemingly complicit in muting feminism and Caribbeanaiety in the critical discourse, she may instead be performing what José Esteban Muñoz described as "disidentification," a form of "cultural, material and psychic survival" that artists operating ("in an artworld too often obsessed with simplistic affirmation of origin of essence") wield in "response to state and global power apparatuses that employ systems of racial, sexual and national subjugation." Disidentification articulates a refusal to concede to the art world's myopic optic, interpretive, and discursive lens. It is a refusal to be Calibanized. It is a rejection not of linkages but of the reduction they too often perform—dissolving the work's complexity into digestible singularity, in effect disappearing and denying the multiplicity engendered by the creolization process in the global Caribbean. Following Césaire, in the 1990s Janine Antoni carved out a transcontinental discursive place that neutered systems intended to occlude her voice and work in the contemporary art world.[86] In *Paper Dance*, she situated her oeuvre as a counterarchive to critical narratives of rejection, erasure, and loss while simultaneously asserting her right to opacity.

During her ascendancy, Dan Cameron noted that Antoni used her body in ways that affirmed it as "a provisional boundary through which identity flows, a heterogeneous site of the play of difference(s) inhabited by the forces that make and unmake the self."[87] Antoni both presupposed and seized power in determining the flow. This same sensibility has underpinned generative artistic production in the global Caribbean during and since the 1990s. This art produced from the margins defines a space that does not concede to the designation of Otherness but is filled with what bell hooks called "radical possibilities." It is work that is postnational and rhizomatic in content, materiality, and form across the spatiotemporal planes it simultaneously occupies. The conceptual arc of Antoni's work is therefore not bound to geopolitical confines or a single story line, though "experiences growing up in The Bahamas lie at the core."[88] It is neither solely nor simply "about" American feminism or the Caribbean, even when the work is situated there. In the words of Caribbean author Michelle Cliff, Antoni and her art are "not outside this history: It is just a matter of recognition."[89]

As with other global Caribbean artists who emerged during the decade, it was also a matter of whether, how, when, and where this recognizing was taking place, and what boundaries and ontologies it maintained, reinforced, or irrupted. Each global Caribbean artist emerging in the 1990s encountered differently arranged problem spaces that all sought to Calibanize the work as "compromised formations," unworthy of critical regard. While Antoni drew on various histories to craft a self-authored practice that resisted marginalization and achieved acclaim in the New York art world, others faced similar challenges in unlikely places. The criticisms that artists such as Belkis Ayón and Edouard Duval Carrié faced further underscore the colonial foundations of art history and the fact that, at the time, the values of the metropole too often shaped how those lying outside its boundaries saw themselves. As we shall see, Ayón and later Duval Carrié forged practices that not only rejected this lens but revealed how the decolonial work Césaire insisted art do was necessary beyond the Caribbean, and within.

CHAPTER TWO

Meeting in the Upper Room

Belkis Ayón's La cena, *1988–1993*

Ousmane Sembène's 1966 film, *Black Girl*, narrativizes the "enslaved African body and soul in pain . . . healed through death."[1] In it, the central character, Diouana, is convinced by the expatriate family she works for in Senegal to return with them to Europe, where she finds herself summarily mistreated, abused, fetishized, and isolated. She resolves to go back, but her employers deny her request, and she has no money to secure her passage. Intent on transporting herself "home," she prepares for the journey and neatly packs her belongings, then goes into the bathroom and kills herself.[2]

On September 11, 1999, the Cuban artist Belkis Ayón ended her own life, with a single gunshot wound to her head. She was thirty-two.

It may seem strange to open a chapter by juxtaposing the suicide of a creative subject with that of a flesh-and-bone creator. In tethering Sembène's work to Ayón's tragic and mythologized death, I am deliberately positioning the artist within a Black Atlantic discourse that underpinned emerging global Caribbean art in the 1990s. This parallelism also foregrounds the specific, strategic, and spiritual understandings of death within African diasporic histories and cultures—the same ones that center Ayón's oeuvre. Within this lineage, physical death is not *the* end; rather, as rendered through the journey of enslaved Africans to the Americas and enacted through Diouana's suicide in *Black Girl*, death is a doorway to freedom, home, and Guinen.[3] But this is not a scripted romance: Ayón's conceptual and aesthetic explorations of death promise neither return nor redemption.

BLACK GIRLS

Janine Antoni and Belkis Ayón enact decolonizing practices that are distinct in form yet interlinked by their transformative ethos. Antoni made her art legible in the New York art world by inserting her whole self into histories of American and feminist art and by architecting the discourse around her work. Ayón's immediate critical landscape was Cuba, and her oeuvre represents a Black feminist decolonizing practice nested in the decolonizing project of revolution.[4] To shatter the silence that stifled discourse on the island, Ayón fashioned a visual discursive practice rooted in its history that resonated beyond its boundaries and rhetoric of revolution to insist on critical reflection and ensure a (Black) woman's seat at the table. Her epistemic intervention generated art that fractured the mythologies of revolution and catalyzed new imaginaries at the intersection of race and gender.

Like Antoni, Ayón used historicization, storytelling, playfulness, and cultural referents to center content and underwrite transformative critique in her voice. *Unlike* Antoni, she remained based in the Caribbean throughout her career, taking advantage of the freedom to travel, exhibit, and retain funds earned from the sale of artworks at home and abroad during what would become known as the Special Period (1991–2000).[5] Although they worked in geographically different problem spaces, the two artists occasionally converged in the same global exhibition sites; for example, both had artwork selected for the 1993 Venice Biennale. In their appropriation and transformation of exclusionary cultural histories, Antoni and Ayón actualized Césaire's vision of decolonizing art forms.

In mapping the critical contours of Ayón's work across media, generations, and localities, I tether her deployment of the concept of Black (female) embodiment and death to Tomás Gutiérrez Alea's film *La última cena*. I consider how Ayón visually, conceptually, and affectively registers unspoken entanglements of race, gender, and history in the unstable rhetoric of postracial, postrevolutionary Cuba as problem space, so as to find historical resonance within a Black Atlantic imaginary that exceeds the island's physical boundaries. This discussion renders another dimension of the prismatic, critical forms that characterized global Caribbean art during this decade and the decolonial work it performed.

Ernesto R. Acevedo-Muñoz proposes that in *Black Girl*, physical liberation (through death) permits the soul and spirit to return to Africa. This vision of life beyond the flesh may seem too metaphysical, romantic, or religious for objective scholarly consideration, yet its relevance is legitimated by the late Cuban scholar Antonio Benítez-Rojo, who as a youth experienced the Cuban Missile Crisis (1962), a moment when Cubans perceived themselves to be on the brink of a nuclear apocalypse. Like most in his Havana neighborhood, Benítez-Rojo's family hunkered down. No one was allowed to leave their homes unless absolutely necessary. But, one day, as he stared out from a cracked window, Benítez-Rojo saw two old Black women out walking together, chatting casually, in defiance of the orders. Something in their deportment convinced him that "there would be no apocalypse," but if it occurred, they (and he) would survive it. The "certain kind of way" the women moved was beyond language's grasp or utterance, imparting a conjoined elusiveness and intimation that materialized death as a passage, not an end.[6]

Like Benítez-Rojo, I consider how Ayón's work *moves*—how it oscillates around an allegorical relationship to the Abakuá secret society and its central sacrificial figure so as to mark itself as generative, contemporary, and deftly critical of Black life and death in Cuba. This chapter embraces an expansive view of the aesthetic, historical, cultural, and philosophical work of Ayón's masterful print *La cena* (1988, 1991, 1993) in order to examine its logic of relations, the polyvocality of its aesthetics, and the historical subterfuge that resonates through its form. In these capacities, *La cena* registers meaning through an epistemological reconfiguration of history and time in the problem space of Cuba and the broader postcolonial Caribbean.

Ayón's work demands intergenerational and transnational engagement in order to illuminate the political and aesthetic stakes it addressed during Cuba's economic crisis, escalating racial inequality, and subjection to searing international critique for its treatment of those afflicted with HIV/AIDS. "The meeting in the upper room" referenced in this chapter's title is used to identify *La cena*'s relationship to canonical Last Supper representations of Jesus and his disciples and to mark the conceptual meeting and Derridean différance between *La cena* and Tomás Gutiérrez Alea's *La última cena*. Both *La cena* and *La última cena* address the past's contemporary resonance in the Caribbean, the way "time unfolds irregularly and resists being captured by the cycles of clock and calendar."[7] Their relationship surfaces the ways Ayón's art articulated the ongoing need for criticality in relation to national, racial, and gender narratives of postrevolutionary Cuba, narratives that even today do not account for the specificities of Black (female) identities.

These systems of erasure are unveiled and engaged through acts of historicization in Alea's film and of defamiliarization in Ayón's art. Produced a generation apart, their temporal distance fosters *La cena*'s projection of an ethically grounded polyvocality at the intersection of race and gender. Like Alea, Ayón produces political work that critiques Cuban society. Like Latamie and Antoni, she broaches historical subjects and silences that sit at the nexus of nation, identity, race, and gender and simultaneously transcend their conceptual and physical boundaries.

SOMETHING MORE

The official narratives of Cuban art history in the 1990s situated Belkis Ayón within the so-called second wave of contemporary artists that emerged after 1980 in the wake of the New Cuban Art, many of whom were represented in the notable exhibition *Volumen Uno / Volume One*. In the 1970s, or "gray years," the Soviet Union's influence had narrowed Cuba's revolutionary articulations and the parameters of acceptable artistic expression.[8] Second-wave artists arose during the Special Period, marked by the Soviet Union's fall and Cuba's ensuing economic hardship. Although the earlier generation of artists had received a measure of international exposure, the second wave was distinctive in that many of them chose to remain on the island while capitalizing on the government's new willingness to permit travel abroad and on the retention of most earnings from the international sale of their work.

Ayón was trained at Cuba's premier institutions and well versed in Western art. But, like Volumen Uno artists José Bedia Valdés and Juan Francisco Elso, both of whom pursued an interest in Santería, and, later, Edouard Duval-Carrié's, interest in Vodoun, she chose to look to her immediate surroundings for inspiration and instruction. Ayón's engagement of the Cuban creole form Abakuá, a tradition considered "primitive" in Western approaches to art history and in Cuba's Marxist society, was strategic. In deploying Abakuá as a conceptual and allegorical frame, she engineered new epistemological configurations for her work. She chose collagraphy, a relatively ancient form of printmaking, as her primary medium. Like Romare

Bearden's collage method, collagraphy involves the artist combining paper and cardboard of varying surface properties, thickness, and textures to tell new stories. Ayón augmented this approach by illuminating mechanisms of power that had gone unchallenged and unchanged during the Cuban Revolution and had become largely normalized in its postrevolutionary landscape.

It is widely known and documented that Ayón's imagery was rooted in the mythos and belief systems of Cuba's all-male Abakuá (secret) society.[9] She began exploring the group's origins as a student at the Escuela Provincial de Artes Plásticas San Alejandro during the 1980s. *La cena* (1988) (figure 2.1) was one of her earliest mature monumental works to center Abakuá's historical and mythical iconography. From the beginning, Ayón was troubled by critics' flattened response to her appropriation of Abakuá:

> El problema está en que yo siento que hay muchas gentes que son muy simples a la hora de hablar de un artista y de una producción. Es mucho más fácil decir: ¡Ah, mira, ella trabaja sobre el abakuá! Está muy bien, pero no hay mucho más que eso.
>
> The problem is that I feel that there are many people who are very simple-minded when it comes to talking about an artist and a production. It is much easier to say: Oh, look, she works on the Abakuá! It's very good, but there's not much more to it than that.[10]

Critics repeatedly failed to thoughtfully and productively engage Ayón's incorporation of Abakuá as concept or allegory. Sidestepping complexity in favor of didacticism, they could neither vocalize nor account for the way that Ayón drew from Abakuá's history to cultivate a Black feminist aesthetic practice that traveled far beyond its narrative frame. This floundering marked yet another instance of the art world's resistance to, anxiety about, and occlusion of artists who were challenging its formal, thematic, philosophical, and geographical frames of reference.

THE PHILOSOPHIES OF ABAKUÁ

The Abakuá society was founded in 1836 in the Cross River cabildo of Havana's Regla district.[11] The members called themselves Èfik Buton.[12] By delineating its linkages with the Cross River region in West Africa, scholars

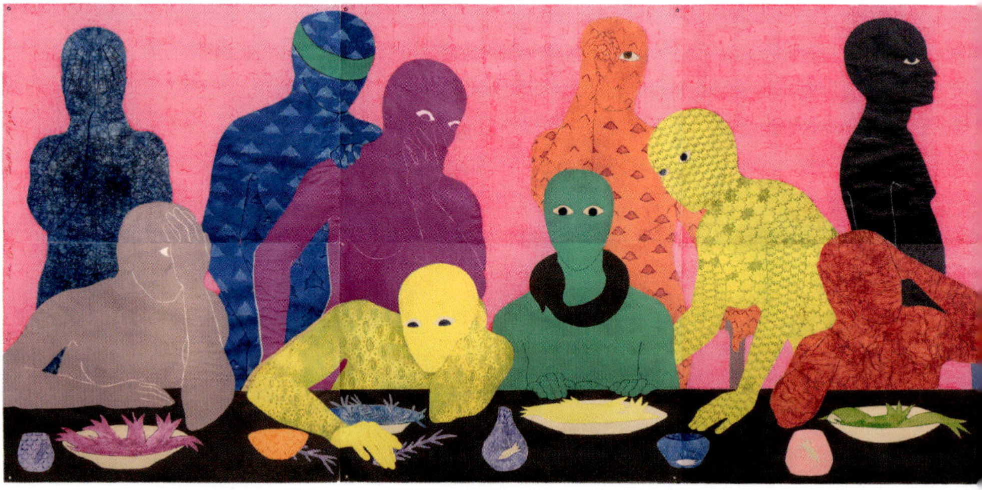

2.1 Belkis Ayón, *La cena*, 1988. Color collagraph mounted on linen. Photographed by José A. Figueroa. Courtesy and copyright © Belkis Ayón Estate, Havana, Cuba.

including Robert Farris Thompson, David H. Brown, Rosemary Branson-Gill, and Ivor L. Miller have categorized the group as a transplanted African society. I diverge from this approach, choosing instead to draw on Wilson Harris's analysis of the practices of reassemblage that accrue within and beyond the limen of the Middle Passage.[13] I position Abakuá as consummately Cuban, situated in and representative of the histories and economies of West Africa and transatlantic slavery.[14]

Abakuá constellates an ideology and philosophy of being created by free and enslaved Africans in Cuba. As a Glissantian plateau, it evidences how creolization generated new cultural arrangements in the wake of fracture. Distinct from Haitian Vodoun, which also took shape in the rupture and devastation of the Middle Passage, it is a cultural practice rather than a religion. Its central humanist liturgical tradition is the *plante* ceremony, which allegorically reenacts its founding myth: the death of a young woman named Sikán.[15] Like most origin stories, there are numerous versions, but several salient features prevail among them.[16]

Abakuá formed in slave cabildos in Havana and Matanzas, where creole Africans interacted with newly arrived Africans and forged novel social configurations. Membership required a pure blood connection to Africa. For the first thirty years, it was an all-male secret society that barred women, whites, and mulattos. The African ethnic groups that merged in cabildos were often themselves an amalgamation of smaller subgroups, most prominently the Èfik (also Ekpe, Efi) and Ejagham (also Ekoi, Efue, Efor, Efo) peoples from the Cross River and Niger Delta regions of today's southeastern Nigeria and western Cameroon, near the Bight of Biafra. The story of their interactions and the development of Abakuá powerfully illustrates the process of autohistoricization—a reworlding in the face of unspeakable trauma.

Cross-disciplinary scholarship on the Americas highlights the formation of religious and cultural groups during and after slavery as evidence of sustained cultural linkages between Africa and the Caribbean,[17] manifestations of creolization, and retentions of classical African traditions previously thought to have been destroyed during slavery.[18] But there is a general lack of critical regard directed toward the Abakuá's formation in Cuba. Like Haitian Vodoun, Abakuá cannot be described as the product of an essentialized African-European mixture, though it is thoroughly syncretic. In fact, there was nothing European about it, until the addition of Catholic imagery when the first white "cabildo" was formed in 1863.[19] Rather, the geographic and social relationships maintained between the cultures emergent from West Africa's Cross River region and their elemental reconstitution in the form of Abakuá (mythologically, liturgically, and formally) reveals the extent to which the Middle Passage was historically reconfigured in Abakuá mythology.

David Brown's extensive study of the Abakuá includes detailed maps of the Cross River region of modern Nigeria and Cameroon. But the distillation of history rendered in the line drawing "Geography of Sacred Memory" reveals the epistemological core of this secret society (figure 2.2). Brown describes the map as a reproduction of the "only known drawing by an African" ever made in Cuba.[20] In spare fashion, it outlines a history of relations between two African societies constantly at war—the Efor people, indicated by a circle, and the Èfik people, represented by the cross form. The mighty Cross River system is imaged as their divider. The drawing shows their relative position to the river and the rest of Africa, as well as the river's merger with the sea, the site of brutal fracture and transformation.

The Middle Passage challenged and renegotiated the groups' previously adversarial relationship. As they emerged on the other side of the Atlantic and were housed together in Cuban cabildos, cooperation was forged by dint of circumstance, and a new narrative was authored to archive the trauma of the Middle Passage and reframe origins. The cabildo was a threshold for the reinvention of personal identity and communal

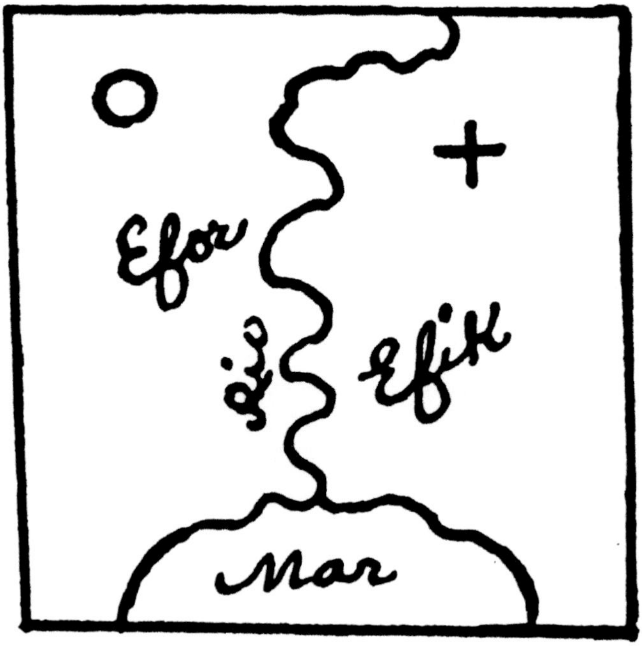

2.2 Geography of Sacred Memory. Drawn by Lydia Cabrera's informant Saibeke, ca. 1940s.

relationships. Cuba was a plantation society, as committed to Catholicism as it was to slavery, which meant it was no longer productive, or even possible, for Cross River Africans to establish an exclusive Efor or Èfik society. A new social formation had to reflect not just the proximity but the *coming together* of peoples from throughout the Cross River territory and other regions. Within this space, the real and symbolic river that had previously divided these groups was erased by the sea that had transported them all to Cuba.

Andrew Apter has suggested that origin narratives articulate the relationship between a newly formed social community and the previous social groupings of its members.[21] Within this theoretical framework, Cross River peoples would have been compelled to explain and reframe their existence in Cuba beyond the irruption of the Middle Passage. Therefore, the Abakuá founding myths had to "rhetorically undercut" the fact of slavery in self-authored and self-directed ways that communicated this new social arrangement but simultaneously reached back to Africa. To be Abakuá meant to retain consciousness of one's African past *and* to compose an identity grounded beyond the Middle Passage and the contemporary enslaved body. This commitment to new social structures—written over and against those of the past—represents autohistoriography, a re-creation myth that is also a self-authored suturing in the wake of trauma.

To be Abakuá was to be a man. In the Middle Passage, enslavers eradicated cultural practices that articulated gender identity and emphasized difference in order to debase and dehumanize men, a fact that sat uneasily within a patriarchal ideological matrix that coupled enslavement and domination with feminization. These complicated and multilayered historical and social valences funneled into the rituals the Abakuá created to formalize their identity. It is no accident that the group's *plante* ceremony, performed to bring initiates into the society, reenacts the sacrificial death of a woman, or the feminine principle.[22]

Ayón leveraged an awareness of the conceptual capacity of gender intersubjectivity in the context of slavery and postrevolutionary Cuba. She discussed her work's historical inflections through narrative and visual signifiers:

> Los antecedentes de esta sociedad secreta hay que buscarlos bien pasados en el tiempo porque surgieron en formaciones económico-sociales muy primitivas donde el hombre se enfrentaba incontables veces a lo desconocido buscando siempre una respuesta satisfactoria a los fenómenos naturales y sociales que la rodeaban, por lo que en mis grabados podrán observar infinidad de puntos coincidentes con el hecho cultural en sí, verificables tanto en el campo de las ideas como en las referencias visuales.
>
> The antecedents of this secret society must be looked for far in the past, because they emerged in very primitive socioeconomic formations in which man faced the unknown countless times, always seeking a satisfactory answer to the natural and social phenomena that surrounded him; so in my engravings you will be able to observe an infinity of points coinciding with the cultural fact itself [the secret society], [and these points of coincidence are] verifiable both in the field of ideas and in visual references.[23]

Ayón's art visualizes the narrative elements and iconography of the founding myth of Abakuá—the death of Sikán and the protection of "the Secret." The story goes that one day, Sikán, the daughter of Mokongo, the most powerful Efor man, went down to the Cross River to draw water.

Unintentionally, Sikán caught Tánze, the fish that Abasí, the supreme god on earth, had embedded his voice in. It was believed that whoever possessed this voice also held the power to subdue others. Sikán didn't realize what had happened until she heard Abasí's voice speaking from her gourd. When the elders found out, they grew concerned about a young woman's possession of such supreme power. They seized the fish and killed it, believing that this would liberate the voice and bring it under their control. Instead, Abasí went silent.

When it became clear that their tactics of dispossession and repossession had failed, they turned their attention to Sikán. They believed she possessed the power to invoke the voice and feared she would be unable to keep it a secret or wield it responsibly. They decided that she must be killed and her blood used to resurrect the god's voice. With her blood, the elders symbolically transferred Abasí's voice to a goat's skin and fashioned a drum. Thereafter, the drumbeat was recognized as the voice of the god. The instrument was central to the Abakuá's formation and to all African-inspired drumming traditions throughout the Caribbean and the Americas.[24]

As Brown and others have noted and the story makes clear, this founding myth reflects a pervasive mistrust of women's character, suspicion that served to rationalize their exclusion from Abakuá and, by extension, public discourse. Like all women, Sikán could not keep a secret; moreover, her inability to control herself portended the inevitable betrayal of her people, which had to be prevented at any cost. Both sacrifice and gift, Sikán's death was rendered as a noble act.[25] What woman other than a dead one could be worthy of inclusion in a male space?

Branson-Gill offers another motivation for Sikán's narrative by looking to the Efor region's gender divide. Because Sikán's story emerged during the shift from matriarchal to patriarchal social organization, Tánze's possession was laden with symbolic meaning and portent. To possess the fish was to hold complete power in the community, to assume a godlike role. Following the deaths (or sacrifice) of Abasí (as Tánze) and Sikán, the only human being with a connection to Tánze, a god vacuum emerged, one that was to be filled by men.

Sikán's death underscored the patriarchal demands of male-concentrated power, desire, and identity in the cabildo.[26] But, in the context of plantation slavery, the cabildo was a space where African men held no true physical authority or control over their bodies. The series of events that culminated in Sikán's death suggests that Abakuá's founding myth is grounded in a psychological and psychosocial need to enact dominance and exert narrative control, an aspiration at odds with the material context of enslavement within which the Abakuá dwelled.

Against this narrowed framing and reading, Ayón beseeched her audience to consider the story's conceptual dimensions in a postrevolutionary context, in "otras condiciones y objetivos muy distintos a los de antepasados africanos" (other conditions and objectives very different from those of the African ancestors).[27] She states:

> My attention centers on Sikán, the woman who discovered the secret that the men longed so very much for and that they took possession of after the sacrifice. I believe my images are more about the various histories of the myths, motivated or encouraged by their lessons on *the human question*, about struggle and survival, about the symbolic and significant coincidences with other, distant cultures across space and time. I am consistently relating vivid personages with feelings or thoughts that sometime grip or disturb us, with feelings of uneasiness (which we do not know how to define), with the spiritual.[28]

The Abakuá founding myth mirrors the Euripidean tragedy *Iphigenia in Aulis*, in which Agamemnon and Clytemnestra's daughter, Iphigenia, is sacrificed so the Greek army can sail to Troy to rescue Helen, Clytemnestra's sister and Agamemnon's brother Menelaus's wife. The story's propelling circumstance is never made clear—either Helen had been "kidnapped" by Paris or had abandoned her husband and children after falling in love with him. This textual ambiguity—and the ways it plays into and with notions of gender and sexuality—is instructive in relation to the Abakuá. Beyond its entertainment value, the play deftly engaged class conflict in contemporary Greek culture by raising questions and casting doubt about forms and notions of authority. It also exposed patriarchy's inconsistencies and incongruities and the ways it perpetuated female dependency and oppression.[29]

Kim Solga has observed that women's sacrifice in Greek culture marks an autoerasure in which the woman is recast as an agent in her own destruction. In these stories, the woman's death reflects, rather than inverts, a benevolent patriarchy, masking violence within a narrative of sacrifice. Through this lens, Iphigenia's story, and Sikán's, naturalize the subordination of women in society.[30] In the context of Cuban slave society, Abakuá manhood was recuperated and affirmed through a woman's symbolic and social death.

To center Sikán's story and give her voice, Ayón interrogates the narratives and knowledge structures that configured Cuban-ness without an active (Black) female presence. Drawing on the Abakuá, Ayón illuminated and resisted the ways Cuba's forms of inequality and oppression were state-sanctioned, gendered, and raced. This was an extraordinary critical position for an artist to adopt and exhibit.

LA CENA, 1988

La cena's original version features an assemblage of figures with seemingly fluid gender identities. However, Ayón has described it as a predominantly female space, inclusive of eight female and two male figures in close proximity around a dinner table.[31] The first standing figure on the left, represented in blue, has her hands cast over her eyes in an expression of disbelief. The next standing figure, also blue, but blindfolded, is being led into the room by a wide-eyed, reddish-brown figure who holds a hand over her mouth. The fourth standing figure from the left is rendered in a muted ochre with flame-like leopard spots, or scales, across her body. She stands with a clenched fist covering her right eye. Leaning into the central figure of Sikán is a fifth woman with blue eyes and dense, yellow-green, scale-like flesh. The final standing figure on the right is a man rendered in shades of black with blue lines detailing his body. His form has been purposely inspired by the seated man in Paul Gauguin's painting, *Spirit of the Dead Watching* (1892) (figures 2.3 and 2.4). Like Gauguin's figure, at first, the man may seem disinterested, since he appears to be exiting the frame, but his side-eyed perspective clearly directs attention toward the scene. He is the only person in the entire composition with a visible mouth. If anyone is going to tell the story of what is happening, it will be him.

Four individuals are seated at the table. On the far compositional left, a woman peeks out from behind the left hand covering her face. Before her, a three-tailed fish swims in a semitransparent gourd, next to a plate of more three-tailed fish. To the right of this woman is a seated man. His body is bright yellow and, except for his hands and face, covered in a dot-and-daub pattern. His pose is a composite representation, drawn from Albrecht Dürer's *Melancholia* (1514) and the Judas figure in countless Russian Byzantine versions of the Last Supper. The plate of bones before him indicates that he has just eaten his fish.

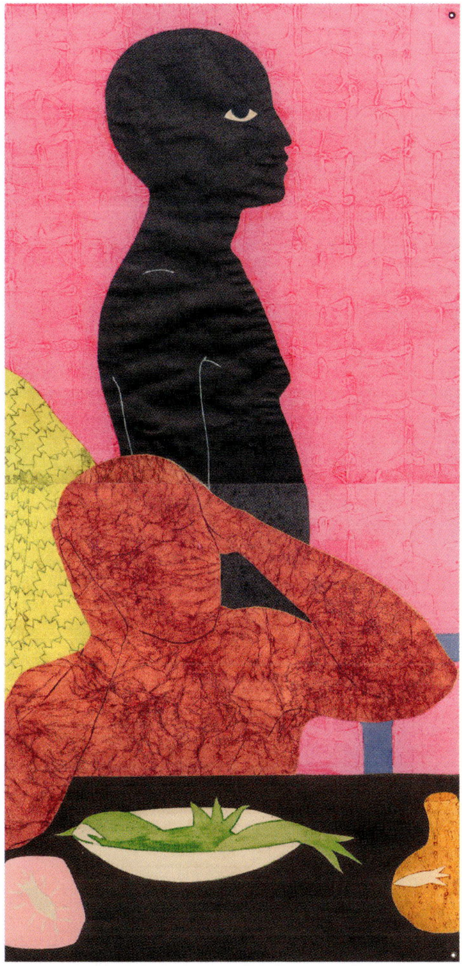

2.3 Belkis Ayón, *La cena*, 1988 (detail). Photographed by José A. Figueroa. Courtesy and copyright © Belkis Ayón Estate, Havana, Cuba.

Sikán sits in the frame's center. She is rendered in bright, verdant green, with a black snake resting languidly around her neck. Her gaze is intent and wide-eyed, fixed directly on the viewer; her expression is one of panic. There is a plate of uneaten fish before her. The final seated figure on the far right is covering her ears and has her eyes closed; her skin's texture is like Japanese rice paper. She, too, has a plate of uneaten fish. A series of vessels are lined up on the table across the compositional plane, each holding a single three-tailed fish. It is clear that something is amiss in this scene. The women don't have mouths to give it voice or definition. Instead, they speak through their bodies—particularly their eyes.

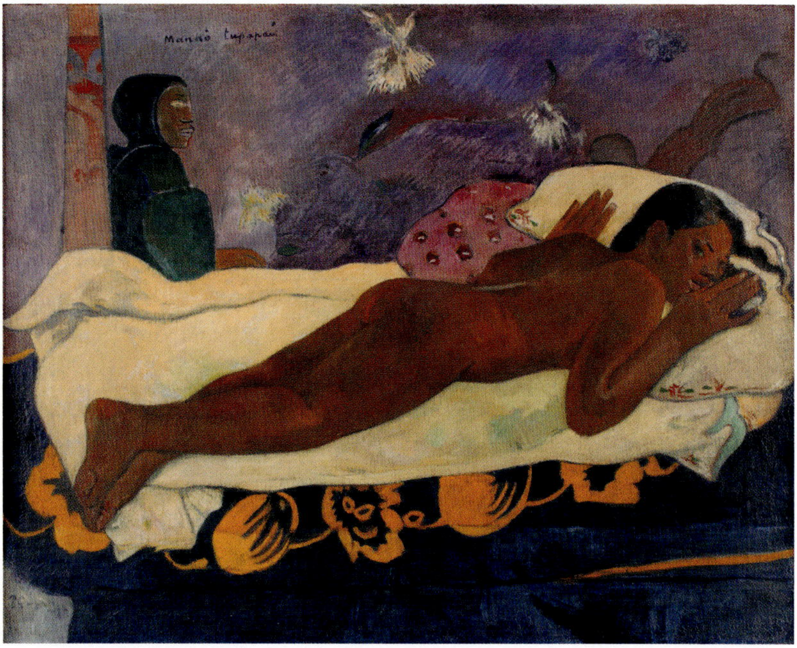

2.4 Paul Gauguin (French, 1848–1903), *Manaò tupapaú (Spirit of the Dead Watching)*, 1892. Oil on jute mounted on canvas, 28¾ × 36⅜ in. (73.02 × 92.39 cm). Collection Buffalo AKG Art Museum. A. Conger Goodyear Collection, 1965 (1965:1). Photographed by Tom Loonan and Brenda Bieger, Buffalo AKG Art Museum.

La cena's background flashes a vibrant neon pink patterned with a grid design of crosses and circles that Ayón described as *anaforuanas*. In African traditions, the cross refers to the Èfik people and the circle to the Efor. The merger of these visual referents into an Abakuá symbolic writing called *oru-bibi* represented the groups' unification in Cuba. Ayón appropriates and transposes this text onto the bodies of select figures.

La cena was first exhibited, in color, in 1988 at Galería de Arte Servando Cabrera in Havana. Although Ayón was initially pleased with the rendering, over time she began to miss the blacks and the tonal values enabled by black-and-white printing.[32] In 1991, for her graduate exhibition at the Instituto Superior de Arte, she modified the work and printed the more widely known black-and-white version (figure 2.5). Ayón articulated her unique approach to color:

> El blanco es un valor. Como el negro. Como los grises. El valor no es el color, el valor es el punto de atención en la obra. Una figura porque es blanca, no es blanco. Una figura es blanca porque es un punto de atención y porque trabajo con blanco, negro y valores. Esa persona pudiera ser negra, pero el valor es blanco.
>
> White is a value. Like the black. Like the grays. Value is not the color; the value is the point of attention in the work. A figure because it is [represented as] white, it is not white. A figure is white because it is a point of attention and because I work with white and black values. That person may be black, but the value is white.[33]

Ayón was undoubtedly aware of the double entendres embedded in her public statements—if one chose to engage them. Her discussion of color values bears traces of Che Guevara's notions of race and Blackness. In a 1959 speech that coincided with a campaign against racial discrimination, Guevara called for a "willed identification" by white and middle-class people with Blacks, mulattos, workers, and peasants to actualize the revolutionary goal of unity and equality.[34] Positioning everyone on an equal footing, he believed that racial identity was subsidiary to a unifying Cuban identity. Despite his assertion and Castro's declaration of the end of racial discrimination in 1960, Cuba continually failed to live up to this stated ideal. On the island, skin color was, and remains, the primary currency of economic and social value.

The revolution's false promise of racial equality reflected across Cuba's social, political, and artistic dimensions. These intersections were poignantly illustrated in the late 1980s when the artist Tomás Esson attempted to exhibit his painting *Mi homenaje al Che* (1987) at Galería 23 y 12 in Havana (figure 2.6). Esson's image depicted a blackened Che peering out from behind a carnal Laocoön, a white beast with red-painted toenails, tiny red horns, and an engorged penis, in the act of mounting a sunburned brown female beast. When Esson's exhibition was installed, state officials were summarily informed about its controversial content. Fidel Castro Díaz-Balart, also known as "Fidelito" because of his striking physical resemblance to his father, visited the gallery to assess the situation; within

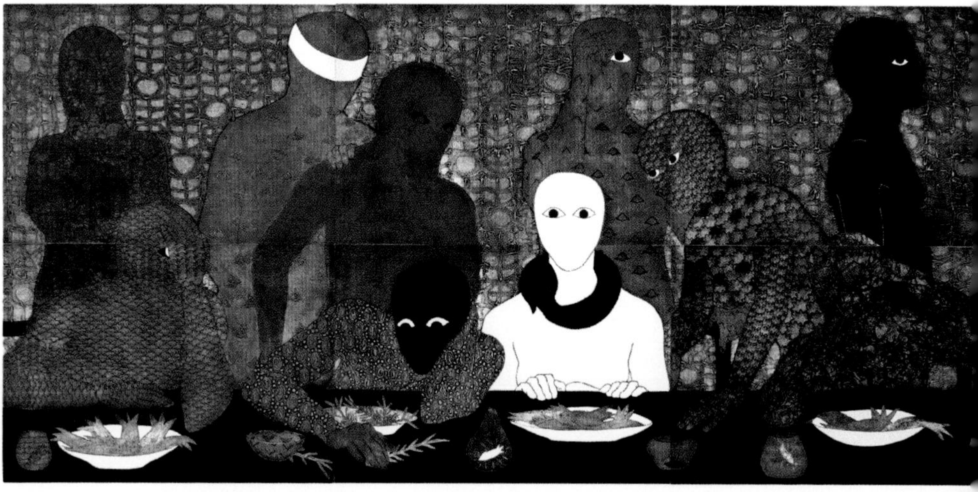

2.5 Belkis Ayón, *La cena*, 1991, 1993. Collagraph on linen, 54⅝ × 118⅛ in. Photographed by José A. Figueroa. Courtesy and copyright © Belkis Ayón Estate, Havana, Cuba.

hours, the exhibition was shut down.[35] The state's objection was not to the painting's carnal nature but to Che's skin color, which they perceived as Black. Although pernicious structural racism and racial hierarchies persisted on the island, they were officially denied in service to the regime's ideological commitment to equality. In fact, despite Castro's claim that "we are all Carabalí," the state treated Blackness as if it was a contagion to be rooted out. As Eric Lott's work on blackface minstrelsy in the Americas suggests, the response to Esson's work reveals the ways Blackness was culturally configured as lack,[36] which simultaneously demanded the preservation of Che's whiteness (and his concomitant distance from Blackness) in ways Che himself never endorsed.

This is the racialized discursive arena that Ayón tentatively entered in 1988, then urgently engaged in 1991, when she altered *La cena*'s palette. If Esson's *homenaje* (homage) revealed the unspoken and unacknowledged subtleties of racial paranoia in postrevolutionary Cuba, artists like Ayón exposed the roots of the government's ongoing refusal to resolve racial inequalities beneath its rhetorical poses. In this context, a formal reading of her color values provides only a partial account of the work's potency. No reproduction can capture its subtle textures and patterning. It is visually stunning. The energy between the figures is heightened in the black-and-white version, and the sense of unease is palpable.

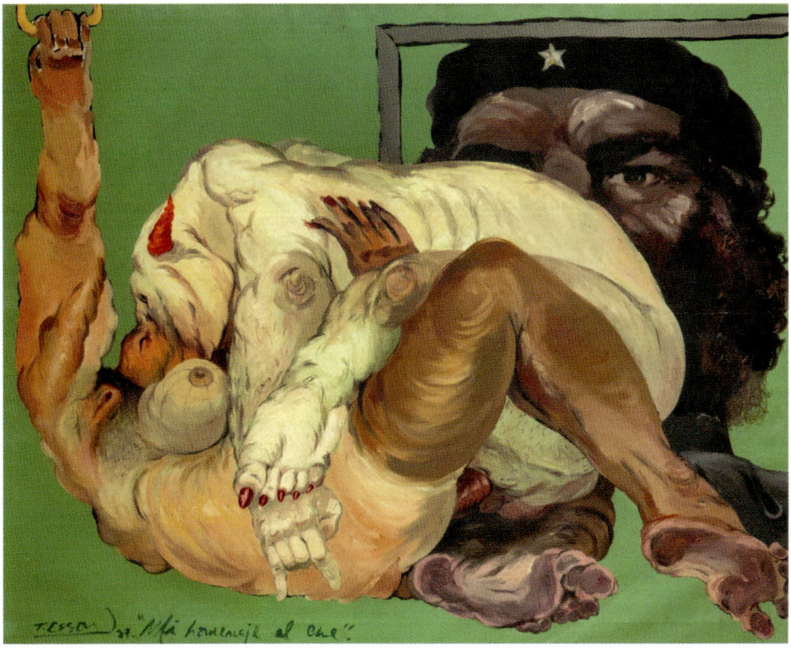

2.6 Tomás Esson, *Mi homenaje al Che*, 1987. Oil on canvas, 62 × 78 in. Collection of Coswell Esson. Courtesy of the artist and ICA Miami. Photographed by Zach Balber.

In a 1999 interview, ethnomusicologist, journalist, and writer Jaime Sarusky asked Ayón whether *La cena* referenced a traditional supper. She quickly answered, "Yes, but only as a conceptual beginning."[37] Accepting the artist's invitation to enact other readings, I engage the work's relationship to Abakuá as a conceptual departure point for its polyvocalism, rendered through allegory, epistle, or something more. Ayón drew on countless resources for visual and narrative cues for each composition. In interviews, she exudes the energy and immersiveness of her process. She told Sarusky in 1999:

> Yo tomo de millones de cosas. Lo que veo que me gusta, lo hago. Hay todo un proceso de tamiz. Yo pienso que esto es como mi hijo, esto es algo que yo creé. Y esto tiene que ver, yo quiero hablar de la insatisfacción, de la intolerancia, quiero hablar de la traición o quiero hablar de sacrificios. Muchas composiciones las tomo, por ejemplo, de la familia. La familia era una pieza que hacía rato tenía machacada en la cabeza. Yo decía, esto tiene que salir por algún lado. Y todo vino por la obra de Gauguin Ana la Javanesa.

> Que a mí me encanta; que es muy importante para mí, que me marcó. . . . Y la familia sale de esa obra, de esa figura sentada tan reposadamente.

> I draw on millions of things. I see something I like, I use it. There is a whole sieving process. I think of this as my child; this is something I created. And this has to do, I want to talk about dissatisfaction, about intolerance, I want to talk about treachery or I want to talk about sacrifices. I draw on many compositions, for example, the family. *The Family* was a piece that for a long time had been pounding in my head. I used to say, this has to come out somehow. And everything started with Gauguin's work *Annah the Javanese*. Which I love, which is very important to me, which impacted me. . . . *The Family* comes out of that work, from that figure so peaceably seated.[38]

La familia (1991) illustrates Ayón's formal linkage of Sikán with Gauguin's *Annah the Javanese Woman* (1893) (figures 2.7 and 2.8), thereby expanding the work's discursive scope beyond Cuba and the Caribbean. In Gauguin's painting, a young Annah sits completely naked on a carved, upholstered blue chair, feet propped on a pillow, a disinterested monkey at her feet. It is a curious composition. Confrontation and pride radiate from the right-facing eye, which is trained on the viewer, but the left-facing lazy eye, which veers off toward the composition's lower-left portion, registers an unwitting ambivalence, degree of shyness, and trace of remorse.

In early twentieth-century Cuban family portraits, the man was typically seated, with the women standing in support of him. In Ayón's *La familia*, Annah's dark body is recast in the figure of Sikán, who is seated in the high-backed chair, realigning the power dynamic. Rendered in flat black, she sits in repose, her legs crossed at the ankles in a levitating chair partly upholstered in fish scales. Her body's only distinguishing marks are the bright whites of her eyes and the white lines defining her toes. Around her neck hangs a cross with the word "Abasi" spelled out vertically on its center column. In her lap or belly is a three-tailed fish. Curled around her feet rests a white ram with black horns whose eyes are also articulated as a three-tailed fish. The serene composition is rattled by a white snake in the lower register, who appears poised to penetrate the white ram nestled behind Sikán's feet. A rooster crowns the butacón chair in which Sikán sits and stares to the right at the man standing there. The man is presented as

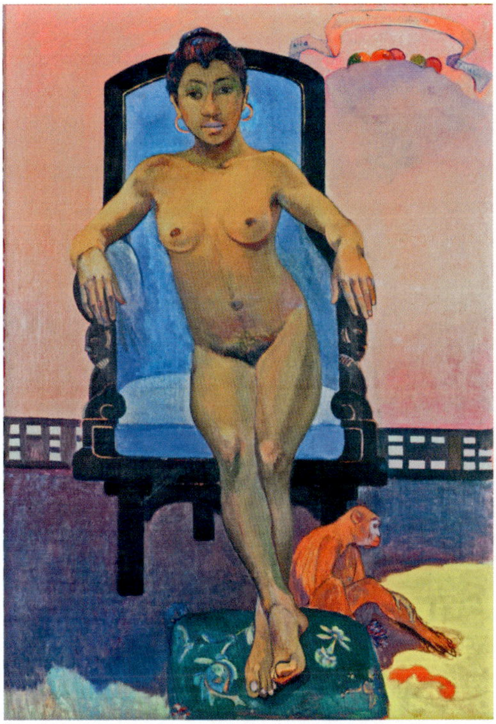

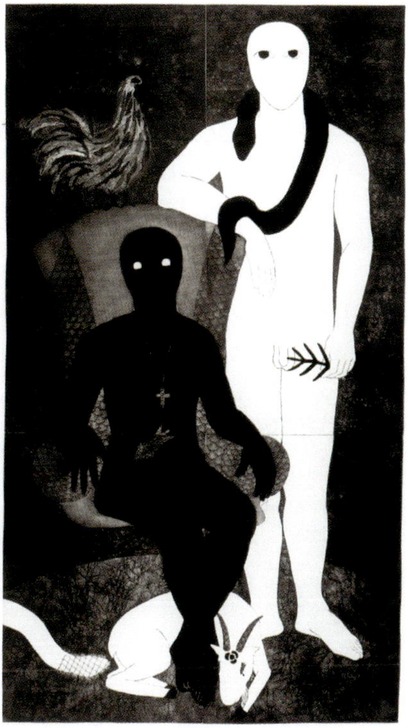

2.7 Paul Gauguin, *Aita tamari vahine Judith te parari (Annah the Javanese Woman)*, 1893. Oil on canvas, 116 × 81 cm. Private collection.

2.8 Belkis Ayón, *La familia*, 1991, 1995. Collagraph on linen, 96½ × 54 in. Photographed by José A. Figueroa. Courtesy and copyright © Belkis Ayón Estate, Havana, Cuba.

a bright-white body, erect but relaxed, his forearm resting languidly over the top of the chair. His hands, feet, genitalia, and eyes are articulated by clean black lines. Around his neck rests a black serpent, and he holds what appears to be a rack of fish bones near his genitalia. Both this snake and the white, partially scaled snake in the lower left corner of the composition are potent symbols in Abakuá.

The serpent around the man's neck evokes Ñangabión, one of two water guardians who witnessed Sikán discover Tánze. Like crocodiles, snakes can navigate both land and water. They present as critical figures in post–Middle Passage narratives, where they are rendered as the embodiment of the god Damballah, who protected Africans during their journey to

Cuba.[39] The goat at Sikán's feet represents the sacrificial offering prepared upon her death, the symbolic source of the Ekpe drum that accompanies the Abakuá *plante* ceremony. This rich world of symbology and historical context expands the painting's conceptual plane by highlighting the dissonance between the composition and its mythical referents.

Following Byzantine formalism and Gauguinesque modern primitivism, the picture plane is shallow. The darkness bears a baroque quality, but light is not engaged dramatically; only tonal values of black, white, and gray are used. Engaging the work within a matrix of resonance generated by Abakuá symbolism suggests that the seated figure represents Sikán. She carries Christ's syncretic cross, the cross of Abasí, and the symbolic cross of the Èfik people around her neck. In her belly rests Tánze, the fish that possessed Abasí's voice. Here, Tánze has morphed into a hybrid being, part eel and part frog, with three tails, reflecting different forms with which to circumnavigate danger and survive in various dimensions and environs. Tánze's presence "inside" Sikán reflects her ordination. She possesses the divine voice and "the Secret" but does not have a mouth with which to share it.

In *La familia*, Ayón further defamiliarizes genre expectations and familial norms by including Ñangabión, Sikán's protector, and highlighting the emanation of light from Sikán's eyes. While the male figure's eyes are darkened, rendering his "light" superficial and shallow, Sikán glows from the inside. Whereas she embodies life, he holds death in the fish bones. The prominence of the seated female's eyes is formally related to the Ireme costumes worn by Ñañigos, or Abakuá members, during carnival. Acquiring sight is a prominent dimension of the Abakuá initiation ritual, as symbolized by the large all-seeing eyes affixed on the costumes. The light in Sikán's eyes is so strong that it has melted her pupils, reflecting a supreme level of consciousness. She has become light itself. In this family portrait, women not only keep the secrets but retain their knowledge as power.

Ayón's visual vocabulary takes viewers beyond the Abakuá's indexical narrative and mythological capacity. In *Arrepentida* (1991) she reimagines "a woman ripping off her skin as a symbol of ambivalence between what we want to be and who we really are" to enlarge the symbolic and narrative possibilities of Sikán's story into a polyversal discourse.[40] Art historian Yolanda Wood suggests that the ripped-off skin can be read "as a zone of misunderstanding," a husk the body must discard to be transfigured.[41] She argues that Ayón's depiction of aesthetic and philosophical transformation in the Cuban context gestures toward the work of Wifredo Lam, whose art was a constant presence in Ayón's studio after her father gave her a substantial retrospective volume of Lam's work, which she treasured.

Lam's monumental productions, such as the exquisite *Huracán* (1945) and the better-known *La Jungla* (1942–43), combined symbolic imagery drawn from and conceived through Cuban religious beliefs of transmorphosis and metamorphosis. On these canvases, human, plant, animal, and symbolic forms synthesize into spectacular hybrid beings that reject conventional boundaries and figurations. Wood observes that, as distinct from Lam, Ayón does not depend on mutating the synthesis of recognized forms to generate meaning. Instead, "surface and bodies function symbolically for their transfiguration, without losing their human form," and the images sustain a "poetics of the body from an essentially philosophical and existential angle."[42]

These articulations register the means through which Ayón's work exceeds its initial evocation of Abakuá mythologies. By citing the way her aesthetic significations travel beyond the fixed frame, I propose that we look not to the work of Cuban visual artists like Lam but to the realm of moving pictures. I believe that Ayón's major interlocutors were also filmmakers like Sara Gómez and Tomás Gutiérrez Alea, the latter of whom she engages in a multigenerational discourse around the nexus of race, gender, and politics.

LA ÚLTIMA CENA, 1976

Fidel Castro championed cultural production as a central means to coalesce revolutionary movements and shape social organization. Three months after the 1959 revolution, he launched the Cuban Institute of Cinematographic Art and Industry (ICAIC) to engage the visual in order to "promote literacy and culture." During this period, filmmaking, alongside other visual mediums, came to be seen as "the most direct and extensive vehicle for education and the popularization of ideas" and as a tool of memory, transformation, and uplift that could be effectively leveraged in the narrative of a new nation.[43] The ICAIC received funding and facilities adequate to producing educational films and documentaries.[44]

Tomás Gutiérrez Alea's *La última cena* became the first historical film the ICAIC produced in postrevolutionary Cuba (figure 2.9). Situated in the context of a relatively young communist society aspiring to situate its achievement in a wider historical struggle against tyranny and oppression,

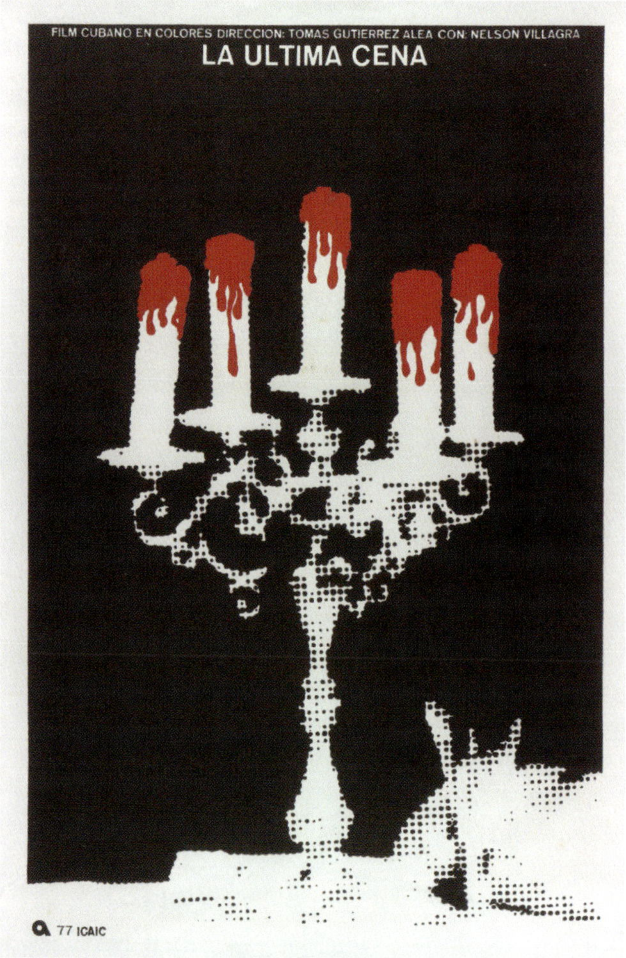

2.9 Film poster for *La última cena* (The Last Supper), 1976. Instituto Cubano del Arte e Industria Cinematográficos (ICAIC). Beinecke Library, Yale University.

Alea's narrative focal point was pitch-perfect. Against the backdrop of the Soviet Union's coercive and repressive influence on the island's art and culture, the film's production coincided with a new push by Cuban artists and intellectuals to build international solidarity.[45] In this broader landscape, Paul Schroeder locates Alea's film within an emergent regional cultural collective that articulated a revolutionary language focused on histories of oppression and hemispheric debates on transatlantic slavery's impact. Carlos Diegues's film *Xica* (1976) and Alex Haley's book and miniseries, *Roots* (1976 and 1977) also exemplify this strand of narrative inquiry and aesthetic innovation.[46]

La última cena was released one year after Angola had gained independence from Portugal under a unified socialist government consisting of three major military factions, supported by the Soviet Union. Within months of Angola's independence, the United States financed an invasion from the neighboring Democratic Republic of the Congo, then led by Mobutu Sese Seko, which resulted in a war that lasted over a decade. Almost fifty thousand Cuban troops were sent to defend Angola; more than half were Black or mixed-race.[47] Ayón's father, a lifelong military officer, was among those deployed. The film, the war, and the island's turn to regionalism constituted the aforementioned "gray years," when Cuba, firmly in the grip of the Soviet Union as a result of the US embargo, the Cuban Missile Crisis, and economic misfires, sought to burnish its reputation as a revolutionary state in the battle against imperialism both at home and abroad. By the 1970s, many of the revolution's promises had not materialized; yet Cuba's military commitments in Angola gestured to its support for international liberation struggles.[48]

Mirtha Ibarra, Alea's widow and frequent collaborator, has said that her husband's films issued from and embodied his belief that critique of one's country is borne from one's love for it.[49] As both supporter and critic of the Cuban Revolution, Alea frames its historical and global contexts in his work to offer space for critical reflection on its utopic aspirations.

In 1959, Alea made *This Is Our Land*, a film about the vital need for agrarian reform. He followed with *The Twelve Chairs* in 1962, which deployed comedy to critique individual greed and elevate an ethos of community above self. By the time he completed *Death of a Bureaucrat* in 1966, Alea had refined his reflections on the widening gap between the promise and reality of postrevolutionary Cuba, registering what Ibarra described as Cubans' habituation to their mistakes and limitations in ways that were desiccating the spirit of the revolution and Cuba itself. Though sometimes cloaked in dissembling humor, Alea's films maintained the revolution's ideals as a central subject and uplifted its goals. Yet he highlighted its inconsistencies by probing its oversights and omissions, specifically around the matrices of race, gender, class, and sexuality.

According to Ibarra, Alea believed his films accomplished their most important work long after the credits had rolled, when spectators had to reconcile their public viewing with their private lives. Natalie Zemon Davis has proposed that *La última cena* propelled Alea into "a group of cinema people and historians who were trying to reconstruct Cuba's past. They were especially interested in slavery and slave activity, which they felt had been ignored or misrepresented in the historical writing of the bourgeois Cuban Republic."[50] Alea approached this discursive and representational landscape as allegory in order to probe Cuba's historical connection to other spaces, particularly Haiti. This is first evidenced in his film *Cumbite* (1964), based on the Haitian writer, indigenist, and avowed communist Jacques Roumain's novel *Masters of the Dew*. Set in Haiti in the small town of Fonds Rouge, the story chronicles the homecoming of the main character, Manuel, after fifteen years in Cuba as a cane cutter. When Manuel returns, the town is suffering from a severe drought. He harnesses special powers to locate a source of water, but a blood feud between families obstructs his intent to use it for the collective good. Manuel is attacked and dies. Although the community's survival depends on ending their feud, they cannot settle it. Ultimately, they propel their own suffering.

Ibarra said that Alea considered *Cumbite* a complete failure. He found its character portrayals inauthentic and the film unfaithful to Roumain's intent. Despite his appraisal, the film was widely praised outside Cuba. Two years after its initial release, it was reviewed in *Variety* as "an arresting film with a tale simply and leisurely told, . . . finely played by an all-Negro cast" and "photographed beautifully."[51] A little more than ten years later, Alea released his second invocation of Haiti in relation to Cuban history and revolutionary ideals, *La última cena*.

La última cena is based on *The Sugarmill* (1964) by Manuel R. Moreno Fraginals. The book offered a blistering historical account of Cuba's sugar industry, which the author argued had been built on the backs of African slaves.[52] The text recalls a historical event that occurred in Cuba during Holy Week in 1727, when the Count de Casa Bayona decided to reenact the biblical Last Supper to express his piety and devotion to Christ.[53] The Count directed his overseer to choose twelve enslaved Africans to play the parts of the disciples; he assumed the role of Christ. On Maundy Thursday, the Count washed and kissed the feet of the twelve slaves, then shared a splendid supper with them (figures 2.10–2.11). During the meal he promised to free an elder slave, return a slave from the fields to the house, and mandate the cessation of all labor on Good Friday. The next morning, Good Friday, the Count left the plantation for town. The overseer, who had not been informed of the Count's promises, woke the slaves for work. They refused, revolted, burned the plantation to the ground, and fled. The remainder of the film depicts the Count's pursuit and capture of ten of his

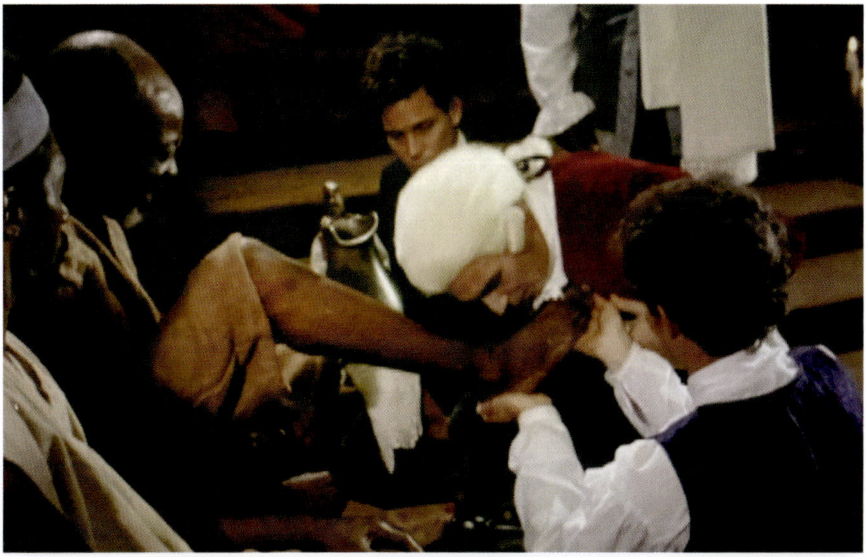

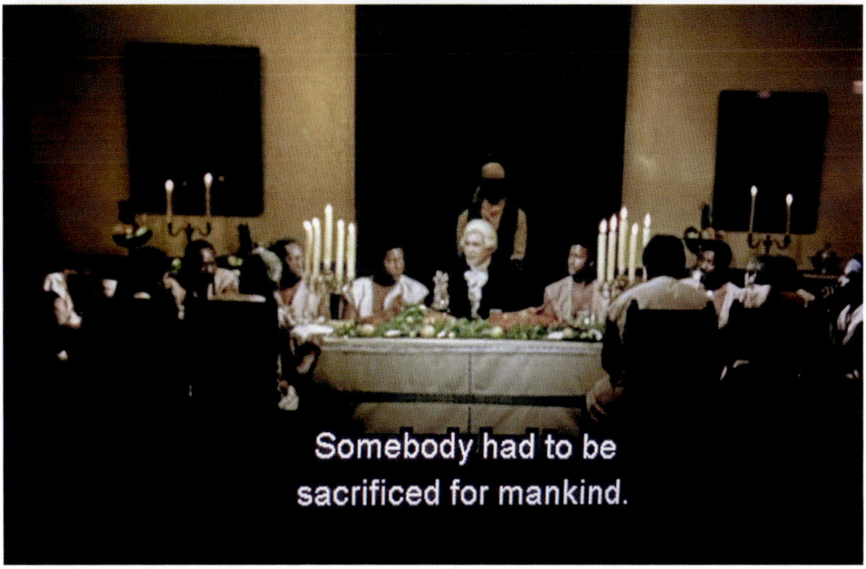

2.10 Tomás Guttiérez Alea, "The Washing of Feet," in *La última cena* (The Last Supper), 1976. Film still.

2.11 Tomás Guttiérez Alea, "Supper Scene," in *La última cena* (The Last Supper), 1976. Film still.

twelve African "disciples," their subsequent execution, and his cautionary exhibition of their heads on spikes.

Although Alea knew that the film's historical events dated to 1727, decades before the Haitian Revolution, he recast its timeline to situate the uprising in 1791. He also introduced a new Haitian character, Don Gaspar, as the mill's manager, who is not cited in the official account or in Fraginals's text. In Alea's version, Gaspar helps one of the insurrection's leaders escape, thereby ensuring the plantation's destruction. Of all the overseers, his is the only life symbolically spared.

Fraginals's book was avowedly Marxist in its approach. It was critical of the economies of slavery and cognizant of its role in fostering the race- and class-based differences the 1959 revolution was meant to expunge. Alea's recontextualization critiques the postrevolutionary present in the guise of history while intimately entangling the Cuban slave economy with the Catholic Church and capitalism. In a narrative choice reminiscent of Suzanne Césaire's treatment of *Youma*, Alea rearranged chronology and added characters with established revolutionary ties to visualize a new historical narrative that linked the events at Casa Bayona to the Haitian Revolution's political, economic, historic, and ideological ideals. These parallels recentered Black Cubans' contributions to modern Cuba's formation, which had been ignored in the pre-1959 era and nationalized and disappeared after the revolution.

ERASING BLACKNESS

As an antecedent to Ayón's *La cena*, *La última cena* exemplifies how local history and culture can generate a globally resonant aesthetic form. It also challenges assumptions of difference and distancing from Cuba's Black heritage and the status of Cubans of African descent to illuminate how slavery's architectures of power and hierarchy persist in postrevolutionary Cuba.

The Cuban elite has long maintained a complicated relationship with Africa. Although official rhetoric purported to recognize Cubans' Congolese or Carabali bloodlines, African-ness was broadly and ideologically subsumed by a postrevolutionary national identity that aspired to erase divisions based on race, gender, and class.[54] In many ways, the 1959 revolution mirrored Jean-Jacques Dessalines's strategic mobilization of "Blackness" in the Haitian context: as an effort to absorb entrenched differences under the rubric of an overarching political identity. In both instances, those who refused to submit to this ideological pretense were viewed as separatists working in contravention of the revolution's goals. And in both societies, Africa was relegated to the "past." Whereas in Haiti, Africa—or Guinen—retained currency within its contemporary figuration of identity, in Cuba, Africa and its traces had to be contained or purposefully and "officially" engineered into folklore and memory.

The African past was cast as regressive to render the postrevolutionary Cuban "New Man," who believed in technology, not gods. Transatlantic Black Cuban religions and social practices were regarded as archaic, primitive, superstitious, and folkloric rather than progressive, future driven, or artistically generative. This approach was both racially charged and ideologically couched in a Marxist framework. It is notable that the first African leader to visit Cuba after 1959 was Ahmed Sékou Touré, president of Guinea. A Muslim who governed as a Marxist, Touré had initiated a purge of traditional religious practices and the art that inspired and grounded them. For decades, cultural groups in Guinea, such as the Baga, were forced to hide their sculptural works or risk their seizure and destruction during government purges. Whether the suppression was legitimated by Islamic anti-idolatry statutes or Marxist atheism, traditions deemed primitive had no place in Guinea's concept of modernity, or in a Cuba led by Touré's friend Fidel Castro.

Although Cubans were intimately connected to Africa, and although Black Cubans had participated in every revolutionary struggle in the island's history, supported the 1959 revolution, and benefited from its ideologies and programs, Black Cubans continued to find themselves defined by forms of racism and racial inequality that coagulated during slavery and persisted in postrevolutionary nationalist, cultural, and industrial formations.[55] Prior to 1959, expressions of racial inequality were partially narrativized through an irrational fear of the Haitian Revolution and articulated through varied channels; for example, racist caricatures of prominent Black Cuban military figures dressed in late eighteenth- or early nineteenth-century French garb (figure 2.12); organized programs, such as *blanqueamiento*;[56] the repression and criminalization of African-derived religions and fraternal orders, including Abakuá;[57] the establishment of American Ku Klux Klan chapters;[58] the repression and criminalization of Black political parties;[59] the massacre of Blacks, including those associated with the Partido Independiente de Color; the denial of jobs to Black war veterans;[60] and the exclusion of Blacks from certain profitable economic sectors, including tourism—unless they worked as entertainers.

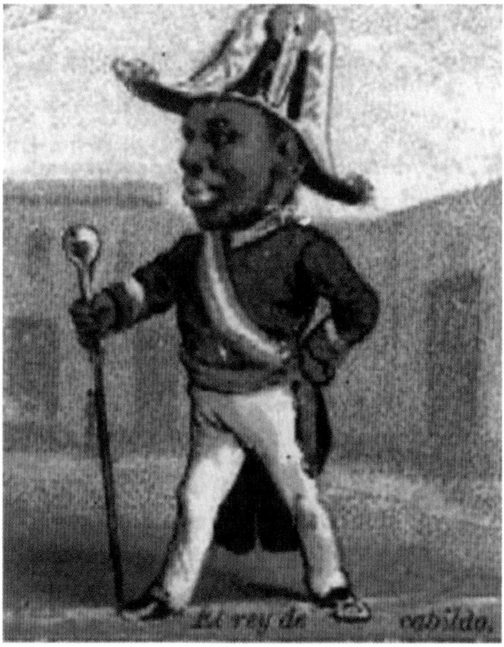

2.12 “The King of the Cabildo.” Chromolithograph from a nineteenth-century cigar box label.

In 1818 the Real Sociedad Económica de Amigos del Pais established the San Alejandro Academy of Fine Arts. As art historian Guillermina Ramos Cruz has noted, prior to the academy's inception, Cuban creative arts had been under the aegis of Black and mixed-race Cubans, but the academy's founders intended to “take the fine arts professions out of the hands of free blacks and pardos.”[61] It is therefore ironic that many of Cuba's most prominent Black and mixed-race artists would not only study there but spearhead the aestheticization of African-derived creolized Cuban traditions. Wifredo Lam and Ayón were part of this group, and Ayón began studying Abakuá while a student at the academy.

Because the revolutionary regime adopted a Marxist framework of class identity and politics after 1959, it refused to fundamentally address existing inequalities embedded in Cuban society and economic systems, in particular those centered on race and, to a lesser extent, gender. Pedro Pérez Sarduy has noted that in its utopic zeal for postrevolutionary equality, “the government targeted disparities of class over race, in the belief that addressing the former would correct the latter.”[62] What resulted was a schizophrenic racial ontology whereby the erasure of race as a primary identifier meant that Blacks who spoke out about the specificities of their history and experience were recast as antirevolutionary.[63]

Cuba's bizarre inconsistencies and false narratives around racial identity and its signifiers are numerous. When Blacks called out their exclusion from high-quality education, they were perceived as ungrateful or maligned for allegedly inferior intellectual capabilities. Research studies on Black Cubans' higher incidence of hypertension were declared invalid "because in Cuba there are no pure races."[64] Wearing "Black" hairstyles was criminalized and only relaxed after Angela Davis and Miriam Makeba visited in 1972.[65] African-derived Cuban religions were discouraged; they have only recently been officially accepted, albeit primarily in the context of folklore and tourism. And Blacks were and still are denied access to certain economic sectors, notably tourism, even though strides have been made in other areas.[66]

These ideological asymmetries have stirred a heated debate on the designation *Afro-Cuban* itself. Some cultural workers, such as the writer Eliseo Altunaga and the anthropologist Jafari Allen, regard the term as an exclusionary conceptual trap that reinforces Africa's difference vis-à-vis its inversion of the European frame. They argue that *Afro-Cuban* does not account for the specificity of a hybridized Cuban culture and reifies tropes that situate European identity at the apex of a racist value system.[67] The composer and choreographer Rogelio Martinez Furé believes that the label's usage and implications compress a diverse, hybrid nation into a homogenizing identity frame that vanishes the density of its African, Asiatic, Chinese, Arab, Hebrew, Hindu, and Indonesian elements and severs it from the broader Caribbean conversation within which it originates. Yet, in the context of this study, if we understand *Cuban* as inherently hybrid, and Africanaeity as its binding agent, the designation *Black Cuban* may serve to fully acknowledge the place of Africa and its diasporas in the epistemological histories of Cuban culture, politics, economies, and social life and the country's lingering racial and gender inequalities.[68]

In the 1970s and '80s, visual artists confronted Cuba's articulation of Blackness and historical connections to Africa in collectives such as Origen (1974–78) and Grupo Antillano (1978–83). Guillermina Ramos Cruz, considered Grupo's official historian, said that the collective "approached the theme of the presence of Blacks in Cuban art as a postcolonial metanarrative in which 'the other' lays claim to the possibility of organizing history based on his [the other's] own categories and from a self-referential ontology."[69] Despite the official practice of linguistically subsuming Blackness under a broader frame—for example, referring to the nation as a "*baragua*" or a "*palenque*" and the people as "Carabali" in national discourse—the government has led no effort to document slavery, abolition, or the Black presence in Cuba since 1959. In fact, access to such information has often been denied or suppressed in libraries and archives. Mirroring Antoni's search for a feminist archive, Ayón encountered difficulties when trying to conduct research on the Abakuá in the late 1980s. Scarcity and obstructions forced her to rely on her uncle's personal library and on texts borrowed from friends and professors. Her clandestine research in these private libraries led to the discovery of Lydia Cabrera and of Enrique Sosa's text *The Ñañigos*, both of which grounded her knowledge of Abakuá.

Ayón's research deepened her interest in Cuba's Black heritage. Yet, as befitting a child of the revolution, she was careful to publicly situate her inquiry in the realm of culture rather than race. She expanded her awareness by attending rumbas on Saturdays and performances of the National Folkloric Company at the Mella Theater. She read UNESCO's magazine, *El Correo*, cultivated an interest in African numerology, and became fascinated by her father's trips to Africa.[70] She also examined posters in her grandmother's house that featured various *íremes*, Abakuá dancers who perform publicly. Ayón described these experiences in a conversation with Jaime Sarusky in which she also mentioned a film by director Sara Gómez, *De cierta manera*.[71]

Ayón's knowledge of Gómez suggests that despite official efforts at suppression, Black Cubans remembered and respected the artist and her work. Ayón would have known that following Gómez's premature death at age thirty-one in June 1974, the ICAIC had censored her work. It released *De cierta manera* (One Way or Another) in 1977 and did not grant access to her remaining work until 1989 and again in 2007. Gómez's cinematic projects wrestled with patriarchy, class distinctions, and lingering racism and often centered the voices, images, and experiences of Black women. Devyn Spence Benson describes *De cierta manera* as "one of the first pieces of non-Western feminist film coming out of the so-called third world to denounce patriarchy and machismo."[72]

Gómez was the only Black female director at the ICAIC in the 1960s. Hired in 1961 as Tomás Alea's assistant, she quickly began making her own films, which showcase concerns and strategies in alignment with those of Ayón. In *De cierta manera*'s script, Gómez renders sites of incongruence between the promise of revolution and its realities for Black and mixed-race Cubans. She subtly questions its subsumption of markers of difference and competing realities by finding value in individual approaches and creativity. Notably, the film includes illustrations of Sikán to illuminate the ways

Abakuá's "patriarchal regime" "created a myth in which the woman SIKAN betrays the great secret of the god ABASI, giving rise to a secret society from which women were excluded for being traitors." Gómez viewed Abakuá as coalescing the "social aspirations, norms and values of machismo in traditional Cuban ways of thinking." Her critique of the fraternity was cogent but classed, vectored through her middle-class origins. She regarded macho Abakuá men as working "against progress and incapable of satisfying the requirements of modern life" and believed that they represented "the last bastion of criminality" in Cuban society.[73]

While Ayón may have been introduced to Abakuá and Sikán's story through Gómez's film, her engagement was profoundly different. Although she shared Gómez's criticism of Abakuá's toxic masculinity and patriarchy, Ayón was far more nuanced in her analysis and approach. She also had direct experience, given that she'd attended *plante* ceremonies with several friends who were initiates.[74] Although Africa and Black culture were officially framed as subsidiary to Cuba's national cultural identity, they presented Ayón with fertile intellectual and conceptual resources and marked the terrain of literal and imposed silences that informed Gómez and erupted in Ayón's work.

PRESENT IN BODY, ABSENT IN ART HISTORY

Whereas Alea situated Cuban history within a regional revolutionary discourse, Origen and Grupo Antillano coalesced around a mutual interest in incorporating aesthetics and philosophical principles linked to pre-Columbian Cuba, Africa, the Antilles, and the African diaspora. As the work of Judith Bettelheim and Alejandro de la Fuente has shown, and various texts delineating Cuban art histories confirm, the contributions of these groups have been and continue to be suppressed on the island and in the written record.

Volumen Uno and its groundbreaking exhibition in January 1981 launched what became known as the New Cuban Art. Although the philosophies of Origen and Grupo Antillano were manifest in this avant-garde group, they are not part of Volumen Uno's official story. While all participating Volumen Uno artists were fully aware of Black Cuban religious and cultural practices, several of the group's more notable figures, including José Bedia and Juan Francisco Elso, both "white-presenting" Cubans, were initiated into Santería and drew heavily from it to conceptually ground their work. Ramos Cruz has credited Bedia's and Elso's art with expressing a "trans-avant-garde vision of modernity in contemporary art." At the same time, she has noted that their adoption of the same Afro-Cuban traditions taken up by Black Cuban artists garnered global attention while Black artists remained in obscurity in the Cuban art world and beyond.[75] This dichotomy also appeared in film: Whereas the state supported Alea's work, despite its critical nature, and the work gained international recognition, Gómez's work was censored with little chance of greater exposure during her lifetime. Much like Grupo Antillano, after her initial explosion onto the local and international scenes, Ayón soon experienced creative suppression in Cuba and was forced to navigate a fraught cultural and political landscape.

Black Cuban artists' double bind was both historically and geographically specific and a universal predicament. On one hand, critics alleged that their engagement with themes rooted in an African diasporic consciousness reflected intimate associations that concomitantly compromised their capacity for intellectual objectivity and conceptual distance. Moreover, incorporating diasporic forms and practices as a Black or mixed-race person was read as anachronistic or primitive—and definitely not contemporary. Even when an artist deflected or outright rejected that narrative, critics endeavored to impose its imprint, fabricating a story line even if it wasn't there.[76]

Given the choice between promoting art locally and internationally, Cuban curators increasingly went the "intellectual" route, which favored white Cuban artists' engagement with diasporic cultural forms (conceived as appropriately distanced and thus nuanced). When Black artists did not include obvious references to Black Cuban cultural practices, their work could be ignored by these very same curators and labeled as mimicry. In the 1980s and '90s, some of the most prominent Cuban curators operated according to value judgments and aesthetic paradigms that would be easily recognizable in the New York art world—blatantly racist, hierarchical, and exclusionary. To navigate this complicated framing, some Black artists foregrounded formalism and technique in public discussions. Although this tactic did not necessarily or entirely prevent the work from being read in narrow anthropological terms, it did open space to circumvent superficial readings increasingly cited as the basis for exclusion from "contemporary" exhibitions. Ayón's work was central to this debate, and it was not left unscathed.

Despite her undisputed success in Cuba and on the global stage and her receipt of the prestigious Maastricht prize for printmaking in 1993, by the latter 1990s, Ayón increasingly found herself hemmed in by the discourse around the New Cuban Art, which stridently excluded the contributions of African-descended artists and of collectives whose work engaged anything viewed as "African."[77] This exclusion applied to contemporary artists and to the historicization of Cuban artistic production as a whole. Wifredo Lam's positioning offers a key example of how this discourse operated. Lam's appearance in Cuban art history narratives has been conditional upon the subsumption of his exploration of Afro-Cuban practices within histories of Surrealism or revolution. By contrast, his work with and honorary presidency of Grupo Antillano and the philosophical approaches to art he shared with the group have been muted.

The term *New Cuban Art*, coined by art historian Gerardo Mosquera, was crafted with Cuba's revolutionary ideals in mind. At the same time, the movement's social practices were aligned with the conventions and prejudices of the international art market. In this context, association with Afro-Cuban belief systems was considered primitive—contemporary art kryptonite—a valuation that increasingly placed Ayón's work in what Cristina Vives described as "classificatory limbo." Depending on the viewer's perspective or interest, as Ayón's career developed, her art was increasingly regarded as "universal enough not to be bothersome from a contextual viewpoint (said the official); ethnic enough that it could be termed 'folkloric' (said the conceptual artist); 'folkloric' enough that it made a difference (said the market); different enough from the topics in vogue that it didn't involve the necessary codes to be termed 'subversive' (said the critic/curator) . . . but so masterfully conceived that it could not be ignored (said all)."[78]

Although Ayón enjoyed gallery representation in New York and Los Angeles and an enviable international exhibition and residency schedule that included biennials and triennials, within Cuba she was increasingly pushed out of the art mainstream. A review of the period's critical literature discloses limited engagement of her collagraphs beyond a superficial and painfully literal connection to Abakuá. By the late 1990s, Ayón was fighting to be included in major local exhibitions, such as II Salón de Arte Contemporáneo (1998) and the 1997 Havana Biennial, whose organizers did not regard her work as "contemporary."[79] Following protests, she was eventually included in II Salón, but the organizers of the 1997 Havana Biennial refused to exhibit her work. She responded by curating a three-person show, with the artists Juan Carlos Menendez and Norberto Marrero, in her grandmother's home in Old Havana. It was a resounding success *and* a rebuke to the curatorial and aesthetic privileging of Western-defined art histories and practices dominant on the island, which eerily aligned with the values of the Cuban state. The show also resulted in an invitation for Ayón to participate in the Gwangju Biennial.

However, despite substantive global interest, Ayón's work was absent in multiple thematic exhibitions that emphatically "launched" those considered the most "conceptual and questioning artists of the 1990s internationally."[80] Latent racism and ambition clouded the lens of Cuban curators just as the global art world and market was being pushed toward reckoning with its Others. The need for a Cuban artist to produce decolonial art in a decolonizing state in the nineties was never clearer. Like Antoni, Ayón was being forced into battle, though in a very different problem space.

Fraginals's text and Alea's cinematic reimagining highlighted the revolution's Achilles' heel. *La última cena* exposed the fissures and frictions that defined post-1959 Cuba, where salient issues of race, gender, and sexuality were sidelined and suppressed. Ayón's *La cena* extended Alea's text by mapping these silences as intergenerational concerns but, this time, without erasing women from the narrative.

LA CENA, 1993

Twenty years after *La última cena*'s premiere, Belkis Ayón completed the first color version of the large-scale collagraph *La cena*. Alea's film and Ayón's print were distinct critical objects emergent and resonant within the same place, in different times and under different conditions. Their respective dinner scenes allude to Leonardo da Vinci's canonical 1498 painting (figure 2.13) and its underlying biblical narrative. Both lend form to Césaire's call for historical reimagination as decolonial action. While Alea's appropriation of history aligns with Cuban revolutionary ideals, Ayón's print bears traces of the filmmaker's racial and economic critique while pivoting its line of sight toward intersectional identities and gender. Ayón's work renders new epistemes beyond the bounds of official Cuban (art) history to include what is unwritten, unspoken, and unacknowledged. In this context, *La cena* presents as a metapicture and speech act: a visualization

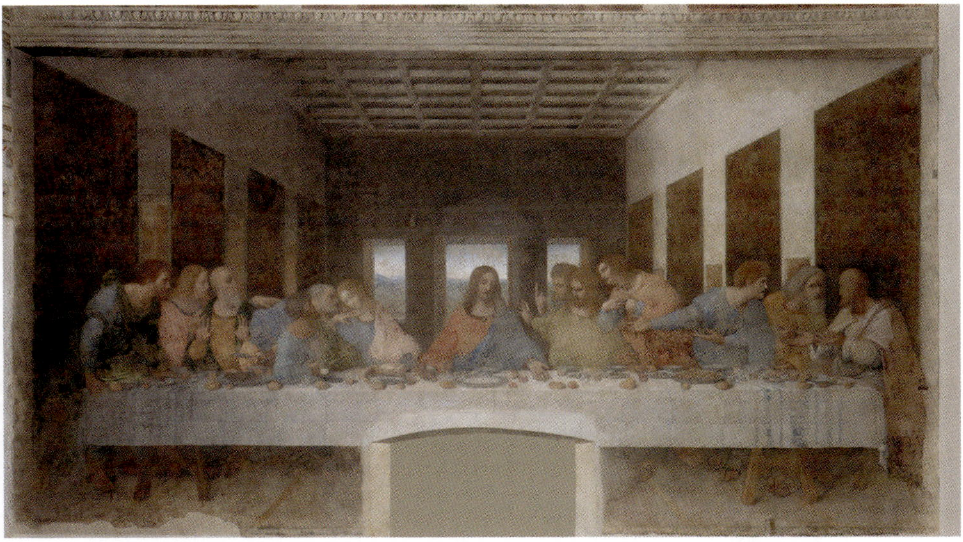

2.13 Leonardo da Vinci, *The Last Supper*, 1495–1498. Fresco, 15 ft., 1 in. × 29 ft. Santa Maria delle Grazie, Milan, Italy.

of silences to rend and expose mythologies of revolution that occlude ongoing tensions and biases around race, gender, and sexuality.

Ayón's experiences were undeniably shaped by geography, gender, and politics, but her role as artist, teacher, and in 1998, the unanimously elected vice president of the National Union of Writers and Artists of Cuba (UNEAC), expanded her horizons. Her large-format prints demonstrate old-school technical mastery alongside evocative, yet enigmatic and discomfiting beauty. In form and composition, they assemble the histories, traditions, and myths Africans brought to the island and the conceptual possibilities that collectives created in response to the presence of enslaved Africans. In these ways, her work surfaced and spoke to the integral role of Black people, Black women, and Black culture in the formation and continued development of Cuban society. Critically, *La cena* depicts an event before Sikán's sacrifice and the Abakuá's formation, allegorizing its history and myths to represent the contemporary oppression, silencing, and disempowerment of Black Cuban women.

In his seminal text *Flash of the Spirit: African and Afro-American Art and Philosophy* (1984), Robert Farris Thompson explored the symbolic writing of the Ejagham (Efo), one of the ancestral peoples of the Abakuá in West Africa. He described how their secret societies' mythology exhibited fluidity of gender roles and conjured an egalitarian ethos. Although men eventually took decisive control, a very powerful group of Nnimm women, from whom Cubans believe Sikán is descended, had once actively participated in Ejagham societies and served as leaders. These women believed that their power transcended their physical bodies and legitimated a divine claim through the myth of the first Nnimm woman's emergence on earth, depicted with a feather in her hair. The feather represented silence and possession of secret knowledge. In Cuba's Abakuá, this relationship was recast as a fatal flaw and a symbol of women's incapacity to fulfill their divine purpose—the safeguarding of secret cultural knowledge.

Thompson explained that "Nnimm women moved, as the forest moves, as the sea moves, in a swaying, chiming mass of fibers, bones, and shells." Exhibiting complete control over their bodies and resisting compartmentalization "as purely instruments of labor," Nnimm women marshaled respect for and fear of their power. They created ritual objects intended to protect their societal position and ensure a balance of power between men and women in society.[81] While their culture did not survive the Middle Passage intact, according to Thompson, many believe that the Abakuá's secret was drawn not from the Cross River region's male societies but from the Nnimm women. He reads the prevalence of silence in Abakuá ritual and the iconographic deployment of feathers as evidence of this lineage.

Black men's continual emasculation through the Middle Passage, slavery, and colonialism and after the revolution fueled the formation of a hypermasculine identity and homosocial space, one that was formally enacted and ritually ordained by the symbolic and violent displacement of femininity and female power.[82] Ayón's oeuvre was grounded in Abakuá, but she rewrote their narrative to envision a world where women's power and values still held sway. The collagraph depicts a solemn initiation supper for women (the initiate is the blindfolded woman being led into the room) that has been infiltrated by men. This portrayal is emphasized by the art historical references to Gauguin's *Spirit of the Dead* and Albrecht Dürer's *Melancholia*, both of which communicate a deep and impenetrable sorrow. It is reiterated through the leopard skin that encases the Judas-like interloper, a link to the all-male Leopard Society found in the Cross River region, and the scales that reference the fish that held Abasí's voice and the feminine secret. Many of the female figures—but not Sikán—have skins that resemble fish scales. The Abakuá insist, *Para ser hombre no hay que ser abakuá pero, para ser abakuá hay que ser hombre* (To be a man you do not have to be Abakuá, but to be Abakuá you have to be a man).[83] In this scene,

Ayón intimates that men who consume the fish not only touch God but anthropophagically consume the feminine essence of (Black) women in order to become men. The work suggests that postrevolutionary and postcolonial patriarchy birthed its very own Gazourmah by repeatedly consuming the life and essence of women, both symbolically and materially.[84]

La cena's political position is sharpened by its compositional dissonance in relation to Da Vinci's *Last Supper*, which places Christ at the center, and to Alea's rendering, which foregrounded the Count but symbolically displaced him by positioning an enslaved African at the top of the central formal triangle. In the middle of Ayón's print, a male's arm and shoulder overlap with Sikán's figure. Here, Ayón declines to replicate the traditional—read patriarchal—hierarchy of these earlier iterations, instead privileging a horizontal discourse, even though it communicates a tragedy—the transition from female (egalitarianism) to male (hierarchy).[85] Whereas all of Da Vinci's and Alea's dinner guests are men, in Ayón's print, they are interlopers.

The distances between Da Vinci's fresco, Alea's film, and Ayón's collagraph can be measured by representations of gender interpolated with Cuba's history and culture. Da Vinci's *Last Supper* represented Christendom's central liturgical practice. Alea rearticulated this frame story to engage Marxist and Christian ideologies in the context of slavery. In both conversions, women were absented. Ayón asks how the story might be transformed and redeployed if women take seats at the table.

The women in *La cena* register apprehension; it is clear that the interloper has crowded out the female initiate at the table. As visualized in Ayón's print, in Abakuá ceremonies, the initiate enters the room wearing a *famba*, or blindfold. Once "the Secret" has been shared, the initiate's eyes are believed to symbolically glow, burning away the blindfold. The bright eyes of enlightenment are registered in the design of the Ñañigo *íreme* mask that initiates wear in public ceremonies. In *La cena*, the women's eyes become a primary means of communication, reflecting recognition that the man's presence and desecration of the feast results in abrogation. Because the women have already transmuted into fish-human form, the man's consumption of the fish engenders horror: the women bear witness to their own destruction and the deracination of societal order. Their lack of mouths—in contravention of the Abakuá founding myth—literally signifies that the secret wasn't given to the enemy by women; it was stolen by men. The eyes' prominence intentionally emphasizes and expands the narrative in specific ways. According to Ayón:

> En realidad los ojos en mi obra es lo que impresiona a la gente, lo que les intriga porque son ojos que te miran muy directamente, entonces creo que no te puedes esconder, donde quiera que te puedes esconder, donde quiera que te muevas ellos están ahí siempre mirándote, están ahí haciéndote cómplice de lo que estás viendo.
>
> Actually, the eyes in my work are what impresses people, what intrigues them, because they are eyes that look at you very directly, so I think you cannot hide; wherever you can hide, wherever you move they are always there looking at you, they are there, making you complicit in what you are seeing.[86]

Ayón's reference to complicity is worthy of pause. What is it that we are complicit in or with? What are we accomplices to? What is the secret? Is it, as Karin Barber suggests, something "constructed by political struggle; through institutional exclusion, rhetoric, and performance," or is it, as Brown proposes, "a 'fetish,' a socially invested repository of symbolic capital, something both sides somehow knew all along"?[87] Although these possibilities are compelling, Ayón isn't interested in simply moving cultural capital from one group to another. By leaving "the Secret" allegorically open as "the voice," or speech itself, the work becomes a self-reflexive composition of what is engendered by the power to speak against one's oppression—the materialization of the subject by the subject. In this context, for Cuban women, particularly for Black Cuban women, *La cena* represents the possibility of an incredibly potent, long-denied achievement.

AT THE CROSSROADS OF RACE, GENDER, AND SEXUALITY IN CUBAN "FEMINIST" ART

La cena (1993) invites us to consider how present inequalities might be reimagined if we disassemble epistemologies and articulate concepts of being that are antisexist, antiracist, antidiscriminatory, nonpatriarchal, and anticolonial. The work's political register is avowedly feminist, and yet Ayón and other Cuban women artists and writers during this period backed away from readings of their work as "feminist." Their collective reticence begs the question, Was feminism, like Blackness, a conceded identity within the rhetoric of revolution that bowed to the exigencies of the time?

In Yoruba, the god Eshu (aka Elegba or Elegua) governs the transition spaces between life and death, future and past, here and there. This is a useful lens through which to read Ayón's work, which resides at the crossroads where race, gender, sexuality, and history in Cuban art collide. Her oeuvre positions the female body as textural and as a contemporary vessel for Eshu's work. In his 1994 text on Cuban art, Luis Camnitzer described the work of Magdalena Campos Pons and Marta María Pérez Bravo as feminist.[88] At the time of his writing, Campos Pons was engaging both Marxism and Santería to challenge mythologies surrounding female sexuality. Against the currents of the New Cuban Art, Campos Pons stated that she wanted her work to be less intellectual and more emotional. After birthing twins, Pérez Bravo had shifted artistic focus toward the female body and its changes during pregnancy. In the United States, such work would automatically be interpreted as feminist, but this qualifier was often rejected or met with profound ambivalence by Cuban women artists, including Ayón. In a 1993 interview with David Mateo, she wrestled with the designation:

> Yo jamás he pensado que mi obra sea feminista. Nunca he tenido ese calificativo ciertamente incorporado. La primera persona que intentó llamar la atención sobre ese aspecto fue el especialista del Centro Wifredo Lam, Eugenio Valdés, y hasta pudiera ser que sí, que tuviera razón, que en realidad mi obra fuera feminista, porque ella refleja mi propia incertidumbre existencial; pero no la he conceptualizado de esa manera.

> I have never considered my work to be feminist. I certainly have never incorporated that qualifier. The first person who tried to draw attention to that aspect of the work was the specialist from the Wifredo Lam Center, Eugenio Valdés, and it could be that, yes, he was right, that my work was actually feminist, because it [my work] reflects my own existential uncertainty; but I have not conceptualized it that way.[89]

Critical literature from this period reveals that Cuban women considered American feminism bourgeois. During the 1990s, the nonprofit women's group the Association of Women Communicators (MAGIN) worked on a range of issues to challenge the postrevolutionary status quo.[90] The organization's efforts not only exposed Cuba as a deeply patriarchal, heterosexist space but also called out its failure to deliver on its promise of gender equality. The Black Cuban poet Georgina Herrera worked with MAGIN to support female sex workers, who were for the most part—especially in the early years of the Special Period—Black women.[91] The state-sanctioned Federation of Cuban Women (FMC) was established by Vilma Espín, Raul Castro's wife, almost immediately after the revolution to manage the bureau for women's affairs. The group MAGIN chose to operate independently from the FMC because it perceived the organization as expressly bourgeois, intended to uphold and protect bourgeois values.[92] Whereas the FMC denigrated sex workers, MAGIN regarded them as valiant, willing to do whatever was necessary to support themselves and their families when faced with dire conditions. MAGIN also maintained that the disproportionate number of sex workers who were Black or mixed-race demonstrated that in Cuba, race could not be separated from gender. When Sara Gómez created the film *Mi aporte* (1972) to attend to the peculiarities of intersected identities and lives within the revolution, Espin and the FMC rejected the film and Gómez as counterrevolutionary.[93] Although Gómez continued to make films, the work was not allowed to be shared publicly for the remainder of her life. In 1996 the FMC deemed MAGIN's work transgressive and counter to revolutionary ideals, and it was "deactivated" by the state.

By devoting sustained and specific attention to critical dimensions and historical reimaginations embedded in Ayón's work, I position her alongside generations of Black women creatives who exposed the specific constraints and experiences they endured at the intersection of race and gender and sought to hold the state accountable for seeing through its revolutionary promise and egalitarian pose. That Ayón faced censorship and exclusion from contemporary exhibitions of Cuban art, despite her global stature, suggests the extent to which her engagement with Abakuá dictated and revealed the art world's limitations and incapacity to consider the contemporary resonances of diasporic social formations and cultural practices. Perhaps, too, someone in power recognized the potency of her critique.

In *Guarding Cultural Memory: Afro-Cuban Women in Literature and the Arts*, Flora González Mandri explores the work of Ayón and Campos Pons. In her discussion of Campos Pons's *When I Am Not Here* (1996), González Mandri argues that the artist "problematizes the black female body as both an object of victimization and a subject capable of perpetuating collective memory."[94] Pons embeds memories in the marks and markings on her skin, similar to Ayón's symbolic etching through and on the flesh. Reimagining her body as site and archive, Pons plumbs the depths of interconnected transatlantic memories to conjure a diasporic memory bank. It is an approach that reverberates in the work of African diasporic women artists working in the 1990s, from Lorna Simpson and Joy Gregory to Alison Saar and Renée Stout.

Mandri emphasizes Ayón's engagement of the mythic over the conceptual and historic. She notes the symbolic potential of the artist's use of her body as model, a frequent observation made by other writers, even though this technique is common practice and often borne from necessity. Ayón once remarked that "I see myself as Sikán, as a bit of an observer, an intermediary and one who reveals . . . Sikán is a transgressor, and as I see her, I see myself."[95] But the elision between artist's body and aesthetic and narrative form is not literal or mythic in *La cena* but semiotic and existential. The composition draws on the Nnimm women's immaterial self-perception, their habitation of the world beyond physical form or limitation. It recalls Antoni's positioning of her body as site and conduit of knowledge. And it suggests that Ayón wants her audience to see themselves in Sikán rather than see *her* as Sikán. The work is not autobiographic, but autohistoriographic. It individualizes reflective experience to illuminate and redirect the lens through which we recognize, interpret, and frame others, and ourselves.

Technically flawless and formally astute, *La cena* engages history through aesthetics to retell a canonical story, recasting a liturgical event with Black women at its center. As with Alea's *La última cena*, allegory is mobilized to situate Sikán's story as part of a longer, ongoing historical narrative and as a sociopolitical critique within an intersected matrix of gender and race. While Ayón's critical eye rests on Black women's place in Cuban society and the myths and ironies that underwrite its revolutionary foundation and reformation, its purview extends beyond this immediate reference point to broader contexts and contemporary spaces.

MEETING IN THE UPPER ROOM

Alea's *La última cena* articulates a claim echoed in Ayón's *La cena*: Freedom is attained not through revolution or emancipation but through epistemological agency and cultural transformation derived from ancestry and history. Echoing Cuba's desire to transcend its increasing isolation, *La última cena* visualized a national narrative aligned with liberation movements in the Americas and beyond. The Haitian Revolution, which was viewed in the nineteenth century as a threat to Cuba's very existence, was narratively repositioned as a historical precedent. Within this paradigm, Cuba was not the exception but part of a universal struggle to manifest Jose Martí's dream of a classless, antisexist, postracial utopia.

The only Africans who escape capture and execution in Alea's film are Sebastian, the rebel slave who recounts an African folktale of transformation, and the man who sings a *mucanda* (a song from Angola/Africa). The film's obvious associations with the Last Supper of Jesus Christ are often read by scholars through Bakhtin's notion of the carnivalesque, such that Sebastian emerges as the *real* Christ figure and the Count as Judas. But this simplification forecloses the representational dissemblance's prismatic nature. In Kafkaesque Cuba, *La última cena*'s supper scene extends for a full fifty minutes. Alea viewed the film's themes much like Fraginals—as fundamental to an understanding of contemporary Cuba and the role of Black people in creating it.

Unlike their Christian referents, in *La última cena*, Sebastian and the Count do not die. The Count occupies three symbolic roles—plantation owner (capitalism), Christ (religion), and Judas (imperialism). Like the story of Sikán/Iphigenia, this triple vision can be interpreted as reflections of the Cuban state. The enslaved African, Sebastian, is not a Christ figure. He gains freedom and his life by destroying the mechanism of oppression—the plantation—and drawing on his cultural heritage to escape death and slavery by transforming into a bird. His transfiguration comes toward the film's end and is registered progressively. First, the audience sees a spike without a decapitated head, then a series of frames imaging Sebastian's conjurations, as the soundtrack shifts from European Baroque music to increasingly urgent African drumming. We watch Sebastian running: as water flowing; as rocks tumbling down a cliff; as horses galloping. He never loses momentum, until his human body finally transforms into a bird that takes flight and effortlessly flies away. As for the Nnimm women and Sikán, life extends past its physical encasement, beyond death. To achieve the condition of freedom still not fully attained by (Black) Cubans today, Sebastian must leave behind his human body.[96]

Toward the end of her life, Ayón referenced the growing feeling of unease that had crept into her work as duly reflected in her circular compositions from the late nineties. In these pieces, the figures appear definitively trapped; the possibility of change, growth, transformation, escape, and renewal is diminished. The light in the figures' eyes, so bright in *La familia* and *La cena*, is increasingly blotted out in *Intolerancia* (Intolerance), *Siempre hay algo* (There Is Always Something), and *Tu amor me condena* (Your

Love Condemns Me). As the compositions' detailing increased, their transcendental possibilities were increasingly foreclosed.

On one level, Ayón's life appears to have been charmed. She was recognized, collected, and exhibited all over the world and enjoyed the freedom afforded to Cuban artists during this period. In 1998, the year she was elected vice president of UNEAC, her imagery began to change. The distance Ayón had carved between herself and Abakuá and herself and Sikán was being whittled away in public discourse. A mythology consolidated about her family's connections to the order, to the point that months before her death, she was compelled to publicly state:

> No es abakuá. Y en mi familia nadie lo es, salvo un primo. Es importante que lo diga porque se han inventado historias de que en mi familia todos los hombres son abakuá. No, en lo absoluto. Somos dos hermanas, nada más.

> He [my father] is not Abakuá. And in my family nobody is, except a cousin. It is important that I say it because stories have been made up that in my family all men are Abakuá. No, not at all. We are two sisters, nothing more.[97]

In addition, Ayón's distanced approach to Abakuá was increasingly framed as anthropological, which disconcerted her because it diminished the conceptual nature and capacity of her oeuvre and legitimized her exclusion from contemporary Cuban art exhibitions. Drawing on Holder, we can say that there was nothing wrong with Ayón's practice. But there *was* something *deeply* unsettling about the curation of Cuban contemporary art and its willingness to feed the global market system's parameters of "contemporary" rather than challenge its perceptions and constraints.

PERPETUAL RETURNS

In 1995 Roberto Fernández Retamar declared Caliban's demise, a fate registered by artists like Antoni and Ayón, who were no longer comfortable with or disposed to seeing themselves or their work through limiting and dehumanizing lenses. Like George Lamming, Retamar had come to believe that, having never been "accorded the power to see," Caliban's capacity to metaphorically embody a postcolonial imaginary capable of producing historically reflective, critically reflexive, anticolonial art was impossible. Lamming had concluded that Caliban was "the excluded, that which is eternally below possibility," and was continually "appropriated and exploited" for the purposes of the imperialists' own "development."[98] Césaire altered the story line, reimagining Caliban as an agent capable of achieving his own liberation in his own voice. By engaging Abakuá in, and conceptually as, the problem space of postrevolutionary Cuba, as Antoni was doing in the New York art world, Ayón performed decolonizing work, in this case centered on Black women finding their voices through Sikán. Although she suffered from curators' and critics' unwillingness to engage her oeuvre's conceptual dimensions, and although she became "frustrated when she realized that the reality she hoped for didn't exist," the work was nevertheless potent in its time and remains relevant.[99] As the following chapter shows with the work of Edouard Duval-Carrié, to do decolonial work often demanded appropriating and transforming the old into the new. In his contemporary deployment of the genre of history painting to reworld Haitian history, like Ayón, Duval-Carrié proceeded to make the invisible visible and the haptic and unspoken seen.

CHAPTER THREE

Historical Drag

Genre, Violence, and History in Edouard Duval-Carrié's Mardigras at Fort Dimanche, *1992*

> Haiti is a country of people who are unfortunately illiterate and the image is essential. . . . Every work of art from Haiti is either a chronicle of history or a very strong statement about aspirations or frustrated aspirations.
>
> EDOUARD DUVAL-CARRIÉ

CHANNELING OGUN

In a *New Yorker* piece in the late 1980s, Mark Danner shared an account of personal significance that took place in Port-au-Prince just before the 1987 general election. On the night he recalls, several reporters, Danner among them, rushed out of their hotel in response to hearing gunfire in the street. Amid the night shadows, Danner spotted a man with a metal rod striding back and forth, chanting, "Toi! Toi! Toi! Toi qui dors! Leve-toi!" ("You! You! You! You who sleep! Rise up!"). Danner refers to the man's call as "bat teneb," the beating of metal objects through which Haitians rouse one another to action in defense of their lives and homes. As he watched the man moving in and out of the shadows, he realized that he wore "an old and ragged flowered dress" over his dirty T-shirt.[1]

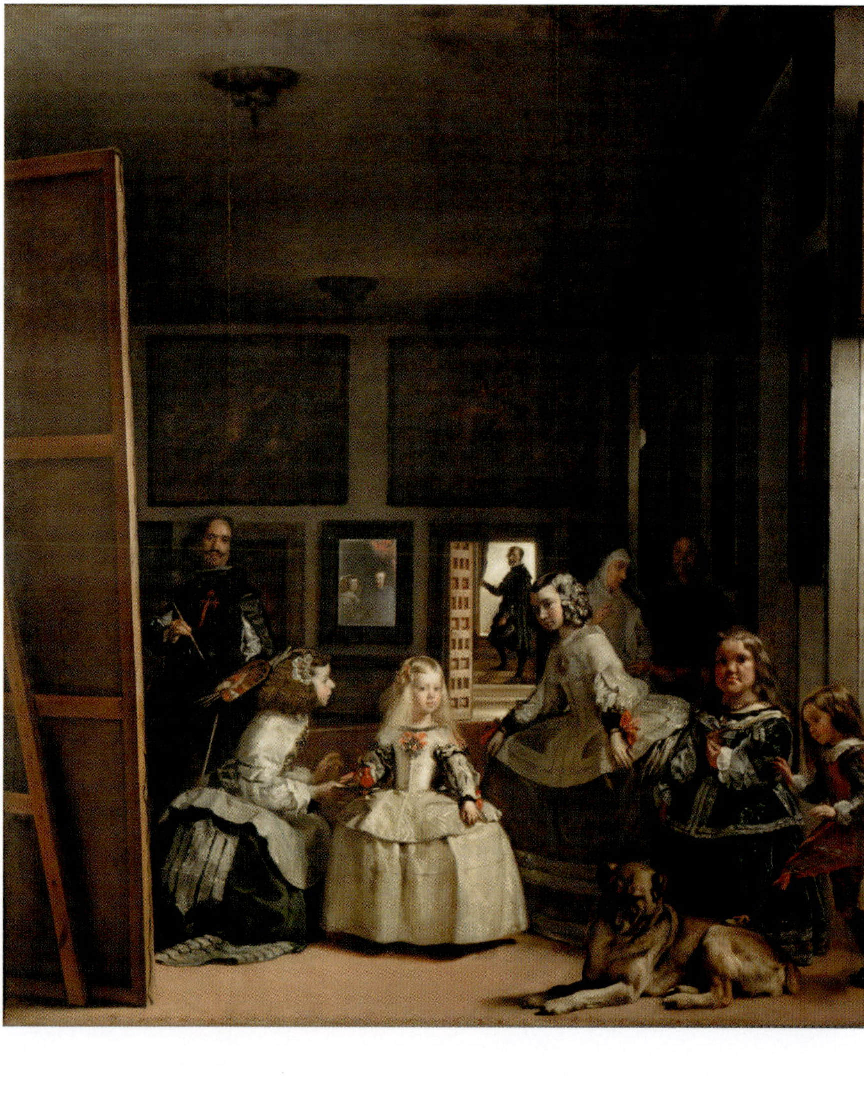

3.1 Diego Velázquez, *Las Meninas* (The Maids of Honor), 1656. Oil on canvas, 10 ft., 5 in. × 9 ft. Museo del Prado, Madrid, Spain.

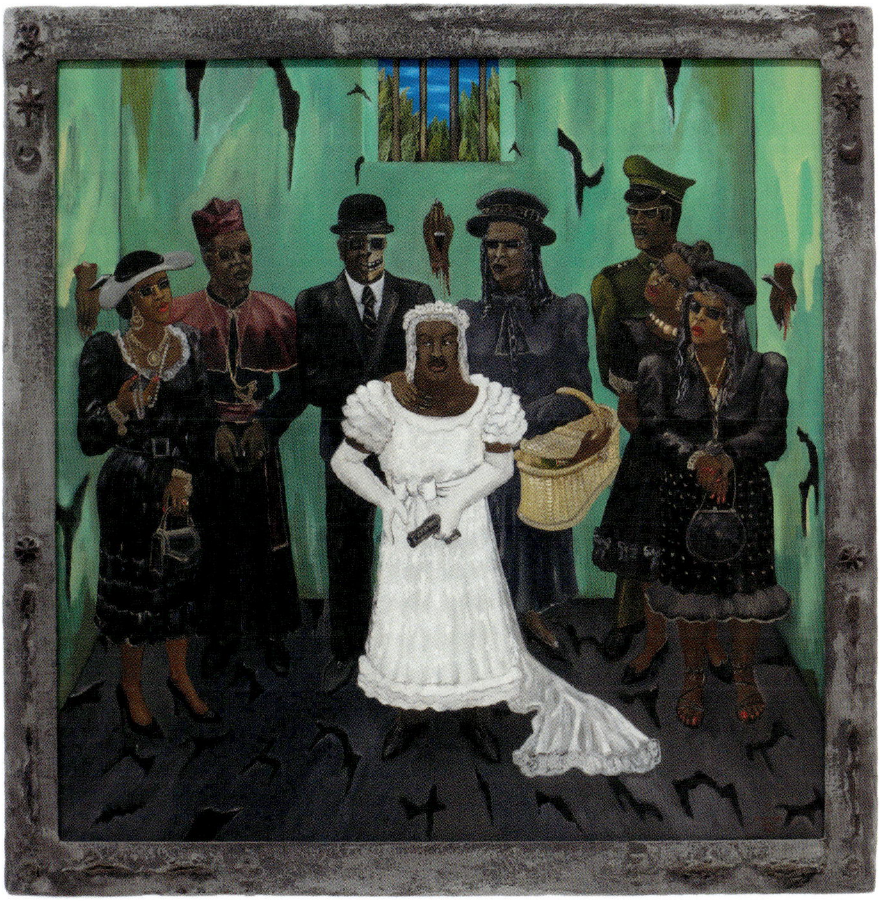

3.2 Edouard Duval-Carrié, *Mardigras at Fort Dimanche*, 1992–93. Oil on canvas, 59 × 59 in. Photographed by Zaire Aranguren. Bass Museum, Miami Beach.

Diego Velázquez's painting *Las Meninas* (1656) (figure 3.1) inhabits a place of honor in Madrid's Prado Museum. For centuries it has been a key punctum in narratives of Western art history, generating endless reconsiderations of Velázquez's extension of representational space, deployment of light, and projection of a double subject, the infanta (situated in the picture plane) and the king and queen of Spain (positioned in the space occupied by the viewer and seen through a mirror in the painting). Edouard Duval-Carrié's history painting *Mardigras at Fort Dimanche* (1992) (figure 3.2) occupies a discursive site between *Las Meninas* and the man in drag, channeling Ogun, the Vodoun god of war, by raising the bat teneb to call his fellow countrymen into battle on the streets of Haiti.[2]

Global Caribbean artists like Duval-Carrié radically deconstructed and reimagined the art historical narrative. But, unlike Antoni and Ayón, who position themselves in relation to feminist, Cuban, and American art histories that excluded them, Duval-Carrié developed a decolonial practice that centered on his work as a *contemporary history painter* intent on aesthetic encounter and redress. His art insists on the right to return, rejecting assumptions intrinsic to the notion and practice of history—that the past is settled. In Duval-Carrié's postcolonial sight lines, historical excavation and accountability are vital, ongoing, and urgent.

Through Duval-Carrié's oeuvre, the seemingly anachronistic genre of history painting played a fascinating role in mapping the contours of contemporary global Caribbean art and its critical encounters. Like Ayón, he confidently deploys Caribbean creolized culture—in this case Vodoun—as a primary conceptual mechanism in his work. His problem space includes the contemporary art metropoles in which he resided and the exclusionary art histories and criticism that circulated therein. It issues from the vantage point of the single most important allegory of Black freedom in the Americas—a revolutionary Haiti that struggled to maintain its sovereignty following the sequential deaths of Toussaint Louverture, Jean-Jacques Dessalines, and Henri Christophe.

In the 1990s, Duval-Carrié responded to Caliban's decolonial cry with a Janus-headed vision of postrevolutionary Haiti, forging a practice that simultaneously looked to its interior landscape and out to the world it inhabited. Through this gesture—at once temporal and spatial—past, present, and future merged in overlapping and contested terrains of representation.

In the spirit of Césaire, and through the lens of a single painting, *Mardigras at Fort Dimanche*, this chapter explores the ways Duval-Carrié contests dominant narratives of his native Haiti and the Caribbean through the manipulation and redeployment of genre as critique. This focus is intended to register the density of his practice, challenge superficial engagement with his art, counter critiques that his work is not contemporary—allegations that parallel those lodged against Ayón—and, most important, to make plain the decolonizing work he performed. Resurrecting and reinventing an anachronistic genre, Duval-Carrié bends past and present to reposition a belief system regarded as primitive by Western modernism and to cast it as thoroughly modern and philosophically foundational to his artistic practice. In the process he employs a postmodern baroque style to reimagine and re-present historical consensus and projections through a contemporary lens.

To describe Duval-Carrié's approach as *postmodern baroque* recalls a European artistic tradition that thrived in the wake of the Renaissance (1500–1750), when opulence, ostentatious decoration, theatrics, sensuality, and emotion coalesced with the rise of plantation slavery in Haiti. His decision to tether *Mardigras at Fort Dimanche* to European artistic traditions through Velásquez's canonical work was a deliberate act of historical drag, intended to pose questions that appear only in the shadow of the canonical referent.

It is worth pausing to consider what and who resides behind the glass that fills the resplendent Hall of Mirrors at Versailles, the palace that came to epitomize the grandeur of the French Baroque era. The room was redesigned by Jules Hardouin-Mansart between 1678 and 1684 in tribute to France's economic, artistic, and political success—success predicated on wealth generated in Saint-Domingue. But there are no references to Haiti's tropical landscapes or the brutalities of its plantation slave economy in a single mural, architectural element, or decorative detail of the Palace of Versailles. While Louis XIV fêted and entertained at Versailles, in Saint-Domingue and France's other colonies, he decreed the infamous Code Noir (1685), which defined slavery and systematized the relations between white French people and enslaved Africans in French territories. A central edict of the French Baroque period, the Code shaped the conditions that led to the Haitian Revolution by delineating what legal (and illegal) brutalities could and could not be inflicted on Black bodies—the bodies that produced the wealth that built the Hall of Mirrors. To mark the terms of his contemporary reckoning, Duval-Carrié seized on the incongruence between the historical reality and material significance of Haiti's plantation economy and the simultaneous erasure of its representational capacity.

"MARDI GRAS" AT FORT DIMANCHE AND THE META CHARACTER OF VIOLENCE IN CARIBBEAN ART

Rather than representing the past as settled, as is typical of the history painting genre, Duval-Carrié's work resists fixity by asking its audience to interrogate accepted historical narratives and the mechanisms of power, privilege, and violence that craft them. *Mardigras at Fort Dimanche* is a key work in a series begun in the late 1980s that problematized and projected Haiti's history into the aesthetic arena. It was painted in the quincentennial year, 1992, during a period of intense military repression and violence following the first coup, which overthrew Jean-Bertrand Aristide. Haitians could be seen toppling statues of Columbus and throwing them into the sea. The landscape seemed ripe for reckoning and re-vision. This context marks *Mardigras*'s problem space as pivoting on the profound violence of Haiti's past and its ripples into the tumultuous present. By centering Duvalierism's institutionalization and deep historical roots, the painting gestures to its enduring affliction long after Duvalier's death and his son's departure.[3] At the same time, the painting draws on and assembles multiple histories and discourses within its single frame—serving as both metapicture á la *Las Meninas* and bat teneb within the contemporaneous global Caribbean art world.

Mardigras is first and foremost an unauthorized family portrait. The Duvaliers are shown caged in a cell at the infamous Fort Dimanche in Port-au-Prince. The US Marine Corps built the fort as a shooting range and military training base during the United States occupation of Haiti (1915–34) (figures 3.3 and 3.4). After François Duvalier entered frontline politics, it was repurposed to house political prisoners. Its incarnation as a prison commenced in 1957, when Daniel Fignole, Haiti's provisional president, who was forced to resign after only nineteen days in office, became its first resident. His imprisonment preceded Duvalier's seizure of power. Soon, the shooting range and military base became training grounds and headquarters for Duvalier's infamous Tonton Macoutes.[4]

After cells and offices were constructed, Fort Dimanche was formally converted into a prison, where horrific acts of interrogation, detainment, and execution occurred at a dizzying and terrifying rate. At the height of Duvalier's power, the prison was known as one of the most deplorable in the world.[5] Jean-Bertrand Aristide later wrote that, more than any other site, Fort Dimanche "was a symbol of the Army and the police and the

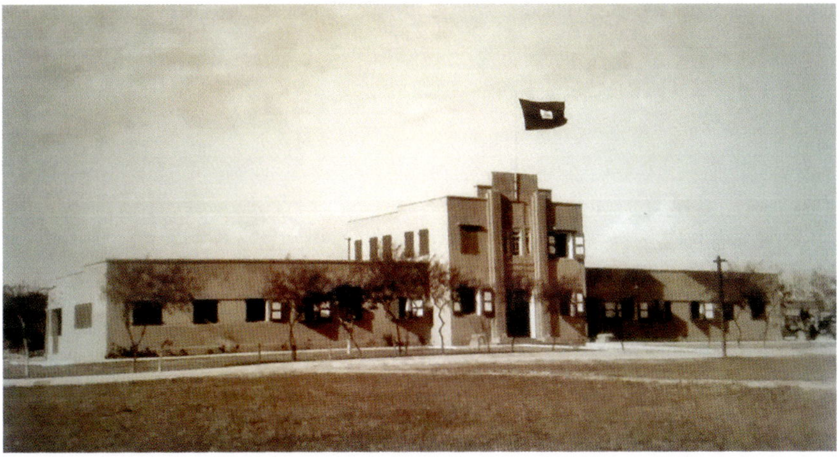

3.3 Fort Dimanche, 1940. Photographer unknown.

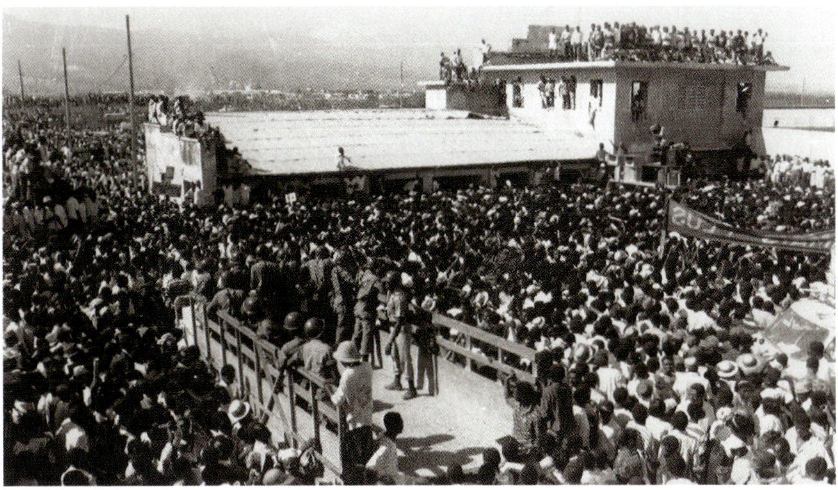

3.4 Liberation of Fort Dimanche, Port-au-Prince, Haiti. Hundreds of Haitians turn out to observe the changing of Fort Dimanche from a torture chamber to a museum, February 8, 1991. The change comes one day after the inauguration of Jean-Bertrand Aristide as president. AP Photo/Daniel Morel.

Tonton Macoutes, all forces organized to destroy us."[6] In one of his first acts after becoming Haiti's first democratically elected president in almost forty years, Aristide ordered the prison's destruction.[7]

In *Mardigras at Fort Dimanche*, Duval-Carrié layers the site's history of brutality with a deliberately overdetermined allusion to Velázquez's infanta. The referent situates the carnivalesque to illuminate the political work of historical drag as a means of implicating canonical (art) histories. Jean-Claude "Baby Doc" Duvalier is positioned at the compositional center, wearing a white dress and carrying a gun. His parents stand directly behind him. François "Papa Doc" Duvalier is presented as the half man, half lwa Bawon Samedi, a figure Duvalier appropriated during his consolidation of power.[8] Papa Doc's right hand features black, razor-like nails and rests like a claw on his son's thick neck. To Papa Doc's right stands Jean-Claude's mother, Simone, dressed conservatively and wearing a black, broad-brimmed hat. She carries a picnic basket with champagne bottles and a severed hand, symbols of the regime's interdependent extremities—opulence and violence encased in a vessel of indifference.

Immediately to Papa Doc's left is the leader of Haiti's Catholic Church. His presence signifies Duvalier's Haitianization of the church in the 1960s and implies support of the regime or, at least, its leader's inclusion in the Duvaliers' circle of influence. Beside the priest stands Michèle Bennett Duvalier, Jean-Claude's wife. At her first official presentation to the Haitian people, she wore a spectacularly resplendent white wedding dress, a gesture that verged on vulgarity against the landscape of an impoverished nation. In Duval-Carrié's depiction, Michèle's sartorial purity is stripped away. She is clad in black, rigidly posed, bejeweled, and adorned with a stylish hat, shoes, bag, and bright-red nails. She clutches a purse in her left hand and a string of pearls in her right, a rosary to the materialism and excess for which she became known.

Three figures congregate on the composition's right side. At the rear is an army colonel, Papa Doc's son-in-law Max Dominique.[9] Dominique's wife and Duvalier's daughter, Marie-Denise, and Duvalier's second daughter, Nicole-Simone, stand in front of him. Marie-Denise and Nicole-Simone are also stylishly clad. All the figures except Baby Doc wear dark shades, a ubiquitous accessory and symbol of the Tonton Macoutes. Their gaze rests on Baby Doc, whose eyes register as dazed, cross-eyed, and zombified.

The Duvaliers' formal dress and deportment contrasts with the markers of decay and destruction that surround them. Severed arms and hands are nailed to the cell's walls, which are rotting and breached by encroaching vegetation from the exterior. Stains and layers of peeling paint recall the skin diseases that afflicted many of the fort's prisoners. The floor cracks portend chasms that seem poised to swallow the family whole. While the cell is riddled with symbols of death and devastation, the sliver of life beyond it (glimpsed through the barred window) is verdant and bright. The earthen vines and greenery press upon the rigor mortis of the prison's interior. The family that sent so many to their demise at Fort Dimanche is now trapped within its walls.

W. J. T. Mitchell coined the term *metapicture* to describe works of art that simultaneously register multiple languages and narratives and thereby counter indexical, singular meanings.[10] Although audiences often seek firm definitions of a work's origins or artistic intent, Mitchell contends that this expectation precludes apprehension of a singular image's multivalent and sometimes antithetical readings. A metapicture elicits not just a "double vision or a dual voice, but a doubling vision," catalyzing a prismatic relationship between language and visual experience that multiplies beyond its frame. By challenging binary approaches to artistic interpretation, metapictures prioritize the interstitial experiences between here and there, artistic intent and audience reception, inside and outside, metropole and periphery, art worlds and other worlds.

Through its codification as a history painting, Velázquez's *Las Meninas* is both metapicture and embodiment of "an episteme, an entire system of knowledge/power relations."[11] The painting shows Velázquez and the household of Spain's King Philip IV assembled in a room in Madrid's Alcazar. The artist is in the process of painting the royal couple, who are positioned outside the frame. The work's title calls attention to the infanta and her attendants, Mari Barbola and Nicolasito Pertusato, whose eyes are wholly focused on their charge. Their gaze is juxtaposed with those of Velázquez and the jester—which rest on the unseen subject(s) lying outside the visible frame, presumably the king and queen. Compositionally, the royal couple occupies the space of the viewer, a strategic positioning that has drawn audiences into the scene for centuries. The painting certainly reflects Velázquez's artistic and symbolic mastery within his contemporary moment—everyone is cast as representational subjects. But conceptually, power resides with the king and queen, whose scope of vision determines and delimits the viewer's.

Las Meninas generates meaning from multiple narrative points. As an artist in service to the Spanish crown, Velázquez was both subject to the court and a subject of the court. He plays with multiple definitions of subjectivity by re-presenting himself as a royal subject (in deference and service to the king and court he paints), narrative subject (he includes himself in the composition), and author (evidenced by the paintings on the wall and his portrayal in the act of painting). This multiply rendered identity interrogates and rearranges established systems of power, relations, and epistemologies. It speaks in tongues.

Duval-Carrié performs a similar feat in *Mardigras at Fort Dimanche*. Drawing on *Las Meninas*'s discursive frames through subject, composition, and form, it becomes contemporary history painting, material object, and metapicture. There is no historical documentation of the gathering it images, and the artist has admitted that it was birthed from desire not reality. As such, the portrait illustrates what Saidiya Hartman has termed "critical fabulation," a necessary reimagination within African Diasporic creative culture in the face of historical negation. Its contemporaneity lies in its reinterpretation of genre, repeated evocation of violence, and supreme act of invention.

FAMILY PORTRAITS

In 1345 BCE, an Egyptian artist made a relief carving of Amenhotep IV (later Akhenaten), his wife Nefertiti, and their children (figure 3.5). Since then, the family portrait has assumed an esteemed place in art history and performed significant ideological labor. While one might not conceive of domestic images as purveyors of violence, Hartman's work on slavery and the archive suggests that family portraiture in the age of transatlantic slavery often revealed the complex relationship between a family's desired representation of power, wealth, and conviviality and its materialization through brutal domination.[12] A famous example of this layered discourse is the delightful conversation painting, *The Family of Sir William Young* (1767–69), by Johann Zoffany (figure 3.6). It is believed that the portrait was commissioned to commemorate Sir William's appointment as governor of Dominica and mark his social arrival.[13] The painting verifies the subject's prestige through a nuanced conversation with its audience; the sitters' pride and privilege are both visible and subdued, in alignment with Georgian moral values.

The Youngs are arranged in an interlocking pattern on what appears to be the side porch of an extensive, manicured estate. Sir William, his daughter, and his wife occupy the painting's physical and emotional cen-

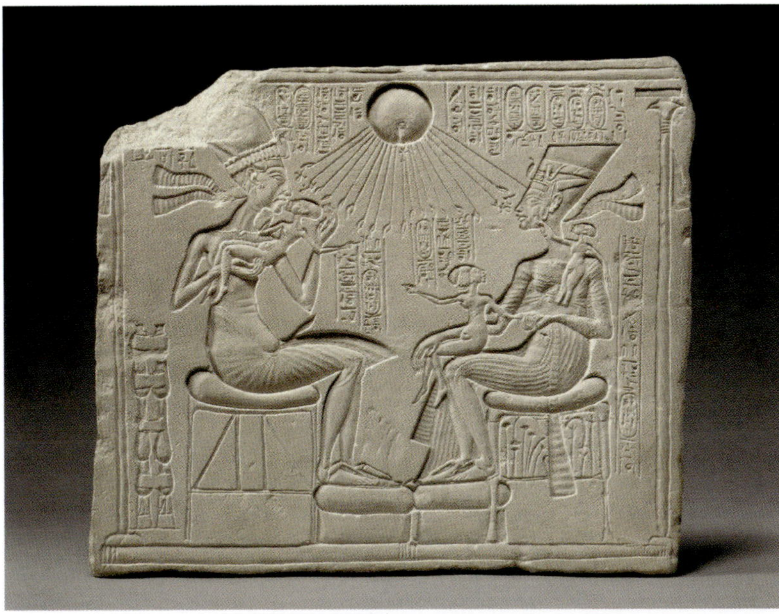

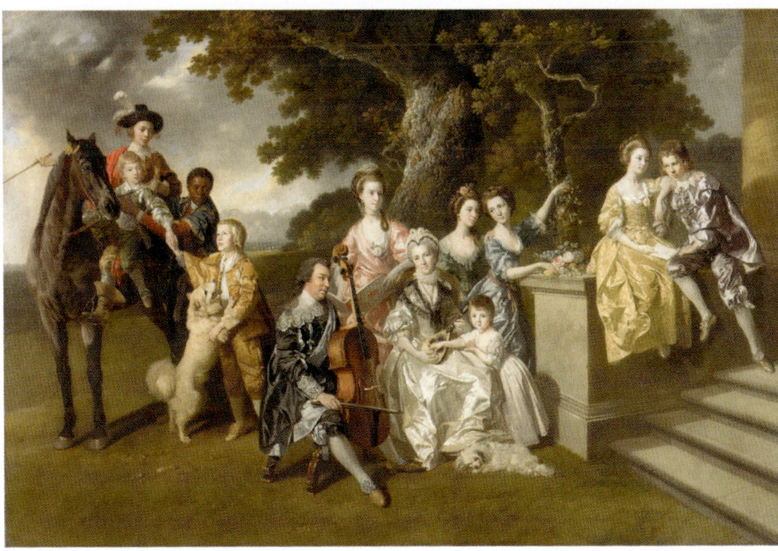

3.5 Artist unknown, A house altar showing Akhenaten, Nefertiti, and three of their daughters. New Kingdom, 18th Dynasty, Amarna Period, reign of Akhenaten, ca. 1353–1336 BCE. Limestone, 12.7 × 15.3 in. Egyptian Museum, Berlin. ÄM 14145.

3.6 Johann Zoffany, *The Family of Sir William Young*, 1767–69. Oil on canvas. Walker Art Gallery.

ter. The family's wealth and prestige transmit through the setting, their opulent Van Dyke dress, and the presence of a Black servant. It is amplified by the backdrop of a mighty oak tree, whose trunk links physically and formally to the bodies of Sir William's daughter, Sarah Elizabeth; his wife, Elizabeth; and, by extension, Sir William, the symbolic root. Their acquired gentility and culture also registers through the family's musical talents: Sir William plays the cello, and his wife holds what appears to be a Renaissance-styled lute. However, it is the presence of the unnamed Black servant boy that completes the painting's official narrative.

Both the employment of Black servants and their inclusion in official family portraiture were quite fashionable during the Georgian era. Beyond this convention, Beth Fowkes Tobin has proposed that the Black boy in *The Family of Sir William Young* also reflects the context of Young's extensive holdings in the Caribbean, specifically that the family's wealth depended on the region's plantation slave economy.[14] Yet even this linkage is coded and layered—the boy's representation adds a grotesque element to the work.[15] He is adorned in silks and taffetas, without the fashionable standard metal collar, and is actively involved with the family, all of which serve to convey and visualize the Youngs' perverse humanity. They were "good" slaveholders.

Despite different hues, environs, and historical contexts, the Duvalier family depicted in *Mardigras at Fort Dimanche* exhibits similar material aspirations and class pretensions, but with a pointed difference: the metanarratives of Duval-Carrié's painting refuse to obfuscate the violence that fuels its materialization. Indeed, *Mardigras* centers historical violence and its afterlives as subject. In a society in which language is simultaneously visual, aural, and performative, in which a gesture is equal to a paragraph, *Mardigras* indicts its representational subjects by casting them as historical objects. In the problem space it references, boundaries are provisional—fluid rather than fixed, transmogrifying rather than permanent—and simultaneously spiritual, sensate, and material. The painting conjures these possibilities through conceptual play. It materializes metamemory in an extended dialogue with the violent incoherence of Haitian history, issuing a cautionary epistle for the future. As in Sir William's family portrait, *Mardigras*'s violence is invisible on the surface plane, but Duval-Carrié's aesthetic act inverts its articulated genre to reveal what was traditionally disappeared—the brutal source of the subject's power and wealth—and etch it into indelibility.

As metapaintings, *Las Meninas* and *Mardigras* reveal a complex intra-ideological web that coheres within them and grows more visible over time. Duval-Carrié's seemingly static composition belies its multivalence, which depends on the specific and pointed ways the artist simultaneously references and distances his painting from Velázquez's famously unstable work. Whereas the discourse around *Las Meninas* has focused on its formal, spatial, and humanist aspects, *Mardigras* images a complex and continuous discourse on time, space, narrative, and history specific to Haiti and the global Caribbean. Here, the concept of history and the act of historicization are conceptually engaged and deployed, and elements of light, space, and genre assume formal and narrative importance. Duval-Carrié exploits expectations embedded in the subgenres of family and royal portraiture to craft a dissonant narrative enunciated in a space of Derridean différance. Like Latamie, Duval-Carrié evokes différance in a way that produces the painting's field of articulation: the concept of history and the power seized to shape historical narrative in the Caribbean. And like *Las Meninas*, *Mardigras at Fort Dimanche* affirms the audience's agency through a visual language central to postrevolutionary Haitian and Caribbean Modernism within a global imaginary.[16]

Duval-Carrié shifts the audience's subjective position from witness, the fundament of the history-painting genre, to self-reflexive author, so that fabulation becomes a generative process that catalyzes through encounter. *Mardigras* does not illustrate a single story or document an isolated event, as is customary in history painting; instead, it initiates a series of layered narratives. Unlike *Las Meninas*, whose size and composition allow the viewer to psychically enter the space, *Mardigras* contains its subjects and creates a purposeful illusion of space between the representational subjects and audience. In this reliquary of state violence, the family poses for us, but at a safe distance.

The gray handmade surface of *Mardigras*'s literal frame is covered with iconography: skulls and crossbones, a crescent moon, snakes, primordial lizards, crosses, and sunbursts enfold time. In Kongo cosmology, many of these symbols refer to Eshu, the god of the crossroads. As a marker of transition or catalysis, this is not a traditional history painting or a simple family portrait. To do its work, *Mardigras* serves as an activator of memory and rememory. Both history painting and portrait, this family and funerary image bears the trace and legacy of unspeakable violence.

Mardigras at Fort Dimanche was once owned by renowned civil rights attorney Sanford A. Rubenstein. It is now part of the collection of the Bass Museum in Miami Beach. Although not on permanent display, it is one of the works most frequently taken out of storage for private viewing.

Generally, the art historical literature praises the painting as a distinctive work in the artist's oeuvre. The two or three lines it merits in exhibition catalogue essays and reviews typically focus on Duval-Carrié's decision to represent Jean-Claude Duvalier in a christening or wedding dress, gesturing to the artist's playful engagement with drag and rumors about the younger Duvalier's bisexuality.[17] Most critics acknowledge the painting's connections with Vodoun and Papa Doc's figuration as Bawon Samedi, a Vodoun god who possesses some of the same qualities as Eshu. But, as with so much of the art historical writing and criticism on 1990s Caribbean art, even from well-intentioned curators and scholars, the discussion ends there.

So let us begin again. Let us consider *Mardigras at Fort Dimanche* as fabulated family portrait and object, history painting, reliquary, bat teneb, and *nkisi*, as a work that decries and contains a virulent and violent history and its echoes in the continuing present.

IMMATERIAL BEINGS

> Our Doc, who art in the National Palace for Life, hallowed be Thy name in the present and future generations. Thy will be done at Port-au-Prince and in the provinces. Give us this day our new Haiti and never forgive the trespasses of the enemies of the Fatherland who spit every day on our Country. Let them succumb to temptation and under the weight of their venom. Deliver them not from any evil. Amen.
>
> JEAN M. FOURCAND, *CATECHISME DE LA REVOLUTION* (1964)

Two men occupy *Mardigras at Fort Dimanche*'s midline.[18] While the spotlight rests on the transgressively dressed Jean-Claude, the narrative pivot is the relationship between him and his father. Everything in the painting frames this central bond, a lineage scripted through co-optation of popular cultural beliefs to consolidate the regime's social and psychic power. As an element of the Haitian political playbook, the lineage narrative often integrates a nonlinear African-derived temporality and spatiality with Vodoun to affirm leadership as divinely ordained and timeless. As Sidney Mintz and Michel-Rolph Trouillot observed, "Vodou was created by individuals drawn from many different cultures. . . . It has never been codified in writing, never possessed a national institutional structure—a priesthood, a national church, an orthodoxy, a seminary, a hymnal, a hierarchy, or a charter."[19] Nevertheless François Duvalier exploited its transcendent belief system to secure and marshal power, even after his death, through his son.

Scholars have cited Vodoun's major role in the oral history of Haiti's revolutionary moments, following its threads through the narratives of François Makandal, Dutty Boukman, Jean-Jacques Dessalines, François Duvalier, and later, Jean-Bertrand Aristide. Each of these men—in Haiti, oral history is primarily the domain of men—openly engaged Vodoun's mythical potentialities. But only one leveraged this constellation to build, consolidate, and assert power: François Duvalier. The historical centrality of Vodoun *and* Papa Doc's violent disfigurement of Vodoun is critical to *Mardigras*'s comprehension as metapicture.

Haiti's revolutionary narratives commence with two triumphant stories. The first articulates a spiritual victory but political failure: Makandal's command of an abortive slave rebellion against the French in 1757.[20] The second registers a triumph in body, mind, and spirit when Boukman, aided by Cécile Fatima, performed a Vodoun ceremony to initiate a rallying cry for revolution at Bois Caïman in 1791. David Geggus, Claude Dayan, Laurent Dubois, and others have indexed these foundational myths as key moments of Vodoun's entry and reentry into Haiti's historical imagination.[21]

The events of Bois Caïman first appear in recorded literature in Antoine Dalmas's *Histoire de la révolution de Saint-Domingue* (1814). Dalmas lived in Haiti at the revolution's onset but conceived the work from memory while in exile in the United States between 1793 and 1794. Although Dalmas did not name Vodoun in the text, his history ties revolution, and its attendant achievement of freedom, to the practice. Vodoun may have been disdained by many, but Haitians recognized it as their own.[22]

Michel S. Laguerre also forges a strong connection between Vodoun beliefs and revolutionary agency. In *Voodoo and Politics in Haiti*, Laguerre declares that Vodoun practitioners and leaders like Fatima and Boukman were central to the movement toward independence through revolution.[23] He contends that Boukman's invocation of the spirits singlehandedly united the people to liberate themselves from the French and, by extension, from slavery. These foundational myths do not emerge out of the type of oral history practiced by the Saramaka Maroons of Suriname, for example, or traditional Western archives.[24] Instead, as Patrick Bellegarde-Smith posits, the story of Bois Caïman is a "*lieu de mémoire*," an unsubstantiated event, possibly drawn from accounts of Frenchmen, perhaps passed down by the enslaved, now agreed upon as truth and history by all.[25] In other words, the events said to have ignited the Haitian Revolution are likely fabulated—composed and agreed upon as historical memory and cited as evidence of the centrality of the creolized practice of Vodoun in accounts of Black liberation.

In these narratives, Boukman and Makandal are described as medicine men, Vodoun priests, or *houngans*. Over the years, the frame of Boukman's story at Bois Caïman has been populated with visual signifiers, including images of a storm, lightning, a forest, and the ritual sacrifice of a black pig. In various retellings, the events assume greater theatricality, and the descriptions accrete increasing specificity. Through these discursive iterations, history is made, fabulously.

Although it is highly unlikely that the Vodoun we understand today could have been named in 1791,[26] as the narrative tightened locally, the ceremony at Bois Caïman assumed aspects that were distinctly Pétro, a branch of Vodoun in which ritual sacrifice centers on pigs and conjures Ogun's adversarial or warlike spirit. Rémy Bastien has argued for this reading most insistently, saying that Boukman performed a Pétro ceremony during a lightning storm that cracked several large trees, thus aligning spiritual strength with nature's might.[27] Just as church architecture in medieval Europe assumed an ecclesiastical role, for Haiti, unifying Boukman's story with Vodoun during a transcendent moment in the nation's history transformed it into an affective ideological cathedral, elevating the Haitian Revolution to divine ordinance.[28]

The conversion of *lieu en mémoire* into narrative, then into a secular ecclesiastical model, was perfected by François Duvalier. His rise mimicked and galvanized the cult of personality first deployed by Jean-Jacques Dessalines, itself modeled on a symbolic narrative and historical extension of the events of Bois Caïman. In his memoir, the naturalist Michel Étienne Descourtilz, whose life was saved by Dessalines's wife, Claire Heureuse, communicates fear, awe, and utter disbelief at Dessalines's masterful defiance of colonial assumptions and capacity to marshal his men to action, even in the face of almost certain defeat. He describes how, in one instance, the soldiers whom Dessalines commanded were deeply moved by his characterization of their foretold deaths as fulfillment of a promised return to Guinen and a reunion with the revolutionary hero Toussaint Louverture. The men responded to his call by attacking their enemy with such vigor—while singing African songs—that the only word Descourtilz could think of to render the scene was "supernatural." Despite witnessing these events, Descourtilz believed that Dessalines's success was possible only because "the Congo Negroes and Guineans were . . . superstitiously affected" by their commander's words.[29] That is, to make his account legible to himself, Descourtilz must simultaneously deny what he in fact witnessed—the agency of Dessalines and his soldiers and their bravery, skill, and sheer determination, even in the face of his countrymen's thorough defeat by those very same men.[30] It was impossible for Descourtilz to register or concede that a former slave could be both respected and authoritative. Duvalier understood the intersections and blind spots facilitated by colonialism and racism that fostered Europeans' misreading and underestimation of Dessalines. Indeed, he would later leverage them to instill fear among the Haitian people and consolidate his power.

Following Descourtilz, French historical accounts dismiss Dessalines as an illiterate, brutal, racist butcher. The truth is far more complicated. Dessalines engaged in a slave war framed as a matter of life and death. Drawing symbolic color lines distilled this imperative. Straightforward in his deliberations and unflinching in his focus, Dessalines rendered a universe where to be considered white meant that you were the adversary. He decimated his enemies with scant consideration of age or gender, committing extraordinary acts grounded in an extraordinarily brutal time and place.[31]

In his seminal text *The Black Jacobins*, C. L. R. James restored Dessalines's humanity in the archive by adopting the recuperative mantle that Baron de Vastey, in *The Colonial System Unveiled*, assumed for Henri Christophe. James asserts that former slaves such as Dessalines sought "their salvation in the most obvious way, the destruction of what they knew was the cause of their sufferings; and if they destroyed much, it was because they had suffered much."[32] Dessalines remains one of the most compelling figures in Haitian history. Though illiterate and a slave until the age of forty, he was a brilliant general who won the hearts of Haitians through his singular vision, countless victories, and conscious cultivation of mythos. His impact and effectiveness are visible not only in the revolution's outcome but in the day-to-day battles he waged and survived. He spoke both French and Kreyòl and strategically deployed them to great effect. For example, he usually referred to past atrocities inflicted on enslaved Africans in Kreyòl, hoping the stories would shore up his men's will to fight. Unlike Louverture and Christophe, he had personally experienced the unmitigated violence of chattel slavery.[33] It is said that his body bore actual scars of that enslavement and that he never hid them, sharing their origin tales to rally his troops to the cause of liberty.

It was Dessalines who restored the ancient Taíno name for the island—Hayti—at the end of an unrelenting march toward liberation in 1804. It was Dessalines who drafted the first Haitian constitution and declared freedom of religion. It was also Dessalines who recognized that unless something was done, there would always be race-based division in the country. To address this portent, he declared that everyone who chose to remain in Hayti after liberation, no matter their race or shade, would be considered Black. In the process, he accomplished what Colin Dayan has described as "nothing less than an epistemological conversion."[34] In the Hayti Dessalines envisioned, Blackness was no longer perceived as a marker of caste grounded in plantation slavery but as synonymous with freedom and a more inclusive national identity.

Dessalines knew that no one had seen a Black man accomplish what he had and cultivated a mythology to explain his successes. It was widely believed that he could double himself so that he could be in two places at once, making him difficult to attack. In this context, the treachery and violence of his murder are notable. After delivering independence, he was betrayed by the monied mulatto class and ambushed. His assailants shot, bayonetted, and stabbed his body repeatedly, then stripped, mutilated, and castrated him. They also cut off his fingers. Their aim was not only to kill but to destroy his body in flesh, spirit, and myth. They made certain that there was no possibility of return and no site to mourn. Yet, unlike Louverture and Christophe (who claimed he could be killed only by a silver bullet), Dayan points out, "Dessalines, the most unregenerate of Haitian leaders, was made into a *lwa* (god, image, or spirit) by the Haitian people. The liberator, with his red silk scarf, was the only 'Black Jacobin' to become a god."[35]

Despite the brutality of his murder and the efforts to suppress his remembrance and influence, new mythologies emerged almost immediately after his death to memorialize him. These tales fabulated his ability to become invisible, his interest in Vodoun, and his use of talismans to protect his body in battle. They told of him killing Haytians who didn't speak Kreyòl and murdering a houngan who provided him with a talisman that, it turned out, could not ward off injury during battle.[36] Murdered in 1806, by 1845, Dessalines had been monumentalized as a hero in the national consciousness on the Champ-de-Mars by descendants of the same mulattos who'd rendered his death (figure 3.7). They canonized Dessalines in the public arenas where they held power, naming the national anthem, "La Dessalinienne," in his honor, while the common people elevated him to the Vodoun pantheon.

For some, Dessalines's resurrection, rehabilitation, and mythic ascendancy might be difficult to absorb, but as Bellegarde-Smith suggests, the

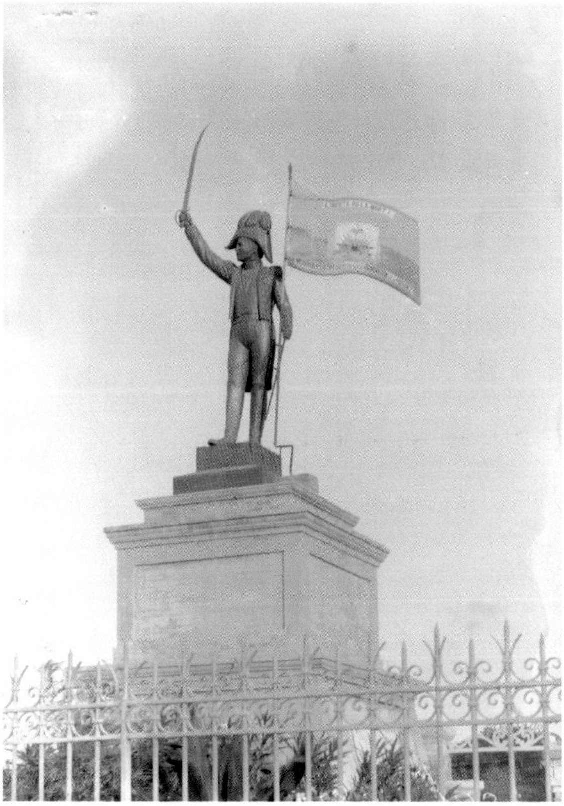

3.7 Normil Charles, sculpture of Jean-Jacques Dessalines on Champ-du-Mars, Port-au-Prince, Haiti. Photographed January 1, 1908, by H. H. Johnston. Royal Geographical Society.

tension between Western and Haitian views of Dessalines reveals a fundamental distinction between cultural frameworks and systems of belief and value. The Haitian worldview did not rely on the dichotomies that organized Western modernism. Instead, as Bellegarde-Smith observes, Haitians possessed a far "more encompassing vision" in which life decisions were made "on a sliding scale, reality and survival brooked compromises, morality was situational, and people understood themselves always as a part of a linguistic, religious, sexual and racial continuum."[37] In this context, Dessalines's societal elevation, particularly within the Vodoun pantheon, recognized simultaneously his courage, leadership, militarism, resolute hatred of the French, societal reforms, gruesome death, and bequeathing of independence to Hayti. In Haiti, interpretations that may seem incoherent when couched in Western binaries permit this incredible yet flawed man to be seen as a national hero, even a god. Like Wilson Harris's evocation of the Black body's reassemblage within the limbo gateway of the Middle

Passage, Dessalines's mutilation and dismemberment allowed for the reconstitution and transformation of his phantom limbs in Vodoun. Though dead, yet shall he live, again and again.[38]

DISFIGURING THE DESSALINES MODEL IN THE "VOODOOISATION" OF HAITI

Many Haitian leaders exploited Dessalines's recouperation and canonization, as well as his high regard in the hearts and minds of the Haitian people. Forging an association with Dessalines was believed to assist in the governance of the masses, blending mythology with brute force. As Bastien suggests, though Vodoun itself lacked a hierarchical system, "a master politician's dream would be to accumulate so much power and create so much fear about his person as to be able to impose himself upon the whole Vodoun clergy."[39] Enter François Duvalier, the critical center of Edouard Duval-Carrié's painting.

After the Catholic Church turned its back on Haiti in 1804, Vodoun helped the masses cohere the chaotic world in which they were immersed. Its belief system was resonant in the here and now and relied on a fusion between a pantheon of gods remembered from West Africa and new ones created in Haiti. Though practiced in the cities, it was in the countryside that Vodoun flourished.

In the late 1940s and '50s, following his medical training, François Duvalier traveled through rural Haiti, distributing medicine for yaws, a skin disease that was raging in the region. In the areas where Vodoun was devoutly practiced, he was thought to possess special healing powers and accorded great respect, earning him the esteemed title "Papa." His extensive interaction with everyday people revealed the depth of their reliance on Vodoun, and he began his immersion in its belief system. He gathered this knowledge in the book *Gradual Elevation of Voodoo* (1944). And he turned his accumulated learnings to brutally manipulative and destructive ends.[40] According to Michel Laguerre, while previous leaders had practiced or made overtures to Vodoun adherents, Duvalier transformed Vodoun from being a "liberating force" to an "oppressive institution."[41] To galvanize support among the middle classes, Duvalier married it with early forms of Négritude and a politicized Blackness, influenced by the Indigenist Movement led by Jean Price-Mars, which had coalesced partly in response to the American occupation of Haiti.

Aligned with the Indigenists but seeking different ends, on June 23, 1938, Duvalier helped found Les Griots, after a Guinean term meaning "the bards." The organization opposed the occupation's repression of African heritage, its imposed religious persecution, and the mulatto elite's perceptions of Black culture as primitive. Duvalier professed the belief that Haiti belonged to Black Haitians, a position that seemingly centered the lives and cultural production of the rural folk who were still the majority population. Les Griots members conducted studies of Haitian life in rural areas and believed that the creative and religious heart of the people found there—namely, Vodoun—should not be denigrated but revered.[42] Their position provided critical affirmation of Vodoun practitioners, who had grown inured to state persecution, and elevated Duvalier's regard in the minds of its adherents.

Emerging from the degradation of the American occupation and its reinstitution of the corvée,[43] many urban and middle-class Haitians grew receptive to Jean Price-Mars and Duvalier's distilled version of Afrocentrism, that is, that as a predominantly Black country, Haiti should be governed by a *visibly* Black president. The power of the visual in a primarily illiterate population cannot be underestimated. Since Christophe, Haiti had been ruled by successive mulatto-led governments that, as Duvalier and his supporters contended, neglected the Black masses, ignored the role of Africa and Africans in the country's development, and sanctioned the Catholic Church's intensive campaigns against Vodoun in the 1920s and 1940s, in contrast to relative freedom of religious expression throughout the nineteenth century. The indigenist call to recognize Africa as the source of Haitian culture aligned with the rise of Haitian modernity in the fine arts, the establishment of the Centre d'Art in the 1940s, and the growing international recognition of painters like Philomé Obin, Hector Hyppolite, and later, Wilson Bigaud. But even as these artists were being lauded abroad for the so-called aestheticization of their Vodoun beliefs, the Catholic Church was persecuting Vodoun initiates at home.[44] In fact, by the time Duvalier took power, the race-based divisions that Dessalines and Christophe had forecast had solidified into a caste system based on a political economy of color. Visibly Black Vodoun adherents occupied its lowest tier, becoming vulnerable to Duvalier's promise of their respect and elevation in society.

Few scholars believe that Duvalier was a true Vodoun adherent. Most contend that he used its symbolic potential and cultural resonance to achieve political ends. Bastien and Courlander analogize Duvalier's relationship to Vodoun to that traditionally maintained between church and state; leaders who are agnostic or atheist often participate in religious ceremonies and appropriate religious iconography for strategic political ends, not because they hold any faith in the belief system or institution. In fact, Bastien and Courlander propose that Duvalier's deployment reveals that "only if he does not believe can he expect to impose his will on his reluctant collaborators." Duvalier's public conformity to Vodoun and use of its faith language in his interaction with the masses was meant to prove "that he possessed magical powers to a superlative degree."[45] The more people believed in his powers, the more power he held.

But, in contrast to the treatment accorded Dessalines, the Haitians did not elevate Duvalier to the status of a god—it was Duvalier himself who aspired to divinity. By exploiting Vodoun's visual language, he became Bawon Samedi, the lwa who resided at the center of its belief structure and led the Gede spirits, guardians of the crossroads of life and death. In panel 1, *Le Départ* (The Departure, 1996), of Duval-Carrié's painting *Milocan, ou la migration des esprits* (Milocan, or Migration of the Spirits; figure 3.8), Samedi is pictured in a stovepipe hat, departing the African rainforest with shackled slaves bound for Haiti. Skeletal images tied to Samedi foreshadow the strange brew of violence and religion Duvalier used to dominate every aspect of Haitian society.[46] His cultivation of Samedi was not only visual but performative. As Paul Johnson argues, his "physiognomy, accoutered in black hat, glasses, and cane as a *Gede* . . . even speaking in that spirit's typical nasal tones, was a bridge that linked representations of religious power and national authoritarian power."[47] Duvalier forged this association so as to wrest ideological control from the Catholic Church; once he secured it, he used it to unite and lead the masses in unprecedented ways.

As president, Duvalier's interest in Vodoun legitimized the religion; in return, he provided key members with access to political power. Through his manipulation of and dominion over its perception and reception, Duvalier critically suppressed Vodoun's creative and catalytic potential. "The Voodooisation of Haitian politics," Laguerre suggests, "became a means to control the local institutions of the masses and to maintain that structure of inequality."[48] Johnson's nuanced study affirms Duvalier's attempts to tie his political ascendancy to Dessalines, but he notes that unlike the former revolutionary who persecuted Vodoun adherents from time to time, Duvalier took "an indigenous and secretist religious group once marginal and even persecuted within the State" and "indigenized [it] as iconic *of* the State, both constitutive of it and a cipher of it, but always without official recognition."[49] That Duvalier achieved this shows him to have been

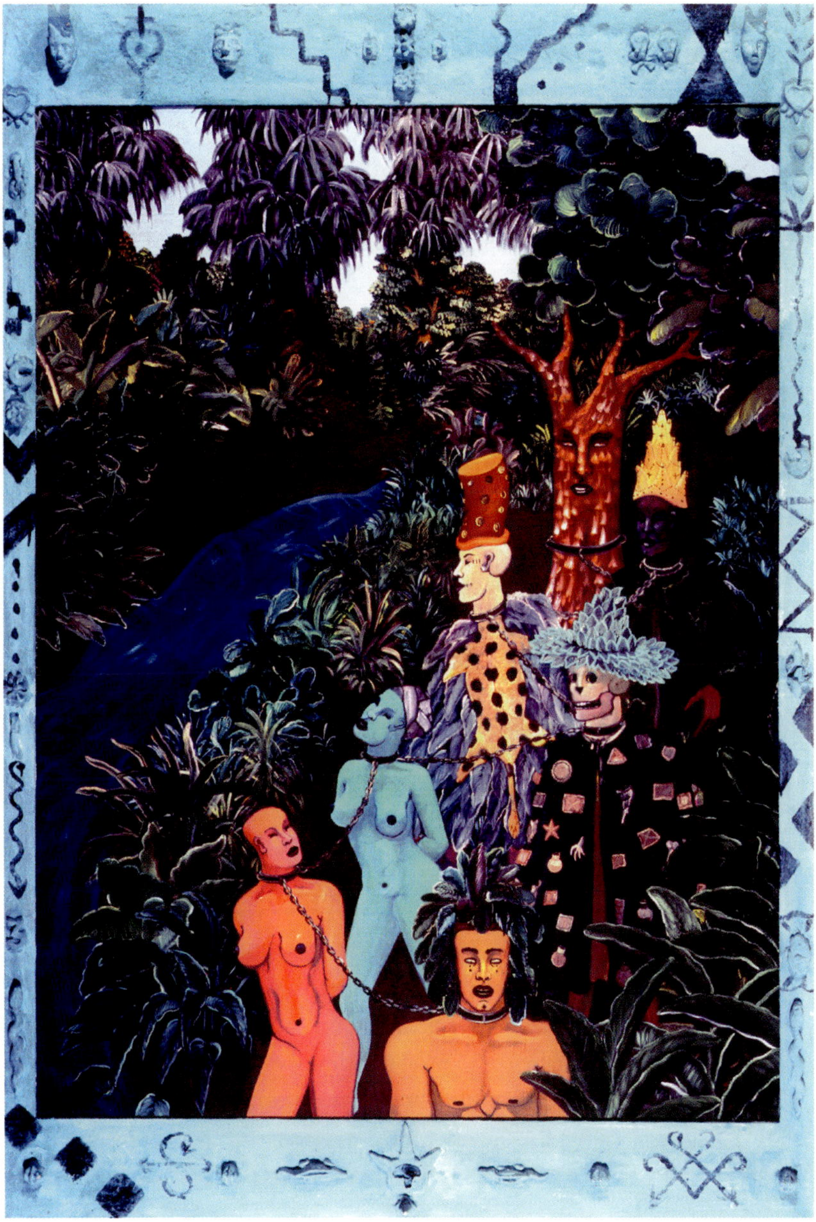

3.8 Edouard Duval-Carrié, *Le Depart* (The Departure), 1996. From *Milocan, ou La migration des esprits* (Milocan, or The Migration of the Spirits) (panel 1 of 4). Oil on canvas in artist frame, 241.5 × 165 cm. Bass Museum of Art, Gift of Dr. Jean Claude Compass.

both brilliant and sociopathic, and it ultimately devastated Haiti and the Haitian people.

Selden Rodman and Carole Cleaver observed that Duvalier's rise meant that Vodoun simultaneously came into its own and "suffered its most serious disfigurement."[50] Rodman and Cleaver recount a now well-known story from the 1960s: Duvalier had various houngans rounded up and brought before him at the palace to announce that he was now their master. The immediate effect was to instill fear, but the long-term impact combined spiritual and political power with brute physical force. This consolidation had never happened before in such a complete, open, and deliberate manner, and it was remarkably effective. Duvalier's concentration of religious power meant the oppression of Haitians would be meted out "in the people's own religious tongue."[51]

Vodoun was not the only means through which Duvalier obtained and sustained power. His rule depended equally on brute force, murder, and intimidation. Vodoun's nonhierarchical structure became a key weakness that Duvalier exploited. By incorporating its priests into the government, he gave them a taste of power. Many houngans were willing to do anything to retain it. They became members of Duvalier's feared Tonton Macoutes: informants, terrorizers, and enforcers. This is how the faith once vested in this revolutionary religion was redeployed to torment and oppress its adherents.

While Dessalines's mythos was only partially constructed during his lifetime and was shaped long after his death, Duvalier left nothing to chance or legacy. By positioning himself as the overseer of the spirits, elected and ordained by the gods, he moved swiftly to solidify political power by changing the Haitian flag, eliminating those who had opposed his election, and simultaneously building on his mythology as arbiter of life and death.[52] He also began to publicly identify himself within Vodoun's narrative and spiritual trajectories, both visually and performatively, cultivating an association with the number twenty-two.[53] Elected president on September 22, 1957, Duvalier subsequently scheduled all major political events to fall on that day. The linkage was so effective, it was believed that Papa Doc had something to do with John F. Kennedy's assassination on November 22, 1963, because the president had instituted an arms embargo against Haiti. To seal the association, when Duvalier officially joined the pantheon of Vodoun spirits, it was as lwa 22.[54]

Duvalier inflicted psychological and physical violence to disappear challengers. The extrajudicial Tonton Macoutes were key soldiers of enforcement. This fluid force and its unchecked reign of terror eventually rendered the army powerless, creating a legacy from which Haiti has yet to recover. Duvalier also expelled European leaders of the Catholic and Episcopal churches and contested the demands of the United States. In the process, he was lionized by Haitians—not out of respect but based on unbridled fear. His exploitation of religion and perpetration of sudden, often spectacular acts of violence represented an inversion that circumvented or destroyed the rules of governance and the traditional hierarchies that the Vodoun faith he had coopted relied on. In the Catholic stronghold of Gonaïves, where Bishop Jean Robert had persecuted Vodoun initiates, Duvalier sought out the houngan Zacharie Delva, a figure believed to possess exceptional "mystical powers," to depose the bishop.[55] Before Duvalier called on him, Delva had reportedly lived a humble existence; aside from his earnings as a houngan, his only form of income was derived from his roadside cart. One of Delva's first acts of service to Duvalier was the bishop's removal and deportation. To celebrate, he held a Vodoun ceremony on the cathedral steps, communicating Duvalier's ascendancy and the transfer of power it represented.

Before Delva's elevation, Clément Barbot was Duvalier's major enforcer as the first leader of the Tonton Macoutes and one of his most loyal and trusted officials. In 1960, however, in a move characteristic of the Shakespearean machinations that defined his leadership, Duvalier inexplicably turned on Barbot and had him imprisoned for eighteen months at Fort Dimanche. Upon his release, whether enraged by his change in fortune or knowing that it was better to strike first than await the inevitable, on April 26, 1963, Barbot organized an attempted kidnapping of Duvalier's children. Their chauffeur and three bodyguards were killed. Although the children were unharmed, Duvalier's wrath was triggered, with exceptional ferocity.

On April 21, less than a week before these events, a rally had heralded the beginning of a "Month of National Gratefulness for Duvalier." The opening speech, delivered by Duvalier's friend and supporter Dr. Jacques Fourcand, warned Haitian exiles and men like Barbot that any attempts to overthrow Duvalier before the May elections would be met with blood and that "the land will burn from the north to the south, from the east to the west. There will be no sunrise or sunset, just one big flame licking the sky; it will be the greatest slaughter in history . . . a Himalaya of corpses."[56] After Barbot publicly admitted to masterminding the kidnapping attempt in an interview with *Time* Magazine, Duvalier, unable to reach him directly, targeted his associates.[57]

Barbot's day of reckoning came in July 1963 when, preparing to mount an attack on Duvalier, he and his brother hid in a straw hut at the edge of a sugarcane field north of Port-au-Prince. Unbeknownst to them, they'd been betrayed. Duvalier commanded his men to set fire to the field, forcing the brothers to flee headlong into a hail of gunfire. Images of Barbot's bullet-riddled body were immediately broadcast throughout Haiti as a stark warning and reminder.

The terror was far from over. Five months after Duvalier was elected president for life in 1964, thirteen Haitian exiles based in New York landed in southwest Haiti intent on overthrowing him. The fate of the group, which called itself Jeune Haiti (Young Haiti), became part of a series of executions that many gave the macabre name the "Vespers of Jérémie." Several of its leaders hailed from the city of Jérémie, and most of their families still resided there. When it became clear that the attack would fail, portents of spectacular brutality loomed. The body of the first group member to be executed, Yvan Laracque, was propped up in a chair and placed at a major downtown intersection to visibly rot in the sun under armed guard. Ten years old at the time, Duval-Carrié recalled passing Laracque's bloated and decaying body every day on his way to school. Although his mother instructed him to cover his eyes as they approached, he couldn't help but look.[58] The image, the smell, and the scene bore extraordinary imprints on the artist's memory.

As Duvalier learned the group members' identities, he drew them out of hiding by systematically arresting and/or killing their family members—the oldest of whom was eighty-five and the youngest only two. Sometimes he publicly humiliated them by parading them naked through the streets before murdering them. After months of fighting that left many dead and saw the rebels picked off one by one, the last two members of Jeune Haiti, Louis Drouin and Marcel Numa, were captured and imprisoned at Fort Dimanche on October 19, 1964. On November 12, they were cleaned, shaved, dressed, and taken to a Port-au-Prince cemetery, the domain of Bawon Samedi, and arrayed before a firing squad. It was Haiti's first public execution in thirty years. Duvalier closed businesses and schools and had the event televised, broadcast, and rebroadcast in the days that followed. Rural folk were transported to the city to watch, and thousands of schoolchildren were forced to attend, including Duval-Carrié's brother, who would later find himself languishing in Fort Dimanche. Unlike many, he survived—barely ninety pounds on his release, but in possession of his life.

The United States government was hamstrung. Duvalier countered any semblance of formal reprimand or intimidation by reminding the United States of its fear of communism in Cuba and the extensive international press coverage that the US civil rights movement was getting. After learning of Haiti's reported human rights abuses, the Kennedy administration issued multiple warnings to the Duvalier government, all of which were ignored. Kennedy responded with threats of invasion and the deployment of warships off Haiti's coast. Capitalizing on his country's memories of the prior occupation, Duvalier asked Kennedy, "If the OAS [Organization of American States] claims the right to intervene because of repressive internal conditions, why don't they land troops in Alabama?"[59] The United States lacked the necessary moral standing to make demands and was easily chastened.

In the wake of the particularly brutal streak that followed the assassination attempt on Duvalier's children, the OAS issued more threats and sent envoys to Haiti. Duvalier threw a carnival. Before the assembled crowd, he declared: "I am here to continue the tradition of Dessalines and of Toussaint Louverture.... I am the personification of the Haitian fatherland.... No foreigner is going to tell me what to do.... Bullets and machine guns capable of daunting Duvalier do not exist. They cannot touch me.... I am already an immaterial being."[60] To the Americans, this statement meant little, but to the Haitian people, it affirmed their leader's cunning and power. Although he spoke perfect English, he addressed American diplomats only in Kreyòl.[61] Duvalier was able to curse them publicly without their immediate knowledge, further embellishing his local legend and presumed invincibility. Small in stature and slight in frame, he nonetheless appeared to possess the power to make America heel. If the great United States could not challenge Duvalier, neither could his countrymen.

Duval-Carrié's *Mardigras at Fort Dimanche* is not merely a representation of a family portrait or a reminder of its brutal legacy. In composition and form, it is a metahistory of the Haitian people that images historical renarrativization as a contemporary exercise and critical decolonial process. The painting references Western art histories, yet through its postmodern Baroque style, antipicturesque form, and evocation of the grotesque, it sets the terms of its engagement through aesthetic points of contact pregnant with historic and symbolic implications that shape the present.

> In Haiti everything is possible, even an egg going back into a chicken.
> EDOUARD DUVAL-CARRIÉ

Like Ayón, in the 1990s, Duval-Carrié increasingly drew on a post–Middle Passage cultural form as a conceptual device to unsettle history.[62] Transcending Négritude's affirmations, his work is representative of the critical, self-reflective oeuvre produced by global Caribbean artists during this period. His fabulation of history actualized contemporary desires to question purported truths embedded in colonial and postrevolutionary narratives, and unmasked how the dual forces of neocolonial economics and political leaders assumed the proverbial overseers' whip to tame and torment the people they had sworn to support, serve, and defend. In *Mardigras*, the Duvalier regime is exhibit A in this masquerade.

When François Duvalier grew increasingly ill in the late 1960s, he began a campaign to ordain his teenage son as successor and used all the tools in his psycho-visual arsenal to convince the people to accept Jean-Claude. One of the more famous visual icons he deployed after becoming president in 1957 was an image of Jesus Christ placing a right hand on his shoulder with the caption "I have chosen him."[63] He repeated this symbolic and rhetorical gesture in 1971, assuming the role of Christ, with his son as "the chosen one" (figure 3.9). The image was papered across the country and broadcast around the world. "I have chosen him" also appeared as its caption.[64] This visual and symbolic relationship is repeated in the gesture at *Mardigras*'s center, to different narrative ends.

While there is no doubt that Duvalier orchestrated a system capable of propping up his son's "presidency," Baby Doc lacked his father's sociopathic tendencies and Machiavellian leadership skills. The untold horrors and repression his enablers unleashed were not grounded in religious or cultural belief systems that might have lent coherence or gained grotesque traction in the minds of his supporters. Jean-Claude failed to understand his own history or his country's. Taking the Haitians' faith for granted, he was never able to replace his father's narrative with robust alternative frameworks, and by destroying established economies of survival, he failed to ensure faith and food for the people. In the process, he contravened agreed-on histories and relations of race, class, and leadership that were centuries in the making. He relinquished narrative control of Haiti's story to people whose interests were served by sustaining his position. Corrup-

3.9 Photograph used in the 1971 Papa and Baby Doc poster "I have chosen him," 1965. Keystone-France. Gamma Keystone Collection.

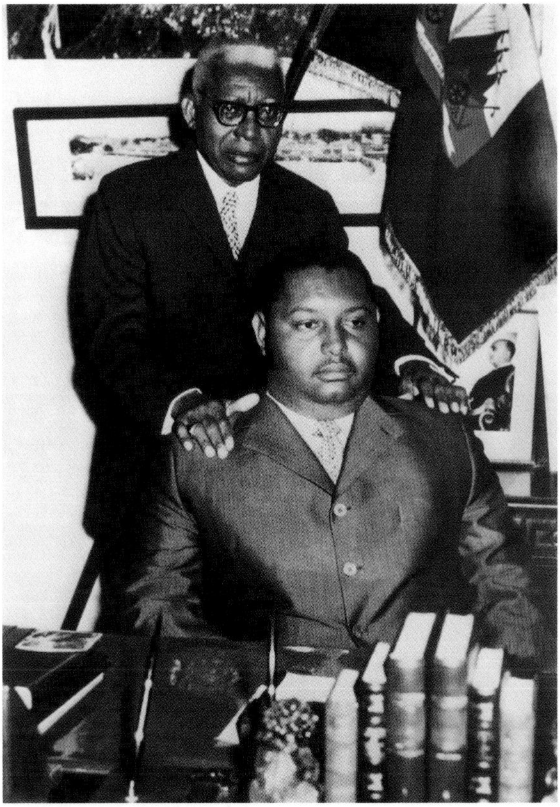

tion was de rigueur, and the opulence of the ruling class was consistently flaunted before the country's poor. In such a landscape, change can happen quickly. And it did.

Many scholars and other observers have discussed Jean-Claude Duvalier's ineffectual leadership, but few stories evidence his incapacities as completely as the real and allegorical fate under his watch of the black creole pig. The pig bears liturgical meaning in Vodoun and deep symbolic and cultural significance in Haitian history and life. Europeans first brought the mammal to Haiti, and in the centuries since, it had adapted to the vagaries of life there so that it needed very little to thrive. According to Abbott, domesticated pigs "ate anything, . . . required little water" and care, and became the "backbone" of the rural community, serving as insurance policies and savings accounts for the rural masses.[65]

In 1978 the Americans discovered African swine fever in the Dominican Republic and urged Jean-Claude to preemptively destroy the black pig, even though no evidence of infestation had yet been found in Haiti. Despite the people's protests, in 1981, Baby Doc agreed to the $16 million eradication plan proposed by the United States, and within eighteen months, the country's black pigs were completely gone.[66] In their place, America introduced, or more specifically sold, a North American pig that required cement piggeries and a special diet—in short, a level of care that the majority of Haitians could not even provide for themselves. The black pig's eradication resulted in the annihilation of an already fragile rural economy. The Haitians who made their living in this economy had always been strong supporters of Baby Doc's father and regarded his son's concession to the US government as a betrayal.

Moreover, in Haitian history, the ceremony at Bois Caïman that symbolically inaugurated the Haitian Revolution centered on the sacrifice of a black pig and the ingestion of its blood. The black pig's destruction now meant that a sacred symbol of Haiti and a fundamental element of its liberation story had been eradicated. The affair also revealed that Baby Doc was out of step with the masses and unable to relate to them in the manner his father had engineered for his political survival.[67]

Baby Doc's marriage further severed him from his father's script and from the people. His wife, Michèle, infamously installed air conditioning in the National Palace so she could comfortably wear her fur coats, and her family was scandalized by numerous financial and criminal entanglements, from cocaine trafficking to luxury-car dealerships. Absent a visible tether to Haiti's narrative and spiritual history, and despite his ongoing exertion of violence through the Tonton Macoutes, Baby Doc's rule was severely compromised.

Prior to Pope John Paul II's visit to Haiti in 1983, images of the pontiff were plastered all over Port-au-Prince. One poster's caption, "Min Mouin! Kote nou?" (Mwen la! Ki kote w ye) (Here I am. Where are you?), was written in Kreyòl.[68] Unlike Baby Doc, who usually spoke to Haitians in French, which the majority could not understand, the pope had learned a few imperfect phrases in Kreyòl, the language of the people. When he arrived on March 9, the words he spoke in Haitian Kreyòl before masses of people made a tremendous impression. His final address, in French, rallied the more than 200,000 people in attendance, who cheered at key moments during the speech. "Something must change here," the pope declared, and he cited the "injustice, excessive inequality, the degradation of the quality of life, misery, hunger, fear of many people." Change would happen much sooner than anyone thought possible.[69]

Mardigras registers the entirety of this complicated story and holds it captive. As a totem and cipher, it quietly renders a period in Haitian history so brutal that few choose to speak of it, a period not fully registered in the visual archive.[70] It issues a call to remember what time may soften and nostalgia may blur but which can never be erased.

HAITIAN HISTORY AND THE WEIGHT OF PSYCHIC TRAUMA

In *Mardigras at Fort Dimanche*, Duval-Carrié mediates between the traumatic world of the flesh and the liberatory sphere of Vodoun. Forged in the crucible of the Middle Passage and slavery, Vodoun functions as a primary conceptual matrix in his paintings from the 1990s. Mintz and Troulliot describe the Middle Passage as "an intensely drastic resocializing process: drastic because it proceeded under the constant threat of violence and even death; resocializing because it demanded the learning of wholly different behavioral patterns by its subjects and victims."[71] What kind of art can expose, image, and heal this trauma? Paul Antze and Michael Lambek argue that societal, individual, and cultural responses to trauma range widely, from multiple-personality disorders; to divisions of mind, self, and soul; to visions and metaphysical experiences, all of which may catalyze new paradigms to cohere chaos. As internal registers and efforts to bridge unfathomable loss, these systems may push at the boundaries of rationality, and even sanity, when viewed from an outsider's perspective.

In the Caribbean, madness is not always perceived as a state of crisis or aberration. Sometimes it is understood as a necessary letting go, or a performance required for the assumption of agency or apprehension of reality. Antze posits that in non-Western cultures (such as Haiti), one does not ask about "the delusions or cognitive impairments imposed by a mental disorder, but rather about the limits of a certain discourse, a certain way of expressing and understanding oneself."[72] To grapple with the Caribbean experience and engage with its art on a historical level involves contesting the limits of a Western-centered discourse that interprets its complex hybridity as impure, its art as mimicry, and its history beyond colonial encounter as nonexistent.

Caribbean religions like Vodoun represent creative responses to prolonged trauma that navigate beyond the binaries and boundaries of Western thought. Though laden by sensationalized visualizations from Hollywood and elsewhere, Africa-descended Caribbean religions and cultural practices like Vodoun, Abakuá, and Santería are examples of coherent transatlantic indigenous philosophies partially remembered and wholly formed in the wake of the slave trade. As Antze and Lambek suggest, memory in Haiti is "more inter-subjective and dialogical than exclusively individual, more act (remembering) than object, and more ongoing engagement than passive absorption and playback." To remember is "never solely to report on the past so much as to establish one's relationship toward it" through the body.[73] In this paradigm, memory is not moored to a fixed event remembered in a fleeting present; it carries across the boundaries of body and spirit, of future and past. This transcendent quality is enacted in Vodoun ceremonies, when the body recalls its spirit and becomes its vessel during rituals. As the spirit mounts the body to possess it, male can become female, and a servant, king.

The nature of the mount is foretold through drawings called *vévé*, made from organic compounds, such as cornmeal and flour, that surround the *pòto-mitan* of Vodoun *houmforts* in a ceremony's early stages. Karen McCarthy Brown describes vévé as "doorways to Guinen."[74] Here Guinen is at once physical and geopolitical reality, site of historical rupture, and spiritual salve: a continent and numinous realm conjured by enslaved Africans where the possibility of return is sited primarily in the spiritual realm. As a repository of historical memory, a home before the severance of the Middle Passage, Guinen is a concept integral to retaining Africa as presence and felt connection. As such, it was a central undercurrent driving Vodoun's inception.

Vodoun lent shape and voice to the relational dynamic between memory (Guinen/Africa) and enactment (Haiti), between trauma and survival. Houmforts offer a doorway for the body trapped in Haiti to reconnect with its homeland, configuring a transcendent arena of physical release and spiritual redemption. The vévé demarcate and signal the threshold of unification and return. Combined with the roadway for the spirits, the pòto-mitan pole, which sits at the houmforts's or Vodoun temple's spiritual center, becomes a place where spirits descend and merge with adherents' bodies.

By drawing on key visual codes expressed in vévé and Vodoun symbolism, *Mardigras at Fort Dimanche* speaks pointedly to the literate and nonliterate. While Vodoun is neither artistic process nor art form, it exhibits the formal innovation intrinsic to avant-garde art. Duval-Carrié's appropriation allows us to "read" *Mardigras* simultaneously as vévé and pòto-mitan. Beyond its representation of severed limbs, "a certain affective dynamic internal to the work" allows one to touch—if only ephemerally—the trauma of its referents. Following Jill Bennett's work, I suggest that *Mardigras* deploys a "communicable language of sensation and affect with which to register something of the experience of traumatic memory," inviting the viewer to recognize and navigate trauma, and thus to survive it.[75]

Antze and Lambek note that adherents' submission to the perceived will of their gods through ritual signifies their trust that the spirits will provide a path forward. The spirits do not mark the past; they carry it into the present.[76] For Dayan, the lwas of Vodoun are "depositories of histories . . . remnants of feelings that cannot be put to rest."[77] Vodoun has attended to contemporary contexts and needs by expanding its pantheon of lwas. While the major gods are linked to a West African pantheon, the majority were created in Haiti after the Middle Passage; all their roles have been subsequently extended or reimagined in response to the experiences of contemporary Haitians.

Bennett's consideration of visual arts in the wake of trauma has implications for a global Caribbean art history project. Suggesting that art can be viewed as the "producer of thought . . . engaged in a synchronous development of theory," she concomitantly asks, "What might it mean to derive theory from the visual . . . affectivity in art—or what [does] art itself [do]?"[78] What does *Mardigras at Fort Dimanche* do? More specifically, what does Duval-Carrié's appropriation and intertwining of African slavery, Haitian history, iconography, and Vodoun in this metapicture enable? These questions are fundamental to the unfolding of Caribbean art in the 1990s, as artists reshaped the discourses, institutions, and markets that anchored art history and the art world.

ZOMBIFICATION, SEXUALITY, AND THE THEORETICAL WORK OF DRAG

After Jean-Claude Duvalier was deposed and exiled in 1986, Haiti underwent a period of transformation and revision. What became known as the *dechoukaj* (uprooting) sought the removal of Duvalierists from positions of power and, in some cases, their trial, imprisonment, and execution. Amid this tumult, Pablo Butcher's 1986 *Haiti libre* poster festooned the streets of Haiti (figure 3.10). Butcher's image is an adaptation of an earlier Duval-Carrié painting of Baby Doc. It shows him cross-eyed, dressed in infanta-lizing regalia, set against the Haitian landscape, with his back to four royal palms (pòto-mitans), and holding a gun to his head. The image was produced six years before *Mardigras*. The critical literature on the poster and the painting it repurposes adhere to the script issued by scholars like Donald Cosentino, who suggests that Baby Doc's costuming drew on rumors about his sexuality, his management by his dominant mother and wife, and the artist's belief that "the Duvalierist kleptocracy is sustained by exploiting the fantasies of the poor, the very source which feeds the excesses of Ezili."[79] For Cosentino, Jean-Claude's representation plays mas—portraying the lwa Ezili Freda rather than Ezili Danto. Like all lwas, Ezili Freda inhabits a multivalent identity. She is known as a fierce lwa who values loyalty and destroys those who betray her or prove themselves unworthy of the gifts life has bestowed on them.[80] She is associated with the Virgin Mary, but is at once materialistic, spoiled, and prone to envy. Baby Doc epitomized these traits. In the poster, Butcher appropriates Vodoun's significations and Duval-Carrié's aesthetic staging and redeploys them to popular, public, political use in a visual language clearly understood in Haiti.

Multiple considerations of Baby Doc's adornment in *Mardigras* present fruitful avenues for exploration, but discourses of the carnivalesque, cross-dressing, and drag are particularly generative of readings that privilege the conceptual over the personal. Randy Conner's work on sex, sexuality, and gender in African diasporic religious traditions explores how cross-dressing oscillates and unsettles identity. He argues that "practices such as cross-dressing may not always or only infer gender diversity nor, by association or extension, sexual diversity."[81] In destabilizing readings of gender, drag disassembles its conventional binary. And while drag performance does not indexically mark sexuality or sexual desire, it is well known that Vodoun as a religion has supported or, at the very least, accommodated homosexuals (*masisi*) and lesbians (*zami*), who have adopted certain lwas, such as Legba and Ezili Danto, as their own. Moreover, in Vodoun, wedding dresses signify beyond gender or sexuality. The Duvaliers arguably played a positive role in making the LGBTQI community visible in Haiti. Though officially illegal, neither regime enforced laws against homosexuality, and both employed known LGBTQI persons in their administrations. While François and Jean-Claude were certainly narcissistic and transactional, neither appeared to be homophobic.

In Haiti and elsewhere in the Caribbean, cross-dressing by cis men is associated with strategic masquerade in service to violence or escape. In addition to recounting the man chanting Ogun, Mark Danner cites a small

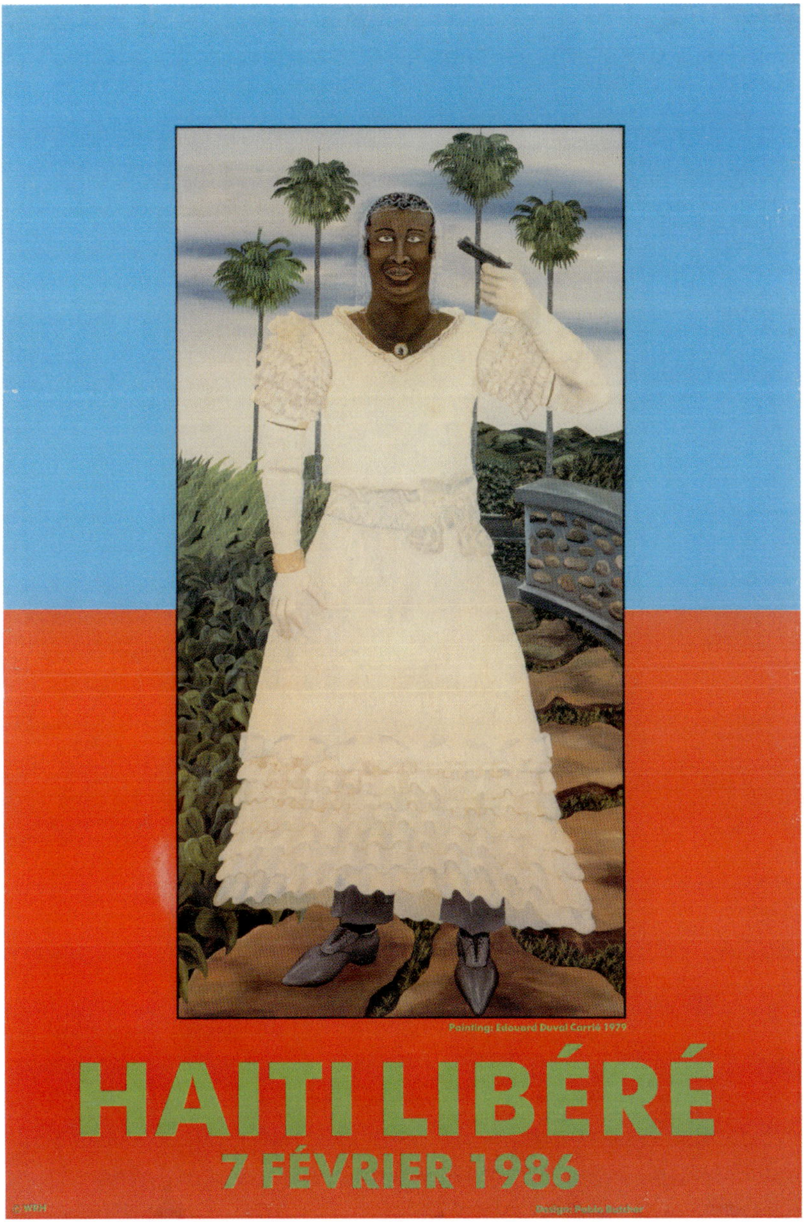

3.10 Pablo Butcher, poster using an Edouard Duval-Carrié painting, created in the months leading up to and following the expulsion of Jean-Claude Duvalier from Haiti, 1986. Collection of Adam King and Signe Prøis, Norway. Painting: Edouard Duval-Carrié, *J.-C. Duvalier en Folle de Marie* (J.-C. Duvalier as a Mad Bride). Collection of Colin McGeehan. Photographed by Evan Jenkins Photography.

group of people he observed gathered around a body on the Rue Nationale. The young man had been hung, hacked to death with a machete, and left in the street for Bawon Samedi. A partially smoked cigarette had been placed between his lips, and various offerings had been arranged near his exposed stomach and entrails. He'd been found earlier that morning in full drag with a can of gasoline in his hand, conceivably about to start a fire that would have killed many of La Saline's residents. Drag was his disguise.[82]

François Duvalier had also donned drag to save his life. Before his election in 1957, Duvalier was forced into hiding to avoid being arrested under President Paul Magloire's policy of rounding up both real and suspected opponents. To move about freely and safely, he dressed as a woman.[83] In the wake of Mikhail Bakhtin's *Rabelais and His World*, it is common to think of the carnival space as a site for inversion and to see its associative masquerades as a medium for the powerless to seize control from the powerful. Joanne Butcher notes that Bakhtin identified the separation between those who watched and those who *were* watched as a primary feature of the carnivalesque. Generated in a space where traditional class hierarchies temporarily dissolved, carnival permitted critique and parody of those normally held beyond reproach and indicated possibilities for change and renewal.[84] While Bakhtin's well-trodden discursive terrain has valence, it is materially and symbolically insufficient to describe the work of mas and the presence of drag as fundamental elements of Caribbean performance.

Like Vodoun and its associative practices, the Caribbean carnivalesque collapses binaries to reject Western modernism's organizational tenets. Following Butcher, rather than reading Jean-Claude's drag through Bakhtin's lens, I align with Efrat Tseëlon's assessment of masquerade's capacity to unsettle and disrupt "the fantasy of coherent, unitary, stable, mutually exclusive divisions. It replaces clarity with ambiguity, certainty with reflexivity, and phantasmic constructions of containment and closure with constructions that are more messy, diverse, impure and imperfect."[85] As a guiding artistic practice in the Caribbean, mas—both in form and in performance—provides clarity of vision and serves as a conduit for ecstatic release. By unmooring modernism's conceptual and perceptual binary of self and other, male and female, mas goes beyond challenging the colonial and neocolonial status quo to affirm, in plain sight, the capacity of the oppressed to recognize regimes of power in the many forms that work to suppress them.[86] Mas creates a space where the oppressed identify and critically assess the source of their degradation. The carnivalesque is thus not limited to the consolation of inversion and release; it can simultaneously embody threat—whether enacted by Haitian peasants or by an artist who plays mas in the aesthetic realm with a despotic president.

The generative quality of mas's shifting terrain is clearly seen in Haitian Rara performances.[87] Rara is a carnival historically controlled by men. It resides at a theoretical crossroads where engagement of a bloody, turbulent history and present is counterposed by lyricism, movement, and form. It is a performance art, catalyzed within and intimately tied to trauma. Linked to Vodoun, the creolized celebration spans Lent and climaxes at Easter, paralleling the Code Noir's mandated period of cessation of labor for enslaved Africans. In the festival, historical memory is expressed not through what is said so much as *how* it is said and how the bodies move fluidly in performance.

In her fieldwork, Elizabeth McAlister has noted that Rara "consists of an outer, secular layer of Carnival 'play' surrounding a protected, secret inner layer of . . . 'work.'"[88] While McAlister sees this work as religious, I believe it is deeply political. In Rara, the performing body enacts the possibility of change through dissemblance. It enables declarations without evidence, transgression without reprimand, and critique without censorship, allowing performers to code switch from political critique to farce in seconds, depending on the audience. It is definitively an evolving performance art, one that adapts to new contexts by changing songs, shifting participatory roles, and composing in real space and time. Rara actively produces a language, or as Bennett puts it, "comes into a language" of address and redress, through a process architected to accommodate and flexible enough to negotiate the challenges posed by the problem space of Haiti.[89]

With these possibilities in play, Duval-Carrié does not present transidentification as intrinsic to the participant's life. Instead, he renders it strategically, as temporary masquerade, deployed to serve a specific purpose. The ritual enactment of the carnivalesque has always allowed for public expression of diverse gender identities and desires, and cis-gendered bodies often perform as their polar opposite in the carnival space. In Haiti and Vodoun, the body as stage for the spirit destabilizes gender identities and lends porousness to the boundaries between man and woman, waking and sleeping, spirit and flesh. Within this semiotic spectrum, Duval-Carrié seized on the wedding dress's connection to the phenomena of zombification in his representation of a cross-eyed Duvalier in drag.

As Colin Dayan suggests, Jean Zonbi, aka Zombie, was a mulatto Creole who fought alongside Dessalines and Christophe during the revolutionary war and was noted for his kill rate of the French. But as a Creole mulatto born into slavery, his story encompasses narratives of slavery that extend beyond the rape, colonialism, and revolution continuously cited as key components of zombification. It is unclear how the term became associated with Jean Zonbi, but a zombie has become the ultimate symbol of "loss and dispossession."[90] Many scholars of Haiti view the zombie as an allegory of slavery and servitude, markers of historical memory interwoven with the Haitian imagination.[91] In this paradigm, the zombie carries the soul of a recently deceased person whose spirit is captured to serve the needs and desires of another. If the possessed soul is akin to the enslaved, the zombie's casket mimics the hold of a slave ship or the perimeter of a plantation. The resurrected zombie re-presents the enslaved in Haiti prior to the revolution. It is a figure that embodies violence, trauma, and the total evisceration of the subjective self: the transformation of the African body from human to dray animal. Today, it also symbolizes asymmetries of power that persisted after slavery.

By representing François Duvalier as Bawon Samedi, Duval-Carrié places him at the center of the zombification process, one that straddles the spirit and material worlds. This crossroads and its ultimate symbol, the graveyard, are Samedi's domain. In *Mardigras*, Jean-Claude is not Ezili but the zombie of his father. Not a leader but a slave. His blank, crossed eyes reveal that his vision has been wholly (dis)possessed.

The wedding dress-cum–christening gown plays a significant role in historical accounts of zombification and its adornment. Lizabeth Paravisini-Gebert has carefully examined the literary and cinematic trove that developed around zombification. Like McAlister, Dayan, Dubois, Depestre, and other Haiti scholars, she links its incarnation to African slavery, the Middle Passage, and the plantation economy, all of which sought to transform human beings into chattel, signifying the loss of individual will.[92] In tracing the development of major aspects of zombification in Haitian culture both inside and outside Haiti, Paravisini-Gebert posits that almost every story can be traced to Zora Neale Hurston's account of the October 1909 case of Marie M. in *Tell My Horse*. Marie M.'s zombification reportedly occurred shortly after her wedding, and she is pictured as a zombie in her wedding dress. The story adds layers of race, class, and sexuality: Marie's zombification is couched not only in terms of mind control but through the appropriation of her white body by a Black male houngan. The spell is eventually broken, but she never returns to her former self or state and descends into complete madness.[93]

Wedding dress zombies are believed condemned until the person who facilitated their zombification has died. But in Duval-Carrié's painting, Baby Doc's *bokor*, or facilitator, is his lwa father, who is perceived as an immaterial and immortal being. There is no death and therefore no possibility of release; Baby Doc is forever bound, a perennial zombie.

The gun in Jean-Claude's hands in Butcher's poster and *Mardigras* echoes a photo taken in 1978, during a period of severe political instability. Jean-Claude is pictured at a public event casually holding a handgun (figures 3.11 and 3.12), recalling his father's tactics: Despite the psychological power he had amassed and the fear he imposed, François Duvalier always traveled with a gun.

As metapicture, *Mardigras at Fort Dimanche* is a "transactive" work: in our act of viewing it, the painting becomes a "catalyst for critical inquiry."[94] Like Rara performances, it is a site of "public ritual through which . . . Haitians in a range of locations remember history. . . . and negotiate power under conditions of insecurity."[95] *Mardigras* affectively externalizes and objectifies the threat of Duvalierism, providing critical distance from the site of trauma so that viewers may reflect and process its implications.

Rara carnivals draw heavily on the performance of Vodoun and songs. Like much of Caribbean music, the songs expertly exploit double and triple entendres as a witty form of wordplay and, at times, literary disguise. *Mardigras* similarly partakes of layered discourses and significations. On one level, by mimicking the "I have chosen him" iconography within the genre of family portraiture and history painting, the work traces and interrogates the narrative of Haitian leadership and the manipulation of deep-rooted belief systems for personal gain. It also illumes the country's historic and ongoing divisions across lines of color, class, and caste. *Mardigras* reminds the viewer that the regime's brutality did not honor "established" boundaries or hierarchies and that recognition of their distinctions rarely intervened in an individual's fate. The arbiter of life and death in Haiti from 1957 to 1986 was a Duvalier.

In *Mardigras*, Duval-Carrié is the Duvalierian court painter in absentia. Here, carnivalesque inversion maps onto the work itself, objectifying the painting as a double nkisi, bearing malevolent forces within the frame and transforming the audience's gaze into the charged Ogun's metal spikes. Robert Farris Thompson's documentation of the Mu Kongo Nsemi Isaki's description, purpose, and use of nkisi is instructive here. Thompson's informant notes:

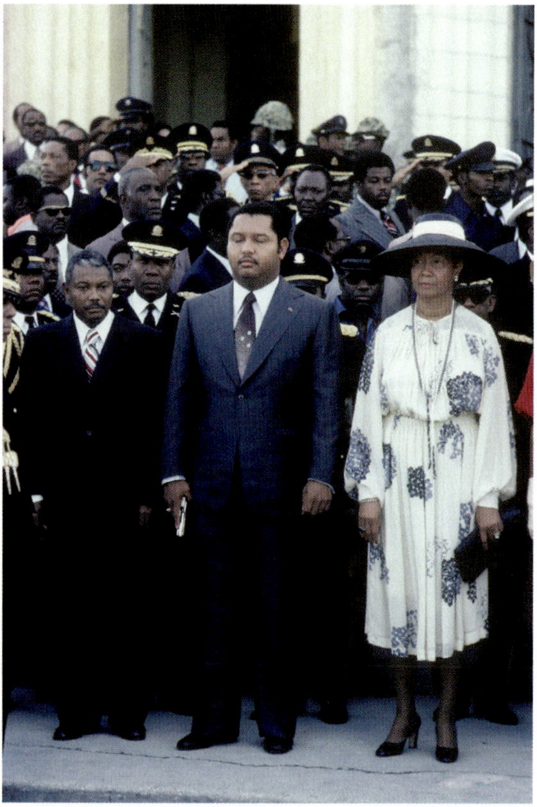

3.11 Jean-Claude Duvalier, President of Haiti, at official function with a gun in his hand, April 1978. Photographed by Gilbert Uzan. Gamma-Rapho Collection.

3.12 François Duvalier, Port-au-Prince, Haiti, May 1963. Photographed by Michael Rougier for Time/Life. ID: TimeLife_image_840549.

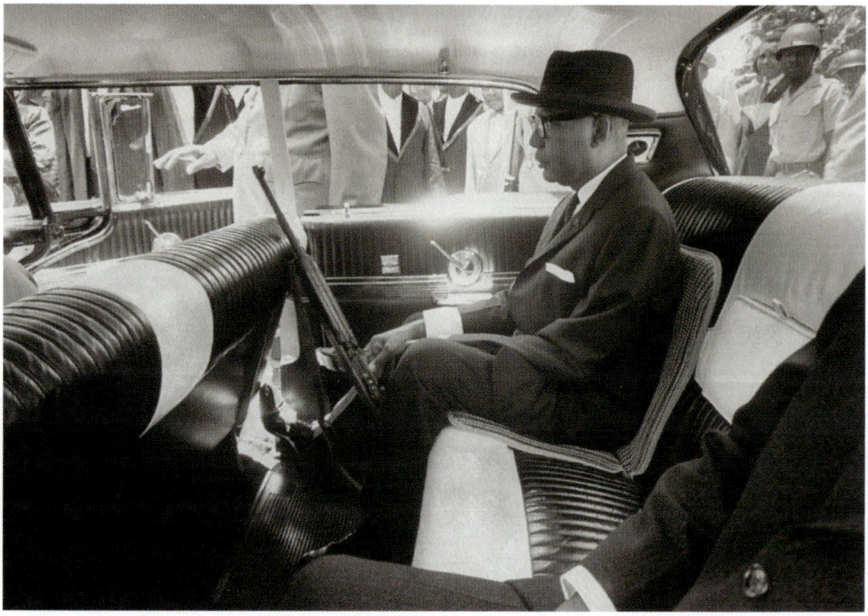

> The name of the thing we use to help a person when that person is sick and from which we obtain health; the name refers to leaves and medicines combined together. . . . It is also called *nkisi* because there is one to protect the human soul and guard it against illness for whoever is sick and wishes to be healed. Thus an *nkisi* is something which hunts down illness and chases it away from the body. An *nkisi* is also a chosen companion, in whom all people find confidence. It is a hiding place for people's souls, to keep and compose in order to preserve life.[96]

Haitians' frequent requests to pull *Mardigras at Fort Dimanche* from storage at the Bass Museum are driven not by nostalgia or consideration of formal or genre innovation but by a *need* to see it: to bear witness to the history it contains. As Martha Minow proposes, drawing from the work of Toni Morrison, "the obligations of witnessing include enabling the practice of re-memory." Morrison deploys the term to describe, in Minow's words, "practices that concretely encourage people to affirm life in the face of death, to hold onto feelings of both connection and disconnection, and to stay wide enough awake to attend to the requirements of just recollection and affirmation and the path of facing who we are, and what we become."[97] Duval-Carrié's achievement is to expand the personal imperative by drawing the history and contemporary reality of all Haitians into the painting's composition. Its content moves beyond the direct experience of violence, imprisonment, and exile to materialize a cathartic space. Using Thompson's phrasing, the painting acts as a "point, a mediating protective grace between the living and the dead."[98]

As a bat teneb, nkisi, family portrait, and contemporary history painting, *Mardigras at Fort Dimanche* fully embodies and expresses the generative capacity of Caribbean modernism after Césaire's Caliban. As seen in the work of Marc Latamie, it fabulates through genre to supplement *and* call into question the veracity of the historical record. It works to reorient our limited perspective on the past, re-presenting it for reflection and regard in the Hall of Mirrors at Versailles and Haiti's National Palace, but also in critical approaches to art history itself.

Duval-Carrié engages a different problem space than Latamie, Antoni, or Ayón do, but the work of the work resonates across these practices. Here, too, art is Césairean in its ability to draw in history, give voice, and decolonize. But as Ayón's oeuvre also makes clear, the critical space that centers Duval-Carrié's practice is not always oppositional or external to the Caribbean but can point within, here to a society illuminated by and at times cornered by the romance of revolution.

Mapping the contours of these artistic practices and attending to the critical heft of this work prepares the textual landscape for a look at Maurizio Cattelan's 6th Caribbean Biennial. Like a modern-day Prospero, Cattelan arrived on the island of St. Kitts in 1999, totally ignorant of the work of Latamie, Antoni, Ayón, Duval-Carrié, and countless others, and declared that in terms of the art world, the Caribbean had no place; it did not exist. However, by the time he arrived, the work of the work of global Caribbean artists was having an impact. Rather than a declaration of fact, the 6th Caribbean Biennial affirmed that the old way of unseeing Cattelan exhibited with this enterprise, and the world to which it belonged, was, as Cesaire's Caliban declared, "crumbling down."

CHAPTER FOUR

The Caribbean Does Not Exist

Maurizio Cattelan's 6th Caribbean Biennial, 1999

Thus far, I have explored three examples of decolonizing art practices within their respective particular problem spaces. Janine Antoni, Belkis Ayón, and Edouard Duval-Carrié shaped their distinct approaches while pushing back against efforts to disappear the complexities of their work or deny them opportunities for its public viewing and engagement. All of them inflected or drew on the Caribbean as a conceptual fulcrum, exhibited work internationally, and circulated globally. All were answering Césaire's call to forge a post-Caliban narrative and creative landscape.

Yet, by the close of the 1990s, emergent Prosperos arose to reinscribe the boundaries these artists had fought so hard to cross. While global Caribbean art and art history are postnational terrains that took shape through decolonizing art practices, the Caribbean is a unique and autonomous problem space, historically shaped and critically grounded. As such, the deeply troubled and troubling performance of the 6th Caribbean Biennial, conceived by Italian artist Maurizio Cattelan and curator Jens Hoffmann, must also be configured as subject in global Caribbean art history and criticism.

This chapter situates the 6th Caribbean Biennial as a Shakespearean *Tempest* redux. The updated yet static paradigm appears as a wolf in sheep's clothing, at direct odds with the energies and synergies manifested by the global Caribbean artists discussed in this book. My analysis of Cattelan's biennial is framed by the personality his project occludes: a Caribbean that is intimately familiar with colonialism and recognizes its afterlives in neocolonial enterprises like commercial tourism; a Caribbean deft in deploying metaphor and reimagining allegory for critical and political ends; a discerning Caribbean that may appear passive in response to global economic forces while enacting decolonization as ongoing process. In form, this chapter follows Marc Latamie, Suzanne Césaire, and Aimé Césaire, miming their decolonizing processes to unmask Cattelan's colonial face, and farce.

Cattelan and Hoffmann's aspirations emanated from a strange brew of revisionist, oppositional, and colonial impulses. Viewing the biennial as an example of the situational or relational aesthetic approach to art-making reveals that many of its participants had become known for work that emphasized "experiences" over "finished products." This position superficially presumed that the work might elude the commercialization of the art market, but it was quickly outed as a "common misperception of Conceptualism's supposed promise."[1] At its core, the 6th Caribbean Biennial was propelled by, and was an exhibition of, navel-gazing narcissism trapped in time and out of place.

From the outset, the biennial's artists and curators appeared either oblivious or indifferent to the fact that the Caribbean, like Africa, was (and continues to be) a diverse space, composed of many nations, peoples, languages, and traditions. They also overlooked that there were *already* several Caribbean biennials in Cuba, Puerto Rico, and the Dominican Republic.[2] Along similar lines, the pre-event coverage did not question why or how an Italian artist based in New Jersey and an American curator were positioned to relaunch a Caribbean biennial, especially at a time when the Havana Biennial was already fifteen years old and a well-known destination on the global art circuit. No one asked about the event's previous iterations—the 1st, 2nd, 3rd, 4th, or 5th Caribbean Biennial. No one. This willful ignorance and myopic vision, on all sides, yielded a vacated signifier—a "Caribbean" that could be encoded with projections, presumptions, and blurred visions.

Using the Caribbean as backdrop, Cattelan and Hoffman drew a line in the sand around the "unchecked" global proliferation of biennials and triennials. They argued that these newer events had been "designed to plug into the international art systems, certain groups of artists, curators, dealers and critics" producing work that was "hot" or "bad" but rarely "good." And why? "Because they fit neatly into an art system designed to control and manipulate both culturally and commercially."[3] With no capacity for self-reflection or irony, their declarations belied the fact that the very system they purported to lambaste was itself responsible for their prestige and the power of their critique. By the time of the event, Cattelan was regarded as one of the most powerful figures in contemporary art. Indeed, the biennial system had not only helped launch his career but extended his market. That he and Hoffmann adopted the biennial's form and mapped it on to the Caribbean reveals these profound tensions and paradoxes.

Like Janine Antoni, in the 6th Caribbean Biennial Cattelan sought to exert an extreme level of authorial control, and the public seemed to take him at his word. His most visible intervention in the biennial space was to disrupt its conventional content. Although, as Alison M. Gingeras notes, "all the rules of the [biennial] game were [still] dutifully followed,"[4] Cattelan did not ask the artists he solicited to exhibit work; instead, he invited them to take a vacation from Art. "It will be a show," he said, "because you will have your list of artists. It will be a show because there are invitations. It will be a show because there will be advertisements. It will be a show because we will do a press conference. It will be a show because, in the end, it will also take a strong position against the proliferation of all the biennales and the trienniales. And a vacation is a nice way to make such a comment."[5] The money flowed in and press packets were distributed. The requisite advertisements appeared in *Artforum*, *Frieze*, and *Flash Art* amid splashy spreads that echoed mass tourism posters—reflecting a genre that, as Ian Strachan, Mimi Sheller, Krista Thompson, Polly Pattullo, and others have shown, etched the Caribbean's imaging as a vacation paradise into the popular imagination (figures 4.1–4.3). None of the participating artists' works were featured in promotional materials. Instead, photographs of fish, palm trees, and former plantation houses repurposed as hotels—essential signifiers of "Caribbean-ness"—backlit the artists' names.[6]

Cattelan's performative critique of *the* art world depended on epistemic architectures of the region that were metaphorical, dehistoricized, and atemporal. Through an anachronistic colonial lens, his perceptual and conceptual vocabulary fixed the Caribbean outside space, time, and history—occluding it entirely. Drawing simultaneously on imperial bifurcations of center and margin, the photographic medium, and globally disseminated, brochure-based advertising campaigns conceived by Madison Avenue, Cattelan exploited a system of Caribbean representation organized around a binary (and static) relationship between tourist and native. Like the

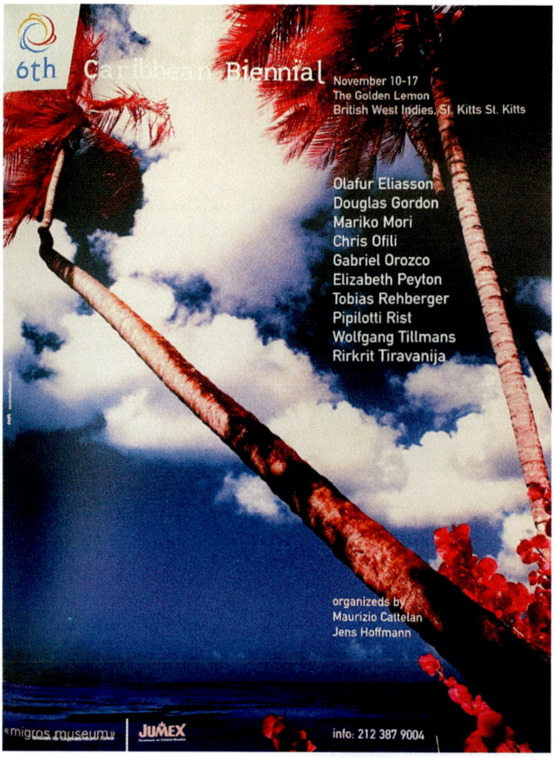

4.1 Full-page advertisement for the 6th Caribbean Biennial, published in *Frieze* 49 (1999).

4.2 Full-page advertisement for the 6th Caribbean Biennial, published in *Artforum* (1999).

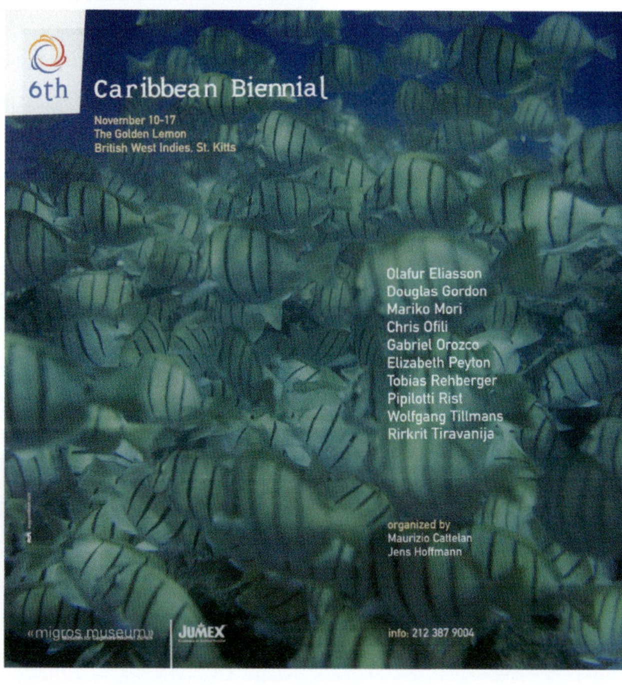

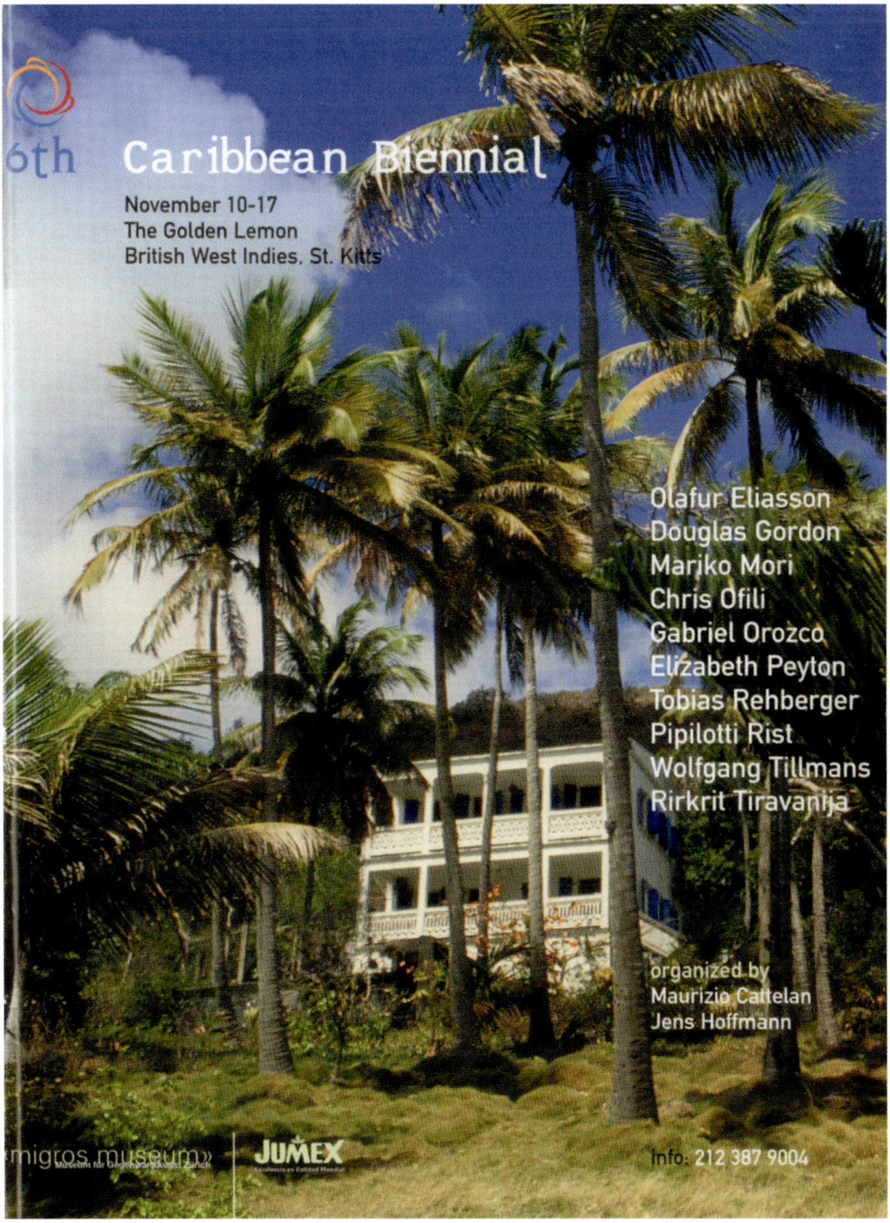

4.3 Full-page advertisement for the 6th Caribbean Biennial, published in *Flash Art* (1999).

ethnographic artifact vis-à-vis the nineteenth-century museumgoer, this social and visual economy vacated the Caribbean of depth, distinction, and complexity. Reduced to sun, sea, and palm trees, the material forces of conquest, slavery, colonialism, anticolonialism, and neocolonialism—forces that shaped and continue to shape the region—receded from view, imaging, and imagining. The Caribbean was a muted paradise beyond time and outside discursive space.[7]

Within the crosshairs of this entanglement rendered by Cattelan's "brochure Caribbean," it is theoretically impossible for natives to produce Art.[8] As I show in this chapter, the tourist paradise's affordance of the opportunity for visiting artists to "go native" on "vacation" from Art, while simultaneously *producing* art (as event), depends on the Caribbean's total effacement, alongside the Calibanization of the people who reside there and the denial of their creative capacity. Within this artist-as-tourist imaginary, the region is reconfigured as superficial backdrop and staging ground, where an Italian artist oblivious of its history and contemporary reality can arrive without any compulsion to excavate origins or account for the present. A modern-day Prospero, Cattelan aggressively marketed and enacted his discovery narrative in the service of postmodern, protoglobal critique or enlightenment—for the good of the colonized. In this vein, he reasoned, "attention can be moved and reorganized for good purposes; like a spotlight that can be pointed in a new direction, illuminating a problem that needs to be solved. That's why this *Caribbean Biennial* is about generosity, too. . . . In any event, the borders between art and the Caribbean have blurred and that's good."[9] By erasing the literal site of his performance, he illuminates his imperialist intent to address and affirm an art world that mirrors his perceptions, despite his feigned intent to challenge them.

Curated by Jens Hoffmann, Cattelan's 6th Caribbean Biennial came to fruition November 10–17, 1999 (figure 4.4). The event was held on St. Kitts, a locale "outside the trade routes of the contemporary art world." In the catalogue, Cattelan characteristically called attention to the scope of his ambition and largesse. Since the "Caribbean does not exist" in the art world, the catalogue explained, the event "sheds new light on the island of St. Kitts and imposes it on the maps of contemporary art. . . . For just one week it felt that all roads led to St. Kitts." And, by and large, initially things seemed to go according to plan.

Cattelan, Hoffmann, and artistic luminaries Vanessa Beecroft, Olafur Eliasson, Douglas Gordon, Armin Linke, Mariko Mori, Gabriel Orozco,

Elizabeth Peyton, Tobias Rehberger, Pipilotti Rist, and Rirkrit Tiravanija arrived on St. Kitts in November 1999.[10] Critics from *Artforum* and *Frieze*, including Jenny Liu, also dutifully voyaged to cover the event.[11] Jenny Liu took some of the press packet's copy at face value, cribbing statements that, for example, declared: "Sixth in a series of rather unsuccessful and under-attended Caribbean Biennials, this one, like the others, was officially intended to raise the Caribbean's barely discernable profile on the global art circuit." But she also sensed that something was amiss. To her credit, Liu nimbly offered a cogent critique and insightful observations. She linked the event to Cattelan's 1995 work *Choose Your Destination: How to Get a Museum-Paid Vacation*, noting that, while the press release promised "that the biennial would engage with its Caribbean location, offering a space for dialogue and building relationships between the international art world and local communities," the participating luminaries made no attempt to interact with the local community.[12] There was also a complete absence of Kittian artists among attendees. All these factors underscore what Cattelan later confessed: the project was propelled by narcissistic impulses, and it was never about St. Kitts or the Caribbean per se. "This biennial is *our* arena," he remarked, "the place where *we* throw our frustrations and tensions and happiness. It is not an opportunistic move; it is an act of generosity [toward the Caribbean]."[13]

Liu aptly labeled the biennial "institutional critique in biennial drag," arguing that "mere replication of one's object, even with a twist," has not been "adequate as critique for a while."[14] Despite its trenchant position, Liu's review is nonetheless enfolded as artifact in the catalogue archive of the biennial to frame the basis of their intervention: Biennials are performances legitimated by their representation in art publications. In this universe, the artist selection and solicitation and the event's ideation, promotion, and documentation—the catalogue, duly edited—are all elements of artwork as spectacle (figures 4.5 and 4.6). While critique of the art world is necessary, Cattelan's biennial exposes the threadbare and disingenuous foundations of its author's provocations.

Cattelan's performance rehearsed the same anxieties and narratives as those that animated colonial encounters and hierarchies. His intervention was a symptom of a bounded art world increasingly discomfited by the participation and influence of non-Western artists and collectors and the consequent decentering this trend augured. It is no accident that the proliferation Cattelan laments occurs outside Europe and the United States—in Havana and Bamako, Cairo, Istanbul, and Gwangju. The 6th Caribbean

4.4 Maurizio Cattelan, 6th Caribbean Biennial, St. Kitts, 1999. Collage of images documenting the event in the catalogue.

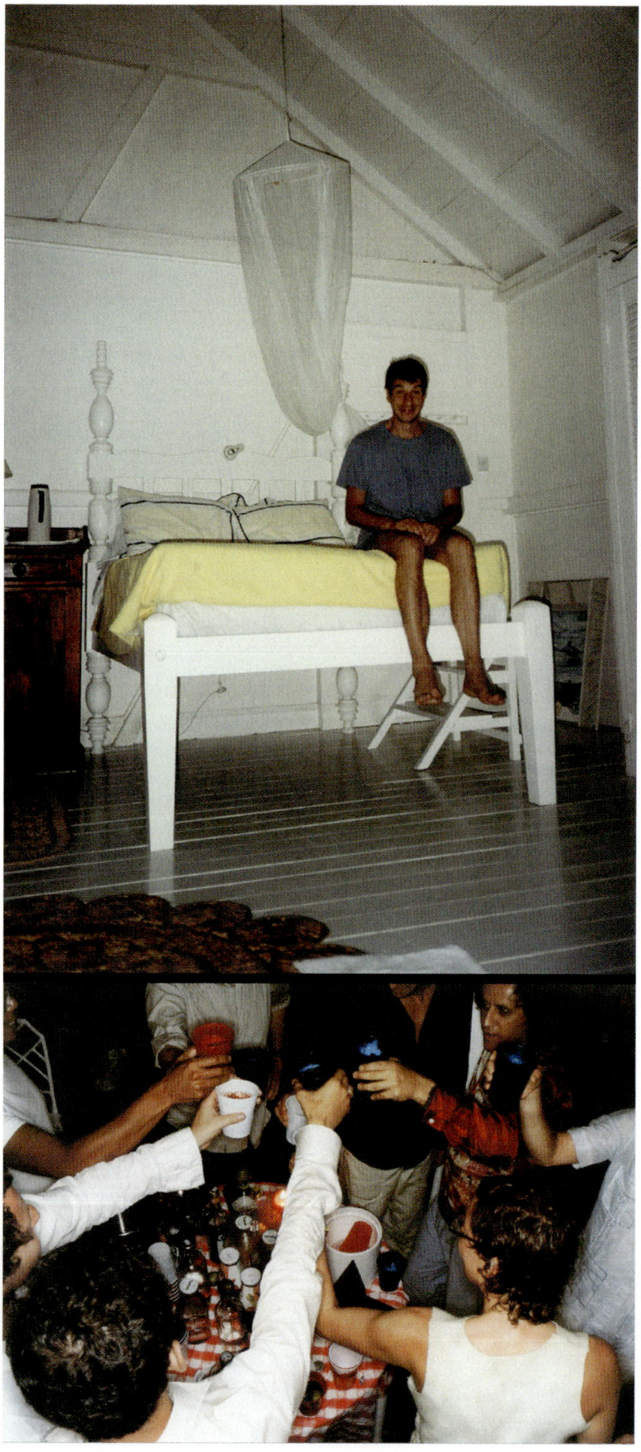

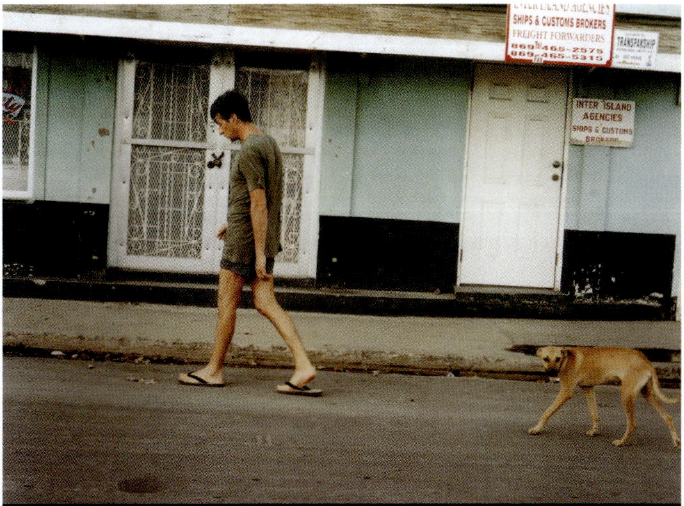
SHIPS & CUSTOMS BROKERS
FREIGHT FORWARDERS
INTER ISLAND
AGENCIES
SHIPS & CUSTOMS

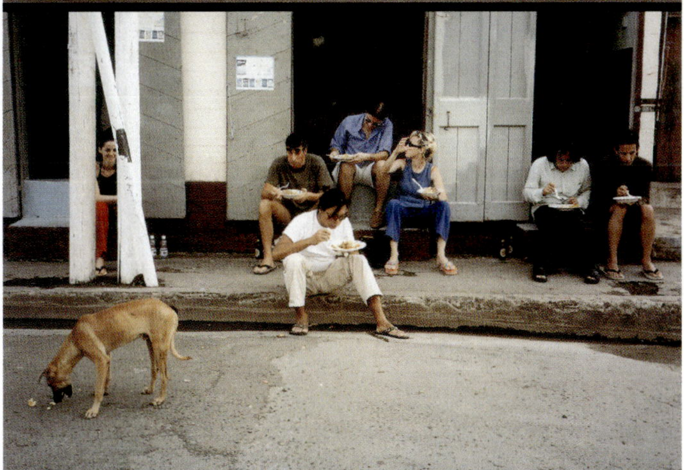

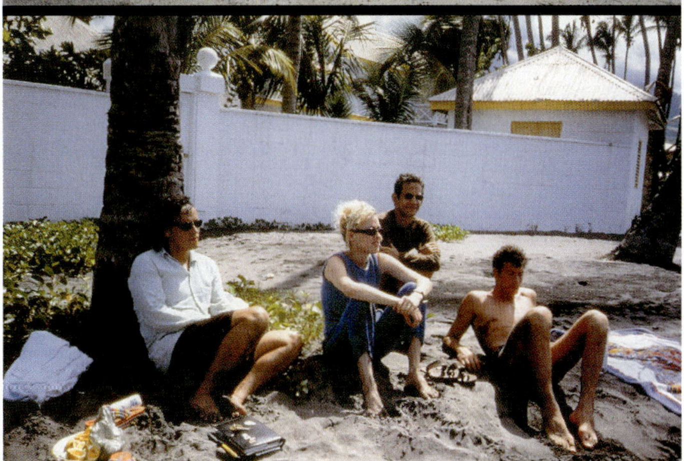

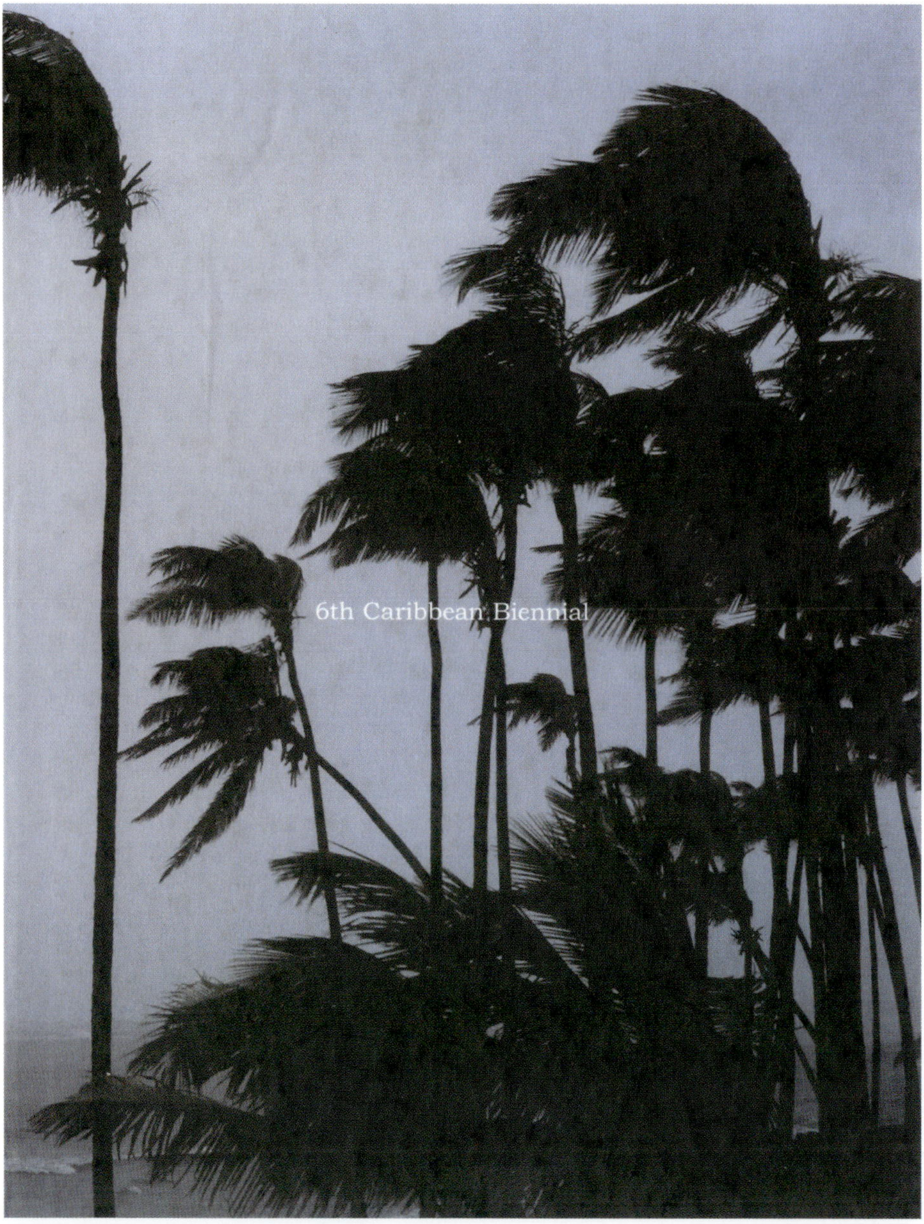

4.5 Catalogue cover for 6th Caribbean Biennale.

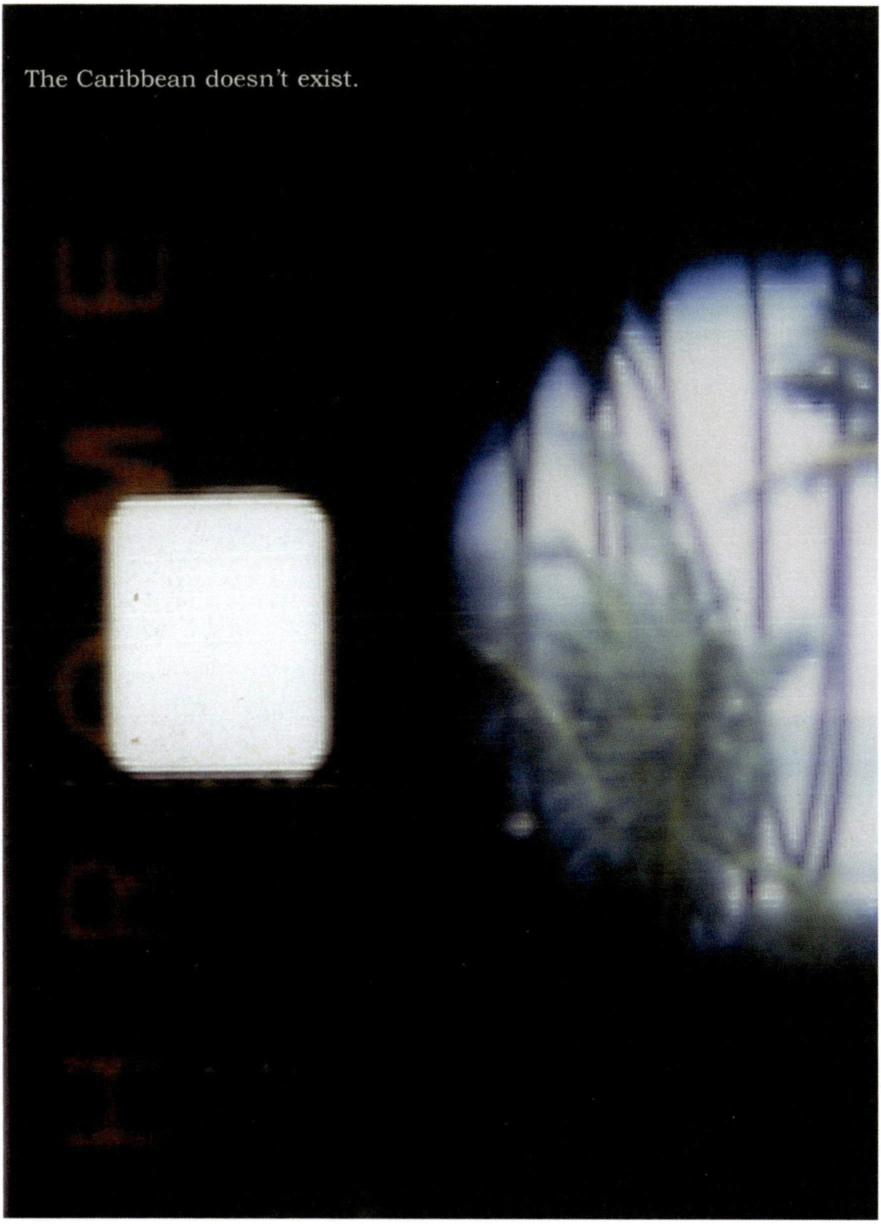

4.6 Page of 6th Caribbean Biennial catalogue: "The Caribbean doesn't exist."

Biennial was the colonizer's last gasp: the conceptual limit of the moribund concept of Western art.

Liu apprehended the vanity and veneer of Cattelan's superficial gloss. Reworking Fanon's experience of objection in *Black Skin, White Masks*, I suggest that his event begs the Other's claim—*Look! A fraud!* Once the surface is pierced, the system of relations that underpin it can be deconstructed and made visible. Drawing on Michel Foucault's work, this excavation requires dehistoricizing the epistemological frameworks that rendered Cattelan's performance both possible and plausible in order to expose his claim that the biennial positioned him as a "Trojan horse" that could "critique" or "unmask" the system that created him.[15]

Plumbing these depths reveals the 6th Caribbean Biennial's disingenuous critical pose and the limits of the discursive formations Cattelan depended on for its legibility. Rather than affecting the reentrenchment of power it sought to affirm, the event in *certain kinds of ways* signaled a shift in hierarchies of power that had hitherto delineated the bounds of citizenship in the contemporary art world. Instead of fueling a postmodern, global art historical enlightenment that values hybridity and functioning "third spaces," mirroring the colonial promise, Cattelan's performance dehistoricized the region, reinstating the power dynamics it purported to dismantle.[16] The biennial was the art world's last-ditch attempt to cannibalize, or Calibanize, the Caribbean.

George Yancy explains colonialism's circuitry from the perspective of the colonizer: "What the colonizer *knows* about the colonized constitutes what the colonized *is*. Perception, epistemology, and ontology are collapsed. With regard to the Black/native/colonized, what is *seen* is what is *known*, and what is *known* is *seen*. Moreover, what is *known* and *seen* or *seen* and *known* is what *there is*."[17] Grounded in these epistemologies, Cattelan arrived on St. Kitts in self-styled postmodern fashion, occluding, without *apparent* resistance, internal discourses that had already produced regional biennials and thousands of artists. Appropriating the biennial form and situating his event within an ordinated lineage, he relied on attendees and a pliable, virtual audience, "the art world," to plug the narrative gaps.

Soon after the biennial, Cattelan, in an interview with Alison M. Gingeras, affirmed his genius, foresight, and remarkable ability to make "everyday life . . . the real agent provocateur."[18] During their *conversation*, Cattelan confessed that the event was a performance and soberly noted that none of the artists "broke character" or ceded celebrity status, even though they were literally "thousands of miles from an art gallery."[19] *Thousands of miles*? Cattelan's ignorant yet telling utterance illustrates Yancy's observation that "what the colonizer *knows* [not much] about the colonized constitutes what the colonized *is*." The Caribbean's displacement—indeed, its disappearance in this supposed dynamic—is both palpable and elusive, mimicking Cattelan's performance cum sociological experiment, in which oblique engagement proceeded through outright occlusion.

The 6th Caribbean Biennial is global Caribbean art history. It crystallizes the region's projected position in 1990s international art circuits by revealing more about the world it defends (and projects) than the postcolonial episteme it confronts. In this constrained and contorted discourse, the Caribbean can provide the stage for exchange, but it has no speaking parts. Unfortunately for Cattelan, by the time he arrived in St. Kitts, the modalities propping up his colonial performance had been utterly fractured, as evidenced by the work of Antoni, Ayón, and Duval-Carrié. In contrast to Derek Walcott's metaphorical vase, the shards could not be sutured.[20] Cattelan's anxious exhibition confirmed that the perceived spatiotemporal distance between the art world and the Caribbean had compressed and attenuated by the close of the nineties, though it was not yet completely stripped of its power. In this vein, Cattelan's conceptual imaginary was both contemporary and anachronistic, rooted in notions of perceived Others tied to race, ethnicity, land, and power that had yielded to historical forces and revolutionary currents. More than a generation after artists like Aubrey Williams, Mavis Pusey, and Frank Bowling had entered the global art scene, alongside the ascendancy of global artists such as Antoni, Ayón, and Duval-Carrié, the 6th Caribbean Biennial showed that Emperor Cattelan had no clothes.

By 1999 many local and global Caribbean artists had already engaged and accessed a space that was not delineated by bounded paradigms of nation, race, or time. Like the region itself, they simultaneously embodied and externalized a critical aesthetic that not only expanded time and space but enfolded them as well, as medium and point of entry. They made it impossible for Cattelan to succeed, regardless of whether his blind spot was looking directly at him or, as with Antoni and Ayón, exhibiting alongside him.[21]

Despite the rattling, nascent transformation of imperial paradigms, Cattelan's absented Caribbean often resurfaced when the work of artists like Antoni and Ayón entered global exhibition spaces. At these junctures, the histories and cultures that informed the artists' production, and often centered it, were typically erased, fetishized, superficially engaged, or, in the case of artists of Haitian descent, such as Duval-Carrié, fantasticated.

The paradoxes spawned by this treatment abounded. Whereas Cattelan could reside in New Jersey yet be perceived as an Italian artist immersed in the history and tradition of Arte Povera, Antoni could not be seen as a New York–based Bahamian artist probing the histories and traditions of Caribbean performance and folklore as part of Western art practices and feminist art histories. Likewise, Ayón's and Duval Carrié's work could not be rendered "contemporary," because it drew on beliefs and faith systems grounded in world views that countered Western norms and were considered primitive within them.

Although the spatiotemporal modalities of centers and margins were increasingly imperiled by the late 1990s, art history and criticism had not yet embraced a rhizomatic, global conversation that generated horizontal conversations. The center-margin binary still directed discourse and imposed cultural erasure on places like the Caribbean, a region that had capitalized on and cultivated its perceived Otherness in the neocolonial orchestrations of mass tourism. Although the Caribbean was seemingly complicit in its own excision from broader conversations around artistic production and value, the impact of these practices produced an art historical "borderclash."[22] As scholars employed the language of universality to intellectualize and aestheticize the work of artists from smaller cultural spaces, local contexts, regional ties, and significations were consistently erased, and art that grappled with ideas and processes resident to the Caribbean but that was produced by artists physically located outside its geographic borders continued to be devalued as inauthentic. Even as these artists conceived work in the context of their unique problem spaces, they often faced pressure to authenticate their work using terms and conditions, or as Édouard Glissant suggests, parameters and plateaus, that were defined by the West which the Caribbean had neither experienced nor benefited from. Art that eluded or was occluded by Western rubrics of land, nation, collective, style, or avant-gardism was inherently disadvantaged, continually placed, like the region itself, outside the main currents of artistic and critical regard.[23]

Shalini Puri has called on scholars to "de-essentialize our reading of form by historicizing it." Given that similar formal aspects may encode different epistemologies and projects depending on historical context, and invoking Stuart Hall's evocation of Derrida, she brings attention to the ways "historical context itself leaves its traces on the form."[24] My discussion seeks to de-essentialize Cattelan's Caribbean by historicizing his colonizing eye, and the Caribbean response to it, in the eye of the neocolonial storm. To plumb anxieties at the heart of his performance, I consider how the contemporary Caribbean was imaged through the development and deployment of the "brochure discourse" Cattelan marshaled to frame his biennial, a strategy that persists in present-day mass tourism. By drawing on Jacques Lacan's theory of perception and the epistemological implications of semiotics in our age of mass marketing,[25] I explore nostalgia, authenticity, fragmentation, and cultural commodification through two artifacts of the tourist experience—the postcard and the photograph. Following Puri, I historicize this conversation alongside the incubation of a multiply expressed Caribbean consciousness focused on decolonial, postindependence, and postrevolutionary autohistoriographies. In the process I seek to render and mobilize a burgeoning discourse around public monuments to highlight the simultaneous generation of alternative and interpenetrating articulations of memory and systems of meaning that counter a totalitarian tourist vision of the Caribbean.[26] Rather than acceding to Cattelan's declaration that "the Caribbean does not exist," I draw on Gayatri Spivak's notion of "worlding" or world-making, not *of* the native but *by* the native(s) as a collective, in order to trouble singular or settled understanding(s) of the relationship between the "smiling native" and the foreign tourist within imperfect Caribbean settings and the work of emergent artists during this critical period.[27]

This is a long road to travel, but historicizing interwoven epistemes both contextualizes and lays bare how Cattelan's biennial and its archive were not simply formal maneuvers on the part of a puckish, witty, slightly unwilling but accolade-loving art star, but exhibit A of colonial frameworks that persist at the core of the art world and art histories.[28] The effort also illuminates the enigmatic excess of Caribbean art vis-à-vis postcolonial art historical writing and criticism to reveal how a commitment to crafting a transformative critical discourse demands dismantlement of the colonial epistemes that shape it.

WORLDING A WORLD

"SMILE. You are a walking tourist attraction,"[29] proclaimed a 1980s poster in Dominica targeted to the native populace. This messaging encapsulates the mirror and screen that frames the native's daily life vis-à-vis the tourists interchangeably shuffling on- and offstage. In this museum installation, as it were, the spectacle demanded that the islander, as Barbara Kirshenblatt-Gimblett suggests, avoided any hint of "performance."[30] The poster acknowledged the absorption of the colonial masquerade as a way of life on Caribbean islands like Dominica and St. Kitts that increasingly relied on mass tourism to sustain their economies following World War II. Here, "One man's life [can become] another man's spectacle."[31]

Alongside their distinctions, the Caribbean islands share many commonalities. They have all been molded by the experiences of indigeneity, genocide, plantation slavery, colonialism (English, French, Dutch, and Spanish), and *post-* periods: postcolonial, postindependence, and postrevolutionary. In tandem with the influx of indentured servants from India, China, and later Java, the region's peoples represent a complex and hybridized lineage traceable to all who have laid claim to it: the original Amerindians, Africans, European colonizers, East Indians, Chinese, Portuguese, Arabs, and Jews. These encounters forged relational cultures from the crucible of African, European, and Asian traditions, and more recently, North American and Chinese power and influence.[32]

The rise of mass tourism in the late twentieth century was unevenly articulated, but by the 1990s, all Caribbean countries and territories were engaged in some form of the enterprise. Some, like The Bahamas, viewed tourism as the goose that kept on laying golden eggs—employing wide swaths of the populace and floating the entire economy. Within this paradigm, tourism was an engine of progress, a surefire way for precariously financed Caribbean nations to gain foreign currency, develop infrastructure, and, if one followed the rhetoric of some contemporary political campaigns, ascend from the so-called Third World to the First World. On paper, it seemed as if the Caribbean was onto something. By the time Cattelan began advertising the biennial, most of the labor force in Bermuda and the Virgin Islands was directly employed by the tourist industry.[33] As these numbers suggest, tourism was and is the business of the Caribbean—ushering in modernity while exacting a devastating toll on the environment, the economic structure, national politics, cultural dynamism, the social structure, and the people.

In his formulation of the "mirror stage," Jacques Lacan described how humans perceive and navigate the world around them by manifesting an imago so as to establish a visual and spatial relationship with their reality (Innenwelt and Umwelt). Lacan characterized the process as "a drama whose internal thrust is precipitated from insufficiency"; we first look into the mirror in an unconscious search for wholeness.[34] Caught in the lure of and desire for spatial identification, this moment precipitates a shift in self-perception from fragmented form to unified living body. But it is a troubled and ambivalent union: The image assumes an identity alien to the body; projection and being are distinguished and yet commingled.

In "Of the Gaze as *Objet Petit a*" (1964) Lacan expanded upon these ideas by exploring the semiotics of self-perception. In this circuit, the eye is a transfer point for activity fueled by our desires, which themselves are shaped by sociocultural meanings encoded onto our surroundings. The gaze represents the objectification of transference, which mystifies or demystifies all that we see *depending on the locus of interpretation*. This is a critical pivot for contextualizing Cattelan's event. He depends heavily on transference to mount the biennial, but all the while, the "empty space" needed to map and materialize his perception has already been claimed by global Caribbean artists and the Caribbean itself. In other words, there is no room on the stage for his solipsistic, anachronistic performance.

Following Lacan, I argue that the gaze frames interactions between the Caribbean native and the tourist. In establishing a zone of encounter and exchange, the gaze permits the native and tourist to switch subject positions. When a native is beheld by the tourist's gaze, they are objectified, and the gaze is uncontested. But when a native person realizes they are being regarded and returns the gaze, the tourist's power to Other, objectify, or devour the native can vanish or invert. In 1999, Cattelan entered a region fully capable of interrupting the circuitry of his Western gaze.

In his early twenties, Lacan traveled to preindustrial Brittany, spurred by a desire to get away from it all and see something different. His quest for authenticity and renewal via touristic exchange offers a theoretical analog for Cattelan's Caribbean native-artist encounter.[35] One day, as Lacan was fishing with a local crew, one of the fishermen pointed to a sardine can floating in the water. Lacan intuitively linked the can to its denotation—the area's role in the sardine industry. But the fisherman introduced an entirely new perspective. He said to Lacan, "You see the can? Do you *see* it? Well, it doesn't see you!" Although the statement seemed nonsensical, it triggered a profound realization for Lacan: He was "not in the picture."[36] The locus of interpretation had shifted and excluded him.

I propose that *both* Lacan's and the fisherman's responses were simultaneously true within circuitries of perception and objectification. The thingness of the sardine can rests in the fact that it was seen, which in turn relies on its possession of language to communicate its can-ness, its being as a can. In the cultural arena, a similar relationship is articulated in the discursive space between Cattelan as prospective colonizer, tourist, and artist (Lacan) and the Caribbean as native (can). In this nexus, the Caribbean possesses the power to refuse the artist's gaze as well as the vocabularies and phenomenologies that inform it.

Lacan attempted to explain the implications of these shifting subject positions in a famous diagram depicting the inherently reciprocal nature of perception. It illustrates the spatial relationships between subjective bodies, the gaze, the image, the screen, and the representational subject. Within his schema, the gaze turns the object into a picture. Mapped onto the tourist-native dynamic, this idea suggests that it is the gaze itself—articulated as an independent action or thing resident beyond either self—that elevates them to a plateau of identification and visibility. The gaze allows natives to be *photo-graphed*, to represent as record what is seen and materialize the parameters of vision as memory.[37]

Within this dynamic, the image and screen jointly inscribe and determine the relationship between tourist and native. The screen encompasses the knowledge that informs interpretation, what something means or signifies. Within the tourism economy, the brochure (visual promotion in any media) functions as a screen to frame expectations of encounter, and the postcard or photograph documents its occurrence. Akin to an anamorphosis, postcards, selfies, and photographs represent efforts to freeze memory.[38] Taken in its most literal sense, Lacan's notion of the screen describes how the brochure, by imaging what is foreign to us, camouflages the intersubjectivity of the tourist-native exchange. In this manner, the screen/brochure functions as a synecdoche for culture and a priori frame of reference, vacating the tourist's actual experience by predetermining it. Lacan's discussion of painting sheds light on this dynamic:

> The painter gives something to the person who must stand in front of his painting which, in part, at least, of the painting, might be summed up thus—You want to see? Well, take a look at this! *He gives something for the eye to feed on*, but he invites the person to whom this picture is presented to lay down his gaze there as one lays down one's weapons. This is the pacifying, Apollonian effect of the image. Something is given not so much to the gaze as to the eye, something that involves the abandonment, the laying down, of the gaze.[39]

Culture, socialization, and epistemes of knowledge shape the gaze. What we "see" depends on what we know, or think we know.

Screens demarcate cognitive spaces that inform perception; readily filled by complex, multivalent semiotic systems, they naturally lend themselves to mythmaking. In a well-known discussion of the image of a Black boy dressed in French military-style clothing on the cover of *Paris Match*, Roland Barthes illuminated how signification drives myth formation. He argued that within a dense semiotic system, the boy doesn't reflect his *own* subjectivity but France's imperial might.[40] According to Barthes, the boy's picture "contained a whole system of values: a history, a geography, a morality, a zoology, a literature. The form has put all this richness at a distance; its newly acquired penury calls for a signification to fill it." Barthes's equation between the image's consolidation of myth and the associative paradox that "myth hides nothing: its function is to distort, not make disappear," gestures toward the semiotic systems at play in the tourist brochure.[41] The brochure presents a Caribbean myth, an image or promise on which the expectations of the tourist as artist are predicated. The gaze itself is ungendered, unraced—it is, at base, human. To activate his performance, Cattelan converts the gaze by deploying the colonial screen as a mechanism that feeds on the Other. His audience, immersed in the same semiotic and epistemological system, takes the artist's manipulation of the tourist advertisement at his word.

Cattelan's techniques are neither novel nor unique; they do not represent or facilitate acquisition of new knowledge per se. His advertisements are distortions that weave together various traces of information in order to influence future perception or assess future experience. They are based on mythology cloaked in the guise of history. Pace Yancy, Cattelan's claim to vision and knowledge is imperial and consuming, and altogether mis-taken. Within the native-tourist dynamic, this distortion equates with a dissociative invisibility, or shadow play of the real, in which the screen's utility articulates at the nexus of colonialism and capitalism—that is, as produced by the desire to control, extract, and exploit. This bare-bones neocolonial capitalism acquires a moral or ethical character through the transfer of funds. Purchasing power valorizes the right to see, which obligates the natives to "SMILE" and comply with their objectification. In this myth of fair exchange, Cattelan's performance trades on counterfeit currency and bad faith—the generosity of the colonial gaze disguises contempt as regard.

SIGNS AND WONDERS, SCREENS AND MYTHS

The image-rich tourist brochure is critical to understanding the biennial's visual and semiotic language. Photographs play a role on both ends of the continuum of perception and experience—as informer of and invitation to experience and as its documentation. Albers and James argue that photographs do not merely confer objective representations of reality but subjectively constitute a *way of seeing*.[42] The tourist brochure, postcard, and souvenir promote this way of seeing through concrete signifiers—sun, sand, sea, and native—framing their interrelationships as well as the tourist's articulation within them.

The Caribbean's ascendancy as a mecca for mass tourism began around 1950 when regular jet service from Europe, Canada, and the United States transported a burgeoning international leisured middle class leading a postwar consumer culture feeding frenzy.[43] Foreign corporations, or Prosperos, packaged the product—the natural environment and the people who dwelled in it—as Caliban-like image-texts to re-present a world that existed outside real time and its attendant challenges and complexities.[44] Photography was the ideal medium for this effort, enabling the encoding of images with ideologies and symbolism that resonated far beyond authorial intention.[45] Hired by native governments, foreign advertising agencies soon began generating slogans and images to stimulate the imagination to travel through time. The Bahamas invited you to "runaway [*sic*] from today."[46] A 1968 Jamaican campaign encouraged the tourist to experience "the life you wished you led," with the promise of Black servants named "Ivy," "Maud," or Malcolm" who would do anything they were asked (figure 4.7).[47]

For the US market that came to dominate Caribbean tourism after World War II, the advertising campaigns enunciated and re-presented a theoretically uncontested naturalization of the racial, class, and gender divisions that were then being summarily challenged and upended in the United States. Framed and contained by these visual narratives, travel to the region promised a haven from reality, an escape to a prior landscape of clearly marked power relations and racialized hierarchies. In these economies of exchange, the Ivys and Malcolms constituted Lacanian screens for the native populace and the tourists' interactions with them.

Exemplifying the commodification of illusion and the promulgation of myth, the Emerald Beach Plantation and Hotel featured as a mainstay of the Bahamian tourism industry's promotional content during the 1960s (figure 4.8). The appropriation of the site's name and its fraught history were all the more fantastical because, as Ian Strachan observes, "the plantation economy never flourished in The Bahamas *until tourism*."[48] In fact, the circulation of the plantation trope sidelined local history to both exploit and satiate the desire for a service model that had long been abolished in The Bahamas but persisted in Americans' emotional attachments and histori-

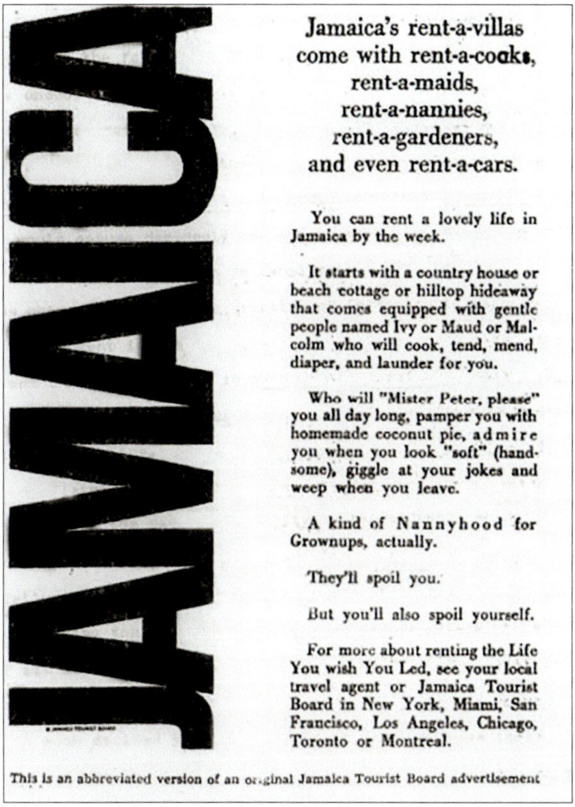

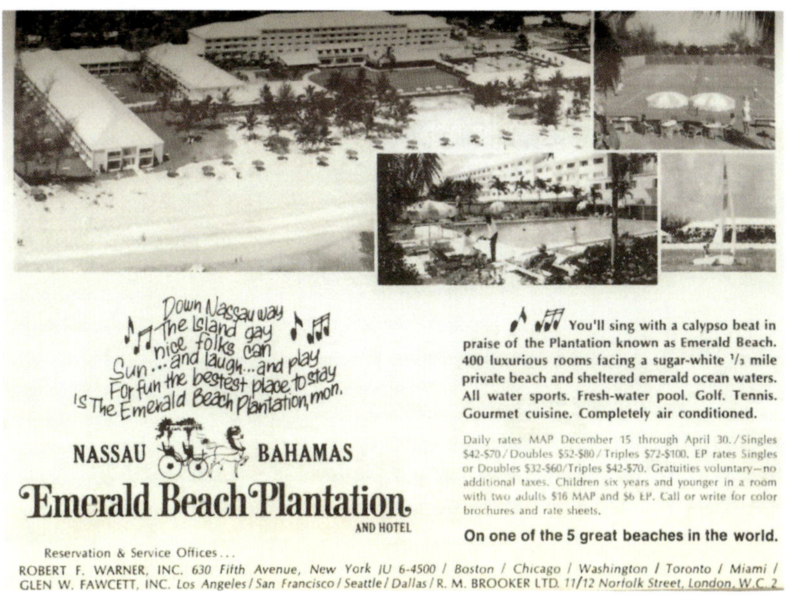

4.7 Jamaica Tourist Board advertisement. Jamaica Tourist Board Archives, Kingston.

4.8 Emerald Beach Plantation and Hotel print ad. *Bahamas Handbook*, ca. 1960. National Archives of The Bahamas.

cal imagination. One can almost hear the happy, at-the-ready hotel workers, singing the advertisement's verse in strange mimicry of native dialect: "Down Nassau way the island gay—nice folks can sun . . . and laugh . . . and play. For fun the bestest place to stay is the Emerald Beach Plantation, mon."[49]

Brochures for the Good Hope Plantation (figure 4.9) also deployed the plantation signifier to reference its history of excessiveness by picturing a deliberately concealed white woman ministered to by no less than four faceless, mechanical, and neutered Black men. In these texts, Blackness was communicated as visual shorthand for an enduring and timeless historical relationship—one that Cattelan would leverage to promote his event decades later.

Tourism advertisements created for the US and European markets both placed emphasis on sexuality, though differently. For example, the "Let's assume I'm an island" campaign tagged as "Print Advertising—USA" feminizes the island within a patriarchal order. Here The Bahamas is a place to casually land and experience on entry (figures 4.10 and 4.11). In the "Are you big enough for The Bahamas?" campaign, intended as "Print Advertising—UK and Europe," one sees a native Black man's musculature and an extremely large fish plunging downward as a surrogate to his imagined manhood. In both instances, the presumed tourist encounters the native through screens, which in the European advertisement commingles visual cues for masculinity, sexuality, race, and the exotic to materialize a simultaneously homosocial and hypersexual image, in turn disassociating the represented from subjecthood. Within this exchange, the native and tourist alike become commodities in a service economy.[50]

W. J. T. Mitchell suggests that image-texts express "the Lacanian triad of imaginary, symbolic, and the real."[51] This layering muddies the waters, enabling the half-story narrated through screens to dominate one's reading of the entire tale. In the material and visual economy of Caribbean tourism, which draws heavily on colonialist ideologies and power dynamics, screens generate and mediate mythologies between natives and tourists, Caribbean and metropoles, art world citizens and aliens.

The linkage between colonialism and Caribbean tourism has been apparent since the earliest years of the industry's rise. In 1885, on a visit to The Bahamas from the United States, William Drysdale noted in his travel diary: "Altogether it was a very proper picture of a morning in the West Indies, where of course nobody has anything to do, and where anybody who has anything to do, don't do it. And that's just the sort of country I

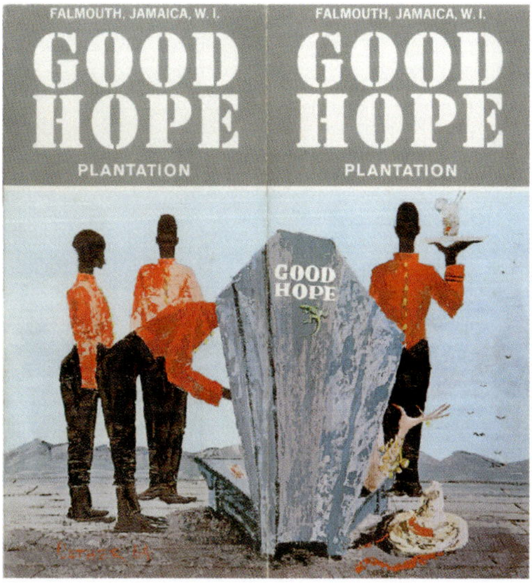

4.9 Good Hope Plantation brochure. Jamaica Tourism Board Archives, Kingston.

like. Here are ten thousand darkies who will do anything you want for a shilling, and I don't see the least reason for any white person doing any work at all—as long as he has a shilling."[52] The racialized capitalist logic that absolves Drysdale's expectations with a shilling came to characterize tourism in the region as well as the "Western" art world's relationship to global Others. It is a logic that Caribbean writers, politicians, and intellectuals, from V. S. Naipaul to Maurice Bishop, have identified as the mirror image of slave economies.[53] This unmasking reveals a neocolonial system of domination fully mobilized during what was described optimistically in the 1990s as a postcolonial age. Like colonialism, tourism represents what Gayatri Spivak might describe as a "worlding" of the native's homeland by global economic concerns. In her discussion of the native escort who assisted Captain Geoffrey Birch on his imperializing mapping project in India, Spivak posits that Birch was "engaged in consolidating the Self of Europe by obliging the native to cathect the space of the Other on his home ground. . . . He is worlding *their own world*, which is far from mere uninscribed earth, anew, by obliging *them* to domesticate the alien as Master." For Spivak, the colonizer's worlding of the native's world commandeers the latter's self-perception; seen through the eyes of the colonizer, the native becomes and simultaneously self-identifies as his Other.[54]

By the close of the twentieth century, the premise that tourism was the region's yellow brick road to wealth was faltering. In 1969, the Bahamian government hired a Washington-based consulting firm to help manage its

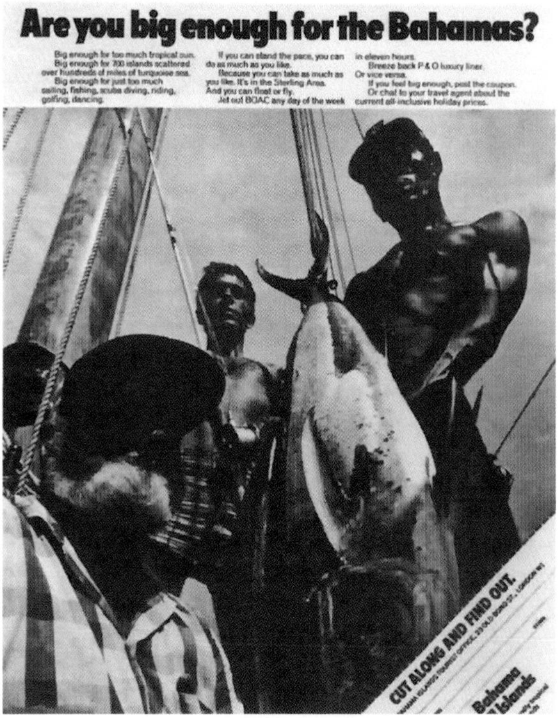

4.10 "Are you big enough for the Bahamas?" Ad for UK and European market. *Bahamas Tourism Report*. National Archives of The Bahamas.

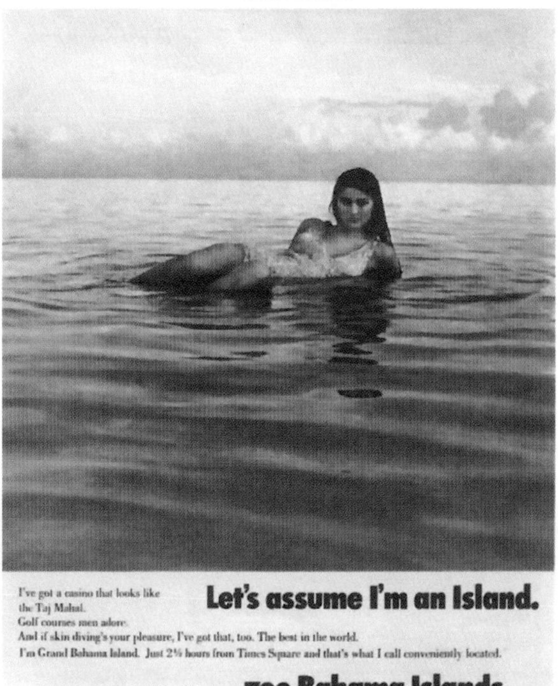

4.11 "Let's Assume I'm an Island." Ad for US market. *Bahamas Tourism Report*. National Archives of The Bahamas.

growth. The firm's report cautions the industry lest it engender domestic resentment: "It is only natural for the Bahamian to resent the inconvenience, which this mass of tourists brings and to think of expatriate workers as a threat to his own job security or to the job security of his friends. Unless these inconveniences and potential threats can be translated into a personal gain for the average Bahamian, the tourism program will not succeed." The government took heed. It soon launched a program of "personalization" to persuade the native population that the industry's wealth and success represented a public investment and social good. Exhortations informed the populace that "two condominiums pay for one school room" and "one foreign worker pays for one new hospital room every year and two trained teachers."[55] Despite this buoyant framing, by the 1990s, many Caribbean countries, overseas departments, and territories, including The Bahamas, were in crisis due to economic stagnation, natural disasters, and rising crime rates resulting from drug trafficking.

Rather than rethink the dominant model or address the social impact of mass tourism, postindependence postcolonial governments began to market tourism to increasingly skeptical native inhabitants, using the same brochure regime employed to lure foreign tourists. They specifically sought to cast natives in a central role within the exchange, an effort that yielded the "SMILE!" promotions in Dominica and the "Bahamas: Our Pride and Joy" campaign in the 1970s and '80s.[56] Mass tourism increasingly influenced local politics, and governments faced criticism from locals when they perceived that foreign interests were taking precedence over their own.

The brochure's anticipation and projection of the tourist's experience encapsulates the inevitability of disappointment, an eventuation that results from the discrepancy between what John Frow describes as a "figural reality," imaged in the brochure's photographic referent, and the "literal reality," what is actually seen or experienced by the tourist.[57] Enmeshed within neocolonial frameworks of perception and attendant mythologies, the photograph-souvenir's authenticating documentation forges a connection between the experience's promise and its trace that was on full display in the 6th Caribbean Biennial.[58] Susan Stewart's seminal work on historical representation and the souvenir is instructive. Stewart observes that historical narrative is always ideological in that "the past it seeks (to render) has never existed except as narrative." In her estimation, Cattelan's performance could be "hostile to history and its invisible origins," yet demonstrate a "longing for an impossibly pure context of lived experience at a place of origin . . . that turns toward a future-past, a past which has only ideological reality."[59] This is especially manifest when it imbricates with the aura of the artist, the final prop in Cattelan's performance.

The visitor's liminality in the Caribbean was documented as early as the eighteenth century.[60] But James Lett's work on contemporary charter yacht tourists' lawlessness and lack of regard exemplifies how "liminoid status encourages [them] to ignore not only the rules of their own society but those of their host society as well."[61] Out of time and place, too often tourists engage in a broadly shallow interaction with the native populace that reflects a patent inability to *see* the native in a way that would generate a deeper social exchange. Cattelan replicated the terms of this foreclosed encounter by packaging the native as mere scenery and ceding possession of the space to tourist artists. Ironically, the liminality of his pointedly insular performance is repeated in the event's catalogue. Absent the typical essays, publication place, year, and page numbers, it, too, exists in a somewhere-nowhere that serves as archive, but not quite. The catalogue might be better perceived as its own art object or a kind of souvenir, emphasizing Stewart's ideological reality, that cleanses the project of its questionable ethics and failure of form in an attempt to align with the creators' perceptions rather than the event's reality. In this way, the catalogue partakes in the same colonialist mechanics and semiotics of desire, erasure, and mythology as the tourist brochure and its attendant verifying document, the postcard. This approach to the past, painfully familiar throughout the length and breadth of the Caribbean, is one that Caribbean people have fought against through less recognized but no less potent approaches to authorship.

WEAPONS OF THE WEAK

Antonio Gramsci contended that the "superstructures of civil society are like the trench systems of modern warfare. In war it would sometimes happen that a fierce artillery attack seemed to have destroyed the enemy's entire defensive system, whereas in fact it had only destroyed the outer perimeter."[62] Drawing on Gramsci's schema, this section examines how tourism and Cattelan's biennial affected the postcolonial Caribbean's outer perimeter.

The discourse on public monuments illustrates how Caribbean people publicly expressed political stances beyond the control or repercussions of colonial and native governments. The lengthy, well-documented history of silenced colonized people voicing opposition to various governmental positions on monuments, using what James C. Scott has described as weapons of the weak, has been observed in the French-, English-, Dutch-, and Spanish-speaking Caribbean.[63] These weapons consist of variously passive and active acts by those who may appear to lack power in the economic, social, and political systems in which they live but who nonetheless claim discrete spaces and distinct methods for contesting them. Because of their public and, at times, spectacular acts, their documentation is often preserved in colonial public records, as Marc Latamie discovered in the story of Lumina Sophie. Through this mechanism, the subjected become visible in history through resistance, as their actions map and mark the articulation of regional decolonial narratives *within* colonial frameworks. In this configuration, Lacan's native gaze buffers the culture from total commodification, creating a space where the native's subjectivity enters the picture.

If, as Lacan suggests, to truly see, we must always consider the reciprocal nature of perception, that is, exercise reflexive engagement with how we see what we see, then to parse the postcolonial perspective within neocolonial economies demands that we challenge the colonial screen's narrative authority and unidirectional regard. Filtered through this lens, the 6th Caribbean Biennial is revealed as contemporary art in colonial drag, in which the performer and performance operate unawares in the shadows of global Caribbean artists' self-authored historiographies.

Spivak maintains that in the imperial colonial project, "meaning/knowledge intersects power" to articulate history as episteme.[64] The Caribbean's public discourse around monuments and memorials maps an attempt to decolonize the past by engaging in autohistoriography. As I show in this section, this effort and conversation began long before the official onset of the postcolonial era and the more recent debate around Laura Facey's Redemption Song Emancipation Monument (2003) in Jamaica.[65] Recognizing Petrina Dacres's work on public monuments in Heroes Park in Jamaica, I discuss the examples that reside outside her intent to chart a publicly realized political discourse across time—from colonial to a postindependent, postcolonial Caribbean.[66] Although my examples are drawn from Jamaica, their contours are not unique to that island. They typify Caribbean people's expression of private opinions in public spaces after centuries of repression, expression wielded as a decolonial weapon articulated through nonarchival processes and mediums. Indeed, it is the public aspect of these debates and actions that is paramount, insofar as it reaffirms postcolonialism as a transborder mindset that enacts and partakes in an ongoing decolonial process rather than a settled spatiotemporal and political condition. Registering demolition by neglect and the expression of a collective voice in ruins, these conversations quite literally frame history as a living field of praxis.

Several years after Jamaica's independence (1962), the United Nations Educational, Scientific, and Cultural Organization (UNESCO) published a document outlining the island's history of historical preservation and commemoration. At the time, as Christopher Tunnard and John Pollaco reported in that document, the Jamaica National Trust Law defined "National Monument" as "any monument or group of monuments and any part or remains of a monument or group of monuments the preservation of which is . . . a matter of public interest by reason of historic, architectural, traditional, artistic or archeological interest." The authors observed that whereas monuments and memorials were traditionally regarded as immovable, this was not the case in Jamaica.[67]

Between the erection of its last Columbus monument in 1958 and the UNESCO report's release, Jamaica established a national heroes and monuments directive to formally address historical omissions. The government commissioned Kamau Brathwaite to compose a short essay, entitled "Jamaican History and the National Heroes," to articulate the initiative's scope.[68] Brathwaite framed the inauguration of national heroes and monuments as a revolutionary, decolonial, and anti-imperial act and a fundamental step in the ongoing struggle for freedom through a reassessment of the historical archive. In the piece, he described a national hero as "a participant in the struggle for freedom at a particular moment of crisis." "Though anchored in a specific period," Brathwaite went on, "he or she illuminates the meaning of the whole, establishing correspondences with each step and stage of the past. . . . The National Hero is and cannot be only a political declaration; he/she is also a folk figure: an expression of the collective memory of the people."[69]

These interventions were both nationalist and epistemological. Brathwaite observed that the Jamaica Maroons had entered the archive only when they confronted or interacted with colonial power: first when they signed a treaty with the British government in 1739 and then almost sixty years later, in 1795, when they revolted against its terms; and again, when they sided with the British to put down the Samuel Sharpe Rebellion. Even Sharpe is remembered, or rendered visible, because he led a revolt against British colonials in 1831–32. Brathwaite gleans two important points from these official inscriptions. First, he observes that as an enslaved, Sharpe engaged a weapon of the weak—passive resistance—to mark his refusal of oppressive labor conditions during the period of British indentureship. This arsenal took many forms, including, for example, a "go slow," or complete cessation of work based on disingenuous claims of illness; purposefully breaking or disabling valuable objects; and claims of earache or temporary deafness impeding one's ability to hear commands. When the plantation owners refused to bend, as they had in Haiti and Cuba a half century before, slaves burned the fields, escalating resistance to full-scale revolt.[70] Second, Brathwaite emphasizes autohistoricization as a generative tool of decolonialism. For people of primarily African descent in the Caribbean, or more inclusively, colonized people in the Caribbean, visibility in the archive and in Caribbean histories was primarily achieved through and thus subject to their encounters with colonials or the colonial system, or both.

The vision Brathwaite presented to the Jamaican government marked a perspectival shift and a reworlding venture. Revisiting and removing monuments and naming new heroes would rewrite a historical record that had become untenable in an independent, postcolonial nation. To enact the process, Brathwaite called on artists' shamanic ability to "restore our sense of an intimate, emotional connection with our past; to restore, in fact our folk myths . . . with the kind of vision [that] makes it possible to leap our discontinuities and connect our fragments."[71] Like the oeuvre of the Césaires in Martinique and of Alea in Cuba, this sentiment would spur the undertow that crested with the work of the generation of artists cited in this text.

The debates surrounding the figure of Nanny illustrate how this process operated. As the leader of the Windward Maroons who defeated the British in the eighteenth century, Nanny appears in archival records only four times, without any mention of her physical attributes. The image that came to represent her is an artist's imaginative rendering based on classical representational sculpture from the Yoruba people of West Africa from whom she is believed to have descended, and histories of representation of epic figures already in the Jamaican art canon. Figures 4.12–4.14 reveal the resemblances between the artist's rendering of Nanny, a Yoruba royal head, and Ronald Moody's seminal sculpture in the facial scarifications of the former and natural wood grains for the latter. Nanny's enduring image, like Duval-Carrié's family portrait, is and was fabulated and agreed on in the absence of a visual or descriptive archive.

Brathwaite's proposal was presented during a period of intense nationalism when everyday Jamaicans were finding their postcolonial voice in domestic concerns. This sentiment was clearly articulated in the public discourse on the memorial statue of Lewis Quier Bowerbank, which began in the years leading up to Jamaican independence and quietly concluded in 1962 (figure 4.15). These proceedings and the political turns they took over the course of a centuries-long conversation, alongside Brathwaite's project, exemplify the critical activity taking place within Gramsci's perimeter, where Jamaica and other Caribbean tourist economies mounted a shield to deflect the colonizing gaze.

On April 11, 1881, a statue struck in Bowerbank's memory was unveiled at the north entrance of Kingston's Victoria Park. The inscription read: "Lewis Quier Bowerbank. This statue was erected by his numerous friends and admirers in memory of him in his private character as a Christian Gentleman. In his professional as a distinguished physician and Sanitary Reformer and in his public as a Custos whose ministration is a tradition and a call. Born in Jamaica 1814,"[72] Bowerbank had distinguished himself by reforming the public hospitals and "lunatic asylum," but his position as Kingston's *custos rotulorum* in the aftermath of the Morant Bay Rebellion eventually led to his departure from the island of his birth for England in 1876 at the age of sixty-two.[73]

In the early 1860s, Jamaica experienced a financial crisis because of the Union trade embargo during the US Civil War. To recover losses, St. Thomas Parish's governing class decided to impose a high tax on its mostly Black and mixed-race farmers. The farmers registered numerous formal complaints, compelling George William Gordon, a successful mixed-race, or "colored," planter, minister, and member of the General Assembly in Kingston, to appeal to the queen on their behalf. The pleas were ignored. Other parish members protested and petitioned the government, also to no avail. The parishioners were led by Paul Bogle, a small farmer and respectable deacon whom Gordon had ordained and who served at the Native Baptist Church in the town of Stony Gut. Bogle was also one of 104 people eligible to vote in the entire parish. Although Gordon and Bogle knew each other and shared similar concerns, they acted independently.

On October 11, 1865, a parish council meeting was held at the Morant Bay Courthouse. Bogle and four hundred farmers from Stony Gut attended, carrying "sticks and cutlasses, accompanied by music of horns, drums and conch shells."[74] The demonstrators clashed with the volunteer police force, which fired into the crowd, killing or wounding about twenty individuals. The crowd responded violently, setting fire to the courthouse, where the volunteers and the council had retreated, killing several people.

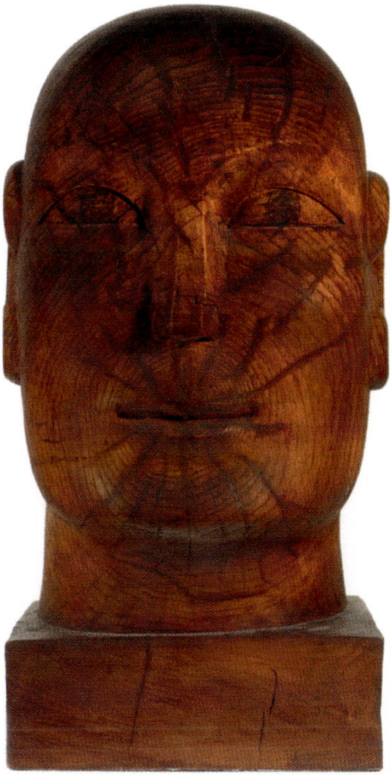

4.12 Ronald Moody, *Tacet*, 1937. Elm wood, $30 \times 13\frac{3}{8} \times 14\frac{3}{16}$ in. National Gallery of Jamaica.

4.13 Artist unknown, *Nanny of the Maroons*. Institute of Jamaica.

4.14 Artist unknown, Yoruba head, Nigeria, twelfth to fifteenth century. Terracotta, $12\frac{1}{4} \times 5\frac{3}{4} \times 7\frac{1}{4}$ in. Minneapolis Institute of Art.

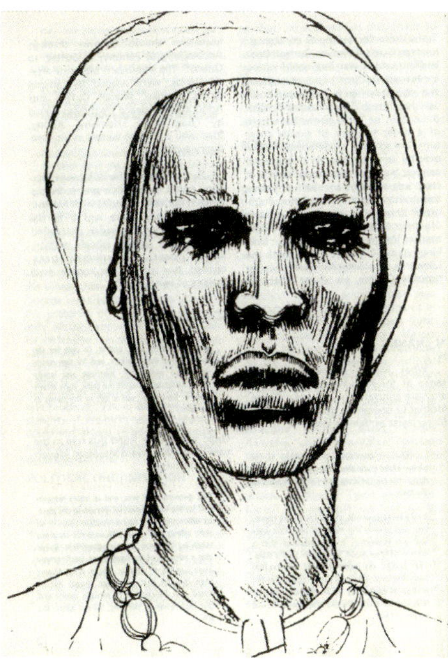

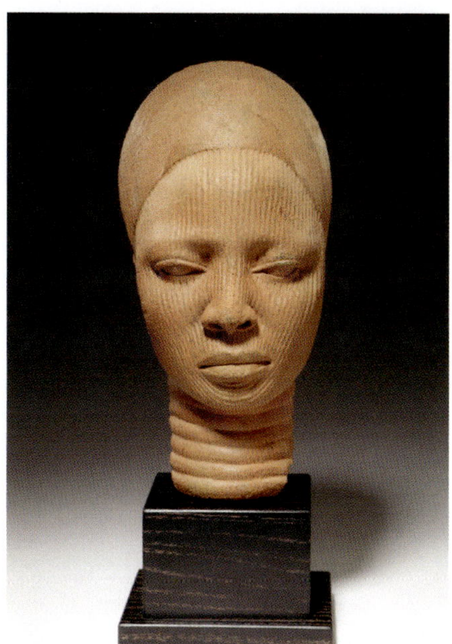

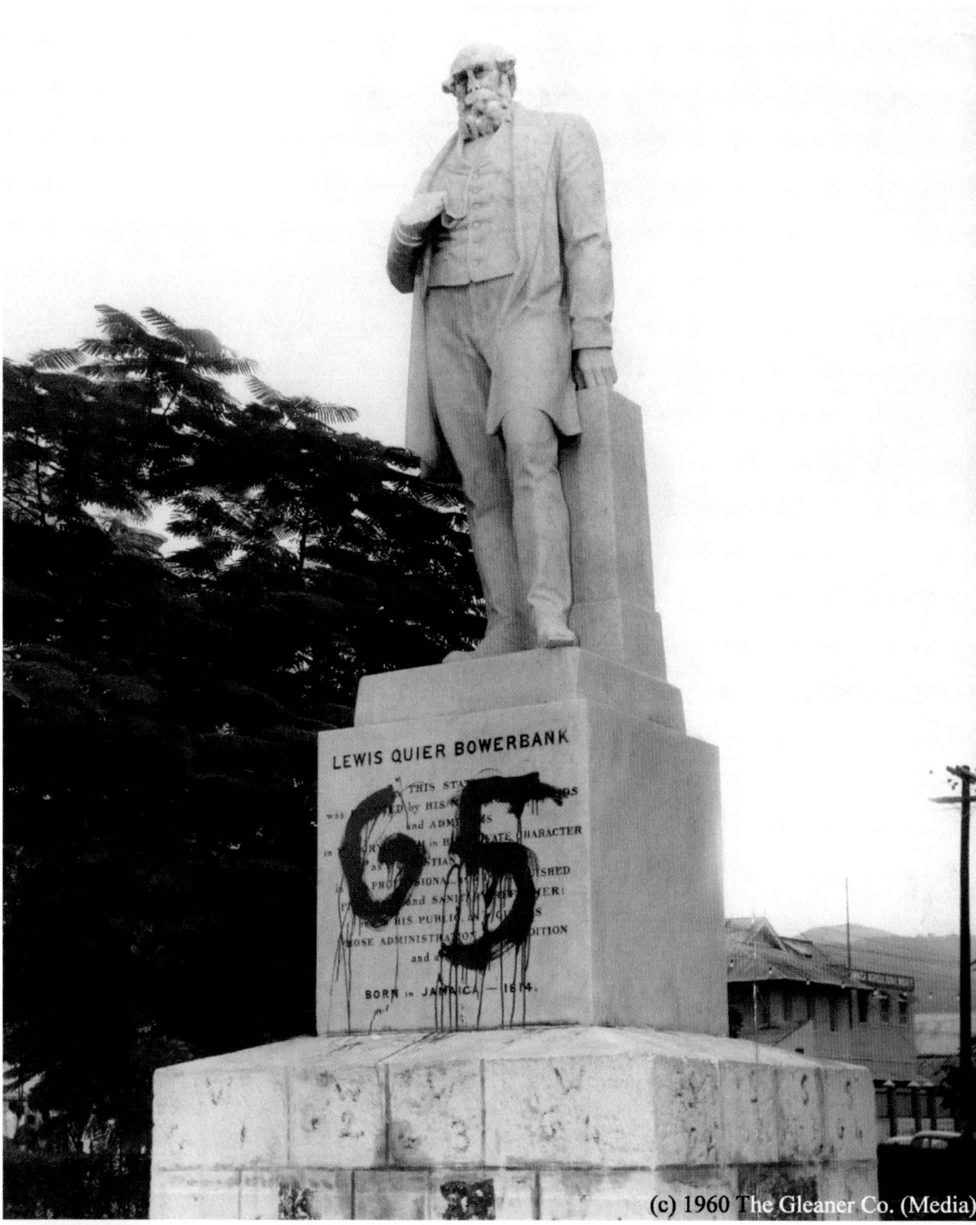

4.15 Defaced statue of Lewis Quier Bowerbank in Queens Park, Kingston, Jamaica, 1962. Photographer unknown. *Jamaica Gleaner*.

The reprisals were immediate and horrific. According to a description from the National Library of Jamaica:

> On the advice of Lewis Bowerbank, Governor [Edward John] Eyre declared martial law and had George William Gordon arrested in Kingston (even though he had no direct involvement in the events of that day) and taken by ship to Morant Bay. There, Gordon was tried and sentenced to death for treason. On Monday 23 October, he was hanged from the centre arch of the burnt out courthouse. Two days later, Bogle and his chief lieutenants were taken and suffered the same fate. . . . Over 430 men and women were killed or sentenced to death by court martial for their alleged involvement in the affair, thousands whipped and harassed and over 1000 homes burnt.[75]

One hundred years later, amid pre- and postindependence historical revision, and in the wake of the dedication of a new monument to Gordon, Bogle, and the 430 people who were massacred, those who now had a voice registered a different view of Bowerbank. The conversation centered on his statue in Victoria Park.

In 1960, two years before Jamaica's independence from Britain, the Kingston and St. Andrew Corporation (KSAC) proposed that Bowerbank's statue be removed from the Parade. But an editorialist in the *Daily Gleaner* rejected this suggestion and reminded Kingston's mayor:

> The statues of a free country indicate the course of its history and the heroes it has revered—or reviled—at different times. Under a dictatorship the erection of statues may be an attempt to falsify history, by representing as a hero of the people, someone to whom most of them object; when the regime is overthrown, it will be natural to regard the statues of the dictator as symbols of tyranny and to remove them or destroy them on the spot. . . . To remove his statue as one unworthy of his place is to impose on 1881 the ideas of today—that is, to lie about 1881.[76]

Here, colonialism is a benevolent force, its legacy both intact and distinct from contemporary realities. The editorialist chides readers for residual bitterness over long-past events and reminds them that Bowerbank was an "earnest medical reformer" and product of his times. He proposes that the blame should instead fall on Governor Eyre, who had made such "a pitiful showing as Governor."[77] There is no acknowledgment of the statue's or colonial government's role in Bowerbank's public redemption or the power of memory and changing cultural currents in the making of history.

It is indisputable that Bowerbank's nineteenth-century reform of the mental health system had less bearing on those who controlled the discourse in 1960 than did his participation in the events at Morant Bay in 1865.[78] If history both reflects and itself adopts a position, then this moment marks the articulation of a new site defined by shifting terrains of power, meaning, and memory. In June 1961, the Ministry of Health denied the KSAC Council's recommendation to relocate the statue from Victoria Park to Bellevue Hospital. In recording this development, the *Daily Gleaner* reported, "The suggestion that the statue should be moved was first raised last December, after the statue which now stands in the Victoria Park was painted and defaced on the 95th anniversary of Gordon's death last October." Although the council dutifully petitioned the hospital, its members' private sentiments were probably best expressed by the irrepressible A. Samuels, who suggested that the "Foreshore Road dump was perhaps the most suitable place for the statue."[79]

For almost a year, Bowerbank's statue remained in place, emblazoned with the number "65," which someone had spray-painted in red on its pedestal to mark the year Bowerbank encouraged the governor to arrest William Gordon, paving the way for his execution. Amid public debate, no action was taken to remove the graffiti and restore the statue, though a directive had been issued to do so. By December 1961, KSAC consigned the removal decision and process to the National Trust, and was "emphatic that any suggestion for placing the statue on any public lot, or in any public road or square would be unacceptable." The statue's fate hung in limbo as council members registered indifference and paralysis. In the *Gleaner*'s phrasing, it lingered in the purgatory of the "Too Hard Basket."[80]

Bowerbank's statue was not the only memorial subject to this treatment. The dispute reflected a rising postcolonial discourse that emerged as central to the ongoing decolonial project. In 1970 the KSAC Council proposed replacing the Queen Victoria statue that adorned the Parade with a commemoration of the Right Excellent Alexander Bustamante, independent Jamaica's first prime minister. Again, a critic from the *Daily Gleaner* weighed in to warn that such an act would signal that "Jamaica is trying to re-write history, to pretend Jamaica has just been invented." He alleged that replacing one monument with another "suggests that this land

and people have no previous history, so bent upon swiftly and unimaginatively creating an explanation for the entity that is Jamaica."[81] The author also cautioned that "a statue is a symbolic expression of history as seen at a particular time."[82] But the intervention was too little too late. The day before the article appeared in print, the *Daily Gleaner* published a photograph of two workers busily installing Bustamante's statue in the place formerly occupied by Queen Victoria. It is still there today.

While Jamaica chose to deinstall colonial figures and replace them with postindependence national heroes, Martinique, still a department of France, traversed a different narrative path. In 1991, during the last decade of Aimé Césaire's spectacular run as mayor of Fort-de-France (1945–2001), a statue installed in 1859 to honor the Martinique-born French Empress Josephine was attacked, decapitated, and emblazoned with the phrase "Respe ba Matinik. Respe ba 22 Mai" (Respect Martinique. Respect May 22). This defiant act recalls Suzanne Césaire's play *Youma, aurore de la liberté* (1952), a work that also countered France's emancipation narrative, which sets the date as March 31, 1848.[83] Many Martinicans believed that this official temporalization denied the role of the slave-led rebellion in securing freedom. After the 1991 attack, the statue was left as is. No effort was made to clean, repair, or restore it. The head remained missing. The marks of the defiant action were left intact as an archive of protest and another chapter in the island's history. The statue is now an empty plinth, following its complete destruction in 2020, during global protests in the wake of American George Floyd's death at the hands of police—presenting yet another chapter in the unfolding of monuments, public memory, and counternarratives in the Caribbean.

These events and conversations coexist with the mythologies of paradise and plantation marketed in tourist economies and redeployed by Cattelan in the 6th Caribbean Biennial. But they face different directions. Despite the colonial power dynamics imposed by tourism, I argue, complex external and internal discourses have altered the Caribbean screen. As Brathwaite noted, "Models after all appear at the abstract zone of our spectrum, continuum; that if they do not change, the reality they seek to explain nevertheless changes around them."[84] Today, the entire Caribbean has abandoned "Ivy and Mister Peter" imagery in tourist promotions. For Jamaica, the concept of national heroes has enabled figures such as Nanny of the Maroons to center discussions on the role of women in Jamaican society and historically rooted intraisland conflicts.[85] In Haiti, in the weeks after the Duvalier regime finally collapsed, "the statue of Christopher Columbus presiding over the harbor of Port-au-Prince was seized and thrown into the sea by persons unknown, who left fastened on the empty pedestal a sheet of paper with a simple scrawled message: 'Pa de blans en Hayti' [Goodbye to white people in Haiti]."[86] These are all examples of spectacular acts of authorship. But rewriting history in the Caribbean can also be devastatingly quiet, weaponized as neglect unfolding over a period of decades.

In his video performance and accompanying documentation *Repairwork* (2007), Blue Curry performs multiple roles, including that of historian. He relays that in 1861, HRH Prince Alfred made his first royal visit to The Bahamas during a tour of his transatlantic colonies. The event was marked by three days of festivities and inaugurated the annual "Prince Alfred Day," subsequently celebrated as a public holiday. An inscription was carved into the iconic caves of New Providence in his honor, and the site of his embarkation was named Prince Alfred's Landing. Five years later, the prince became the Duke of Edinburgh, and the Bahamian Parliament commissioned a bust for permanent installation at the Nassau Public Library.

The following year, the duke sat for sculptor Charles Bacon, who created a marble bust reportedly held in such esteem that it was displayed at the ninety-ninth exhibition of the Royal Academy of Arts in London. When the bust arrived in Nassau and was unveiled, Governor Rawson William Rawson deemed it a "good likeness," and a celebratory regatta and ball were held to mark the occasion. With similar pomp and circumstance, the bust was officially installed at the library. It was subsequently relocated when the library moved to its current site, a former jail, just behind the Houses of Parliament.

In 1910, a decade after the duke's death, "Prince Alfred Day" was quietly removed from the roster of public holidays. Yet his bust remained dusted and on permanent display at the library through two world wars, the age of bootlegging, the Duke of Windsor's appointment as governor, labor unrest and the Burma Road Riots of the 1940s, the 1958 general strike, the fight for women's suffrage and its ratification in 1962, the majority rule movement of the 1960s, and the march to Bahamian independence in 1973. Until something happened.

As Curry documents, in the 1980s, "Eli and Reds" visited the library and inscribed their names into the duke's face. By 2001, when Curry first noticed the bust, it was sitting on the floor of the library's verandah, decapitated, and splattered with paint, presumably after a renovation. In 2005 Shawndell@hellokitty.com visited the library and posted an image of the bust online with the tag, "A statue of a man beside himself! True subject unknown." In 2007 Curry "restored" the bust, which had by that time been placed atop a table on the library's verandah, dragged in blue eye makeup, and adorned with a penciled-in moustache and eyebrows. He reattached the head with duct tape and documented the process and the bust's history in his film (figures 4.16 and 4.17). While beyond the temporal scope of this text, the artist's contemporary intervention via the evidentiary qualities of documentary film embodies the spirit and intent of the artists centered in this book.

As a synecdoche for colonialism, the bust's subjection to the intertwined processes of neglect and forgetting concretizes a silence, a refusal to see, that can be read as a speech act that communicates what is valued as memory and becomes art, visual, or cultural history in the present. This achievement bypasses the traditional colonial archive to document an absented perspective that is at the same time irreducibly historical. Through aesthetic intervention, *Repairwork* marks the presence of and shifts in postcolonial consciousness across space and time.

These permutations are co-resident with recent historical preservation efforts, ironically fueled by native desire and to some degree by tourists' dissatisfaction with the perceived homogeneity and superficiality of their experience. They include the restoration and preservation of slave quarters on Bonaire and Nassau, the restoration of Port Royal in Jamaica, and the restoration and erection of national museums and galleries of art in Bermuda, The Bahamas, Cuba, and throughout the region. These recalibrations in the region's screen shun romanticization and mythologies and have become occasions for the Caribbean to confront and reflect on its past, providing opportunities to see itself beyond the limiting narratives of colonial histories.

A SPIRAL RETELLING

In 1999 Maurizio Cattelan performed the 6th Caribbean Biennial. Curator Jens Hoffmann would later explain that to make their point, they "wanted to find the biggest stereotype of an exotic holiday place." Enter the Caribbean. Using the tourism frame, artist and curator exploited the region's entangled perception as both paradise and plantation to render it

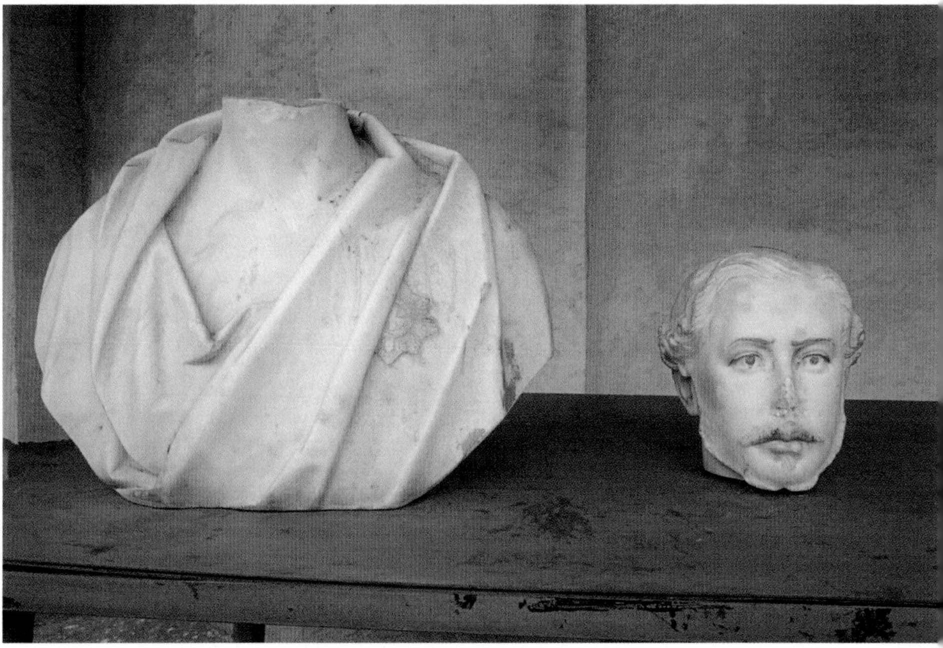

4.16 Blue Curry, *Repairwork*, 2007. Still. Courtesy of the artist.

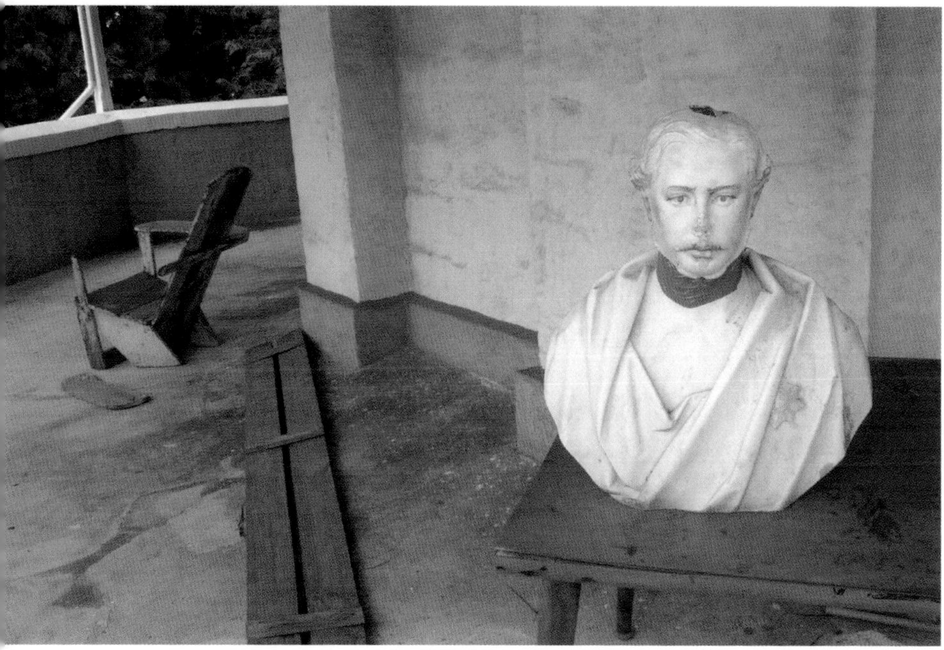

4.17 Blue Curry, *Repairwork*, 2007. Still. Courtesy of the artist.

as a blank slate for the colonizing imagination. It was a deeply cynical project situated within (yet theoretically in contradistinction to) an art world shifting in tremendously unsettling ways for some.

In framing and documenting the performance, Cattelan reasoned that "increasingly globalization and new 'peripheral' biennials such as La Habana, Johannesburg, or Istanbul" were problems because they "are putting into question that exhibition model." As "artist knight" and defender of "good art," he questioned how recent downturns in the global economy had impacted "art centers in America and Europe and the rise of so-called voices from the margins," such that "artists from countries that have been sidelined as secondary and unimportant, are receiving attention in the art world arena." But rather than see this shift in positive terms or attribute it to talent or ingenuity, Cattelan read the artists' rise as the result of "racist paternalism," global economics run amok, and the appropriation of subaltern voices. His ability to produce a biennial in a somewhere-nowhere like the Caribbean was not only proof of this assertion but also evidence of the biennial form's lack of meaning and import. The 6th Caribbean Biennial was Cattelan's "declaration of indignation, retaliation, and endless anger." Following Prospero's playbook, he was there to save art and the market through his critical intervention and material presence.

Cattelan's colonial gaslighting has played to decisively mixed reviews, both at the time and in the years since. The event has been described as navel-gazing and white tears. His overt reprimand of the new biennials was read as completely disingenuous; after all, his own success depended in part on the form. Following the Columbus and Prospero prototypes, the contemporary Italian artist redrew hierarchical and value-based geographical distinctions between center and periphery in lieu of engaging the artists from the rising margins who were dissolving them.

In its concluding pages, without breaking character, Cattelan postulates: "The Caribbean Biennial is an institution, admittedly of Western persuasion, and for this very reason it is imperative that it ask basic questions about the coexistence of cultures. What must continue today is the flow of information from the margins of the community back into the mainstream, so that western institutions may benefit from these innovative experiments and move towards an even greater openness."[87] It's unclear whether this benediction is meant to be tongue-in-cheek or marks the performance as a painful and extended one-liner. For whose benefit was the event enacted and at whose expense? Cattelan's words reawaken what Stuart Hall describes as the "trauma of the colonial experience," a grotesque disfigurement resident not in the actions, bodies, or minds of the colonized but in those of the colonizer.

The performance demonstrated how the region *had* been "positioned and subjected in the dominant regimes of representation" and the extent to which the process of Othering employed by the artist was a "critical exercise of cultural power and normalization."[88] Its conclusion sought to reaffirm the perceived periphery's service as a feeder society for dominant cultures and economies, where colonial presence is interpreted as benevolence and the colonized are infantilized and unseen except through the colonizer's screens or epistemes. That one of the artist-produced works included a postcard of St. Kitts featuring artists in the landscape secures the project's limits and the colonial narcissism at the heart of its critical pose (figure 4.18).

The region's deployment as screen reflects a persistent perception of the Caribbean in global art historical discourses during the 1990s: as lacking internal direction and as located outside "Western" time, unaware of and unaffected by continental epistemological machines of modernism and postmodernism. In this schema, a primitive cultural space can only mimic and provide the backdrop for high art; it cannot itself philosophically generate art. According to the centers of power that determined global art trends at the time, the Caribbean was a dream and Caribbean art a misnomer. As mime and mirror, Cattelan's 6th Caribbean Biennial embodied the art world's self-imposed blinders to global currents and ingenuity. It unmasked the dis-ease concerning what was already in motion by 1999: the inevitable decentering of the West's linear historical formation and authorial claim over artistic processes and media, conceptual approaches, the notion of the avant-garde, market strength, and, in a word, power.

The biennial also revealed the threat posed by the Caribbean artists who had fully emerged in global circles by 1999. Unified approaches to form, style, and medium and ties to specific nationalized geographic spaces that were once used to define legibility in and to the so-called mainstream could not be imposed on the contemporary work of these artists. They claimed intersectional identities, labored beyond national borders, deployed Caribbean histories and culture as content and concept, and enacted representational and rhetorical innovations. They did not just see

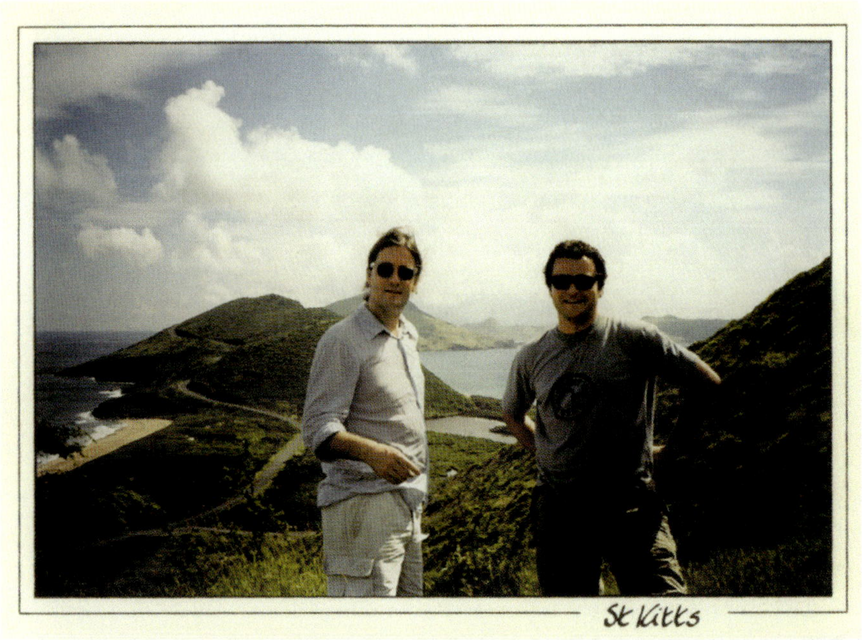

4.18 Postcard of Olafur Eliasson and Tobias Rehberger, standing in front of a sweeping view of St. Kitts.

themselves as historical interventions but as actors fully capable of *making* history in and through their work. Employing a new language of contemporaneity, they negated conventional understandings of authorship, studio, medium, object, and nationalism to reworld a world where Caribbean art unbound would be immanent and visible. It is not without irony that ultimately the Caribbean completely ignored the 6th Caribbean Biennial. Cattelan was right—the Caribbean he had imagined did not exist.

CONCLUSION

"Wrong Way" Lenny, Tempests, and Other Détournements

> Decoloniality means first to delink (to detach) from that overall structure of knowledge in order to engage in an epistemic reconstitution.
>
> WALTER MIGNOLO

> People deprived of their history can make up their own, and what better job can there be for an artist shifting through the anxieties of a Post-Colonial society, where the divide between myth and actual experience often disintegrates and we find ourselves in a unique contemporary space.
>
> IRÉNÉE SHAW

As Maurizio Cattelan was preparing for his journey to St. Kitts, a strong, late-season hurricane was coalescing in the Caribbean Sea. Ill-fated and unprecedented, the storm did not move east to west, as hurricanes typically do, but rather performed an ecological détournement by proceeding in reverse. It was dubbed "Wrong Way" Lenny, and just days after Cattelan and his artists arrived, it wreaked havoc and menace on the island. St. Kitts was assailed by 20-foot waves that extended 600 feet inland, causing flooding and more than $40 million in damage. Island residents were confined to their homes, and the visiting artists to their hotel. This tempest's extraordinary path wryly suggested that in the Caribbean, nature could mount its own decolonial event.

Like "Wrong Way" Lenny, this book détournes. It contests art historical epistemes and the critical archive by focusing on global Caribbean artists who emerged in problem spaces that sought to minimize their presence and marginalize their work. Mirroring Césaire's recasting of Caliban and reconception of *The Tempest* from a philosophical, ethical, and methodological perspective, I reengage the work produced in the 1990s to probe its contours and provocations in ways that seemed contemporaneously impossible. My consideration of a relatively small sample highlights and juxtaposes the massive output of a venerable generation of artists whose oeuvres boldly grapple with history, enacting what Walter Mignolo has described as "epistemic reconstitution," thus repositioning a global Caribbean imaginary as a center of regard.

Inspired by T. J. Clark's methodology, this book examines the social context of artistic creation and relies on Caribbean theorists active during twentieth-century colonial, decolonial, independence, and postindependence periods to shape it. These figures provided the critical and intellectual foundation for Caribbean studies and the corpus that shaped the interventions of the artists considered in this text, aesthetic theoreticians of nonlinear art histories. Their work was also foundational in my transition from artist to curator and art historian.

At the University of Chicago in the mid-1990s, I enrolled in the seminar "Other Modernisms," taught by newly minted art historian Paul Rogers. The class addressed seminal questions I'd been unable to articulate in my Western survey–oriented art history classes: *What about the rest of the world? What about my world?* As we studied modernism's global eruptions—in Egypt, Sudan, and Nigeria for example—it became clear that modernism did not belong to the West; that it, in fact, marked a creative catalysis that was replicated and generated across spaces and beyond linear time.

Until this encounter, I had been taught a single story, a story I loved but was simultaneously unsettled by. The seminar's rhizomatic conceptualization of art history opened ways of seeing that stamped my critical lens and the landscape of my work. Like Janine Antoni, I responded to this awakening by scouring institutional libraries for resources related to Caribbean modernism and the art histories of the Americas outside the United States, as well as those of Africa and its diasporas. Aside from a few artist biographies and survey-based exhibition catalogues, there was scant engagement.

Library materials on a single figure like Picasso dwarfed the available scholarship on broad swaths of the world. Eventually, my pursuit led me to a short essay entitled "Searching for a Way Out," by the Trinidadian artist Christopher Cozier, published in 1994 in the *Massachusetts Review*.

As Latamie, Antoni, Duval-Carrié, and Ayón entered global spaces in the 1990s, Cozier, a member of the same generation, détourned. After living in New Jersey and New York for several years, he felt compelled to return to the Caribbean.[1] Warned by his mentors Joan Semmel and Leon Golub not to go back to the region, where they believed he would face oblivion, Cozier and his wife, the artist Irénée Shaw, nonetheless made the move. The decision to return to Trinidad was the first step on what he humorously describes as a rocky path filled with broken bottles and spiders. However, the return propelled him into becoming one of the most influential artists of his generation.

Once he was back in Port of Spain, Trinidad, Cozier's practice transformed. No doubt, this new-again problem space demanded something different than when he had first left it. While Shaw had found her métier in painting and continued working in that medium, Cozier moved from painting monumental canvases engaging the sonic energy of carnival (figure C.1) to conceptual art, installation, sound, sculpture, performance, film, writing, and curation—engaging whatever medium, process, or form best served his emergent ideas.

He also began to write art criticism centered on work being made on the island. Between 1989 and 1994, at the invitation of Lloyd Best, he contributed a monthly column to the *Trinidad and Tobago Review*. And between 1994 and 1996, Cozier wrote occasionally for the *Trinidad Guardian*, the periodical that had published his first piece of writing after his return to Trinidad. This archive reveals his pervasive and authentic concern with the island's arts ecosystem. He called out its commerce, which, he believed, disadvantaged artists and, at times, took advantage of them. He criticized the timidity he witnessed in the work of artists whom he characterized as making pictures. He hailed the efforts of artists like Wendy Nanan, John Stollmeyer, Susie Dayal, and Francisco Cabral, whose work stimulated and brought clarity to his own critical practice. These articles shone a light on a small but growing group of sculptors, performance artists, and conceptual artists working in Trinidad and across the Caribbean, a group that now also included Cozier.

In the early nineties, he began exhibiting a series of works that by 1995 had become known collectively as the Cultural Autopsy Series. *Conversation*

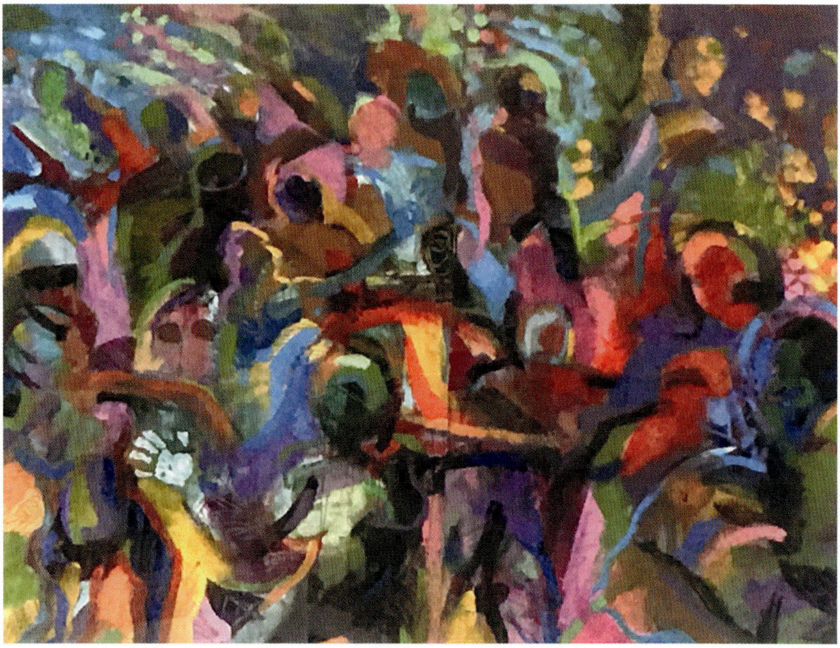

C.1 Christopher Cozier, Untitled, ca. 1985. Acrylic on paper, 6 × 8 ft. Private collection. Photographed by Erica Moiah James.

with a Shirt Jac (1991); the extended performance, video, and sculpture work *Blue Soap* (1994); and *Art and Nation: Things We Must Learn from Day 1* (ca. 1997) became key pieces in the series (figures C.2 and C.3).[2] *Conversation with a Shirt Jac* began as a performance piece in which Cozier literally sits in a red chair and speaks to a sartorial icon of male, University of the West Indies–trained teachers, public servants, priests, politicians, and nationalists—the Shirt Jac—positioning it as synecdoche for the independence generation, his parent's generation. In Cozier's words the performance "was a way of defining the relationship of people of my generation to the discourses of the nationalist agenda with its ideas of social responsibility and its cultural conventions such as a romance with revolutionary languages and/or stances."[3] It asked the public to consider postindependence ideas regarding "respectability vs reputation" and the friction between "middle class ascendancy and privilege" and the simultaneous desire to retain "'grassroots' populist viability" through a kind of problematic "bad man" masculinity. Such direct provocation in Caribbean art at the time was unusual.

Other seemingly ordinary icons of the nation-building period also appear in the series, such as the classroom blackboard, the crested school shirt, the tamarind whip used to discipline students, sliced bread, and blue soap. In this expanding group of works, Cozier continually posed critical questions of his audiences and engaged in ongoing conversation with his publics around the promise, disappointments, and potentialities of independence and nationhood. In each case he pushed against simple readings, choosing to press toward the harder work of nuance, complexity, and critical awareness rather than resolution. The series showcases the evolving visual language through which his mature practice enunciates. Everyday items register a rising tide of doubt about the promise of the region's postrevolutionary and postindependent nations.

Blue Soap was the first extended performance and video piece exhibited in Trinidad. Each scene plays on the increasingly layered significations of blue soap, in which its ubiquitous use before Trinidad's independence was gradually supplanted by imported commodities that became associated with postindependence modernity and middle-class aspirations. As parapraxis, the work points to multiple issues, ranging from women's fate in postindependence Trinidad to the ongoing colonial value systems upheld by so-called Afro-Saxons. *Blue Soap*'s broad, ambivalent character is tempered by moments of Caliban-like clarity—none more powerful than one toward the end of the performance when the main female character quotes Octavio Paz's poetry as she destroys her oppressors, declaring "I am a history, a memory that invents itself!"[4] In layered and compelling ways, through this work Cozier uncovers the romance of creolization and postcolonialism, simultaneously gesturing to the ongoing need for the intentional yet persistently nuanced work of decolonization.

In "Searching for a Way Out," Cozier echoed Caliban's speech of recognition to Prospero as he articulated and unpacked the challenges faced by contemporary global Caribbean artists in the wake of Peter Minshall's debut of ManCrab in the Trinidad Carnival of 1984 (figure C.4). The sculptural form and character of ManCrab dominates the penultimate scene in Minshall's epic mas *The River* (discussed in chapter 1), where, according to Cozier, Minshall uses Carnival "as a raw material, a form, to express himself; to animate *our* theatrical sensibility. [The work] dared to say that as a society, *we* had a point of view and a vital means to express it; a voice." In the article, he positioned Minshall's work as a plateau in contemporary art that demanded consideration by all artists who identified as Caribbean. Although they faced "conditions of value and understanding [that] are

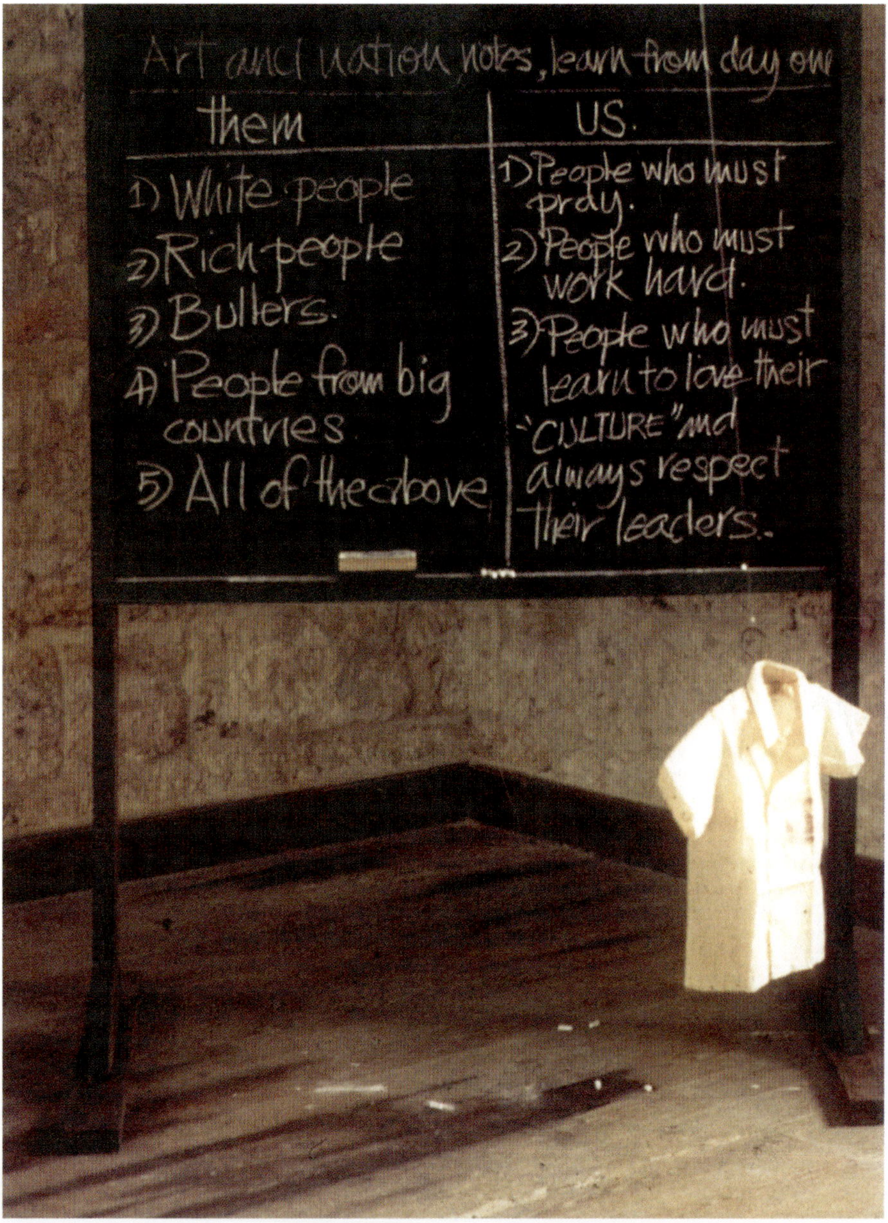

C.2 Christopher Cozier, *Art and Nation: Things We Must Learn from Day 1*, ca. 1997. Cultural Autopsy Series. Courtesy of the artist.

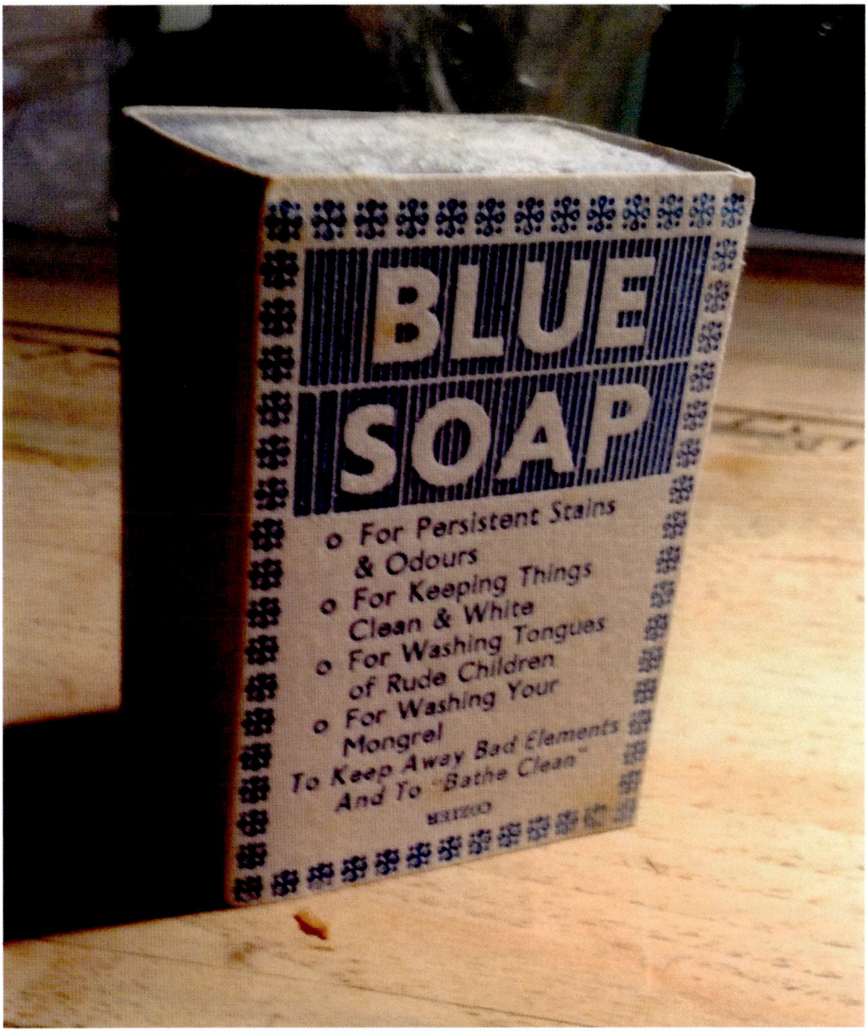

C.3 Christopher Cozier, *Blue Soap*, 1994. Cultural Autopsy Series. Courtesy of the artist.

never asserted by [them]," and although their "work may at best be seen as a coy or gratuitous attempt to render a prescribed form, their flotsam, or at worst an anthropological artifact, perpetually 'representative,'" although their art is continuously read as "the product of a[n already known] context rather than that of an individual," and although the "real meaning, the life of the work is never approached," ManCrab as epic art form signaled that these assessments had been imposed on Caribbean art and artists, and revealed them as lies. Minshall's work illumes the colonizing, limiting, and purposefully totalizing premise that my project seeks to contest. Heeding Cozier's call, I work to build a context within which Caribbean art is seen on its own terms and Caribbean art and artists are "allowed to speak."[5]

As Cozier explored the work of a growing number of artists whose processes and output reflected the ingenuity demanded of daily life in the region, he noted that practitioners like Minshall, John Stollmeyer, Guy Beckles, and Francisco Cabral were working expansively with everyday and unconventional materials, obtained from hardware stores or scoured from the streets, that bore specific local histories and significations. Uninterested in making pretty paintings or sculptures, these artists produced visceral art shored from the island's detritus that both registered and at times satirized contemporary conditions. The article affirmed that Cozier's generation was doing the exact work he longed for, within a global archipelago he would come to recognize, occupy, and cultivate.

Four years after "Searching for a Way Out" was published, Cozier began working with David Scott and his team at *Small Axe*, an academic journal focused on the Caribbean and based at Columbia University. Cozier encouraged the editors to attend more purposefully to Caribbean art. Two months before Cattelan's biennial, *Small Axe* devoted an issue to visual art and globalism debates.[6] The editors, who now included Cozier, cited the many Caribbean nations that had significantly invested in arts institutions during the postcolonial era, noting recent phenomena that bore evidence of their impact. They called attention to the seminal AICA (Association Internationale des Critiques d'Art) meeting in Barbados in 1998; the all-female artist exhibition *Lip, Sticks and Marks*, mounted in Barbados and Trinidad that year; the publication of Thames and Hudson's *Caribbean Art* (1998) by Veerle Poupeye; *Carivista* (1998), organized by the Barbados Art Museum and Big River Workshop (Trinidad and Tobago), in collaboration with CCA7 (Caribbean Contemporary Art Space 7, founded in Trinidad and Tobago in 1997); and the Triangle Workshop in England. They also cited the 24th São Paulo Biennial (1998), curated by Virginia Pérez

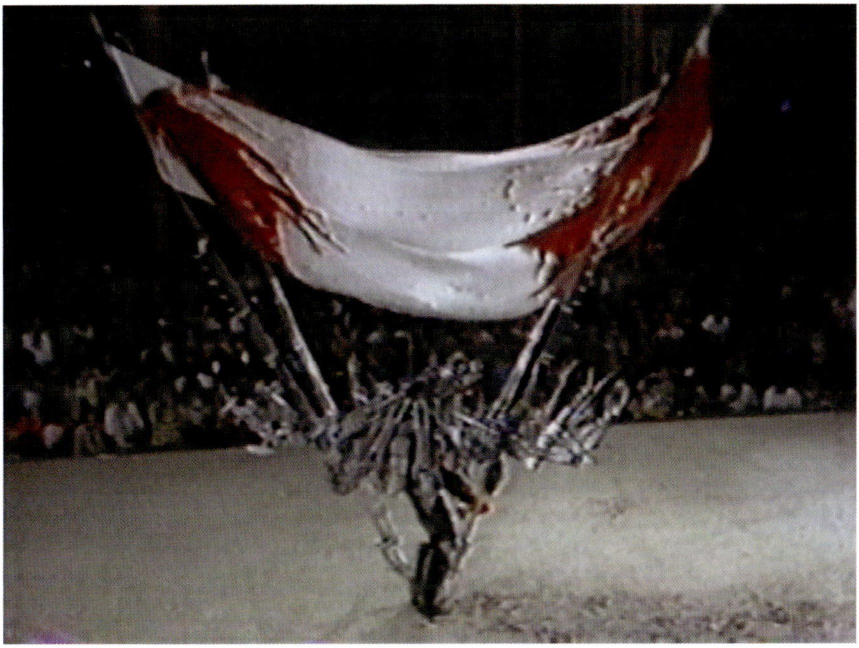

C.4 Peter Minshall, ManCrab from the mas *The River*, 1983. Still from Carnival main stage footage. Trinidad Tobago Television (TTT).

Ratton and featuring a number of Caribbean artists; the Havana Biennials of 1991, 1994, and 1997; and countless exhibitions mounted by local artists in every global Caribbean space on both sides of the Atlantic. The special issue argued cogently that the Caribbean and the hemispheric south were animate and fertile creative spaces. Alongside transformative events occurring in the United States, it was clear that the art world's boundaries were being pervasively challenged and redrawn.

Cozier's response to this turning tide in the special issue of *Small Axe* was entitled "Between Narratives and Other Spaces."[7] In the article, he contended that nationalist art histories followed the monument theory of history, which served to deprive art of its animate and critical engagement and limit its significations in global spaces. His perspective situated the contemporary Caribbean artist in a familiar position: resisting a so-called postcolonial frame eerily similar to the one they had only recently transcended.

As an artist critical of national narratives and international styles in the 1980s and 1990s, Cozier challenged their linearity and assumed indexicality, and dramatized the interstices between personal and collective expression.

Reflecting on the period he said, "I felt as if I was in motion between two non-discernable points," interested in making "Art or representation that doesn't just display us, but rather what we or at least one of us might be thinking."[8] He openly questioned whether the absence of sustained critical inquiry in and about the region had rendered it incapable of issuing a more forceful global defense of its art. Yet he simultaneously marveled at the diverse ways Caribbean (as opposed to Trinidadian, Jamaican, or Cuban) artists turned inward to native and folk cultures and regional histories to invert postcolonial markers of local authenticity for more expansive possibilities. As he continued to develop in his practice within a broader concept of "Caribbean," Cozier realized that the tendency to organize the art world into center and peripheries, us and them, was also a construct designed to control the terrain; quietly he acknowledged, "*There is no 'them' out there.*"[9]

The beauty of creolization is found not only in what it pulls together but also in what it breaks apart and thus ushers in. Cozier's generation forged genuinely global relationships and practices. Their work testifies to the undeniable fact that Caribbean art has always been made "in many places at once . . . wherever Caribbean people have settled and continue to imagine and respond to the world around them."[10] To creolize art history while attending to this work comes with a promise that something beautiful will be ushered in.

THE GLOBAL CARIBBEAN: A UNIQUE CONTEMPORARY SPACE

In the early aughts I returned to The Bahamas to help establish the National Art Gallery of The Bahamas, where I served as its founding director and chief curator. With an unusually vibrant local art scene, most contemporary work did not push beyond market expectations and thus nestled comfortably within the consumable and respectable genre of postcolonial impressionism. Many local artists expressed frustration at the critical and creative limitations this market imposed.

To cultivate a broader community for Bahamian artists that would challenge their thinking and expand their creative processes, I worked to foster dialogue between local artists and others practicing in what I increasingly regarded as a global Caribbean and turned to Christopher Cozier for help.

Since the 1990s, he had continued to publish, curate, and expand his professional art practice. This achievement was well represented in a then-recent series of installations of the work *Attack of the Sandwich Men*, in which he manipulated an icon of postcolonial societies—sliced-bread sandwiches—wrapped them in wax paper, pierced them with miniature Trinidadian flags, and arranged them in a neat grid reminiscent of military and classroom formations. In this juxtaposition, Cozier vivified how a simple symbol of modernity, namely, access to commercially produced sliced bread, became a means to foster division among the people. His ability to mobilize material and form to critical effect had remained strong, and I invited him to inaugurate the dialogue the art community urgently needed.

Cozier began his visit by sharing his concerns, processes, and work in a gallery talk. It was left to attending artists to decide whether they wanted to meet with him one-on-one. From the moment he completed his presentation at the National Art Gallery, Cozier was in conversation. He met with artists of every stripe, from the Sunday painter to dedicated artists. After the fifth day of nonstop meetings, he was exhausted. I was elated.

His engagement with the community of artists working in Nassau lit a match that has not abated in the years since. Cozier's visit was followed by talks and studio visits from an array of artists and curators, including Peter Minshall, LeRoy Clarke, Ras Ishi Butcher, Ras Akyem Ramsay, and Veerle Poupeye, to name just a few.

Building on these connections, in the following years, the gallery led group trips to regional art events such as the Havana Biennial; Art Basel, Miami; and CARIFESTA, Guyana (2008). For many artists who joined these trips, being in another "Caribbean" country was new and powerfully demystifying, a means to break the colonial imposition of difference that had cultivated a palpable and psychological sense of disconnection among the islands. Broader dialogue with artists and exposure to other regional art spaces opened the critical plane and allowed artists to see their work in relation to the Caribbean and the rest of the world.

In Guyana, Kishan Munroe, Blue Curry, John Cox, and Alan Wallace shared their work with audiences at Castellani House. Groups of traveling artists attended panels featuring Derek Walcott, David Dabydeen, Earl Lovelace, and Austin Clarke. They conversed with such fellow artists and intellectuals as Annalee Davis and Winston Branch and, in the process, reoriented themselves intellectually, historically, and aesthetically beyond the Bahamian frame.

The artists also met the Trinidadian writer Nicholas Laughlin in Guyana. Laughlin, along with Cozier and the architect Sean Leonard, had recently launched "a ting" called Alice Yard, in Leonard's grandmother's yard in Port of Spain. The idea for the space emerged following the closure of Caribbean Contemporary Art Space 7 (CCA7), launched with great expectations in Port of Spain in 1997 by a small group that included Cozier, Charlotte Elias, and two renowned British artists then living on the island, Chris Ofili and Peter Doig. By the early 2000s, however, CCA7 had discontinued operations, leaving an institutional vacuum on the island, which Alice Yard came to fill. Like CCA7, the Yard was interested in cultivating Caribbean contemporary art in conversation with the world. It was a small space, committed to big ideas.

After CARIFESTA 2008, Alice Yard invited Blue Curry, Heino Schmid, and other artists, along with art historians and curators, including me, to spend time thinking and working at the Yard. It was there that I met the Nigerian artist Bright Eke. Trained under El Anatsui, Eke was, when we met, in the Yard piecing together discarded plastic bottles to create massive sculptural objects grounded in his formal training and ethical concern for the environment. Embodying Alice Yard's function as a site of catalysis, Eke's work spurred my interest in African diasporic environmental art, which has since become a key part of my pedagogical and research practice.

Alice Yard's work in cultivating contemporary global Caribbean art practices specifically, and the interconnectedness of global art practices more generally, has been extraordinary. It exemplifies the important role a growing transnational network of small, often artist-led nongovernmental concerns has played in the cultivation of contemporary global Caribbean art. This list includes Alice Yard's project space Granderson Labs, a revitalized Le Centre d'Art in Haiti, Instituto Buena Bista (IBB) in Curaçao, The Current in Nassau, Fresh Milk Barbados, Tembe Art Studio in Suriname, NLS (New Local Space, Ltd.) Kingston, Ruby Cruel–London, the virtual space Tilting Axis, and many others. Working across languages and national boundaries, these organizations encourage experimentation, innovation, and curation while nurturing community, connection, and sustained critical conversations. These spaces embody the postcolonial hope and liberatory work of Césaire by crafting what Irénée Shaw describes collectively as "unique contemporary spaces."

Global Caribbean artists emerging in the 1990s imagined a story generated and resident beyond Shakespeare's Caliban. Their work precipitated ongoing détournements within the discipline of art history. I had the pleasure of hearing Kamau Brathwaite speak in a series of intimate settings in the early 2000s. The talks were capped by a large public lecture in Bridgetown, Barbados, in 2009. Over the course of the decade, Brathwaite often reflected on loss across multiple dimensions: years of work; home; life; his spouse; his archive, due to the combined impact of Hurricane Gilbert, heat, rot, and theft; and the threat of displacement from his family home in Barbados. He spoke of survival, forced migration, and the surfacing of will required to assemble and create from the detritus of ruin. His consistent humility and vulnerability were fortifying and inspiring. These talks transported me to his 1970s essay "Caribbean Man in Space and Time." Presented publicly for the first time just three years after Césaire's *A Tempest* and shortly after CARIFESTA 1972, the piece gestured toward the postcolonial future envisioned by Césaire, Fanon, Wynter, Hall, Glissant, Wilson, Spivak, Lima, Mignolo, and other theorists on whom this text draws. Like his lectures, the essay displayed Brathwaite's intellectual vulnerability. In this text, he considered, reconsidered, reworked, and repositioned not only his subject but his approach to Caribbean arts and scholarship.

"Caribbean Man in Space and Time" is known to live in three published versions.[11] In each version, it models the need for and usefulness of critical détournement as dialogic locus for the artists documented in this study, as well as in the discipline of art history. In the work, Brathwaite dramatizes his internal struggle to articulate a methodology that could account for a Caribbean creative universe beyond binary constructs. When the essay appeared in John Hearne's edited volume for CARIFESTA '76, it documented a clear cognitive shift. Midway through the piece, Brathwaite détournes. He concedes that organizing the Caribbean around binaries, the very approach he had hitherto foregrounded, would ultimately fail, "since binary models are predicated on continuities, and in so doing miss and devalue knowledge found in the discontinuities inherent in Caribbean life and knowledge systems."[12] His willingness to change direction when the critical model he inherited failed him aligns with Césaire's re-vision of the allegorical possibilities of Shakespeare's Caliban. It echoes in a generation of artists who possessed an acute awareness of the way history and art history were generated and their failure to mark a space of regard for their work. It affirms the need to throw off old, ill-fitting models as decolonial action, and encourages the development of new methods through new fields, such as global Caribbean art history.

This text recognizes the Caribbean as a space of generative discontinuities, propelling nonconformity with binaries, notions of purity, and markers of authenticity that predicate value in Western art. Whereas Césaire issued a call for decolonial action, Brathwaite's détournement responded by advancing interdisciplinary, nonlinear, interteleological approaches to Caribbean (art) history.

This book traverses numerous fields of inquiry and endeavor, but at heart, it is a quarrel with the discipline of art history and the boundaries it demarcates in relation to the study of global Caribbean art. By focusing on seminal pieces or small groups of works produced during the 1990s, made by an even smaller group of artists, this text demonstrates the profundity of their contribution in plain sight, despite its relegation to the margins of regard. I chose this constellation of artists because their work articulates varied positions—local and global, historic and contemporary—that compel us to ask: If such a small sampling can generate this depth and range of inquiry, what else must and can we retrieve to calibrate a decolonial gaze in art history?

The book's unconventional structure and methodological range both challenge and sideline epistemological certainties inherent in the notion and practice of disciplinarity. They testify to the ways history itself became a multivalent zone of engagement for decolonizing Caribbean global artists who linked presents and pasts to see the world anew. The generation whose work grounds this text exposed, challenged, and at times disarmed and neutered epistemic, aesthetic, and disciplinary constraints by integrating and animating Caribbean mythologies, narratives, cultural practices, and unofficial histories.

Although the terms *postrevolution*, *postindependence*, and *postcolonial* all suggest conditions that exist in the wake of a transformative event, this text does not view them as equivalent conditions or treat them as unobstructed pathways to visions of freedom prospected by decolonial forebears or contemporaries. David Scott suggests that the word *post* gestures toward an "anti-colonial revolutionary romance" that demands an origin trajecting toward a triumphant, often progressive goal, even though realities of "post-" conditions have slowly squeezed and crushed such aspirations. Seeming to share in this view, many global contemporary Caribbean artists emerging in the 1990s questioned the romantic assumptions of *the post-* and insisted on binding histories with the present in ways that demanded accountability for what had been suppressed or ignored in the problem spaces they chose to occupy. Their work registers decolonization as an ongoing process in the postcolonial turn. Rather than embrace a grand narrative of postcolonial redemption or a totalizing art historical frame based on Western modernism's concept of shared location, community, and formal uniformity, these artists drew on multiple mediums and creolizing processes to rethink past, present, and future. In rejecting overdetermined teleologies, they resisted claims of authenticity and authority and presented creolization itself as a disruptive and creative act.

The groundwork laid in this text reveals the lie at the heart of Cattelan's biennial performance. The critical heft and creative energy of this period's global Caribbean art register his anachronistic pose by evidencing the formal, conceptual, and aesthetic range of what I believe to be the most transformative decade of contemporary art. By evading limiting critical frames and affirming formal and narrative complexity, the artists profiled in this text set the stage for future generations of contemporary global Caribbean artists who will deploy abstract and conceptual languages to explore the Caribbean's unstable presence. In this thinking space, creolizing processes confidently dissemble, misdirect, and obfuscate theoretical limits to transcend them. Here Caribbean-ness is not viewed as a sign of alterity but as a mode of seeing within a critical global imaginary.

Growing up on the island of Grand Bahama, Janine Antoni dreamed of traveling far and wide to move freely through space, beyond the horizon's farthest point, where the sun met the sea. Many years later, just a few months after Cattelan's performance, Antoni returned to her childhood home as a globally recognized artist to reengage the skyline that had framed her youthful visions. She erected two poles, between which she balanced a rope to align with the visible horizon, then filmed herself walking across it—slowly, determined, occasionally unsteady. The performance, entitled *Touch* (2000), was exhibited for the first time in the Caribbean at the Inaugural National Exhibition (INE), which I curated at the newly launched National Art Gallery of The Bahamas in 2003 (figure C.5).[13] Observing the audience, I noticed that, despite the narrative looping, spectators lingered, reliving Antoni's journey across the horizon again and again. Like much of the work discussed in this text, the spatial and temporal heart of the global Caribbean beat through every breath of her piece. Although the film documents her return home, its conceptual punctum is defined by the dream of transcending its narrative and physical frame; Antoni can now walk along the same horizon she once longed to leave behind. With full knowledge of what lay beyond its sight line, Antoni's informed return resonates with Cozier's homecoming and the way it invited him to see differently and articulate relationships from this new scope of vision. He soon recognized that 1990s global Caribbean artists were increasingly adept at understanding themselves in relation to the art world, one made not of fixed points but of sites and practices that they themselves were actively generating and circulating.

The ongoing dematerialization of long-held critical, market, and scholarly boundaries has been key to the rise of contemporary global Caribbean art. In 2003, Tavares Strachan sealed the windows in his dorm room at the Rhode Island School of Design and installed a lamp linked via the internet to a light meter placed atop his parents' home in The Bahamas. It was calibrated to reflect the intensity of sunshine registered by the meter, which shifted as the sun rose, set, or was obscured by clouds. Entitled *Color of the Sun*, the resulting work creates a symphonic experience of light across space and time. A deeply moving, densely layered, and discursively active piece, it cultivates a critical, self-reflexive experience that exceeds the perceptive capacity of closed models and disciplinary frames. It labors in the service of Césaire's post-Caliban future and reflects the work of artists who enunciate themselves unbound by place, singular narratives, specific ideologies, or weaponized notions of race, class, gender, sexuality, or nation. Potent, generative, and beautiful, the light materializes the invisible, casting a much larger critical space than one defined by a physical place. In *Color of the Sun*, the Caribbean enters the conversation as illumination. It is seen, felt, absorbed, and powerful, yet also immaterial and untethered.

In dissolving boundaries between here and there, *Color of the Sun* surfaces the art world's fictive center-margin cartography. For contemporary artists like Strachan, who've built practices on the momentum generated by earlier generations, boundaries have fallen and *there is also no "them" out there*. There is no negation, obfuscation, sidestepping, or softening of the Caribbean in the work of rising contemporary artists; it is always present.

Deborah Anzinger, Firelei Báez, La Vaughn Belle, April Bey, Charles Campbell, Blue Curry, Morel Doucet, Adler Guerrier, Versia Harris, Lucia Hierro, Deborah Jack, Marlon James, Leasho Johnson, Kachelle Knowles, Kandy G. Lopez, Tessa Mars, Carlos Martiel, Jeffrey Meris, Joiri Minaya, Lavar Munroe, Luis Manuel Otero Alcántara, Ada Patterson, Ebony G. Patterson, Kenny Rivero, Asser Saint-Val, Giovanna Swaby, Rodell Warner,

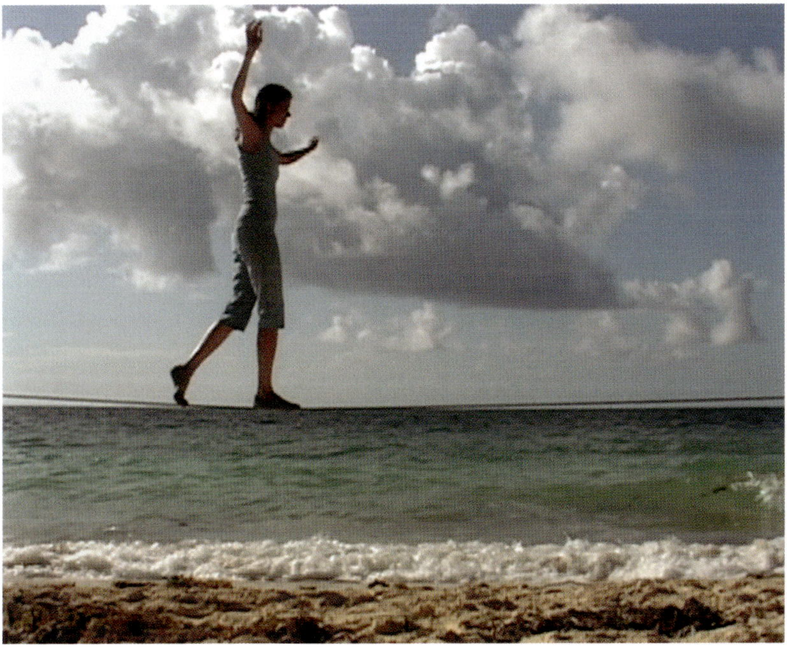

C.5 Janine Antoni, *Touch*, 2000. Still. DVD with Beta master tape. 9.37 minutes.

Cosmo Whyte, Didier William, and many others belong to the waves of contemporary global Caribbean artists who have emerged in the wake of those who first demarcated its imaginary. Some have moved beyond the global to explore the conceptual possibilities of deep space and time, creating new worlds that have sloughed off the vestiges of colonialism and neocolonialism. Strachan led the way, with *Blast Off* (2008–9) and *Orthostatic Tolerance: It Might Not Be Such a Bad Idea If I Never Went Home Again* (2010), but there is also April Bey's ongoing Atlantica series and Gilles Elie Dit-Cosaque's film *Zétwal* (Stars) (2008) to consider. *Zétwal* foretold the possibly real, possibly fictional story of a Martinican handyman named Robert Saint-Rose, who, in the 1970s, sought to build a spaceship from scrap metal to become the first Antillean in space. The film's narrative quickly enters the cosmic mindscape of the imaginary; Saint-Rose's spaceship didn't depend on fossil fuels or nuclear energy but on the philosophical heft of Aimé Césaire's poetry. For artists like Strachan, Bey, and Dit-Cosaque, global or interstellar spaces have emerged as sites of possibility that reside beyond the reach of state power and the domain of national borders and suggest liberation from the weight of slavery, colonialism, and perhaps history itself. Utopian and speculative, these are places of imagination, canvasses of the marvelous, and rhizomatic plateaus that extend the boundaries of human selves and relations.

The decolonial call Caliban issues and the methodology Césaire models forecast the ethos embedded in 1990s global Caribbean art. It is an ethos that extends to our present, affirming art that is expressive but also exploratory, ideational, and theoretical; art capable of centering what was once sidelined by dismantling seemingly intractable epistemes and the West's material, historical, conceptual, and colonial occlusions. It is art that opens up the global imaginary, insisting that art history follows, in ways that have only just begun.

NOTES

INTRODUCTION

Epigraph: Geoffrey Holder, interview with John Lahr, Metropolitan Museum of Art, New York, 2003.

1 Poupeye, "Trading Across the Black Atlantic"; Poupeye, *Caribbean Art*, 1st ed.; Tawadros, *Changing States*; Zaya, "Trading Plots."

2 The event occurred at the Americas Society in New York City, an institution dedicated to expansive engagement with the arts and culture of the Caribbean and the Americas from a postcolonial perspective.

3 I argue that by the 1990s, Caribbean artists of Latamie's generation had far surpassed the allegorical limits and subaltern positionality embodied in the trope of Shakespeare's Caliban, recognizing its patent incapacity to signify Caribbean (postcolonial) futures. Nonetheless, the trope has been employed widely, across disciplines, temporalities, locations, and discourses of colonialism and postcolonialism. The literature and curatorial engagement of this figure in relation to the Caribbean is extensive. Notable examples include Retamar, "Caliban" and "Caliban Revisited," reissued collectively in *Caliban and Other Essays* (1989); Lamming, *Pleasures of Exile*; Hulme, *Colonial Encounters*; Henry, *Caliban's Reason*; Spivak, *Critique of Postcolonial Reason*; López Springfield, *Daughters of Caliban*; Meeks, *Critical Interventions in Caribbean Politics and Theory*; and Jackson, *Creole Indigeneity*. Some of these texts, particularly those of Spivak and Jackson, align with Césaire and openly seek to move beyond Shakespeare's Caliban as trope for all inescapably colonized people.

4 Hall, "Cultural Identity and Diaspora," 24.

5 *Dechoukaj* is a Haitian Kreyòl term meaning "to completely root up and destroy."

6 Linebaugh and Rediker, *The Many-Headed Hydra*.

7 Scott, *Refashioning Futures*, 12.

8 Hulme, *Colonial Encounters*, 108.

9 Hulme, *Colonial Encounters*, 108.

10 Césaire, *Discourse on Colonialism*, 33.

11 Vergès, *Resolutely Black*.

12 Vergès, *Resolutely Black*, 21.

13 Significantly, Vergès cited an introduction Césaire had penned for Daniel Guérin's *Les Antilles Decolonisées* in 1986, which suggested that he was baffled by the persistence of opposition to his advocacy for departmental status based on what had unfolded in the interim. Césaire wrote: "How hard is it to understand that the first step of a people considered for centuries as official citizens of the state, but whose citizenship is given a marginal status, wouldn't be to reject the hollow and debilitated form of their citizenship, but rather to demand that it be fully recognized and respected by the state?" Vergès, *Resolutely Black*, 60–61.

14 *Béké* is an Igbo-derived term used to describe a small European-descended class that has controlled the economy of French Caribbean islands like Martinique and Guadeloupe since the days of the transatlantic slave trade. See Winer, *Dictionary of the English/Creole of Trinidad and Tobago.*

15 Véron, "Césaire at the Crossroads in Haiti," 431.

16 Véron, "Césaire at the Crossroads in Haiti," 439.

17 Vergès, *Resolutely Black*, 32.

18 Vergès, *Resolutely Black*, 31, 32.

19 Frost and Lefevre Tavárez, "Tragedy of the Possible," 34.

20 Vergès, *Resolutely Black*, 15.

21 Vergès, *Resolutely Black*, xxi, 17–18.

22 Frost and Lefevre Tavárez, "Tragedy of the Possible," 30.

23 Bonilla, *Non-Sovereign Futures*; Wilder, *Freedom Time*, 2.

24 Wilder, "Here/Hear Now Aimé Césaire!," 586.

25 Frost and Lefevre Tavárez, "Tragedy of the Possible," 30.

26 Wilder, "Here/Hear Now Aimé Césaire!," 586.

27 Rabbitt, "History into Story," 7–8.

28 Rabbitt, "History into Story," 2, 14.

29 Rabbitt, "History into Story," 14.

30 In an interview with Sonia Arátan published in *Casa de Las Americas*, Césaire concluded that the "Congo did not exist except in Lumumba's head. . . . This is why what can be seen as utopian was for him essential in order to advance reality." In other words, as Frost and Tavárez conclude, as a leader, Césaire viewed Lumumba as "dialectically driven to act from the perspective of the future." Aratán, "Entrevistas con Aimé Césaire," 132; Frost and Lefevre Tavárez, "Tragedy of the Possible," 41–42.

31 Murdoch argues that France's attempt to use the exposition to recast itself as a plural society failed miserably in its refusal to acknowledge societal hierarchies based on theorizations of racial difference. Though he cannot affirm whether Césaire attended the exposition, Murdoch posits that the 1946 decision reflects Césaire's demand for accountability from France in the shadow of this willful blind spot. Murdoch, "Aimé Césaire," 66.

32 Murdoch, "Aimé Césaire," 66–67.

33 This view aligns with that of Yarimar Bonilla, who argues that though Césaire was against Martinican independence, he did not regard the colonizers' presence or absence as a primary factor in the achievement of liberation. In colonialism and postcolonialism, the ultimate battlefield for Césaire, though it was tied to land and plantation economies, was psychological. Bonilla, *Non-Sovereign Futures*.

34 The conceptual ideas and positions that undergird *A Tempest* are powerfully stated, albeit differently, in Césaire's *Discourse on Colonialism*.

35 Aimé Césaire, *A Tempest*, Act III, Scene 5, 62–63. Though not as well-known as it should be, this is perhaps one of the more notable passages in modern Caribbean literature. It significantly grounds Audre Lorde's famous and, in my view, famously misread speech-essay "The Master's Tools Will Never Dismantle the Master's House, 1984," reprinted in *Sister Outsider*, 110–14.

36 Thompson, *Flash of the Spirit*, 84; Dogbeh-David et al., "Palabre," 230–33.

37 Wilder, "Here/Hear Now Aimé Césaire!," 592.

38 Wilder, "Here/Hear Now Aimé Césaire!," 592; quoted from Césaire, "The Man of Culture and His Responsibilities," 130–31.

39 Marc Latamie, conversation with the author, May 29, 2012.

40 Pago, *L'histoire tragique de Marie-Philomène Roptus dite Lumina Sophie dite Surprise*. For a more extensive discussion of the significance of the island's oral histories, specifically in the context of the 1870 rebellions and state histories, see Chivallon, "Mémoires de l'esclavage à la Martinique," 235–61.

41 The image's label states, "Marc Latamie. Pencil on paper. Courtesy of the artist." He renders Lumina Sophie in the same manner and style used by the French artists and leaves her similarly unnamed, adding another dimension to the exhibition's critical labor.

42 Situational aesthetics describes the creative result of an artist's fabrication of social situations or encounters in an exhibition space where the audience participates, willingly or unwillingly. These encounters are performative, self-reflexive, and ethereal. The emphasis is not on the contemplation of a discrete work of art but on the process or experience initiated by the artist. The artists Rirkrit Tiravanija, Michael Asher, and Fred Wilson, in his seminal exhibition *Mining the Museum*, employ elements of situational aesthetics to create their "work."

43 Mignolo, "Epistemic Disobedience."

44 Césaire, *Discourse on Colonialism*, 51–52.

45 Martinique has had several occasions to renegotiate its relationship with France and define a path to independence or greater autonomy, in opposition to Césaire's vision of a way forward. The most recent opportunity occurred in a 2010 referendum. There are many ways to view the outcome. Perhaps one would expect that in the wake of his death, Martinicans would choose to chart a course counter to the 1946 decision. Others might argue

that it was too late, that Martinicans had assimilated and were no longer willing or able to cut ties with France. Neither view encompasses the complexities of the island's position in a neoliberal capitalist world. As Césaire might have observed, the ghosts were in the machine, but the machine had mutated.

46 Diawara, "Conversation with Édouard Glissant," 59.

47 Diawara, "Conversation with Édouard Glissant," 61. Glissant suggests that Caribbean people had, by and large, failed to recognize the generative potential of their formation and fully deploy it as strategy.

48 Diawara, "Conversation with Édouard Glissant," 61.

49 For a brilliant discussion of the ways the phenomenon of heterogeneity has functioned in Caribbean archives and museum spaces, see Modest, "We Have Always Been Modern." For an example of art history that rejects the implications of Western models and assessments of the Caribbean and Caribbean art as pure mimicry and as anachronistic and thus without value, see James, "Decolonizing Time."

50 Deleuze and Guattari, *A Thousand Plateaus*, 6.

51 Deleuze and Guattari, *A Thousand Plateaus*, 7.

52 McKittrick, *Sylvia Wynter*.

53 Benítez-Rojo, *Repeating Island*, 18.

54 Scott, *Refashioning Futures*, 8.

55 In *Conscripts of Modernity*, David Scott argues that dreams of a postcolonial future funneled through the independence project have been dashed. His work supports Césaire's position. However, Césaire takes the argument a step further by positioning the arts as a way to move beyond the limited freedom that independence brings Caribbean countries.

56 This phrasing draws on Eric Williams, who explained that "Massa was more often than not an absentee European planter exploiting West Indian resources, both human and economic." Here I use Massa day as a metaphor for colonial discourse. Williams, "Massa Day Done."

57 As the language suggests, this definition is deeply influenced by my early encounter with Toni Morrison's work, specifically *Playing in the Dark*.

58 "Whether in the Francophone, Anglophone, Arab, Chinese, Japanese world," Glissant said, "what's specific in the definition of the Other is that this Other is not just considered different. The Other is considered as contrary. Now, in the world, there is no contrary. The dialectic of differences is something I agree with, but not the dialectic of contraries, because the dialectic of contraries assumes that there's a truth over here, and its contrary over there. . . . I don't believe there is a truth." Diawara, "Conversation with Édouard Glissant," 63.

59 This number includes the artists discussed in this project as well as Nicole Awai, John Beadle, José Bedia, Ricardo Brey, Ras Ishi Butcher, Magdalena Campos Pons, Tony Capellán, Annalee Davis, Jean-Ulrick Désert, Joscelyn

Gardner, Kcho, Roshini Kempadoo, Tirzo Martha, Steve Ouditt, Marcel Pinas, Jorge Pineda, Belkis Ramírez, Arnaldo Roche Rabell, Ras Akem Ramsay, and a host of others. My selection hinges on my level of engagement with their work and the range of critical discourses it commands and challenges. The art produced by this study's subjects resonates independently and interdependently in illuminating, generative ways.

60 James, "Prismatic Blackness."

61 I also appreciate how the work of these artists converses across languages—engaging English, Spanish, French, Haitian Kreyòl, and other regional languages. This is particularly notable in the context of the multilingual field of global Caribbean art history, where the tendency has been to historicize according to language, thus prioritizing colonial disjuncture while ignoring historical connections stemming from the shared experience of colonialism itself.

62 See "We Have Always Been Modern," in which anthropologist Wayne Modest compellingly assesses how Caribbean cultural production has been situated in the discipline of anthropology and in institutional spaces like natural and cultural history museums.

63 The term *prismatic* draws on the prism's effect as a beam of light passes through it. A prism takes a single beam of white light, or in the context of art, the object, then fractures it into every spectrum on the color scale and multiplies its signification or affect, or both. In this project's lexicon, *prismatic* also describes the artistic will to fracture colonial perceptions of Caribbean creativity that animated the generation under consideration.

64 The discourse around authenticity in African art is extensive. See, for example, Cornet, "African Art and Authenticity"; Shelton, "Fakes, Fakers, and Fakery"; Kasfir, "African Art and Authenticity"; and Theodossopoulos, "Laying Claim to Authenticity." The discourse illuminates the ways disciplinarity and critical foundations are (pre)determined by Western and colonial values imposed on other societies and the ways those societies account for them.

65 Leon Wainwright has unpacked the critiques of belatedness in relation to the work of Caribbean artists in Britain in *Timed Out*.

66 Kempadoo, *Creole in the Archive*. *Black Martinik* is a local creole term for the island of Martinique and its Black majority, which Aimé Césaire and Marc Latamie were/are members of.

67 Muñoz, *Disidentifications*.

68 James, *Beyond a Boundary*.

69 Wilson Harris's "History, Fable and Myth in the Caribbean and Guianas" is one of the most brilliant theorizations of Caribbean art, culture, creativity, and identity in the wake of the Middle Passage. Harris described the Passage as a "limbo gateway" (157) for the enslaved, to illuminate the importance of autohistoriography in the process of reconstituting the broken

African body of the enslaved in the Americas. Harris sees the "philosophy of history . . . buried in the arts of the imagination" (156) as an "inner corrective" (159) that heals the enslaved and later colonized body from systemic disassembly.

70 If one can read Cattelan's 2016 Guggenheim Museum retrospective as a cumulative statement of his artistic practice, it is evident that the 6th Caribbean Biennial has quietly been excised from the artist's oeuvre. Hoffmann, on the other hand, has boldly asserted its importance, including it in his book on the greatest contemporary art shows. See Spector, *Maurizio Cattelan*; Hoffmann, *Show Time*.

71 Lamming, *Pleasures of Exile*, 107.

CHAPTER ONE: FROM BEHIND GOD'S BACK

Epigraph: Lynette Antoni (Janine Antoni's mother). The phrase *behind God's back* is used to describe a place so insignificant that even God has forgotten about it. Transcript of Janine Antoni's talk and conversation with David Bailey, Whitechapel Gallery, London, November 2003.

1 Raven, "Womanhouse," 64.

2 Janine Antoni was born in Freeport, Grand Bahama Island, The Bahamas, on January 19, 1964. Through her Trinidadian parents, she can trace her family's Caribbean heritage back more than two hundred years. The Bahamas celebrated its independence on July 10, 1973.

3 To *play mas* means to participate in the Lenten, Christmas, New Year's, or harvest masquerades in the Caribbean. It is a term that bears great cultural and political significance as a strategic weapon of the weak and oppressed to contest power structures that deny them participatory rights. For an excellent introduction to Trinidad's carnival, see Hill, *Trinidad Carnival*.

4 Scott, *Refashioning Futures*, 3.

5 Antoni quoted in Cottingham, "Janine Antoni," 104–5.

6 Antoni quoted in Trippi, "Untitled Artists' Projects by Janine Antoni," 148. This chapter depends substantively on the artist's voice, owing in large part to its centrality in Antoni's critical strategy.

7 James, *Beyond a Boundary*, 195. This creative participatory dynamic is crucial to Antoni, so much so that she sometimes includes the audience in performance (e.g., in *Slumber 1993*) and invites collaboration in the process of making work.

8 James, *Beyond a Boundary*, 196.

9 Fanon, *Black Skin, White Masks*, 112.

10 James, *Beyond a Boundary*, 197.

11 James, *Beyond a Boundary*, 142. This is an earlier phase than Jacques Lacan's mirror stage, as discussed in "The Mirror Stage as Formative of the

Function of the *I* as Revealed in Psychoanalytic Experience," chapter 1 in *Écrits*. Here, knowledge of self is obtained through immediate and direct sensation; there is no intermediary.

12 Janine Antoni, artist talk and conversation with David A. Bailey.

13 Cembalest, "Fast Forward." This biennial was derided by critics who objected to the art's perceived political content, which in this case meant that the work of women and artists of color dominated the show. *Gnaw* was reviewed as a highlight of the exhibition and immediately purchased by Charles Saatchi, a preeminent 1990s art collector, for $30,000. It is now in the permanent collection of the Museum of Modern Art, New York.

14 Antoni quoted in Trippi, "Untitled Artists' Projects by Janine Antoni," 144.

15 Cameron, "Habeas Corpus" (unpaginated).

16 Carson, "Response to 'The Reception of the Sixties,'" 144.

17 Kapur, "Globalisation and Culture," 21.

18 For an extensive discussion of *The River* in the context of the artist's other contemporaneous productions, see Schechner and Riggio, "Peter Minshall."

19 For a discussion of the politics of hair in the Caribbean, see James, "Fatima, circa 1886."

20 Cottingham, "Janine Antoni," 104 (square-bracketed addition mine).

21 hooks, "marginality as site of resistance," 343.

22 The importance of seeing the self as part of an archive threads through this book, as an idea resonant with feelings of rootedness that allow a person who is destabilized by various isms to center themselves on solid ground. Antoni's story is an episode in a long chain of omission and recovery. Chicago, a brilliant thinker, ardent feminist artist, pioneer, and educator who founded the first feminist art program at Fresno State, recalled that when she came to the university in the late 1960s, she began to receive publications issuing from New York feminist circles. The documents attenuated her isolation and empowered her to speak publicly about long-held beliefs and emotions. But when she started teaching, there was no archive to support the movement; it had to be created. This act demanded the rewriting of the grand narrative of American art to render the work of women artists visible. Broude and Garrard, "Conversations with Judy Chicago and Miriam Schapiro," in *The Power of Feminist Art*, 66–67.

23 Broude and Garrard, "Conversations with Judy Chicago and Miriam Schapiro," 67.

24 Schor, *Wet*, 50.

25 Schor, "Patrilineage."

26 Schor, email communication with the author, September 29, 2019.

27 Schor, email communication with the author.

28 Schor, *Wet*, 113.

29 Schor, *Wet*, 113.

30 Schor, *Wet*, 114. In a footnote, Schor specifies that, like Connor, she had taught Antoni. After issuing her comments, Schor learned that Antoni had indeed cited her as an influence in an interview with Laura Cottingham for *Flash Art*, but that the editor had forced Cottingham to omit the reference in favor of better-known 1980s feminist artists, such as Sherman, Levine, Barbara Kruger, and Jenny Holzer. "Apparently," Schor writes, "even a woman artist's (and a feminist art critic's) good faith effort to credit a specific woman mentor may be occulted by a generic reference to the usual suspects, although at least in this case they are female." Schor, *Wet*, 226–27n25.

31 I am intentionally drawing here—somewhat tongue in cheek—on Fidel Castro's famous speech "History Will Absolve Me," which he delivered on October 16, 1953, while he was on trial for leading a military assault on the Moncada Barracks. Made seven years before the Cuban Revolution, the address is rife with expressions of his aspirations and Cuba's revolutionary ideals. I reference it here to register the possibility that, like Castro's raid, many may find Antoni's tactics off-putting but her intentions noble.

32 Later in this chapter I cite the work's resonance and surfacing of a counter-hegemonic narrative issuing from the Caribbean postcolonial feminist lens. Antoni's case is peculiar and specific to her experience or to, recalling David Scott, her "problem space." Hailing from The Bahamas, she was without a history, model, or mentor and thus searched for "other mothers" to validate her thinking and creative impulses. In addition to the West, Cuba, Haiti, and Jamaica had well-established art histories from which this generation's artists could draw. The same was not true for Antoni.

33 Buskirk, *Contingent Object of Contemporary Art*.

34 The piece bowed out on its stand and collapsed while on exhibition at the Sandra Gering Gallery in 1992.

35 Antoni is having similar problems with her soap heads for *Lick and Lather*, which were acquired by the National Gallery of Art in Washington, DC, in April 2016. Since then, two of the heads have turned yellow or orange in spots, and she has had to replace them. On no less than three occasions, Antoni has had to replace the chocolate ones as well, and not always due to decay; when the objects have been exhibited, visitors have been known to nibble at the nose when no one is looking. Antoni, interview with the author, Miami Beach, FL, January 6, 2008. In 2011 she worked with Hirshhorn Museum curators to develop a process that stabilized the works. See Gupta, "Art of Chocolate (and Soap)."

36 Buskirk, *Contingent Object of Contemporary Art*, 6, 7.

37 Janine Antoni, artist talk and conversation with David A. Bailey.

38 Janine Antoni, artist talk and conversation with David A. Bailey.

39 Tawadros, "Beyond the Boundary," 133, 145. For Antoni, it's not just the kitchen but the home in general and the public space of the gallery.

40 Janine Antoni, interview with the author.

41 An African-rooted Bahamian street festival, Junkanoo marked the performance of power. Like many regional carnivals, its arena was the street. Each year, participants—mostly economically and politically disenfranchised Blacks—would take to the streets and seize possession of the city center, the site of parliament, the supreme court, the economic nerve center, and later, the entire country for a few hours. With drums, bells, costumes, and conch shells moving in syncopated rhythm, the people would engage in what Clement Bethel describes as "a mass occupation of Bay Street for a night." Bethel, *Junkanoo: Festival of The Bahamas*; James, "Elegy."

42 Antoni, artist talk and conversation with David A. Bailey.

43 Said, *Representations of the Intellectual*, 39.

44 Bahamas Association of Cultural Studies (BACUS) Conference, College of The Bahamas, June 4–6, 1998. In my presentation, I cited Antoni as an example of an artist who generates meaning through conceptualizations of aesthetic form broader than those typically associated with the region. While the overall response to my argument was sympathetic, several audience members questioned my characterization of Antoni as a "Bahamian" artist. To them, her art did not engage issues pertinent to their lives and concerns as Bahamians and Caribbean people. While attentive to their views, I respectfully disagreed, partly because I understood the conservative nature of contemporary art at the time and the stranglehold of this singular viewpoint on artistic expression, and partly because I recognized that the loudest voices danced around the elephant in the room—race and, specifically, the place of "whiteness" in national identity.

45 The pressure to "represent" both formally and politically is an ongoing issue for artists living both outside and inside the region, but things have opened up. Today, Antoni is fully recognized as a global Caribbean artist, and her work expresses the same constellation of influences and discursive interests.

46 *Caribbean white* refers to people who may or may not present as white but are regarded as white socially and culturally. Racial mixture is assumed, or always remains in play, in designations of Caribbean white.

47 Edmondson, "Race, Privilege, and the Politics of (Re)Writing History," 190.

48 Edmondson, "Race, Privilege, and the Politics of (Re)Writing History," 190.

49 Mercer, *Welcome to the Jungle*, 248.

50 Mercer, *Welcome to the Jungle*, 241; Gilroy, "Cruciality and the Frog's Perspective," 35.

51 Mercer, *Welcome to the Jungle*, 35.

52 For a discussion of the white creole body, see Belinda Edmondson's "Race, Privilege, and the Politics of (Re)Writing History," 180–81. Like much of the scholarship cited in this chapter, this essay, published during the 1990s, shaped the conversation at the time in necessary ways. It still offers one of the sharpest discussions in print of racialized embodiment in the Caribbean.

53 I draw on the concept of racial passing as performance to illuminate how it can be deployed to undercut social power that restricts access on other terms. Passing is not always grounded in racial self-hatred; it can be seen as a tool to reject oppressive racial constructs. For a personal discussion on the practice of racial passing in the Caribbean, see del Valle Casals, "Passing for a White Woman."
54 Epigraph to this section: Janine Antoni's recollection of her mother's occasional comments on reading "new" writings on her daughter's work, in Antoni, interview with the author, 2008.
55 Antoni, interview with the author, 2008
56 Email communication with the author, April 2, 2024.
57 Fisher, "Interperformance."
58 Schor, *Wet*, 60, 86.
59 Lajer-Burcharth, "Antoni's Difference," 151.
60 Lajer-Burcharth, "Antoni's Difference," 152.
61 Here I rely on Emily Apter's discussion of late nineteenth-century eroticism in "Splitting Hairs," 168.
62 Nichols, "Seeing Food," 818.
63 Hall, "Spectacle of the Other," 240.
64 Hall, "Spectacle of the Other," 240; McClintock, *Imperial Leather*, 34.
65 Hall, "Spectacle of the Other," 241. McClintock argues that "the first point about the Pears' [Soap] advertisement is that it figures imperialism as coming into being through domesticity. At the same time, imperial domesticity is a domesticity without women" (32). Although Antoni's 2002 exhibition at the Museum of Modern Art did not use soap, it actively engaged aspects of imperialism's and patriarchy's historical imprint on the art world. She unstitched the "A" letters from the MoMA banners until all that remained was "MoM." The work highlighted, with a bit of humor, the irony of women's exclusion from the grand narrative of Western art at MoMA, an institution founded by three women. Janine Antoni, Shahzia Sikander, and Kara Walker, *Projects 70*, Museum of Modern Art, New York, 2000.
66 Cameron, "Habeas Corpus."
67 Cembalest, "Fast Forward," 122.
68 Trippi, "Untitled Artists' Projects by Janine Antoni," 150.
69 Allen, "Caribbean Bodies," 293.
70 McAlister, *Rara!*, 73.
71 Mohammed, "'But Most of All Mi Love Me Browning,'" 30–31. See also Tobin, *Picturing Imperial Power*; Kriz, *Slavery, Sugar, and the Culture of Refinement*; and Bagneris, *Colouring the Caribbean*.
72 Cooper notes that from the inception of Jamaica's participation, light-skinned or white women have been routinely chosen to represent Jamaica in international beauty competitions such as Ms. World and Ms. Universe. Jamaica is not singular; it was bittersweet to observe the overwhelmingly

positive response when Ms. Jamaica, Davina Bennett, wore her naturally curled hair in an afro at the 2017 Ms. Universe pageant. It's worth asking exactly whose values are positioned as official or normative in these spaces. Cooper, "Dancehall Dress," 81.

73 Lady Saw left the dancehall stage in December 2015 and later reemerged as a Christian evangelist, her body fully covered, at times to comical excess.

74 Lady Saw's music evinces a profound sense of humor and acerbic wit, an extremely important and severely ignored aspect of Caribbean culture and historic survival. On turning thirty-six in 2005, she said, "Yes, mi no fraid fi talk mi age, mi ah 36 looking like 16, and feeling like a virgin. The old woman no ketch me up yet, she caan find my address, but she find some gal roun ere and beat dem wid the old stick." "Lady Saw's Buzzing About," *Jamaica Online Star*, July 25, 2005, http://old.jamaica-star.com/thestar/20050725/ent/ent3.html#google_vignette.

75 Cooper, "Sweet and Sour Sauce," 1.

76 Cooper, "Dancehall Dress," 81.

77 Cooper, "Dancehall Dress," 77.

78 Antoni quoted in Weintraub, *Art on the Edge and Over*, 126.

79 Even the lauded Lady Saw, who undertook great pains to separate her stage persona from her life as "Marion Hall," has had to navigate a patriarchal Caribbean value system that regards womanhood as defined by childbirth. Although she has adopted three children and raised them as her own, her battle with infertility has become grist for male DJs in dancehall who ridicule her by referring to her as a "mule" on the very stage she commands. She has affirmed her power and resilience by speaking back to this assault through her music and performance.

80 Hall, "Spectacle of the Other," 267–68. This tactic is fraught with danger and complexities around the mechanics of desire. Graham Huggan has argued that postcolonial writers working in the metropole recognize that their work's commodified value depends on a measure of exotic appeal. Huggan notes that in engaging this expectation, writers risk complicity with the cultural imperialism they purport to denounce. Considering the developing discourse on Antoni's art, I would argue that she sidesteps dependence on this lever by engaging it as generative content in and for her work. Huggan, "Postcolonial Exotic," 24.

81 Ryan, *Trickster Shift*. Milla C. Riggio has also observed that in Trinidad carnival, the act is "fortified by calypso's . . . tradition of social criticism satirizing everything from government, racial prejudice, and ethnic stereotypes to gender and sexual repression." I propose that Antoni has brought this type of trickster "mas" into the institutionally sanctioned spaces of galleries and museums. Riggio, "Resistance and Identity," 8.

82 Antoni, artist talk and conversation with David A. Bailey. *Touch* was the first piece Antoni exhibited in the Caribbean. It was included in the Inaugural

National Exhibition at the National Art Gallery of The Bahamas in 2003, which was curated by the author and is discussed further in chapter 5.

83 Antoni, interview with the author, 2008.

84 Trippi, "Untitled Artists' Projects by Janine Antoni," 148.

85 From the 2008 interview with the author:

(JA) Well I have rewritten the history. There is so much work before and after *Wean* that I've just . . . [*gestures as if to push away*]. My husband says I am a magician, to just make work disappear. [*Laughter*]

(EJ) I have to ask you about that.

(JA) I have tried to make my history very specific so there are a lot of dead ends. I just decided they weren't clear; they were not serving the purpose of the new work.

86 Muñoz, *Disidentifications*, 161, 165. The parenthetical words are those of Robert Storr, whom Muñoz quotes in relation to the concept of disidentification and the artist Félix González-Torres.

87 Cameron, "Habeas Corpus."

88 Antoni and Odenbach, "Advertisement for Myself," 33.

89 Cliff, *No Telephone to Heaven*, 194. See also Edmondson, "Race, Privilege, and the Politics of (Re)Writing History," 185.

CHAPTER TWO: MEETING IN THE UPPER ROOM

1 Acevedo-Muñoz, "End of the Line," 168.

2 *Black Girl* is intimately tied to the Caribbean and the Black diasporic currents discussed in this text. Though considered an "African" film, it blurs all lines within diaspora as a quintessential Pan-African work of art. The voice of the film's narrator, Diouana, is that of the Haitian actress and singer Toto Bissainthe, who would later gain recognition in Raoul Peck's films *Haitian Corner* (1987) and *Man by the Shore* (1993). Bissainthe met Sembène in Paris in the 1950s after she cofounded Les Griots, the first Black, African-diasporic theater group in Paris, with the French-Guadeloupean filmmaker Sarah Maldoror. The poster for their first production, Jean-Paul Sartre's *No Exit / Huis clos*, was designed by the Cuban artist Wifredo Lam. Their second production was Aimé Césaire's *La Tragédie du Roi Christophe* (The Tragedy of King Christophe), and their third, Jean Genet's *Les Nègres* (The Blacks), directed by Roger Blain. These important transatlantic crosscurrents illustrate the arc of my research practice, which explores how geographic boundaries are negotiated and transcended through history, art, culture, and politics.

3 *Guinen* is an older term for what has become known in modern times as West Africa. During plantation slavery, people spoke of returning to Guinen, not Africa. In my family, for example, the earliest known African ancestor is recorded as "Emme from Guinen."

4 Devyn Spence Benson suggests that Fidel Castro, in his famous 1961 speech "Some Words to the Intellectuals," "depicted the revolution as a battle for the re-education or decolonization of Cuban minds." Benson, "Sara Gómez," 138.

5 *Special Period* refers to the years of economic crisis Cuba faced and the societal changes it induced after the end of the Cold War, the dissolution of the Soviet Union, and its subsequent withdrawal of economic support for Cuba in 1991. See Weppler-Grogan, "Cultural Policy, the Visual Arts, and the Advance of the Cuban Revolution."

6 Benítez-Rojo, *Repeating Island*, 10–11.

7 Benítez-Rojo, *Repeating Island*, 11.

8 By 1997, Cuba had partially rebounded from the economic crisis of the Special Period due to its reemphasis on (art) tourism. Even after Ayón gained international success and could afford to employ any process she desired, she chose to continue using collagraphy. See Weiss, *To and from Utopia in the New Cuban Art*, 154–57, for a dense discussion of the period and the state's return to a tourism model to which art was joined.

9 See Bettelheim, *AfroCuba*; Branson-Gill, *Belkis Ayón*; Brown, *Light Inside*; Wood, *Siempre Vuelvo*; Ayón and Vives, *Nkame*; and Miller, *Voice of the Leopard*.

10 Sarusky, "Hablar de los mitos y el arte." All Spanish texts in this book were translated by Lilianne Lugo Herrera and the author.

11 A cabildo is a living arrangement born in slavery, designed to acclimatize or "season" newly arrived enslaved Africans to life in Cuba. Individuals were grouped according to areas of common language and ethnicity in Africa. Each group had different jobs; some cabildos focused on stevedore-type work, others on crafts, others worked on plantations, and so forth. The practice was intended to divide the population. But, as the birth of Abakuá indicates, it also served to maintain African cultural forms and became a fertile ground for reconfigured social relationships. There were less formal organizations of Abakuá cabildos in the eighteenth century. The 1836 date indicates the first named association of Abakuá. Miller, *Voice of the Leopard*, 78; Brown, *Light Inside*, 4; Martínez, *Cuban Art and National Identity*.

12 In 1881, forty-five years after Èfik Buton (or Efi Kebutón) was founded, there were eighty-three known Abakuá cabildos in Havana alone. Brown, *Light Inside*, 15. As the secret group grew in numbers and strength, it became more visible, particularly during the festival of Epiphany, in the form of the Ñañigo Iremé masquerade. This masquerade's design established the importance of eyes or sight to symbolize enlightenment in Abakuá and became a key motif in Ayón's practice.

13 Harris, "History, Fable and Myth," 156–59.

14 Branson-Gill, *Belkis Ayón*; Brown, *Light Inside*; Wood, *Siempre Vuelvo*; Miller, *Voice of the Leopard*.

15 Although there is occasional use of religious terms to discuss aspects of Abakuá, it is not itself a religion, nor is it simply a fraternal order. I regard Abakuá as a way of life or philosophy of living, albeit a sexist one, that is deeply engaged with historical knowledge preservation that extends far in the past, before the trauma. Many Abakuá were also initiated in the more obviously liturgical Palo Monte or Lucumí religions and were deeply involved in grassroots political movements, such as the labor leader Aracelio Iglesias, who was killed in a Havana wharf dispute in 1948. As Brown notes, "Iglesias was an Abakuá officer, a priest of Shango and a babalawo." Brown, *Light Inside*, 26.

16 Ivor Miller, in *Voice of the Leopard*, proposes that there is no single master narrative or founding myth of the Abakuá's origin and posits that each constellation developed its own story. While this approach makes the Cuban version more specific and significant in its problem space, the main characters in the story and the description of Sikán's death remain the same despite variations in the overall narrative. In this text, I draw on the essential myth as Ayón understood it.

17 For a thorough engagement of these practices, see two seminal texts: Thompson, *Face of the Gods*, and Price, *First-Time*. *Face of the Gods* (1993) was the first exhibition I ever worked on as a museum curatorial assistant at the DuSable Museum in the 1990s. It centered on ritual traditions of African-derived religious practices in the Americas. Price's *First-Time* documents the gatherings, perceived as religious and thus harmless by Europeans, that offered opportunities for enslaved Africans to meet, imagine, plan, and, as we have come to understand, eventually seize their freedom. The text attends to what an activity or "picture" appears to be from the vantage point of the powerful versus what it is from the vantage point of those perceived to be powerless and therefore subject. It has substantially shaped my scholarship and methodological approaches to Caribbean art history.

18 Barnet, *Afro-Cuban Religions*; Thompson, *Flash of the Spirit*.

19 Readers should bear in mind two things: First, Black male slave habitation in cabildos may be seen by some as a positive outcome of horror, conducive to the spread of fraternalism and generation of creativity. However, this chapter complicates this kumbaya version of the story. Second, even as we use the term *Black*, in Cuba, as in much of the wider Caribbean and Americas, race is determined or constructed differently than in the United States via a complex and uneven combination of skin color, hair texture, wealth, class, societal roles, and desire. Historically, in Cuba, one could appear visibly Black but obtain legal status as a white person.

20 Here the term *African* means a person born in Africa or who is phenotypically "black," or both, and living in Cuba. This image was composed by Lydia Cabrera's informant Saibeke (ca. 1940–50) and obtained by Brown from the estate of Lydia Cabrera. Brown, *Light Inside*, 10, 11.

21 Apter, *Black Critics and Kings*; Brown, *Light Inside*, 12.

22 I am not suggesting that similar groups or secret societies like Abakuá did not exist in West Africa prior to 1836. Oral histories attest that during the eighteenth century an "Èfik" or "Ekpe Society" existed in the Cross River region. It, too, was a male organization and consisted of prominent merchants who governed the area economically. One can think of it as an analogue to a contemporary chamber of commerce, though there also appeared to be a strong moral and ethical dimension, reflected in the intent to enforce contractual agreements and ensure debt repayment and honorable exchange of goods. Sometimes these "goods" included slaves, and sometimes the slaves became the Èfik people themselves. No doubt members of this very group found themselves in the belly of a slave ship from time to time. However, beyond their all-male aspect, these groups do not correspond to the contemporary apprehension of Abakuá or to the way Ayón came to understand it in the context of Cuba. Even so, as Ivor Miller's rich fieldwork in Cuba and the Cross River region makes clear, it is useful and necessary to position Abakuá within both a specific African teleology and a self-authored Cuban narrative. Miller, *Voice of the Leopard*.

23 Ayón, "Confesiones, 1991," Alex and Carole Rosenberg Papers.

24 Branson-Gill, *Belkis Ayón*, 6. In another version of the story, after capturing Tánze, Sikán marries into the Èfik and is killed by them out of fear that she will tell her father, an Efor, the secret that she can communicate with god. Yet another story relates that she marries into the Efor and is then killed by her people, the Èfik, because they do not want her sharing the secret with her husband. Slight variations abound, but the main characters remain the same, and all the stories end in Sikán's murder, couched in the language of sacrificial death.

25 Brown, *Light Inside*, 44.

26 In the eighteenth century, cabildo life and Cuban slavery were predominantly male enterprises. The Cuban economy underwent a dramatic shift after the Haitian Revolution as Cuba sought to control the sugar market once dominated by Saint-Domingue. This process demanded free labor. In the two hundred years prior to the Haitian Revolution, an estimated ninety thousand Africans were imported directly to Havana. This number almost doubled in the ensuing twenty years. Notably, the population of female slaves increased proportionally to maintain trade and sugar production. It would be interesting to explore what impact these changing demographics might have had on the formation of the Abakuá society in 1836 and the question of Black male sexuality within the group. Palmié, *Wizards and Scientists*.

27 Branson-Gill, *Belkis Ayón*, 6; Ayón, "Confesiones, 1991." Alex and Carole Rosenberg were Ayón's American gallerists. Early in this project they granted me complete access to their gallery and personal files on Ayón, including letters, artist statements, and sales records. Carole was especially

close to Ayón and delivered the eulogy at her service. The Rosenbergs also owned a print of *La cena*, one of three black-and-white versions I have been able to study in situ. This version and another, in a private collection in Miami, represent collagraphy of the highest order.

28 Ayón, "Confesiones, 1991."

29 Nikoloutsos, "Appropriating Greek Myth"; Lush, "Popular Authority in Euripides' *Iphigenia in Aulis*."

30 Solga, "Body Doubles, Babel's Voices."

31 This is based on Belkis Ayón's own written description of the work. Alex and Carole Rosenberg Papers.

32 Ayón, "Confesiones, 1991."

33 Sarusky, "Hablar de los mitos y el arte," 70.

34 Ernesto "Che" Guevara was from an upper-class Argentinian family. The quotation is taken from a speech he gave at the Universidad las Villas on his acceptance of an honorary degree, during which he highlighted the need to open up the institution to the former peasant class, Blacks, and others who'd been historically excluded. He described the trajectory of his social mobility and awareness, from his "career as a university student, as a member of the middle class, as a doctor with middle-class perspectives" to his abandonment of middle-class comforts and the respectability of the medical profession when he became a revolutionary. In terms of self-regard, he claimed that he now saw himself as one with the people. The speech is partially reprinted in Fernández Retamar, *Caliban and Other Essays*, 44–45. See also Hulme, "Calibán," 114–22.

35 I engage the censoring of this painting extensively in James, "Theriantropic Beasts and the Mystic Revelation of Tomás Esson."

36 Lott, *Love and Theft*, 36.

37 Sarusky, "Hablar de los mitos y el arte," 68.

38 Sarusky, "Hablar de los mitos y el arte," 71.

39 Brown, *Light Inside*, 40. The snake is a central figure in Abakuá as well as Haitian Vodoun, where it represents the powerful Damballah, the holder and giver of life.

40 Ayón quoted in Mateo, "Volver sobre los sentidos," 8.

41 Wood, *Siempre Vuelvo*, 4–7.

42 Wood, *Siempre Vuelvo*, 4–7.

43 Schroeder, *Tomás Gutiérrez Alea*, 1–2.

44 Prior to 1959, there was no Cuban film industry. Having studied law at the University of Havana, upon graduation in 1951, Tomás Gutiérrez Alea left Cuba to study filmmaking in Rome at the Centro Sperimentale di Cinematografia, where he was influenced by Italian Neo-Realism. In the years before the revolution, Alea worked at a Mexican-owned production company making short films. His first film for the ICAIC was *This Is Our Land* (1959), which focused on agrarian reform on the island.

45 At the time, Grupo Antillano was the major visual arts group on the island and was committed to forging connections between Cuba and the broader Caribbean. It consisted primarily of Cuban artists of African descent. Wifredo Lam supported the group's vision and efforts. Ramos Cruz, "Tribute to Grupo Antillano."

46 Schroeder, *Tomás Gutiérrez Alea*, 9.

47 Bettelheim, *AfroCuba*, 44.

48 The Castro government's missteps, outright failures, and miscalculations during this period are engaged across multiple arenas by Weppler-Grogan, in "Cultural Policy, the Visual Arts, and the Advance of the Cuban Revolution"; Guerra, in *Visions of Power in Cuba*, epilogue; and Lynch, in "Cuban Architecture Since the Revolution."

49 Mirtha Ibarra, *In Conversation*, Council for Latin American and Iberian Studies and the MacMillan Center, Spring Film Series in Honor of Tomás Gutiérrez Alea, Luce Hall, Yale University, April 22, 2016.

50 Davis, *Slaves on Screen*, 56.

51 *Variety* (Archive: 1905–2000) 243, no. 6 (June 29, 1966): 6.

52 Moreno Fraginals was reprimanded by the Cuban revolutionary government for this text, partly because it did not align with the teleology the government wished to construct by marking 1959 as an inevitability centuries in the making. He was denied teaching posts locally but lectured globally in subsequent years. By the time Moreno Fraginals reemerged as a teacher in the mid-1970s in Cuba, during the film's production, he was at the University of Arts of Cuba (Instituto Superior de Arte; ISA), where Belkis Ayón became a student and, later, a teacher and colleague of Moreno Fraginals before he emigrated to Miami.

53 The Count of Casa Bayona appears in the earliest Cuban painting to include a Black person, *Family of the Count of Casa Bayona* (ca. 1750–79), painted by José Nicolás de Escalera, an artist of mixed racial origins. It is situated in a chapel built on the site of the sugar mill that was destroyed in 1727. The Black man included in the lower right register is shown prominently wearing a necklace with a large cross pendant, indicating his Christianity and fealty to the family. Lugo-Ortiz, "Between Violence and Redemption."

54 De la Fuente, *A Nation for All*; de la Fuente and Rodríguez Valdés, *Queloides*.

55 De la Fuente and Rodríguez Valdés, *Queloides*, 10.

56 *Blanqueamiento* was the official practice of promoting the migration of whites of Spanish descent to Cuba through the promise of free land and employment. This was intended to balance the number of Black slaves being imported to the sugar plantations. According to Robin Moore, "Between 1898 and 1916, approximately 440,000 Spanish-speaking settlers came to live in Cuba either from Spain itself or former colonies. By 1929 this figure had increased to 900,000. . . . At the same time, laws restricting immigration

from Asian and other non-Caucasian countries were strengthened." Moore, *Nationalizing Blackness*, 28. This group of immigrants has benefited economically and politically from Spain's own, twenty-first-century population incentive, which offers Cubans who can prove Spanish descent citizenship and passports, even if they choose to remain primarily in Cuba.

57 David Brown's work offers a detailed analysis of what being Abakuá meant over time, from "exotic but frightening" in the pre-emancipation nineteenth century, to "delinquent, vagrant, promiscuous, atavistic" after emancipation, then to a "pathogen or contagion" in the first part of the twentieth century. Brown, *Light Inside*. While multiple cabildo raids were carried out by the police in the early twentieth century, many intellectuals, including the renowned Fernando Ortiz, once supported the government stance against related cultural practices, called for the prohibition of Santería, supported the view that African religions represented social pathologies—aiding in their criminalization—and endorsed the ban on musical performances of rumba, comparsa, and son as proof of African barbarism. See Juncker, *Afro-Cuban Religious Arts*, 12–40.

58 Groups such as the "Liga Blanca de Cuba and El Orden de los Caballeros . . . were formed with the express purpose of 'whitening' Cuba" and removing people of color from "every facet of national life." Moore, *Nationalizing Blackness*, 30.

59 Helg, *Our Rightful Share*.

60 A tragic story is told, in official and unofficial versions, of the great Black Cuban general Quintín Bandera. Moore recounts a story of the August Revolution of 1906, which resulted from the protests of Black soldiers, including Banderas, over their inability to find work after serving with honor in the War of Independence and their exclusion from government: "Seventy-year-old Quintín Banderas [*sic*], a central figure in the uprising, was [soon after] assassinated in his sleep by soldiers under orders from the Estrada Palma administration." Moore, *Nationalizing Blackness*, 29. The oral history rendition of the same incident, provided by the Black Cuban journalist Reynaldo Peñalver Moral, differs from official accounts. Moral states that after the Liberation War of 1898, "the black General Quintín Bandera was reduced to being a garbage collector. The story goes that one day in Old Havana, he approached the first U.S.-approved president of Cuba, Don Tomás Estrada Palma, who liked to walk down Obispo Street greeting the populace, his car behind him. When Quintín Bandera said he was without a job, Estrada Palma threw him a five-peso gold coin. Quintín Bandera set about him with his stick. Not long after, Quintín Bandera was found slashed with a machete on the corner of Vies and Figuras streets. The press headlines of the assassination ran, 'Quintín Bandera dead in Ñañigo brawl' [code for "killed by fellow Blacks"]. People said it was Estrada Palma who had him killed." Peñalver

Moral, "A Journalist's Story," 48. See also Kutzinski, *Sugar's Secrets*; Helg, *Our Rightful Share*; and de la Fuente, "The New Afro-Cuban Cultural Movement."

61 Ramos Cruz, "Tribute to Grupo Antillano," 20.

62 Pérez Sarduy and Stubbs, *Afro-Cuban Voices*, 5.

63 In a conversation at Yale University in 2016, Mirtha Ibarra shared that Alea often said, "If Kafka had been born in Cuba, we would have considered him a realist!" Exhibiting profound contradictions, postrevolutionary Cuban society could certainly be described as Kafkaesque. Ibarra, *In Conversation.*

64 Cordiés Jackson and Sesma, "Issues of Black Health," 62.

65 De La Torre, "Masking Hispanic Racism." According to Devyn Benson, following Stokely Carmichael's visit to Cuba in 1967, Sara Gómez began wearing her hair natural; Ayón later did the same. Today the practice may seem a simple thing, but in 1960s and 1990s Cuba, and even today, as previously discussed in relation to Janine Antoni, to do so was, as Alea asserted, revolutionary. Benson, "Sara Gómez," 150, 153.

66 Perhaps the most obvious irony is the case of Varadero Beach, which until 1959 had been the exclusive, favored leisure resort for Cuba's upper classes, which were predominantly "white." "Decades later Varadero was to become yet again exclusive, when Cuba's opening to international tourism made the modern hotels of this former enclave of Cuban-style segregation out of bounds to cash-stricken Cuban nationals." Segregation was nationalized through tourism and entailed excluding Cubans of every stripe from certain beaches. Molina et al., "The Only Black Family on the Block," 49.

67 Allen, "Looking Black at Revolutionary Cuba"; Altunaga, "*The Dead Come at Midnight*," 91, 93.

68 Martinez Furé, "A National Cultural Identity?," 155, 156, 157.

69 Ramos Cruz, "Tribute to Grupo Antillano," 19.

70 Ayón's father was a military police officer assigned to Fidel Castro. He accompanied Castro on several trips to Africa.

71 Sarusky, "Hablar de los mitos y el arte," 69–70.

72 Benson, "Sara Gómez," 137.

73 Lord et al., *Cinema of Sara Gómez*, 136–37.

74 Benson notes that as a result of the limited release of Gómez's work, "until recently . . . Gómez was largely unknown on the island of her birth"—except in certain households—until the National Film Institute "dedicated a special edition of *Cine Cubano* to her life in 1989." Benson, "Sara Gómez," 127; *Cine Cubano*, special issue on Sara Gómez, no. 127 (1989).

75 Here, Ramos Cruz speaks directly of Volumen Uno's membership, which besides Bedia and Elso, included Flavio Garciandía and at least one Afro-Cuban, Ricardo Brey. Ramos Cruz reads the variable reception of artwork grounded in the same ideas as an incursion into Black culture without Black artists. Grupo Antillano was not an exclusively Black group, but its attempt

to focus on African diasporic linkages was nonetheless suppressed by the state. See Ramos Cruz, "Grupo Antillano and the Marginalization of Black Artists," 148. Through its five-year run, Grupo Antillano consisted of a vast number of artists, writers, scholars, and musicians. Founding members included the artists Ramón Haití Edouardo, Rogelio Rodríguez Cobas, Arnaldo Larrinaga, Rafael Queneditt, Roberto Diago (symbolic, as he was deceased), Wifredo Lam, and Rogelio Martínez Furé. This group brought the work of Fernando Ortiz back into the discourse of Cuban culture and was committed to Black aesthetics. It should be noted that the work of Grupo Antillano and a greater desire among Afro Cubans to know more about their relationship to diasporic cultures were significantly influenced by CARIFESTA. The filmmaker Gloria Rolando recounts: "In 1979 CARIFESTA was held in Cuba and I first saw a steel band and heard a lot about the plantation world. Suddenly, all these figures in Latin American history that had seemed isolated to me came together, and I was fascinated. The seeds had been sown." Rolando, "Africa, the Caribbean, and Afro-America in Cuban Film," 133.

76 Pascual Castillo, "Fleeting Anecdotes and Stories of Escape from Slavery," 50.

77 In 1998, the year before she died, Ayón had solo exhibitions in Los Angeles, Zurich, New York, and Tokyo. Between 1988 and 1998, she held twenty solo and two-person exhibitions, six mounted in Cuba. During this decade, her work was included in almost one hundred exhibitions around the world, including the Havana, Maastricht, Venice, and Gwangju biennials. Artist files, Catherine Couturier Gallery, Los Angeles.

78 Vives, "Belkis Ayón: Su propia voz" / "Belkis Ayón: Her Own Voice," 26|263.

79 Brossard, "Era muy exigente, pero también muy flexible" / "She Was Very Demanding, but Also Very Flexible," 123|291.

80 Vives, "Belkis Ayón: Su propia voz" / "Belkis Ayón: Her Own Voice," 27|265.

81 Thompson, *Flash of the Spirit*, 235.

82 In my interviews with Volumen Uno artist Ricardo Brey in 2022–23, he recounted Thompson's visit to Havana in 1984, shortly after the publication of *Flash of the Spirit*. Thompson spoke to a room filled with artists of every stripe and level. A few precious copies of the book were distributed among those gathered. The copy that Brey and Juan Francisco Elso obtained that night was passed from one person to the next, among artists and students, to be read and devoured. Although she was only sixteen at the time, given the size and cohesion of Havana's artistic community, I'd like to believe that Ayón was aware of Thompson's talk and had access to the book. The Nnimm sensibility in her oeuvre is very strong, and Thompson's work would have been one of the few ways—if not the only way—for her to make this connection. She produced *La cena* two years after the visit. See James, "The Light of Things / La luz de las cosas."

83 Menéndez, "Para destruir un miedo" / "Banishing Fear," 63|273.

84 Gazourmah is a central character in Filippo Marinetti's novel *Mafarka, the Futurist* (1909–10). He is the son whom the main male character gestates and literally gives birth to. He is described as having "Black" features and was intended to demonstrate men's futurist power to produce life without women. See Kanz, "Queering Violence and Masculinity in Marinetti."

85 Although the focus is on Abakuá, the snake's presence in *La cena* and *La familia* draws one to Damballah, the oldest god in the Vodoun pantheon. He is the lwa of creation but can also precipitate death. In addition, the presence of the spotted figure behind Sikán alludes to male aggression, as well as to the Leopard societies of Africa and later of Haiti that believed in the possibility of transmutation from human into other animal forms.

86 Ayón quoted in Sarusky, "Hablar de los mitos y el arte," 69.

87 Barber, "How Man Makes God in West Africa"; Brown, *Light Inside*, 152.

88 Camnitzer, *New Art of Cuba*, 215, 217.

89 Mateo, "I Always Come Back: Irregular Conversations with Belkis Ayon, November 1993," Carole and Alex Rosenberg Papers, New York.

90 Founded in 1993, MAGIN was increasingly viewed as a transgressive group by the Cuban government and was "deactivated" in 1996. See Fernandes, "Transnationalism and Feminist Activism in Cuba"; and Hormilla, *Mujeres en crisis*.

91 "Black" Cubans have not left the island in the same numbers as whites, because, for the most part, they did not have recourse to foreign family remittances to weather the economic crisis of the Special Period. Faced with limited resources, Black women were the first to go into *jineterismo* (prostitution). But in reading accounts of Cuban women facing debilitating poverty and instability, one notes that one of their main battlegrounds was the domain of morality; specifically, they contested the perception that poverty is linked with immorality.

92 Herrera, "Poetry, Prostitution, and Gender Esteem," 123.

93 Devyn Benson provides a fascinating account of how the FMC and Espin handled Sara Gómez's work in order to highlight the experience of Black women activists in Cuba, and of the events that led to their being branded as counterrevolutionary and their organization being deactivated. Benson, "Sara Gómez," 134–58.

94 González Mandri, *Guarding Cultural Memory*, 10.

95 González Mandri, *Guarding Cultural Memory*, 104–5.

96 Two subsequent films by Alea, *Los Sobrevivientes* (The Survivors, 1978) and *Hasta cierto punto* (Up to a Certain Point, 1983), were both critical of the revolution but in different ways. About the first, Alea explained, "Revolutions are like Saturn, they devour their own children," and in the latter film, he wanted to bring attention to the heterosexism that was ingrained in

Cuba after the revolution, believing that the revolution had done nothing to solve the oppressions that had spun out of patriarchy.

97 Although more is known about depression and suicide today, persisting rumors regarding Ayón's tragic passing have appeared in print—for example, Bettelheim, *AfroCuba*. None of the rumors explain her suicide. She used her father's gun. There was no note. Many people have heard that she was depressed over a failed love affair in summer 1999. However, her work on the problem of love began in 1998. In addition, when I spoke with the curator of the final exhibition Ayón participated in, they said she showed no visible signs of distress or change in personality. She was generally quite bubbly and pleasant and publicly presented that way until the day she died. Within the context of Cuba at this time, such a prominent figure's death by suicide would be most likely linked to severe depression, public disgrace, or an illness that could not be faced. Any of these scenarios could have made Ayón's life intolerable and a continued career at the level of prominence she enjoyed impossible, but there is no concrete evidence that she faced any of these challenges, which makes her disappearance even more difficult to bear.

98 Lamming, *Pleasures of Exile*, 107.

99 Vives, "Belkis Ayón: Su propia voz" / "Belkis Ayón: Her Own Voice," 27|265. A detail of an Ayón print served as the signature image for the 2022 Venice Biennale, "The Milk of Dreams." A suite of her works opened the main exhibition at the Arsenal, the same place she had made her biennale debut almost thirty years earlier. The biennale capped an intense exhibition scheduled for her work that began with a comprehensive retrospective exhibition, *Nkame*, which traveled for several years to various venues after opening at UCLA's Fowler Museum in 2016.

CHAPTER THREE: HISTORICAL DRAG

Sections of this chapter and various approaches to the ideas discussed therein were previously published in "Speaking in Tongues: Metapictures and the Discourse of Violence in Caribbean Art," *Small Axe: A Caribbean Journal of Criticism* 16, no. 1 (2012): 119–43, https://doi.org/10.1215/07990537-1548137; *Edouard Duval Carrié: Historical Retelling and the Postmodern Baroque* (Miami: Oolite Arts and Bass Museum, 2020); and "Outta' Line: Decolonial Enlightenment and the Genre of History Painting in Contemporary Caribbean Art," in *The Imagined New (or What Happens When History Is a Catastrophe?)*, edited by Anthony Bogues, Leora Farber, Zamansele Nsele, and Surafel Wondimu Abebe (Johannesburg: University of Johannesburg and iWale Books, 2023).

Epigraph: Quoted in McCarthy Brown, *Tracing the Spirit*, 76.

1 Danner, "Reporter at Large—I," 81.

2 In Vodoun, Santería, Palo Monte, and other West African Yoruba- or Kongo-derived religions in the Americas, Ogun, or Oggun, is the god of iron, metal, and war.

3 I thank Kate Ramsey for helping me clarify this link between Haitian history in the 1990s and the nonlinear aspects of the artist's history work.

4 Tonton Macoutes was the name Duvalier gave to an unpaid terror squad officially known as Volunteers of National Security, or VSN. The group operated independently of the police and the army and reported only to him, effectively circumventing the military's power to challenge Duvalier's rule.

5 In the early 1970s, Amnesty International released several assessments of Haiti's prisons and rated the conditions in Fort Dimanche as among the world's most deplorable. Elizabeth Abbott has noted that severely malnourished prisoners would scrape the lime off the walls to mix with the scant food on offer, in the hope of stemming illness. Duval-Carrié's own brother was sentenced to Fort Dimanche for almost two years. A tall, athletic man when he was arrested, he weighed ninety pounds and was almost to the point of death when released. Edouard Duval-Carrié, interview with the author, Nassau, The Bahamas, March 7, 2008; Abbott, *Haiti*, 135.

6 Aristide quoted in Danner, "The Prophet," 32.

7 Shortly after the dust cleared, more than three thousand Haitians moved onto the grounds of the former prison, swallowing it up in the slum known as Citi Soleil. Aristide's connection with the prison was not lost on the artist; he is also implicated in the work, given his appropriation of the Duvalierist playbook to secure power.

8 In the Vodoun pantheon, a lwa, or loa, refers to a spirit deity or god. Bawon Samedi is the lwa associated with death, sexuality, and children. His domain is the cemetery, the symbolic crossroads between life and death and the arena of the zombie. See glossary of terms in Cosentino, *Sacred Arts of Haitian Vodou*. The name of Haiti's creolized religion is spelled many different ways. This text uses the spelling *Vodoun* following a discussion of the term by Harold Courlander in the 1980s. However, in citations, the spelling used by the cited author is followed as written. See Courlander, "The Word Voodoo."

9 Max Dominique was a senior army officer and known to be an extremely tall, distinguished-looking man. His presence has a double meaning: He is literally "in the family," and as he goes, so goes the army, and his family.

10 Mitchell, *Picture Theory*, 35–82.

11 Mitchell, *Picture Theory*, 58.

12 Hartman, *Scenes of Subjection*, 7.

13 From time to time, I use the phrase *it is believed* to refer to instances in which oral history has forged a common belief whereby, despite the absence of written records, something is spoken of as fact.

Mary Webster's work on the artist Johann Zoffany dates the painting to 1767–68; she notes that John Young, presumably the child in blue silks on the horse, was baptized in Antigua in 1761 and appears to be no more than six years old in the painting. Webster, *Johan Zoffany*, 162.

14 Tobin, *Picturing Imperial Power*, 39–49.

15 This reading is in opposition to that of Tobin, who views the glint of white around the African's neck as a collar. The collar, if represented at all, would have been clearly articulated. This is not the case in the painting. In Webster's 2011 text on Zoffany, there is no mention of a collar; at the same time, she does describe the young man as "a black boy brought no doubt from Antigua," the location of several of Young's extensive Caribbean plantations. Webster, *Johan Zoffany*, 163.

16 For an exegesis on Caribbean Modernism, see James, "The Light of Things / La luz de las cosas."

17 The interpretation of "dress" is impacted by the exhibition format itself and the institutional location of the engagement: art gallery, art museum, history museum, or ethnographic museum. Mintz and Trouillot, "Social History of Haitian Vodou," 123–47; Roberts, *Edouard Duval-Carrié*.

18 The epigraph quotation is from François Duvalier's state-issued text, *Catechism of a Revolution* (1965), in which he employed the liturgical form to envisage his divine ascension to Haitian rule through the lineage of Toussaint and Dessalines. For different assessments of this text, which was distributed widely and in English, see *Time* magazine, May 7, 1965; and Abbott, *Haiti*, 133.

19 Mintz and Trouillot, "Social History of Haitian Vodou," 123.

20 François Makandal was believed to be of Guinean origin and possibly Muslim. He was an older slave who escaped his plantation and devised a plan to poison whites. The plan was discovered, and he was captured and burned at the stake. After his death, any slave found engaging in the use of herbs was said to be committing "makandals." See Mintz and Trouillot, "Social History of Haitian Vodou."

21 Geggus, *Haitian Revolution*; Dayan, *Haiti, History, and the Gods*; Dubois, *Haiti*.

22 Dayan, *Haiti, History, and the Gods*, 29.

23 Laguerre, *Voodoo and Politics in Haiti*, 1.

24 Price, *First-Time*.

25 Bellegarde-Smith, "Spirit of the Thing," 53; Dayan, *Haiti, History, and the Gods*, 27.

26 What is understood as Vodoun today is rooted in Africa but took shape in response and relation to the needs of the Caribbean people and the conditions they found themselves in. I argue that what was being summoned in the eighteenth century by enslaved Africans in Haiti was not what we understand today as Vodoun but rather an early form of African spirituality that emerged out of the Middle Passage, like Abakuá in Cuba, to make sense of its forced rupture.

27 Bastien's position that Boukman performs a Pétro Vodoun ceremony, as opposed to a Rada one, is significant; Rada is seen as African-derived and

deemed a passive or conciliatory spirit. "The Rada gods or loas," Bastien writes, "came from Africa and their role during the slavery period was one of appeasers and conformists, giving solace to their 'children.' The Pétro were born in Haiti and some of them were deified priests and leaders. They were bent on action through fire, poison, and massacre." Bastien, "Vodoun and Politics in Haiti," 42–43. Pétro, created out of the brutality of slavery, was used to combat the violence imposed on Black bodies in Haiti. For Bastien, it stands to reason that if a ceremony was in fact performed, Boukman would have employed a Pétro spirit to call for revolution. However, such an iteration would have required the existence of a fully articulated and distinct Vodoun religion and a consciousness of its revolutionary potential among Haitians, which was highly unlikely at the time. Bastien's argument is cyclical in that it describes the application of a spirit by revolutionaries in the same instant it comes into being. It is both a phenomenon *and* proof that the phenomenon occurred. Even so, his theory has become established history at this point, despite the fact that the distinction between Pétro and Rada sects is a modern phenomenon and one for which I have found no evidence in the late eighteenth century.

28 I propose that Duval-Carrié's chosen setting of Fort Dimanche performs a similar ecclesiastical role for contemporary audiences.

29 Dayan, *Haiti, History, and the Gods*, 30.

30 In a scene from the 2002 film *Roble de Olor* (Scent of Oak), by Cuban filmmaker Rigoberto López, a band has been dispatched by the courts to find the members of what had been described as an orchestra made up of slaves. When the posse arrives at the group's practice space, the leader literally goes mad, unable to register what he sees and hears. In response, he kills all members of the orchestra—effectively erasing the record of their existence and validating, in a macabre sense, his refusal to acknowledge their existence. A similar ethos runs through accounts by individuals like Descourtilz.

31 On occasion, he was known to spare the lives of "physicians, priests and artisans." Niles, *Black Haiti*, 58.

32 James, *Black Jacobins*, 88.

33 James, *Black Jacobins*, 316.

34 Dayan, *Haiti, History, and the Gods*, 24–26.

35 Dayan, *Haiti, History, and the Gods*, 17.

36 For Dessalines, language was a key marker of Haitian identity—a means of recognizing a community born of the experience of the Middle Passage and slavery.

37 Bellegarde-Smith, "Spirit of the Thing," 54.

38 Harris, "History, Fable, and Myth."

39 Bastien, "Vodoun and Politics in Haiti," 52.

40 Shiflett, "World News Makers."

41 Laguerre, *Voodoo and Politics in Haiti*, 4–5.

42 Laguerre, *Voodoo and Politics in Haiti*, 103; Danner, "The Prophet."

43 The corvée was a forced labor system that first appeared in Haiti in the mid-nineteenth century but had long been abandoned by the time of the occupation. The Americans reinstituted it when they arrived in 1915, in order to build roads and other infrastructure. Conditions were extremely harsh, and some described the system as another iteration of slavery.

44 The pattern of recognition of Vodoun artists abroad and persecution of adherents at home goes much deeper. In the essay "Artists of Haiti: Reflections on a Narrative," Richard J. Long examines the international perception of Haitian art, the narrative's institutionalization through the texts of Selden Rodman, and its contestation within Haiti. Long suggests that many Haitians felt that Rodman's book *Renaissance in Haiti: Popular Painters in the Black Republic* (1948) presented a narrow view of Haitian art. Although several texts contradicted his reading, such as *Treatise on Haitian Art* (1959), it was too little too late. Rodman's interpretation was considered definitive, and Haiti entered metropolitan exhibition spaces amid the perception that all art created there was rendered through the veil of Vodoun. Long notes the influence of the United States and the role of the Centre d'Art in shaping this narrative. The Centre d'Art was founded in 1944 as an English-language teaching program under the stewardship of Howard University's Mercer Cook. A 1978 exhibition of Haitian art presented work by both "primitives" and trained artists, though only the work of the "primitives" appeared in the catalog. The trained artists were subsequently included after protesting their exclusion. See Lerebours, "Indigenist Revolt"; and Long, "Artists of Haiti."

45 Bastien, "Vodoun and Politics in Haiti," 60.

46 Roberts, *Edouard Duval-Carrié*, 18.

47 Johnson, "Secretism and the Apotheosis of Duvalier," 422.

48 Laguerre, *Voodoo and Politics in Haiti*, 107.

49 Johnson, "Secretism and the Apotheosis of Duvalier," 424.

50 Rodman and Cleaver, *Spirit of the Night*.

51 Johnson, "Secretism and the Apotheosis of Duvalier," 424.

52 Duvalier's first attempt to change the flag was symbolic and portentous. The proposed alteration was from blue-and-red horizontal to black-and-red vertical. Instead of the coat of arms designed by mulatto President Alexandre Pétion, Duvalier wanted a "guineafowl perched on a conch (the *lambi* which called the slaves to rebellion).... The bird signifies constant vigilance and the conch represents the call to massacre. There can be no clearer warning." Bastien, "Vodoun and Politics in Haiti," 61.

53 It is believed that in "early March 1958, ... Duvalier and a houngan ... took a trek up to [the cave] Trou Foban." Abbott, *Haiti*, 81–82. The cave was believed to be the lwas' dwelling place, and Duvalier's ceremony was

intended to encourage them to follow him to live in the palace. According to the story, the lwas agreed and followed Duvalier down the mountain. It's important to remember that it isn't the legend's truthfulness that matters but the belief it compels and sustains. Many Haitians were believers.

54 This association was reinforced through his death. Duvalier died on April 21, 1971. One day later, a windstorm blew in, and on April 24, Bawon Samedi Day, he was buried. After his son was deposed in 1986, angry Haitians rushed to his grave with the full intention of mutilating his body, but playing the myth to the end, they found that akin to Jesus's rendered fate, the tomb was empty.

55 Abbott, *Haiti*, 106.

56 Fourcand, *Catechisme de la Revolution.*

57 *Time* magazine, May 3, 1963.

58 Edouard Duval-Carrié, interview with the author, Nassau, The Bahamas, March 7, 2008.

59 Abbott, *Haiti*, 111.

60 Danner, "Reporter at Large—II." Duvalier never left Haiti after becoming president, but two events occurred that shielded him and Haiti from outside influence in ensuing years. The only chief of state to visit was Haile Selassie in 1966, of major symbolic importance to the Rastafari Movement in the region; and in 1967, Duvalier won the support of Israel when Haiti cast a deciding vote to recognize the state.

61 Abbott, *Haiti*, 111.

62 Epigraph to this section quoted in McCarthy Brown, *Tracing the Spirit*, 77.

63 The visual record of the Duvalier years is remarkably and, one must conclude, purposely scant. This image is recounted and verbally described in Haitian history texts such as Abbott's, but despite lengthy efforts, I have not located a physical copy of the poster.

64 Abbott, *Haiti*, 159.

65 Abbott, *Haiti*, 241–42.

66 Cody, "To Snuff Out Swine Fever, Haiti Slaughters Its Pigs."

67 Abbott, *Haiti*, 203–4, 336–37.

68 Solomon, "Pope's Visit Treated as National Holiday in Haiti," UPI, March 10, 1983; Pullella, "Ending His 8-Nation Tour Pope John Paul II . . . ," UPI, March 10, 1983.

69 "Pope in Haiti, Assails Inequality, Hunger, and Fear," *New York Times*, March 10, 1983, A-8. Father Jean-Bertrand Aristide capitalized on the popular success of the pope's visit to build a political movement that would hasten Duvalierism's swift collapse. As a Catholic priest, Aristide, like the majority of middle- and working-class Haitians who heard the pontiff speak, spoke and understood French. To extend his reach, like Duvalier and Dessalines before him, he employed visual codes and cultivated mythologies to fuel his ascendancy.

70 It is a fascinating aspect of the Duvalier regime that it was not widely photographed—on purpose. Papa Doc rarely recorded himself, his family, or his crimes in photographs and videos, unless the visualization could be leveraged in targeted ways. He also forbade news agencies from printing photographs. A shrewd observer of photography's presumed capacity to reflect truth, Duvalier understood the power of rumor over fact and accordingly used documentation mediums sparingly.

71 Mintz and Trouillot, "Social History of Haitian Vodou," 126.

72 Antze and Lambek, *Tense Past*, 3.

73 Antze and Lambek, *Tense Past*, 239, 240.

74 McCarthy Brown, *Tracing the Spirit*, 14.

75 Bennett, *Empathic Vision*, 2–5. Bennett fleshes out this idea using Hal Foster's *The Return of the Real*, in which Foster presents the subject as simultaneously "evacuated and elevated."

76 Antze and Lambek, *Tense Past*, 241.

77 Dayan, *Haiti, History, and the Gods*, xviii.

78 Bennett, *Empathic Vision*, 150.

79 Cosentino, *Sacred Arts of Haitian Vodou*, 35.

80 Duval-Carrié, *Vodou Pantheon*.

81 Conner, "Rainbow's Children," 143.

82 Danner, "Reporter at Large—I," 55.

83 Similar subterfuge has been attempted in other, spectacular and, at times, comical instances throughout the Caribbean, more recently with the apprehension of the infamous Jamaican drug lord, or don, Christopher "Dudus" Coke in 2010.

84 Butcher, "Peter Minshall," 39, 48.

85 Tseëlon, "Introduction," 3.

86 Tseëlon, "Introduction," 3.

87 Rara is a public carnival performance that usually occurs around Lent. Historically, it was performed primarily in the countryside, but it is now seen in urban areas as well. Groups of men and women associated with specific *houmforts*, or Vodoun temples, parade through the streets for miles, accompanied by music, singing, spontaneous and choreographed dancing, and religious rituals. The songs and movements are decidedly secular and sexual in nature, but, as McAlister demonstrates, they can also be politically astute and subversive. As the celebrants proceed through the streets, they solicit monetary donations from the public. A figure called the *major-jonc* precedes the procession, preparing the spectators for what is to come. McAlister, *Rara!* For more on this specific form of carnival, see Deren, *Divine Horsemen*.

88 McAlister, *Rara!*, 31.

89 Bennett, *Empathic Vision*, 2.

90 Dayan, *Haiti, History, and the Gods*, 37.

91 McAlister, *Rara!*, 102.
92 Paravisini-Gebert, "Women Possessed," 39.
93 Paravisini-Gebert, "Women Possessed," 40; Hurston, *Tell My Horse*; Seabrook, *Magic Island*.
94 Bennett, *Empathic Vision*, 7.
95 McAlister, *Rara!*, 7.
96 Thompson, *Flash of the Spirit*, 117.
97 Minow, *Between Vengeance and Forgiveness*, 147; Das, *Remaking a World*, 13.
98 Thompson, *Flash of the Spirit*, 127.

CHAPTER FOUR: THE CARIBBEAN DOES NOT EXIST

1 Horowitz, *Art of the Deal*, 101.
2 The Havana (Cuba) Biennial (est. 1984), the San Juan (Puerto Rico) Biennial of Latin American and Caribbean Engraving (1970–2001), and the Dominican Republic Biennial of Visual Art (est. 1942) are some examples of the form in the Caribbean.
3 Funcke et al., *6th Caribbean Biennial* (unpaginated).
4 Gingeras, "Sociology Without Truth," 52.
5 Cattelan quoted in Bonami et al., *Maurizio Cattelan*, 35. This text is a compilation of interviews with the artists, statements that Cattelan made in the late 1980s through the early 2000s, writings on his work, and texts he considered important. Note the difference in spelling of the terms *biennial* and *biennale*. Spelling may shift depending on the cited reference.
6 Ads were printed in *Artforum*, *Frieze*, and *Flash Art* in November 1999. Cattelan later interspersed this promotional form with half-truths and lies; for example, "Armando Garcia's" official introduction to the biennial as "Councilor for Culture of the Caribbean Region and Director of the Caribbean Biennial" is pure pose; no such position or person existed. Though prominently included in the advertised roster of participating artists, Chris Ofili, arguably the most controversial artist of 1999, never made it to the event. Yet Ofili, the only Black artist on the list, "appears" in the "exhibition" catalogue, stereotypically represented by disembodied gold chains and a large pendant, along with a quote from Rudy Giuliani on civilization. The catalogue was published long after the event. His reputation colonized, Ofili is nonetheless archived as a key player in a performance he never participated in. Even the catalogue's subtitle, *Blown Away*, subsumed nature's unpredictability by centralizing the unforeseen, devastating hurricane that passed over St. Kitts while the biennial was in full swing.
7 Ian Strachan's *Paradise and Plantation: Tourism and Culture in the Anglophone Caribbean* (2002) was one of the first literary and cultural analyses of tourism's promotional imagery in the making of the Caribbean. This

lesser-known text is a key precursor to Krista Thompson's in-depth engagement of the role of early photography in the formation of the Caribbean picturesque, *An Eye for the Tropics: Tourism, Photography, and Framing the Caribbean Picturesque* (2006). Thompson examined the disarticulation or rearticulation of these tropes in the work of contemporary artists such as David A. Bailey and Christopher Cozier. My text draws on Strachan's insightful research and shares Thompson's desire to look at these phenomena as a means to call into question postcolonial theory as currently imagined, effecting a more generative movement of the art historical discourse.

8 The term *brochure Caribbean* was coined by Polly Pattullo, and its meaning was expanded by Ian Strachan.

9 All quotes purporting to be the voice of Cattelan in this book are from the previously cited event catalogue as archive, an unpaginated text edited by Bettina Funcke, Cattelan, and Hoffmann.

10 It is unclear how much the artists knew about the "biennial" before they agreed to travel, but at least one participating artist, Mariko Mori, is known to have grown increasingly uncomfortable with the premise as the days passed, and left early.

11 I have always suspected that the journals might have been "in on the joke," but their writers do not appear to have been.

12 Liu, "Trouble in Paradise." Liu notes the emptiness and hypocrisy of this supposed "anarchic" performance. The biennial made the artists "the object of contemplation" yet suppressed the coverage of the performance by the performing objects.

13 Funcke et al., *6th Caribbean Biennial*, 2001.

14 Liu, "Trouble in Paradise."

15 Foucault, *What Is an Author?*, 116–18.

16 It calcified the power dynamics embedded in the relationship.

17 Yancy, "Colonial Gazing," 7.

18 Gingeras, "Sociology Without Truth," 53.

19 Gingeras, "Sociology Without Truth."

20 Walcott, "The Antilles."

21 Considering the ways Cattelan's work encountered that of global Caribbean artists before and after the 6th Caribbean Biennial is sometimes amusing. Not only was his artwork featured alongside that of Antoni, Ayón, and other global Caribbean artists in major exhibitions and biennials, but their convergence also materialized in texts. For example, in *Fractured Figure: Works from the Dakis Joannou Collection* (2007), Antoni's *Saddle* (2000) faces off against Cattelan's *Now* (2004) on facing pages.

22 The concept of the "borderclash" was theorized by Carolyn Cooper in *Noises in the Blood.* Dancehall, Cooper argues, is a Caribbean way of seeing and expression that contravenes the ways these expressions have been read in the West.

23 Glissant and Dash, *Caribbean Discourse*, 64.

24 Puri, *Caribbean Postcolonial*, 142.

25 Barthes, *Mythologies*; Lacan, "The Mirror Stage."

26 Here I am drawing on Walter Benjamin's "Author as Producer" (1937), in which he noted the communal nature of art and its specific relevance to the production of national or anticolonial discourses through the creation and destruction of public monuments.

27 Spivak, *Critique of Postcolonial Reason*, 118, 211, 228.

28 Various scholars have theorized and deployed the term *zombification*, discussed in the previous chapter. Here I extend the reading in the previous chapter through Shalini Puri's discussion of its use in Erna Brodber's novel *Myal* (1999). The term offers Puri a gauge by which to discuss and redefine cultural theft as a kind of "spirit thievery" or "zombification." This fascinating idea is also explored as a metaphor for a colonized mind in, for example, Benítez-Rojo, *Repeating Island*; and Dayan, *Haiti, History, and the Gods*.

29 Pattullo, *Last Resorts*, 62.

30 Kirshenblatt-Gimblett, *Destination Culture*, 48.

31 Kirshenblatt-Gimblett, *Destination Culture*, 47.

32 The term *forged* is used to specifically reflect back to the difficult processes involved in forming the Caribbean. It is a creolized culture, but one in which inequalities of power, race, ethnicity, and gender have not magically disappeared. The concept as it relates to Caribbean hybridity is discussed with particular richness in Puri, *Caribbean Postcolonial*.

33 By 1990, the World Tourist Organization (WTO) reported, tourism represented the largest employment sector in many Caribbean islands, 35 and 37 percent of the Bahamian and Jamaican labor force, respectively. Harrison, *Tourism and the Less Developed Countries*, 15.

34 Lacan, "The Mirror Stage," 4.

35 Lacan, *Four Fundamental Concepts of Psycho-Analysis*, 95.

36 Lacan, *Four Fundamental Concepts of Psycho-Analysis*, 96.

37 Lacan, *Four Fundamental Concepts of Psycho-Analysis*, 106.

38 Lacan, *Four Fundamental Concepts of Psycho-Analysis*, 92. I am using *brochure* and *poster* in the literal sense, but the observation extends to any information delivered through a digital, visual, ekphrastic, or aural medium that grounds the tourist's perception of the place to which they will travel.

39 Lacan, *Four Fundamental Concepts of Psycho-Analysis*, 101.

40 Barthes, *Mythologies*, 116. This young man can be read on multiple levels: as an empty signifier that makes him a symbol of French imperialism; as a full signifier that recognizes the "truth" that the young Black boy is only an alibi and that he understands the distortion; and finally as a mythical signifier whereby the Black boy comes to represent, or embody French imperiality, the implication being that he has been civilized and has benefited from imperialism.

41 Barthes, *Mythologies*, 118, 121.

42 Albers and James note photography's deployment as an anticipatory frame to inform the tourist's experience and as the primary means through which they certify their experience. Photographs distill chaotic experiences and verify the *reality* and historical trace of a given experience. Albers and James, "Tourism and the Changing Photographic Image," 126.

43 Craton and Saunders, *Islanders in the Stream*, 302.

44 The importance of engaging the brochure and television commercial as an image-text comes from my reading of W. J. T. Mitchell's proposal that it conceptually provides a way of "trying to capture the sense that even the 'atomic unit' of semiotics—the sign—is a heterogeneous structure of representation, a mixed medium." Wiesenthal and Bucknell, "Essays into the Imagetext," 17.

45 Albers and James, "Tourism and the Changing Photographic Image," 127.

46 Commonwealth of The Bahamas, Annual Report on Tourism, 1969–1975.

47 Pattullo, *Last Resorts*, 151.

48 Strachan, *Paradise and Plantation*, 94 (emphasis added).

49 *The Bahamas Handbook*.

50 Although not addressed here, sex tourism is a Caribbean reality. While sex workers have been present in the Caribbean since the earliest contact with Europe, mass tourism created a demand that intersects with a native desire to compete economically. This intersection has dramatically increased the number of individuals engaged in the sex business. The tendency has been to describe this relationship from the outside in, using the trope of the "exotic" as lure for the innocent tourist. Certainly the brochures I have thus far discussed would support this approach. This notion of the "exotic" fits neatly into Western paradigms and is general enough to allow the men and women who patronize the Caribbean sex worker to relinquish responsibility, regardless of race, age, or ethnicity. It is a business that includes male (referred to as "rent-a-dread" in Jamaica) and female prostitutes. But it is also a "business" that attracts violence and panders in the sexual abuse of children. These factors should give everyone pause and call into question neat readings of exoticism and Caribbean sex work. See Kempadoo, *Sun, Sex, and Gold*; de Albuquerque, "In Search of the Big Bamboo"; Padilla, *Caribbean Pleasure Industry*; and Nixon, *Resisting Paradise*.

51 Wiesenthal and Bucknell, "Essays into the Imagetext."

52 Drysdale, *In Sunny Lands*, 6; Strachan, *Paradise and Plantation*, 109.

53 In *The Middle Passage*, V. S. Naipaul remarked that "every poor country accepts tourism as an unavoidable degradation. None has gone as far as some of these West Indian islands, which, in the name of tourism, are selling themselves into a new slavery" (210). It can be said that Maurice Bishop's stand against neocolonial forces in Grenada contributed to his death.

54 Spivak, *A Critique of Postcolonial Reason*, 211, 212.

55 Checchi and Co., *A Plan for Managing the Growth of Tourism*, 153–54.

56 Strachan, *Paradise and Plantation*, 210.

57 MacCannell, *The Tourist*, 109–17 (inevitability of disappointment); Frow, *Time and Commodity Culture*, 67.

58 Frow, *Time and Commodity Culture*, 94.

59 Stewart, *On Longing*, 23.

60 Chloe Chard notes a desire on the part of eighteenth-century European and American travel writers to obscure "the boundary between the foreign and the familiar by the construction of a second boundary: the line of separation between the traveller as spectator and the pictorial spectacle of the foreign." In the process, the traveler becomes distant from both domains of their normal reality and exists in a type of liminal space. As one individual on the Grand Tour stated, "I am a nameless person, a mere bird of passage, it [any disturbing thing they may encounter] concerns me not." Chard, "Crossing Boundaries," 127, 138.

61 Lett, "Ludic and Liminoid," 49.

62 Gramsci, *Prison Notebooks*, 235.

63 Scott, *Weapons of the Weak*.

64 Spivak, *Critique of Postcolonial Reason*, 215.

65 While a discussion of this monument is outside the scope of this project, the public dialogue and scholarly work that developed around it are notable. See Poupeye, "Monument in the Public Sphere."

66 Dacres, "Monument and Meaning."

67 Tunnard and Pollaco, *Jamaica*, 20. The authors gave the example of the statue of Lord Rodney, who saved the country from invasion by the French in 1782. In 1873 Rodney's statue was moved by state mandate from Spanish Town to "the foot of King Street in Kingston, against the wishes of the former community's inhabitants, who hauled it back again."

68 Brathwaite, *Wars of Respect*, 3.

69 Brathwaite, *Wars of Respect*, 4.

70 Brathwaite, *Wars of Respect*, 6.

71 Brathwaite, *Wars of Respect*, 6.

72 "The Statue of Lewis Quier Bowerbank," Compilation of the West India Reference Library, May 16, 1970, from *Journal of the Institute of Jamaica*, vol. 1: *1891–1898*, Institute of Jamaica.

73 "The Statue of Lewis Quier Bowerbank."

74 The Historical Sites of Jamaica, Morant Bay Courthouse, West India Reference Library, National Library of Jamaica, Kingston.

75 The Historical Sites of Jamaica.

76 "Dr. Bowerbank," *Daily Gleaner*, December 19, 1960, Archives of the *Jamaica Gleaner*.

77 "Dr. Bowerbank," *Daily Gleaner*, December 19, 1960.

78 In the guise of evenhandedness—or the "both sides disease"—the writer performs the role of Spivak's native escort by attempting to subsume the native's right to reinterpret the past.

79 "Bowerbank Won't Go to Bellevue," *Daily Gleaner*, June 13, 1961.

80 "Bowerbank Statue Still No Decision," *Daily Gleaner*, December 16, 1961.

81 "Decision to Replace Statues, 'Trying to Rewrite History,' Says Seneca," *(Jamaica) Star*, May 17, 1970. The Bowerbank debate was resurrected in this defense when a citizen critic writing in the *Gleaner* faulted the KSAC for erroneously accusing Bowerbank of being involved in Gordon's execution, preferring to remember him instead as a "humanitarian administrator who had been responsible for transforming a slave hospital on North Street into the Kingston Public Hospital."

82 "Decision to Replace Statues."

83 Barnes, in *Cultural Conundrums*, prologue, discusses the statue in the context of Caribbean gendered and racialized cultural politics. While Barnes reads the beheading as retribution, I see it as a defiant act of autohistoriography on the part of marginalized Caribbean voices, a weapon of the weak. The story continued in 2020 when the statue was destroyed during protests in Martinique in the wake of George Floyd's death.

84 Brathwaite, "Caribbean Man in Space and Time," *Carifesta Forum*, 202.

85 The public monument to Nanny was highly contested. In "Nanny Stands Tall," published in the *Kingston Daily News* on October 21, 1981, Jean Jackson suggested that this position was based on the fact that she was a Maroon and that the "patriotic parishioners of Paul Bogle maintained that no Maroon should be a Hero." This is because, after Nanny's death, colonial governments enlisted Maroons to hunt runaway slaves. "In October of 1865," Jackson recounts, "there was a price of 400 pound sterling on Bogle's head and it was in fact the Maroons who hounded, arrested and took him to Morant Bay, heralded we are told by the blowing of conch shells. . . . Needless to say, Nanny had been dead for well over a century when Paul Bogle was captured." She posits that the history of the Maroons cannot be narrowed to that period or to that incident and argues that Nanny deserved National Hero status and a monument because "she personifies many of the ideals for which, as a people we are still striving—discipline, self-sufficiency, courage, strength and dignity. She commanded the respect of both friend and foe, and was a force to be reckoned with, as the British had to recognise, even at that stage." Nanny's monument is currently in National Heroes Park, Kingston.

86 Danner, "Beyond the Mountains (Part II)."

87 Funcke et al., *6th Caribbean Biennial.*

88 Funcke et al., *6th Caribbean Biennial.*

Epigraphs: Walter Mignolo in Hoffmann, "Interview—Walter Mignolo/ Part 2"; Irénée Shaw in Hezekiah, "Conceptualizing the Boundaries of Nation-Space."

1 All references to Christopher Cozier and his practice are based on a series of conversations and formal interviews that occurred between artist and author in Nassau, Port of Spain, New York, and Miami and online between 2005 and 2023.

2 Cozier's work can have multiple elements or feature extended engagements, taking various forms throughout. *Blue Soap* is a work that had performance, video, and sculpture iterations or elements.

3 Untitled essay dated 1998, Christopher Cozier personal archives.

4 Gugolati, "A Detergent Artwork in Trinidad and Tobago."

5 Cozier, "Searching for a Way Out," 420, 422.

6 Cozier and Paul, "Debating the Contemporary in Caribbean Art."

7 Cozier, "Between Narratives and Other Spaces," 19.

8 Cozier, "Between Narratives and Other Spaces," 21.

9 Cozier and Tancons, "No More Than a Backyard on a Small Island," 45.

10 Cozier and Tancons, "No More Than a Backyard on a Small Island."

11 This essay was first presented as a talk in Barbados shortly after CARIFESTA '72. It was then published in 1974 as a standalone pamphlet entitled "Caribbean Man in Space and Time: A Bibliographic and Conceptual Approach," by Savacou, and again as "Caribbean Man in Space and Time," *Savacou* 11–12 (September 1, 1975): 1–11. The following year, another version was published as "Caribbean Man in Space and Time," in *Carifesta Forum: An Anthology of 20 Caribbean Voices*, edited by John Hearne.

12 Brathwaite, "Caribbean Man in Space and Time," in *Carifesta Forum.*

13 The INE was one of three shows installed at the launch of the National Art Gallery of The Bahamas in 2003. It featured Bahamian artists who had been working in The Bahamas and abroad since 1973, the year of The Bahamas' independence from Britain. The other exhibitions were *Bahamian Visions: 1870–1920*, a photography exhibition curated by Krista A. Thompson, and *One Man's Vision: The Vincent D'Aguilar Collection*, curated by Petrine Archer-Straw.

BIBLIOGRAPHY

ARCHIVES

Archives of the *Jamaica Gleaner*, Kingston. Online.
Artist files. Catherine Couturier Gallery, Los Angeles, CA.
Lydia Cabrera Papers (1910–91). Cuban Heritage Collection, University of Miami.
Chris Cozier personal archives.
National Archives of The Bahamas, Nassau.
National Library of Jamaica. Institute of Jamaica, Kingston.
Selden Rodman Papers. Library Archives, University of Wyoming, Laramie.
Selden Rodman Papers. Sterling Library Archives, Yale University, New Haven, CT.
Alex and Carol Rosenberg Papers. New York, NY.
Rachel Weiss Papers. Cuban Heritage Collection, University of Miami.

BOOKS AND ARTICLES

Abbott, Elizabeth. *Haiti: The Duvaliers and Their Legacy*. New York: Touchstone Simon and Schuster, 1988.

Acevedo-Muñoz, Ernesto R. "The End of the Line: Africa, Death, and Freedom in Caribbean Cinema." In *Healing Cultures: Art and Religion as Curative Practices in the Caribbean and Its Diaspora*, edited by Margarite Fernández Olmos and Lizabeth Paravisini-Gebert, 165–78. New York: Palgrave, 2001.

Albers, Patricia C., and William R. James. "Tourism and the Changing Photographic Image of the Great Lakes Indians." *Annals of Tourism Research* 10, no. 1 (1983): 123–48.

Alea, Tomas Gutierrez, and Julianne Burton. "'Individual Fulfillment and Collective Achievement': An Interview with Tomas Gutierrez Alea." *Cinéaste* 8, no. 1 (1977): 8–15, 59.

Allen, Caroline. "Caribbean Bodies: Representation and Practice." In *Caribbean Portraits: Essays on Gender Ideologies and Identities*, edited by Christine Barrow, 276–93. Kingston, Jamaica: Ian Randle, 1998.

Allen, Jafari Sinclaire. "Looking Black at Revolutionary Cuba." *Latin American Perspectives* 36, no. 1 (2009): 53–62.

Altunaga, Eliseo. "*The Dead Come at Midnight*: Scripting the White Aesthetic / Black Ethic." In *Afro-Cuban Voices: On Race and Identity in Contemporary Cuba*, edited by Pedro Pérez Sarduy and Jean Stubbs, 87–96. Gainesville: University Press of Florida, 2000.

Amalfitano, Lelia. *Self/Made Self/Conscious: Janine Antoni and Bruce Nauman.* Boston: School of Museum of Fine Arts, 1994.

Antoni, Janine. Artist talk and conversation with David Bailey. Whitechapel Gallery, London, November 2003.

Antoni, Janine. *The Girl Made of Butter: Janine Antoni.* Ridgefield, CT: Aldrich Museum of Contemporary Art, 2000.

Antoni, Janine. "Janine Antoni: Born 1964." In *Modern Sculpture: Artists in Their Own Words*, edited by Douglas Dreishpoon, 323–25. Berkeley: University of California Press, 2022.

Antoni, Janine. *Moor.* Stockholm: Magasin 3 Stockholm Konsthall; Santa Fe: SITE Santa Fe, 2003.

Antoni, Janine, and Marcel Odenbach. "Advertisement for Myself: Marcel Odenbach in Conversation with Janine Antoni." *PAJ* 21, no. 2 (1999): 33–41.

Antze, Paul, and Michael Lambek, eds. *Tense Past: Cultural Essays in Trauma and Memory.* New York: Routledge, 1996.

Apter, Andrew. *Black Critics and Kings: The Hermeneutics of Power in Yoruba Society.* Chicago: University of Chicago Press, 1992.

Apter, Emily. "Splitting Hairs: Female Fetishism and Postpartum Sentimentality in the Fin de Siècle." In *Eroticism and the Body Politic*, edited by Lynn Hunt, 164–90. Baltimore, MD: Johns Hopkins University Press, 1991.

Aratán, Sonia. "Entrevistas con Aimé Césaire." *Casa de Las Américas* 49 (July–August 1968): 130–37.

Aristide, Jean-Bertrand. *In the Parish of the Poor: Writings from Haiti.* Translated and edited by Amy Wilentz. Maryknoll, NY: Orbis Books, 1990.

Ayón, Belkis, and Cristina Vives. *Behind the Veil of a Myth = Tras el velo de un mito: Belkis Ayón.* Houston: Station Museum of Contemporary Art, 2018.

Ayón, Katia, and Cristina Vives, eds. *Nkame: Belkis Ayón.* Madrid: Turner, 2010.

Bagneris, Mia L. *Colouring the Caribbean: Race and the Art of Agostino Brunias.* Manchester: Manchester University Press, 2018.

The Bahamas Handbook. Nassau: DuPuch, 1969.

Barber, Karin. "How Man Makes God in West Africa: Yoruba Attitudes Towards the *Orisa.*" *Africa* 51, no. 3 (1981): 724–45.

Barnes, Natasha. *Cultural Conundrums: Gender, Race, Nation, and the Making of Caribbean Cultural Politics.* Ann Arbor: University of Michigan Press, 2006.

Barnet, Miguel. *Afro-Cuban Religions.* Translated by Christine Renata Ayorinde. Princeton, NJ: Markus Wiener; Kingston, Jamaica: Ian Randle, 1995.

Barson, Tanya, and Peter Gorschlüter, eds. *Afro Modern: Journeys Through the Black Atlantic.* Liverpool: Tate, 2010.

Barthes, Roland. *Mythologies*. New York: Hill and Wang, 1972.

Bastien, Rémy. "Vodoun and Politics in Haiti." In *Religion and Politics in Haiti—Two Essays*, edited by Harold Courlander and Rémy Bastien; preface by Richard P. Schaedel, 39–68. Washington, DC: Institute for Cross-Cultural Research, 1966.

Bellegarde-Smith, Patrick, ed. *Fragments of Bone: Neo-African Religions in a New World*. Urbana: University of Illinois Press, 2005.

Bellegarde-Smith, Patrick. "The Spirit of the Thing: Religious Thought and Social/History Memory." In *Fragments of Bone: Neo-African Religions in a New World*, edited by Patrick Bellegarde-Smith, 52–69. Urbana: University of Illinois Press, 2005.

Benítez-Rojo, Antonio. *The Repeating Island: The Caribbean and the Postmodern Perspective*. Translated by James E. Maraniss. 2nd ed. Durham, NC: Duke University Press, 1996.

Benjamin, Walter. "Author as Producer." In *Walter Benjamin: Selected Writings*, vol. 2, part 2: *1931–1934*, translated by Rodney Livingstone et al.; edited by Michael W. Jennings, Howard Eiland, and Gary Smith. Cambridge, MA: Belknap Press of Harvard University Press, 1999.

Bennett, Jill. *Empathic Vision: Affect, Trauma, and Contemporary Art*. Stanford, CA: Stanford University Press, 2005.

Benson, Devyn Spence. *Antiracism in Cuba: The Unfinished Revolution*. Chapel Hill: University of North Carolina Press, 2016.

Benson, Devyn Spence. "Sara Gómez: *Afrocubana* (Afro-Cuban Women's) Activism After 1961." *Cuban Studies* 46 (2019): 134–58.

Benson, Devyn Spence, Daisy Rubiera Castillo, and Inés María Martiatu Terry, eds. *Afrocubanas: History, Thought, and Cultural Practices*. Translated by Karina Alma. New York: Rowman and Littlefield International, 2020.

Bethel, E. Clement. *Junkanoo: Festival of The Bahamas*. Edited and expanded by Nicolette Bethel. London: Macmillan Caribbean, 1991.

Bettelheim, Judith. *AfroCuba: Works on Paper, 1968–2003*. Seattle: University of Washington Press, 2005.

Bonami, Francesco, Nancy Spector, Barbara Vanderlinden, and Massimiliano Gioni. *Maurizio Cattelan*. London: Phaidon, 2000.

Bonilla, Yarimar. *Non-Sovereign Futures: French Caribbean Politics in the Wake of Disenchantment*. Chicago: University of Chicago Press, 2015.

Bottinelli, Silvia. "*In & On*: Herbs, Fish, and Janine Antoni's Touch." In *The Taste of Art: Cooking, Food, and Counterculture in Contemporary Practices*, edited by Silvia Bottinelli and Margherita d'Ayala Valva, 107–19. Fayetteville: University of Arkansas Press, 2017.

Boyes, Johanna Morgan. "Genre and Subjectification in Janine Antoni's *Loving Care*." *Journal of Student Research* 7, no. 2 (2018): 14–17.

Branson-Gill, Rosemary. *Belkis Ayón: Early Work*. Boston: Massachusetts College of Art, 2003.

Brathwaite, Edward Kamau. "Caribbean Man in Space and Time." *Savacou* 11–12 (September 1975): 1–11.

Brathwaite, Edward Kamau. "Caribbean Man in Space and Time." In *Carifesta Forum: An Anthology of 20 Caribbean Voices*, edited by John Hearne, 199–208. Kingston, Jamaica: CARIFESTA, 1976.

Brathwaite, Edward Kamau. *Wars of Respect: Nanny and Sam Sharpe*. Kingston, Jamaica: Agency for Public Information, 1977.

Brodber, Erna. *Myal*. London: New Beacon Books, 1999.

Brossard, Janette. "Es muy exigente, pero también muy flexible" / "She Was Very Demanding, but Also Very Flexible." In *Nkame: Belkis Ayón*, edited by Katia Ayón and Cristina Vives, 120|289–123|291. Madrid: Turner, 2010.

Broude, Norma, and Mary D. Garrard, eds. *The Power of Feminist Art: The American Movement of the 1970s, History and Impact*. New York: Harry N. Abrams, 1996.

Brown, David H. *The Light Inside: Abakuá Society Arts and Cuban Cultural History*. Washington, DC: Smithsonian Books, 2003.

Brown, David H. *Santería Enthroned: Art, Ritual, and Innovation in an Afro-Cuban Religion*. Chicago: University of Chicago Press, 2003.

Buck-Morss, Susan. *Hegel, Haiti, and Universal History*. Pittsburgh: University of Pittsburgh Press, 2009.

Bundy, A. J. M., ed. *Selected Essays of Wilson Harris: The Unfinished Genesis of the Imagination*. London: Routledge, 1999.

Buskirk, Martha. *The Contingent Object of Contemporary Art*. Cambridge, MA: MIT Press, 2003.

Butcher, Joanne. "Peter Minshall: Trinidad Carnival and the Carnivalesque." *International Review of African American Art* 8, no. 3 (1989): 39–48.

Cameron, Dan. "Habeas Corpus." In *Janine Antoni: Slip of the Tongue*, edited by Nicola White and Brenda McPharland, n.p. Glasgow: Center for Contemporary Art; Dublin: Irish Museum of Modern Art, 1995.

Camnitzer, Luis. *New Art of Cuba*. Austin: University of Texas Press, 1994.

Carnegie, Charles V. *Postnationalism Prefigured: Caribbean Borderlands*. New Brunswick, NJ: Rutgers University Press, 2002.

Carson, Juli. "Response to 'The Reception of the Sixties.'" *October* 71 (1995): 144–45.

Cartelli, Thomas. "After *The Tempest*: Shakespeare, Postcoloniality, and Michelle Cliff's New, New World Miranda." *Contemporary Literature* 36, no. 1 (1995): 82–102.

Cembalest, Robin. "Fast Forward: Janine Antoni." *Art News* 92, no. 9 (1993): 122–23.

Césaire, Aimé. "Cahier d'un retour au pays natal / Notebook of a Return to the Native Land" (1939). In *Aimé Césaire: The Collected Poetry*, translated by Clayton Eshleman and Annette Smith, 32–85. Berkeley: University of California Press, 1983.

Césaire, Aimé. *Discourse on Colonialism*. Introduction by Robin D. G. Kelley. 1955. Reprint, New York: Monthly Review Press, 2000.

Césaire, Aimé. "The Man of Culture and His Responsibilities." *Présence Africaine* 24–25, no. 1 (1959): 125–32.

Césaire, Aimé. *A Season in the Congo*. Translated by Gayatri Chakravorty Spivak. Introduction by Souleymane Bachir Diagne. London: Seagull Books, 2010.

Césaire, Aimé. *A Tempest*. Translated by Richard Miller. Alexandria, VA: Alexander Street, 2000.

Césaire, Aimé. *Toussaint Louverture: La Revolución Francesa y el problema colonia.* Havana: Instituto del Libro, 1967.

Césaire, Aimé. *The Tragedy of King Christophe: A Play*. Translated by Paul Breslin and Rachel Ney. Evanston, IL: Northwestern University Press, 2015.

Césaire, Suzanne. *The Great Camouflage: Writings of Dissent (1941–1945)*. Edited by Daniel Maximin. Translated by Keith L. Walker. Middletown, CT: Wesleyan University Press, 2012.

Chanan, Michael. *Cuban Cinema*. Minneapolis: University of Minnesota Press, 2004.

Chard, Chloe. "Crossing Boundaries and Exceeding Limits: Destabilization, Tourism, and the Sublime." In *Transports: Travel, Pleasure, and Imaginative Geography, 1600–1830*, edited by Chloe Chard and Helen Langdon, 117–50. New Haven, CT: Yale University Press, 1996.

Checchi and Company. *A Plan for Managing the Growth of Tourism in the Commonwealth of The Bahamas*. Nassau: The Bahamas Ministry of Tourism, 1969.

Cheng, Anne Anlin. "Wounded Beauty: An Exploratory Essay on Race, Feminism, and the Aesthetic Question." *Tulsa Studies in Women's Literature* 19, no. 2 (2000): 191–217.

Chivallon, Christine. "Mémoires de l'esclavage à la Martinique: L'explosion mémorielle et la révélation de mémoires anonymes" [Memories of Slavery in Martinique: Eruption of Memories and the Revelation of Anonymous Ones]. *Cahiers d'Études Africaines* 50, no. 197 (2010): 235–61.

Church, Emily Musil. "In Search of Seven Sisters: A Biography of the Nardal Sisters of Martinique." *Callaloo* 36, no. 2 (2013): 375–90.

Cliff, Michelle. "Caliban's Daughter." *Journal of Caribbean Literatures* 3, no. 3 (2003): 157–60.

Cliff, Michelle. "Caliban's Daughter: The Tempest and the Teapot." *Frontiers* 12, no. 2 (1991): 36–51.

Cliff, Michelle. *No Telephone to Heaven*. New York: Plume, 1996.

Cody Edward. "To Snuff Out Swine Fever, Haiti Slaughters Its Pigs." *Washington Post*, April 2, 1983.

Collihan, Kathleen M., and Constantine P. Danopoulos. "Coup d'Etat Attempt in Trinidad: Its Causes and Failure." *Armed Forces and Society* 19, no. 3 (1993): 435–50.

Conner, Randy P. "Rainbow's Children: Diversity of Gender and Sexuality in African-Diasporic Spiritual Traditions." In *Fragments of Bone: Neo-African Religions in a New World*, edited by Patrick Bellegarde-Smith, 143–66. Urbana: University of Illinois Press, 2005.

Cooper, Carolyn. "Dancehall Dress: Competing Codes of Decency in Jamaica." In *Black Style,* edited by Carol Tulloch, 68–83. London: V&A, 2004.

Cooper, Carolyn. "Lady Saw Cuts Loose: Female Fertility Rituals in the Dancehall." In *Sound Clash,* edited by Carolyn Cooper, 99–123. New York: Palgrave Macmillan, 2004.

Cooper, Carolyn. *Noises in the Blood: Orality, Gender, and the "Vulgar" Body of Jamaican Popular Culture.* Durham, NC: Duke University Press, 1995.

Cooper, Carolyn. "Sweet and Sour Sauce: Sexual Politics in Jamaican Dancehall Culture." The 2005 Jagan Lecture, Center for Research on Latin America and the Caribbean (CERLAC), York University, North York, 2007.

Cordiés Jackson, Lliliam, and Nuria Pérez Sesma. "Issues of Black Health." In *Afro-Cuban Voices: On Race and Identity in Contemporary Cuba,* edited by Pedro Pérez Sarduy and Jean Stubbs, 61–74. Gainesville: University Press of Florida, 2000.

Cornet, Joseph. "African Art and Authenticity." *African Arts* 9, no. 1 (1975): 52–55.

Cottingham, Laura. "Janine Antoni: Biting Sums Up My Relationship to Art History." *Flash Art* 26, no. 171 (1993): 104–5.

Cosentino, Donald J., ed. *Sacred Arts of Haitian Vodou.* Los Angeles: UCLA Fowler Museum of Cultural History, 1995.

Cosentino, Donald, and Edouard Duval-Carrié. *Divine Revolution: The Art of Edouard Duval-Carrié.* Seattle: University of Washington Press, 2005.

Courlander, Harold. "Vodoun in Haitian Culture." In *Religion and Politics in Haiti—Two Essays,* edited by Harold Courlander and Rémy Bastien; preface by Richard P. Schaedel, 1–26. Washington, DC: Institute for Cross-Cultural Research, 1966.

Courlander, Harold. "The Word Voodoo." *African Arts* 21, no. 2 (1988): 88.

Cozier, Christopher. "Between Narratives and Other Spaces." In "Debating the Contemporary in Caribbean Art," edited by Christopher Cozier and Annie Paul, special issue, *Small Axe: A Caribbean Journal of Criticism* 3, no. 2 (1999): 19–36.

Cozier, Christopher. "Searching for a Way Out." *Massachusetts Review* 35, no. 3/4 (1994): 419–28.

Cozier, Christopher, and Annie Paul, eds. "Debating the Contemporary in Caribbean Art." Special issue, *Small Axe: A Caribbean Journal of Criticism* 3, no. 2 (1999).

Cozier, Christopher, and Claire Tancons. "No More Than a Backyard on a Small Island." *Fillip* 16 (Spring 2012): 42–51, 127.

Craton, Michael, and Gail Saunders. *Islanders in the Stream: A History of the Bahamian People.* Volume 2: *From the Ending of Slavery to the Twenty-First Century.* Athens: University of Georgia Press, 1998.

Dacres, Petrina. "Monument and Meaning." *Small Axe: A Caribbean Journal of Criticism* 8, no. 2 (2004): 137–53.

Dalmas, Antoine. "Histoire de la révolution de Saint-Domingue [Paris, 1814]." In *The Haitian Revolution: A Documentary History*, translated by David Geggus, 117–18. Indianapolis: Hackett, 2014.

Danner, Mark. "Beyond the Mountains (Part II)." December 4, 1989. https://markdanner.com/1989/12/04/beyond-the-mountains-part-ii/.

Danner, Mark. "The Prophet: Review of *Aristide: An Autobiography* by Jean-Bertrand Aristide, with Christophe Wargny, Translated by Linda M. Maloney, and *In the Parish of the Poor: Writings from Haiti* by Jean-Bertrand Aristide, Translated and Edited by Amy Wilentz." *New York Review of Books* 40, no. 19 (November 18, 1993): 28–36.

Danner, Mark. "A Reporter at Large. Beyond the Mountains—I." *New Yorker*, November 27, 1989, 55–100.

Danner, Mark. "A Reporter at Large. Beyond the Mountains—II." *New Yorker*, December 4, 1989, 68–78, 111–41.

Danner, Mark. "A Reporter at Large. Beyond the Mountains—III." *New Yorker*, December 11, 1989, 100–131.

Das, Veena, Arthur Kleinman, Margaret M. Lock, Mamphela Ramphele, and Pamela Reynolds, eds. *Remaking a World: Violence, Social Suffering, and Recovery*. Berkeley: University of California Press, 2001.

Dash, J. Michael. "The Theater of the Haitian Revolution / The Haitian Revolution as Theater." *Small Axe: A Caribbean Journal of Criticism* 9, no. 2 (2005): 16–23.

Daut, Marlene. *Baron de Vastey and the Origins of Black Atlantic Humanism*. New York: Palgrave Macmillan, 2017.

Davis, Gregson. *Aimé Césaire*. New York: Cambridge University Press, 1997.

Davis, Natalie Zemon. *Slaves on Screen: Film and Historical Vision*. Cambridge, MA: Harvard University Press, 2000.

Dayan, Colin. "Out of Defeat: Aimé Césaire's Miraculous Words." *Boston Review* (September–October 2008): 50–52.

Dayan, Joan (Colin). *Haiti, History, and the Gods*. Berkeley: University of California Press, 1996.

de Albuquerque, Klaus. "In Search of the Big Bamboo." *Transition* 77 (1998): 48–57.

de la Fuente, Alejandro, ed. *Grupo Antillano: The Art of Afro-Cuba / El Arte de Afro-Cuba*. Santiago de Cuba: Fundación Caguayo, 2013.

de la Fuente, Alejandro. *A Nation for All: Race, Inequality, and Politics in Twentieth-Century Cuba*. Chapel Hill: University of North Carolina Press, 2001.

de la Fuente, Alejandro. "The New Afro-Cuban Cultural Movement and the Debate on Race in Contemporary Cuba." *Journal of Latin American Studies* 40, no. 4 (2008): 697–720.

de la Fuente, Alejandro, and Elio Rodríguez Valdés, eds. *Queloides: Race and Racism in Cuban Contemporary Art / Raza y racismo en el arte Cubano contemporáneo*. Pittsburgh: Mattress Factory, 2011.

De La Torre, Miguel A. "Masking Hispanic Racism: A Cuban Case Study." *Journal of Hispanic/Latino Theology* 6, no. 4 (1999): 19–56.

Deleuze, Giles, and Félix Guattari. *A Thousand Plateaus: Capitalism and Schizophrenia*. Translated by Brian Massumi. Minneapolis: University of Minnesota Press, 1987.

del Valle Casals, Sandra. "Passing for a White Woman." In *Afrocubanas: History, Thought, and Cultural Practices*, edited by Devyn Spence Benson, Daisy Rubiera Castillo, and Inés María Martiatu Terry; translated by Karina Alma, 161–72. New York: Rowman and Littlefield, 2020.

Deren, Maya. *Divine Horsemen: The Living Gods of Haiti*. London: Thames and Hudson, 1953.

Diawara, Manthia. "A Conversation with Édouard Glissant Aboard the *Queen Mary II* (August 2009)." Translated by Christopher Winks. In *Afro Modern: Journeys Through the Black Atlantic*, edited by Tanya Barson and Peter Gorschlüter, 58–63. Liverpool: Tate, 2010.

Dogbeh-David, R., J.-C. Bahoken, L. Balthazar, Iwiyé Kala-Lobé, Abdias do Nascimento, and Mbella Sonné Dipoko. "Palabre." *Présence Africaine* 58 (1966): 215–34.

Drysdale, William. *In Sunny Lands: Out-Door Life in Nassau and Cuba, with Illustrations of Places and People*. New York: Harper Books, 1885.

Dubois, Laurent. *Haiti: The Aftershocks of History*. New York: Henry Holt, 2012.

Duval-Carrié, Edouard. *The Indigo Room; or, Is Memory Water Soluble?* Fort Lauderdale: Fort Lauderdale Museum of Art, 2004.

Duval-Carrié, Edouard. *The Vodou Pantheon*. Miami Beach: Bass Museum of Art, 2006.

Duval-Carrié, Edouard, Paul B. Niell, Michael Carrasco, and Lesley A. Wolff. *Decolonizing Refinement: Contemporary Pursuits in the Art of Edouard Duval-Carrié*. Tallahassee, FL: Museum of Fine Arts Press, 2018.

Duval-Carrié, Edouard, and Michelle Robinson. *Edouard Duval-Carrié: Migration of the Spirit*. Davenport, IA: Figge Art Museum, 2005.

Edmondson, Belinda, ed. *Caribbean Romances: The Politics of Regional Representation*. Charlottesville: University Press of Virginia, 1999.

Edmondson, Belinda. "Race, Privilege, and the Politics of (Re)Writing History: An Analysis of the Novels of Michelle Cliff." *Callaloo* 16, no. 1 (1993): 180–91.

Edwards, B. H. "Aimé Césaire and the Syntax of Influence." *Research in African Literatures* 36, no. 2 (2005): 1–18.

Fanon, Frantz. *Black Skin, White Masks*. Translated by Charles Lam Markmann. London: Pluto, 1986.

Fanon, Frantz. *The Wretched of the Earth*. New York: Grove, 1961.

Fernandes, Sujatha. "Transnationalism and Feminist Activism in Cuba: The Case of Magín." *Politics and Gender* 1, no. 3 (2005): 431–52.

Fernández Olmos, Margarite, and Lizabeth Paravisini-Gebert, eds. *Healing Cultures: Art and Religion as Curative Practices in the Caribbean and Its Diaspora*. New York: Palgrave, 2001.

Fernández Retamar, Roberto. *Caliban and Other Essays*. Minneapolis: University of Minnesota Press, 1989.

Fisher, Jennifer. "Interperformance: The Live Tableaux of Suzanne Lacy, Janine Antoni, and Marina Abramovic." *Art Journal* 56, no. 4 (1997): 28–33.

Fisher, Jennifer, and Jim Drobnick. "Janine Antoni: Performance and Its Objects." *Liminalities: A Journal of Performance Studies* 16, no. 4 (2020): 1–20.

Font, Mauricio A., and Alfonso W. Quiroz, eds. *Cuban Counterpoints: The Legacy of Fernando Ortiz*. Lanham, MD: Lexington Books, 2005.

Forsdick, Charles. "Haiti and Departmentalization: The Spectral Presence of Toussaint Louverture." *International Journal of Francophone Studies* 11, no. 3 (2008): 327–44.

Foucault, Michel. "Authorship: What Is an Author?" *Screen* 20, no. 1 (1979): 13–34.

Fourcand, Jean M. *Catechisme de la Revolution: En L'honneur du docteur Francois Duvalier President Constitutionel a vie de la Republique d'Haiti et de Madame Simone O. Duvalier Premiere Marie-Jeanne d'Haiti*. Port-au-Prince: Edition Imprimerie de L'Etat, 1964.

Fraginals, Manuel R. Moreno. *The Sugarmill: The Socioeconomic Complex of Sugar in Cuba, 1760–1860*. New York: Monthly Review Press, 1976.

Frost, Jackqueline, and Jorge E. Lefevre Tavárez. "Tragedy of the Possible: Aimé Césaire in Cuba, 1968." *Historical Materialism: Research in Critical Marxist Theory* 28, no. 2 (2020): 25–75.

Frow, John. *Time and Commodity Culture: Essays in Cultural Theory and Postmodernity*. Oxford: Clarendon, 1997.

Funcke, Bettina, Maurizio Cattelan, and Jens Hoffmann. *6th Caribbean Biennial: A Project by Maurizio Cattelan*. Paris: Les presses du reel, 2001.

Galoustian, Naregh. "Paths to Decolonization in the French Caribbean: Aimé Césaire and Frantz Fanon." *Caribbean Quilt* 2 (2013): 143–50.

Ganase, Pat. *Blue Soap. Recent Art Works by Christopher Cozier*. Port of Spain: Aquarela Galleries, 1994.

Garber, Marjorie B. *Vested Interests: Cross-Dressing and Cultural Anxiety*. New York: Routledge, 1997.

Gaspar, David Barry, and David Patrick Geggus, eds. *A Turbulent Time: The French Revolution and the Greater Caribbean*. Bloomington: Indiana University Press, 2002.

Geggus, David. *The Haitian Revolution: A Documentary History*. Cambridge, MA: Hackett, 2014.

Geggus, David, ed. *The Impact of the Haitian Revolution in the Atlantic World*. Columbia: University of South Carolina Press, 2001.

Gilroy, Paul. *The Black Atlantic*. Cambridge, MA: Harvard University Press, 1993.

Gilroy, Paul. "Cruciality and the Frog's Perspective: An Agenda of Difficulties for the Black Arts Movement in Britain." *Third Text* 2, no. 5 (1988): 33–44.

Gilroy, Paul. "It Ain't Where You're From, It's Where You're At . . . : The Dialectics of Diasporic Identification." *Third Text* 5, no. 13 (1991): 3–16.
Gingeras, Alison M. "A Sociology Without Truth." *Parkett* 59 (2000): 50–53.
Giroux, Henry, and Stanley Aronowitz. "The Politics of Clarity." *Afterimage* (1991): 5, 17.
Gleijeses, Piero. "The First Ambassadors: Cuba's Contribution to Guinea-Bissau's War of Independence." *Journal of Latin American Studies* 29, no. 1 (1997): 45–88.
Glissant, Édouard. *Poetics of Relation*. Translated by Betsy Wing. Ann Arbor: University of Michigan Press, 1997.
Glissant, Édouard, and J. Michael Dash. *Caribbean Discourse: Selected Essays*. Charlottesville: University Press of Virginia, 1989.
González Mandri, Flora María. *Guarding Cultural Memory: Afro-Cuban Women in Literature and the Arts*. Charlottesville: University of Virginia Press, 2006.
Gramsci, Antonio. *Prison Notebooks*. New York: International, 1999.
Guerra, Lillian. *Visions of Power in Cuba: Revolution, Redemption, and Resistance, 1959–1971*. Chapel Hill: University of North Carolina Press, 2012.
Gugolati, Maica. "A Detergent Artwork in Trinidad and Tobago: Christopher Cozier's *Blue Soap*." *Esclavages and Post-Esclavages*, no. 5 (2021). https://doi.org/10.4000/slaveries.5352.
Gupta, Anika. "The Art of Chocolate (and Soap)." *Smithsonian Magazine*, February 10, 2015. https://www.smithsonianmag.com/smithsonian-institution/art-chocolate-and-soap-180954180/.
Hall, Stuart. "Cultural Identity and Diaspora." In *Diaspora and Visual Culture: Representing Africans and Jews*, edited by Nicholas Mirzoeff, 21–33. London: Routledge, 1999.
Hall, Stuart. "The Spectacle of the Other." In *Representation: Cultural Representations and Signifying Practices*, edited by Stuart Hall, 225–76. London: Open University, 1997.
Hall, Stuart. "When Was 'the Postcolonial'? Thinking at the Limit." In *The Postcolonial Question: Common Skies, Divided Horizons*, edited by Iain Chambers and Lidia Curti, 242–60. London: Routledge, 1996.
Harris, Wilson. "History, Fable and Myth in the Caribbean and Guianas." In *Selected Essays of Wilson Harris: The Unfinished Genesis of the Imagination*, edited by A. J. M. Bundy, 152–66. London: Routledge, 1999.
Harrison, David, ed. *Tourism and the Less Developed Countries*. New York: Halsted; Toronto: Belhaven, 1992.
Hartman, Saidiya. *Scenes of Subjection: Terror, Slavery, and Self-Making in Nineteenth-Century America*. Oxford: Oxford University Press, 1997.
Heartney, Eleanor. "Thinking Through the Body: Women Artists and the Catholic Imagination." *Hypatia* 18, no. 4 (2003): 3–22.
Helg, Aline. *Our Rightful Share: The Afro-Cuban Struggle for Equality, 1886–1912*. Chapel Hill: University of North Carolina Press, 1995.

Henriques, Fernando. *Children of Caliban: Miscegenation.* London: Secker and Warburg, 1974.

Henry, Paget. *Caliban's Reason: Introducing Afro-Caribbean Philosophy.* New York: Routledge, 2000.

Heon, Laura. "Janine Antoni's Gnawing Idea." *Gastronomica* 1, no. 2 (2001): 5–8.

Herrera, Georgina. "Poetry, Prostitution, and Gender Esteem." In *Afro-Cuban Voices: On Race and Identity in Contemporary Cuba*, edited by Pedro Pérez Sarduy and Jean Stubbs, 118–26. Gainesville: University Press of Florida, 2000.

Hezekiah, Gabrielle. "Conceptualizing the Boundaries of Nation-Space: Some Thoughts on Art, Criticism, and the Creation of a Canon." *Small Axe: A Caribbean Journal of Criticism* 3, no. 2 (1999): 79–81.

Hill, Errol. *The Trinidad Carnival: Mandate for a National Theatre.* Austin: University of Texas Press, 1972.

Hoffmann, Alvina. "Interview—Walter Mignolo/Part 1: Activism and Trajectory." *E-International Relations*, January 21, 2017. https://www.e-ir.info/2017/01/17/interview-walter-mignolopart-1-activism-and-trajectory/.

Hoffmann, Alvina. "Interview—Walter Mignolo/Part 2: Key Concepts." *E-International Relations*, January 21, 2017. https://www.e-ir.info/2017/01/21/interview-walter-mignolopart-2-key-concepts/.

Hoffmann, Jens. *Show Time: The 50 Most Influential Exhibitions of Contemporary Art.* London: Thames and Hudson, 2014.

hooks, bell. "marginality as site of resistance." In *Out There: Marginalization and Contemporary Cultures*, edited by Russell Ferguson, 341–44. Cambridge, MA: MIT Press, 1990.

Hormilla, Helen Hernández. *Mujeres en crisis: Aproximaciones a lo femenino en las narradoras cubanas de los noventa* [Women in crisis: Women's issues in the work of Cuban women writers of the 1990s]. Havana: Publicaciones Acuario, Centro Félix Varela, 2011.

Horodner, Stuart. "Interview with Janine Antoni." *BOMB* 66 (1999): 50.

Horowitz, Noah. *Art of the Deal: Contemporary Art in a Global Financial Market.* Princeton, NJ: Princeton University Press, 2011.

Huggan, Graham. "The Postcolonial Exotic: Salman Rushdie and the Booker of Bookers." *Transition*, no. 64 (1994): 22–29.

Hulme, Peter. "*Calibán*: Roberto Fernández Retamar's American Intelligence." *Small Axe: A Caribbean Journal of Criticism* 20, no. 3 (2016): 114–22.

Hulme, Peter. *Colonial Encounters: Europe and the Native Caribbean, 1492–1797.* London: Routledge and Kegan Paul, 1987.

Hurbon, Laënnec. *Voodoo: Search for the Spirit.* Translated by Lory Frankel. New York: Harry N. Abrams, 1995.

Hurston, Zora Neale. *Tell My Horse: Voodoo and Life in Haiti and Jamaica.* New York: Harper and Row, 1990.

Jackson, Jean. "Nanny Stands Tall." *Kingston Daily News*, October 21, 1981.

Jackson, Shona N. *Creole Indigeneity*. Minneapolis: University of Minnesota Press, 2012.

Jaehne, Karen. "*The Last Supper* by Tomas Gutiérrez Alea." *Film Quarterly* 33, no. 1 (1979): 48–53. https://doi.org/10.1525/fq.1979.33.1.04a00090.

James, C. L. R. *Beyond a Boundary*. Introduction by Robert Lipsyte. Durham, NC: Duke University Press, 1993.

James, C. L. R. *The Black Jacobins*. New York: Vintage, 1963.

James, Erica Moiah. "Decolonizing Time: Nineteenth-Century Haitian Portraiture and the Critique of Anachronism in Caribbean Art." *Nka: Journal of Contemporary African Art* 44 (2019): 8–23.

James, Erica Moiah. *Edouard Duval-Carrié: Historical Retelling and the Postmodern Baroque*. Miami: Oolite Arts and Bass Museum, 2020. https://thebass.org/wp-content/uploads/2020/09/EDOUARD_BROCHURE_9.16.pdf.

James, Erica Moiah. "Elegy." In *En Mas': Carnival and Performance Art of the Caribbean*, edited by Claire Tancons and Krista A. Thompson, 174–81. New York: Independent Curators International, 2015.

James, Erica Moiah. "*Fatima*, circa 1886." In *Victorian Jamaica*, edited by Wayne Modest and Timothy Barringer, 105–7. Durham, NC: Duke University Press, 2017.

James, Erica Moiah. "The Light of Things / La luz de las cosas." In *Juan Francisco Elso: Essays on America / Ensayos sobre America*, edited by Olga M. Viso, 106–49. New York: El Museo del Barrio, 2023.

James, Erica Moiah. "Outta' Line: Decolonial Enlightenment and the Genre of History Painting in Contemporary Caribbean Art." In *The Imagined New (or What Happens When History Is a Catastrophe?)*, edited by Anthony Bogues, Leora Farber, Zamansele Nsele, and Surafel Wondimu Abebe, 154–84. Johannesburg: University of Johannesburg and iWale Books, 2023.

James, Erica Moiah. "Prismatic Blackness: Art Aesthetics and Being in the Global Caribbean." In *The Image of the Black in Latin American and Caribbean Art*, edited by David Bindman and Alejandro de la Fuente, 476–529. Cambridge, MA: Harvard University Press, 2023.

James, Erica Moiah. "Speaking in Tongues: Metapictures and the Discourse of Violence in Caribbean Art." *Small Axe: A Caribbean Journal of Criticism* 16, no. 1 (2012): 119–43.

James, Erica Moiah. "Theriantropic Beasts and the Mystic Revelation of Tomás Esson." In *Tomás Esson: The GOAT*, edited by Gean Moreno, 18–37. Miami: ICA Miami; Munich: Hirmer, 2021.

Jameson, Fredric, and Masao Miyoshi. *The Cultures of Globalization*. Durham, NC: Duke University Press, 1998.

Jaskari, Minna. "Tomás Gutiérrez Alea and the Post-Revolutionary Cuba." In *Artikkelit Marraskuu*, November 1997. http://www.helsinki.fi/hum/ibero/xaman/articulos/9711/9711_mj.html.

Joannou, D., U. Fischer, C. MacLeod, and J. Deitch. *Fractured Figure: Works from the Dakis Joannou Collection*. Athens: Deste Foundation for Contemporary Art, 2007.

Johnson, Paul Christopher. "Secretism and the Apotheosis of Duvalier." *Journal of the American Academy of Religion* 74, no. 2 (2006): 420–45.

Juncker, Kristine. *Afro-Cuban Religious Arts: Popular Expressions of Cultural Inheritance in Espiritismo and Santería*. Gainesville: University Press of Florida, 2014.

Kamugisha, Aaron, and Yanique Hume, eds. *Caribbean Cultural Thought: From Plantation to Diaspora*. Kingston, Jamaica: Ian Randle, 2013.

Kanz, Christine. "Queering Violence and Masculinity in Marinetti." In *Gender, Agency, and Violence: European Perspectives from Early Modern Times to the Present Day*, edited by Ulrike Zitzlsperger, 123–31. Newcastle upon Tyne: Cambridge Scholars, 2013.

Kapur, Geeta. "Globalisation and Culture." *Third Text* 11, no. 39 (1997): 21–38.

Karem, Jeff. *The Purloined Islands: Caribbean-U.S. Crosscurrents in Literature and Culture, 1880–1959*. Charlottesville: University of Virginia Press, 2011.

Kartofel, Graciela. "Island Thresholds: Contemporary Art from the Caribbean" [review]. *Art Nexus* 4, no. 58 (2005): 164–65.

Kasfir, Sidney Littlefield. "African Art and Authenticity: A Text with a Shadow." *African Arts* 25, no. 2 (1992): 40–53, 96–97.

Kelley, Robin D. G. "A Poetics of Anticolonialism." Introduction to *Discourse on Colonialism*, by Aimé Césaire, translated by Joan Pinkham. New York: Monthly Review Press, 2000.

Kempadoo, Kamala, ed. *Sun, Sex, and Gold: Tourism and Sex Work in the Caribbean*. Lanham, MD: Rowman and Littlefield, 1999.

Kempadoo, Roshini. *Creole in the Archive: Imagery, Presence and the Location of the Caribbean Figure*. Lanham, MD: Rowman and Littlefield, 2016.

Kendall, Michelle D. "Co-Opting Haitian History in Martinican Theatre." *Journal of Haitian Studies* 19, no. 1 (2013): 184–97.

Kirshenblatt-Gimblett, Barbara. *Destination Culture: Tourism, Museums, and Heritage*. Berkeley: University of California Press, 1998.

Kriz, Kay Dian. *Slavery, Sugar, and the Culture of Refinement: Picturing the British West Indies, 1700–1840*. New Haven, CT: Yale University Press, 2008.

Kutzinski, Vera M. *Sugar's Secrets: Race and the Erotics of Cuban Nationalism*. Charlottesville: University Press of Virginia, 1993.

Lacan, Jacques. *The Four Fundamental Concepts of Psycho-Analysis*. New York: W. W. Norton, 1981.

Lacan, Jacques. "The Mirror Stage as Formative of the Function of the *I* as Revealed in Psychoanalytic Experience." In *Écrits: A Selection*, translated by Alan Sheridan, 1–7. New York: W. W. Norton, 1977.

Laguerre, John. "The 1990 Violent Disturbance in Trinidad and Tobago: Some Perceptions." *Caribbean Quarterly* 54, no. 4 (2008): 129–39.

Laguerre, Michel S. *Voodoo and Politics in Haiti*. New York: St. Martin's, 1989.

Lajer-Burcharth, Ewa. "Antoni's Difference." *differences* 10 (1998): 129–70.

Lamming, George. *The Pleasures of Exile*. London: M. Joseph, 1960.

Larson, Kay. "Women's Work (or Is It Art?) Is Never Done: Freeport-Born Artist Janine Antoni Pays Tribute to Pioneers of Feminist Performance Art." *Nassau Tribune*, January 16, 1996, 7.

Lavigne, Julie. "Janine Antoni's *Lick and Lather*: Eroticism as Identity Subversion." In *Precarious Visualities: New Perspectives on Identification in Contemporary Art and Visual Culture*, edited by Johanne Lamoureux, Christine Ross, and Olivier Asselin, 283–301. Montreal: McGill-Queen's University Press, 2008.

Lerebours, Michel-Philippe. "The Indigenist Revolt: Haitian Art, 1927–1944." In "Haitian Literature and Culture, Part 2," special issue, *Callaloo* 15, no. 3 (1992): 711–25.

Lett, James. "Ludic and Liminoid Aspects of Charter Yacht Tourism in the Caribbean." *Annals of Tourism Research* 10 (1983): 35–56.

Lindner, Stacie. "Janine Antoni: Finding a Room of Her Own." Master's thesis, Georgia State University, 2006.

Linebaugh, Peter, and Marcus Rediker. *The Many-Headed Hydra: Sailors, Slaves, Commoners, and the Hidden History of the Revolutionary Atlantic*. 2nd ed. Boston: Beacon, 2013.

Liu, Jenny. "Trouble in Paradise." *Frieze* (UK) 51, no. 3 (2000): 50–52.

Long, Richard. "Artists of Haiti: Reflections on a Narrative." In *Caribbean Visions: Contemporary Painting and Culture*, edited by Samella Lewis, 65–70. Alexandria, VA: Art Services International, 1995.

López-Calvo, Ignacio. "'Coloniality Is Not Over, It Is All Over': Interview with Dr. Walter Mignolo (Nov. 2014, Part I)." *Transmodernity* 6, no. 1 (2016): 175–84.

López-Calvo, Ignacio. "'Coloniality Is Not Over, It's All Over': Interview with Dr. Walter Mignolo (Nov. 2014, Part II)." *Transmodernity* 6, no. 2 (2016): 171–96.

López Springfield, Consuelo, ed. *Daughters of Caliban: Caribbean Women in the Twentieth Century*. Bloomington: Indiana University Press, 1997.

Lord, Susan, María Caridad Cumaná, and Víctor Fowler Calzada, eds. *The Cinema of Sara Gómez: Reframing Revolution*. Bloomington: Indiana University Press, 2021.

Lorde, Audre. "The Master's Tools Will Never Dismantle the Master's House." In *Sister Outsider: Essays and Speeches*, 110–14. Trumansburg, NY: Crossing, 1984.

Lott, Eric. *Love and Theft: Blackface Minstrelsy and the American Working Class*. New York: Oxford University Press, 1993.

Lugo-Ortiz, Agnes. "Between Violence and Redemption: Slave Portraiture in Early Plantation Cuba." In *Slave Portraiture in the Atlantic World*, edited by Agnes Lugo-Ortiz and Angela Rosenthal, 201–26. Cambridge: Cambridge University Press, 2013.

Lush, Brian V. "Popular Authority in Euripides' *Iphigenia in Aulis*." *American Journal of Philology* 136, no. 2 (2015): 207–42.
Lynch, James. "Cuban Architecture Since the Revolution." *Art Journal* 39, no. 2 (1979): 100–106.
MacCannell, Dean. *The Tourist: A New Theory of the Leisure Class*. New York: Schocken Books, 1976.
Mackie, Erin Skye. "Cultural Cross Dressing: The Colorful Case of the Caribbean Creole." In *The Clothes That Wear Us: Essays on Dressing and Transgressing in Eighteenth-Century Culture*, edited by Jessica Munns and Penny Richards, 251–70. Newark: University of Delaware Press, 1999.
Magnuson, Ann. "Caribbean Castaway." *Artnet*, February 24, 2000. http://www.artnet.com/magazine/features/magnuson/magnuson2-24-00.asp.
Marinetti, Filippo-Tommaso. *Mafarka the Futurist*. 1909. London: Middlesex University Press, 1998.
Martínez, Juan A. *Cuban Art and National Identity: The Vanguardia Painters, 1927–1950*. Gainesville: University Press of Florida, 1994.
Massé, Guirdex. "Cold War and Black Transnationalism: Aimé Césaire and Mercer Cook at the First International Congress of Black Writers and Artists." *Palimpsest* 4, no. 2 (2015): 115–33.
Mateo, David. "Volver sobre los sentidos." In *Siempre Vuelvo: Colografías de Belkis Ayón—Exposición Homenaje*, edited by Yolanda Wood. Havana: La Galeria Habana, 2000.
McAlister, Elizabeth. *Rara! Vodou, Power, and Performance in Haiti and Its Diaspora*. Berkeley: University of California Press, 2002.
McCarthy Brown, Karen. *Tracing the Spirit: Ethnographic Essays on Haitian Art from the Collection of the Davenport Museum of Art*. Seattle: University of Washington Press; Davenport, IA: Davenport Museum, 1995.
McClintock, Anne. *Imperial Leather: Race, Gender and Sexuality in the Colonial Contest*. London: Routledge, 1995.
McKittrick, Katherine, ed. *Sylvia Wynter: On Being Human as Praxis*. Durham, NC: Duke University Press, 2015.
Martínez Furé, Rogelio. "A National Cultural Identity? Homogenizing Monomania and the Plural Heritage." In *Afro-Cuban Voices: On Race and Identity in Contemporary Cuba*, edited by Pedro Pérez Sarduy and Jean Stubbs, 154–61. Gainesville: University Press of Florida, 2000.
Meeks, Brian. *Critical Interventions in Caribbean Politics and Theory*. Jackson: University Press of Mississippi, 2014.
Melas, Natalie. "Untimeliness, or Négritude and the Poetics of Contramodernity." *South Atlantic Quarterly* 108, no. 3 (2009): 563–80.
Menéndez, Lázara. "Para destruir un miedo" / "Banishing Fear." In *Nkame: Belkis Ayón*, edited by Katia Ayón and Cristina Vives, 53|271–73|279. Madrid: Turner, 2010.
Mercer, Kobena. *Welcome to the Jungle*. London: Routledge, 1994.

Mignolo, Walter D. "Delinking: The Rhetoric of Modernity, the Logic of Coloniality and the Grammar of De-Coloniality." *Cultural Studies* 21, nos. 2–3 (2007): 449–514.

Mignolo, Walter D. "Epistemic Disobedience, Independent Thought and Decolonial Freedom." *Theory, Culture and Society* 26, nos. 7–8 (2009): 159–81.

Miller, Ivor. "A Secret Society Goes Public: The Relationship Between Abakuá and Cuban Popular Culture." *African Studies Review* 43, no. 1 (2000): 161–88.

Miller, Ivor. *Voice of the Leopard: African Secret Societies and Cuba.* Jackson: University Press of Mississippi, 2009.

Miller, Nicola. "A Revolutionary Modernity: The Cultural Policy of the Cuban Revolution." *Journal of Latin American Studies* 40, no. 4 (2008): 675–96.

Miller, Paul B. *Elusive Origins: The Enlightenment in the Modern Caribbean Historical Imagination.* Charlottesville: University of Virginia Press, 2010.

Minow, Martha L. *Between Vengeance and Forgiveness: Facing History After Genocide and Mass Violence.* Boston: Beacon, 1998.

Minshall, Peter. "River: A Mas' in Two Acts." *TDR: The Drama Review* 42, no. 3 (1998): 184.

Mintz, Sidney, and Michel-Rolph Trouillot. "The Social History of Haitian Vodou." In *Sacred Arts of Haitian Vodou*, edited by Donald Cosentino, 123–47. Los Angeles: UCLA Fowler Museum of Cultural History, 1995.

Mitchell, W. J. T. *Picture Theory.* Chicago: University of Chicago Press, 1994.

Modest, Wayne. "We Have Always Been Modern: Museums, Collections, and Modernity in the Caribbean." *Museum Anthropology* 35, no. 1 (2012): 85–96.

Mohammed, Patricia. "'But Most of All Mi Love Me Browning': The Emergence in Eighteenth and Nineteenth-Century Jamaica of the Mulatto Woman as the Desired." *Feminist Review* 65, no. 1 (2000): 22–48.

Molina, Elpidio de la Trinidad, Jorge Molina, and Egipcia Pérez. "The Only Black Family on the Block." In *Afro-Cuban Voices: On Race and Identity in Contemporary Cuba*, edited by Pedro Pérez Sarduy and Jean Stubbs, 49–60. Gainesville: University Press of Florida, 2000.

Moore, Robert J. "Colonial Images of Blacks and Indians in Nineteenth Century Guyana." In *The Colonial Caribbean in Transition: Essays on Postemancipation Social and Cultural History*, edited by Bridget Brereton and Kevin A. Yelvington, 126–58. Cave Hill: The Press, University of the West Indies; Gainesville: University Press of Florida, 1999.

Moore, Robin D. *Nationalizing Blackness: Afrocubanismo and Artistic Revolution in Havana, 1920–1940.* Pittsburgh: University of Pittsburgh Press, 1997.

Moral, Reynaldo Peñalver. "Under the Streetlamp: A Journalist's Story." In *Afro-Cuban Voices: On Race and Identity in Contemporary Cuba*, edited by Pedro Pérez Sarduy and Jean Stubbs, 41–48. Gainesville: University Press of Florida, 2000.

Morrison, Toni. *Playing in the Dark: Whiteness and the Literary Imagination.* Cambridge, MA: Harvard University Press, 1992.

Muñoz, José Esteban. *Disidentifications: Queers of Color and the Performance of Politics*. Minneapolis: University of Minnesota Press, 1999.

Murdoch, H. Adlai. "Aimé Césaire, the Colonial Exhibition, and the Modernity of the Black Atlantic." *International Journal of Francophone Studies* 14, nos. 1–2 (2011): 57–74.

Museum of Modern Art. *Projects 70*. Janine Antoni, Shahzia Sikander, Kara Walker. November 22, 2000–March 13, 2001. MoMA, New York, 2000.

Naipaul, V. S. *The Middle Passage*. London: Penguin Books, 1962.

Nichols, Stephen G. "Seeing Food: An Anthropology of Ekphrasis, and Still Life in Classical and Medieval Examples." *MLN* 106, no. 4 (1991): 818–51.

Nikoloutsos, Konstantino P. "Appropriating Greek Myth: Iphigenia and Argentine Patriarchal Society in Inés de Oliveira Cézar's *Extranjera*." *Classical Receptions Journal* 2, no. 1 (2010): 92–113.

Niles, Blair. *Black Haiti: A Biography of Africa's Eldest Daughter*. New York: G. P. Putnam and Sons; London: Knickerbocker, 1926.

Nixon, Angelique. *Resisting Paradise: Tourism, Diaspora, and Sexuality in Caribbean Culture*. Jackson: University Press of Mississippi, 2015.

Ortiz, Fernando. *Cuban Counterpoint: Tobacco and Sugar*. Durham, NC: Duke University Press, 1995.

Padilla, Mark. *Caribbean Pleasure Industry: Tourism, Sexuality, and AIDS in the Dominican Republic*. Chicago: University of Chicago Press, 2007.

Pago, Gilbert. *L'histoire tragique de Marie-Philomène Roptus dite Lumina Sophie dite Surprise, 1848–1879: Femme-flamme de l'insurrection du sud de 1870 en Martinique*. Matoury, French Guiana: Ibis rouge, 2008.

Palmié, Stephan. *Wizards and Scientists: Explorations in Afro-Cuban Modernity and Tradition*. Durham, NC: Duke University Press, 2002.

Paravisini-Gebert, Lizabeth. "Women Possessed: Eroticism and Exoticism in the Representation of Woman as Zombie." In *Sacred Possessions: Vodou, Santería, Obeah, and the Caribbean*, edited by Margarite Fernández Olmos and Lizabeth Paravisini-Gebert, 37–58. New Brunswick, NJ: Rutgers University Press, 1997.

Pascual Castillo, Omar. "Fleeting Anecdotes and Stories of Escape from Slavery or—From Queloides I to Black Cuban Groove, a Racial Reading of the New Cuban Art." In *Queloides: Race and Racism in Cuban Contemporary Art / Raza y racismo en el arte Cubano contemporáneo*, edited by Alejandro de la Fuente, 44–58. Pittsburgh: Mattress Factory, 2011.

Pattullo, Polly. *Last Resorts: The Cost of Tourism in the Caribbean*. New York: Monthly Review Press, 2005.

Paul, Annie. "Chris Cozier: A State of Independence." *Caribbean Beat Magazine*, no. 50 (July–August 2001). https://www.caribbean-beat.com/issue-50/chris-cozier-state-of-independence#axzz8djZlIMZh.

Paul, Annie. "The Enigma of Survival: Traveling Beyond the Expat Gaze." *Art Journal* 62, no. 1 (2003): 48–65.

Paul, Annie, and Christopher Cozier. "Christopher Cozier." *BOMB*, no. 82 (2002): 66–73.

Penn, Dianne. "Grand Bahamian 'Bites' Big Apple Art Scene." *Nassau Tribune*, April 7, 1993, 1B, 7B.

Pérez Sarduy, Pedro, and Jean Stubbs, eds. *Afro-Cuban Voices: On Race and Identity in Contemporary Cuba*. Gainesville: University Press of Florida, 2000.

Poupeye, Veerle. *Caribbean Art*. London: Thames and Hudson, 1998.

Poupeye, Veerle. "A Monument in the Public Sphere: The Controversy About Laura Facey's *Redemption Song*." *Jamaica Journal* 28, nos. 2–3 (2004): 36–48.

Poupeye, Veerle. "Trading Across the Black Atlantic: Globalization and the Work of Marc Latamie." *Australian and New Zealand Journal of Art* 3, no. 2 (2002): 77–102.

Powell, Richard J. *Black Art: A Cultural History*. London: Thames and Hudson, 2003.

Price, Richard. *First-Time: The Historical Vision of an Afro-American People*. Baltimore, MD: Johns Hopkins University Press, 1983.

Pullella, Philip. "Ending His 8-Nation Tour Pope John Paul II . . ." UPI, March 10, 1983. https://www.upi.com/Archives/1983/03/10/Ending-his-eight-nation-tour-Thursday-Pope-John-Paul-II/7413416120400/.

Puri, Shalini. *The Caribbean Postcolonial: Social Equality, Post-Nationalism, and Cultural Hybridity*. New York: Palgrave Macmillan, 2004.

Rabbitt, Kara M. "History into Story: Suzanne Césaire, Lafcadio Hearn, and Representations of the 1848 Martinique Slave Revolts." *Anthurium* 12, no. 2 (2015). https://anthurium.miami.edu/articles/10.33596/anth.291.

Ramos Cruz, Guillermina. "Grupo Antillano and the Marginalization of Black Artists." In *Afro-Cuban Voices: On Race and Identity in Contemporary Cuba*, edited by Pedro Pérez Sarduy and Jean Stubbs, 147–53. Gainesville: University Press of Florida, 2000.

Ramos Cruz, Guillermina. "Tribute to Grupo Antillano / Homenaje a Grupo Antillano." In *Grupo Antillano: The Art of Afro-Cuba / El Arte de Afro-Cuba*, edited by Alejandro de la Fuente, 17–34. Havana: Fundación Caguayo, 2013.

Raven, Arlene. "Womanhouse." In *The Power of Feminist Art: The American Movement of the 1970s, History and Impact*, edited by Norma Broude and Mary D. Garrard, 48–65. New York: Harry N. Abrams, 1996.

Riggio, Milla C. "Resistance and Identity: Carnival in Trinidad and Tobago." *TDR: The Drama Review* 42, no. 3 (1998): 7–23.

Roberts, Brady. *Edouard Duval-Carrié: Endless Passage*. Phoenix: Phoenix Art Museum, 2002.

Rodman, Selden. *Renaissance in Haiti: Popular Painters in the Black Republic*. New York: Pellegrini and Cudahy, 1948.

Rodman, Selden, and Carole Cleaver. *Spirits of the Night: The Vaudun Gods of Haiti*. Foreword by Jay Livernois. Dallas: Spring, 1992.

Rolando, Gloria. "Africa, the Caribbean, and Afro-America in Cuban Film." In *Afro-Cuban Voices: On Race and Identity in Contemporary Cuba*, edited by Pedro Pérez Sarduy and Jean Stubbs, 129–39. Gainesville: University Press of Florida, 2000.

Ryan, Allan J. *The Trickster Shift: Humour and Irony in Contemporary Native Art*. Seattle: University of Washington Press; Vancouver: UBC Press, 1999.

Said, Edward. *Representations of the Intellectual: The 1993 Reith Lectures*. London: Vintage, 1994.

Saltz, Jerry. "The Artist Who Fell to Earth." *Village Voice* 48, no. 40 (2003). http://www.artnet.com/magazine/features/saltz/saltz10-2-03.asp.

Sarusky, Jaime. "Hablar de los mitos y el arte." *Revolución y Cultura* 2–3 (1999): 68–71.

Schechner, Richard, and Milla C. Riggio. "Peter Minshall: A Voice to Add to the Song of the Universe: An Interview." *TDR: The Drama Review* 42, no. 3 (1998): 170–93.

Schor, Mira. "Patrilineage." *Art Journal* 50, no. 2 (1991): 58–63.

Schor, Mira. *Wet: On Painting, Feminism, and Art Culture*. Durham, NC: Duke University Press, 1997.

Schroeder, Paul A. *Tomás Gutiérrez Alea: The Dialectics of a Filmmaker*. London: Routledge, 2002.

Scott, David. *Conscripts of Modernity: The Tragedy of Colonial Enlightenment*. Durham, NC: Duke University Press, 2004.

Scott, David. *Refashioning Futures: Criticism After Postcoloniality*. Princeton, NJ: Princeton University Press, 1999.

Scott, James C. *Weapons of the Weak: Everyday Forms of Peasant Resistance*. New Haven, CT: Yale University Press, 1985.

Seabrook, William. *The Magic Island*. New York: Harcourt, Brace and Company, 1929.

Sheller, Mimi. *Consuming the Caribbean: From Arawaks to Zombies*. London: Routledge, 2003.

Shelton, Marie-Denise. "Fakes, Fakers, and Fakery: Authenticity in African Art." *African Arts* 9, no. 3 (1976): 20–31, 48–74, 92.

Shiflett, Vance. "World News Makers." *World Affairs* 122, no. 3 (1959): 87–88.

Skura, Meredith Anne. "Discourse and the Individual: The Case of Colonialism in *The Tempest*." *Shakespeare Quarterly* 40, no. 1 (1989): 42–69.

Solga, Kim. "Body Doubles, Babel's Voices: Katie Mitchell's *Iphigenia at Aulis* and the Theatre of Sacrifice." *Contemporary Theatre Review* 18, no. 2 (2008): 146–60.

Sollins, Susan, and Marybeth Sollins, eds. *Art 21: Art in the Twenty-First Century 2*. New York: Abrams, 2003.

Solomon, Digby A. "Pope's Visit Treated as National Holiday in Haiti." UPI, March 10, 1983. https://www.upi.com/Archives/1983/03/10/Popes-visit-treated-as-national-holiday-in-Haiti/5024416120400/.

Spector, Nancy. *Maurizio Cattelan: All / [a Cura Di]*. New York: Guggenheim Museum; Milan: Skira, 2011.

Spivak, Gayatri Chakravorty. *A Critique of Postcolonial Reason: Toward a History of the Vanishing Present*. Cambridge, MA: Harvard University Press, 1999.

Stewart, Susan. *On Longing: Narratives of the Miniature, the Gigantic, the Souvenir, the Collection*. Baltimore, MD: Johns Hopkins University Press, 1984.

Strachan, Ian G. *Paradise and Plantation: Tourism and Culture in the Anglophone Caribbean*. Charlottesville: University of Virginia Press, 2002.

Sussman, Elisabeth. "Then and Now: Whitney Biennial 1993." *Art Journal* 64, no. 1 (2005): 74–79.

Tancons, Claire, and Krista A. Thompson, eds. *En Mas': Carnival and Performance Art of the Caribbean*. New York: Independent Curators International, 2015.

Tawadros, Gilane. "Beyond the Boundary: The Work of Three Black Women Artists in Britain." *Third Text* 3, nos. 8–9 (1989): 121–50.

Tawadros, Gilane, ed. *Changing States: Contemporary Art and Ideas in an Era of Globalisation*. London: Institute of International Visual Arts, 2004.

Theodossopoulos, Dimitrios. "Laying Claim to Authenticity: Five Anthropological Dilemmas." *Anthropological Quarterly* 86, no. 2 (2013): 337–60.

Thompson, Krista A. *An Eye for the Tropics: Tourism, Photography, and Framing the Caribbean Picturesque*. Durham, NC: Duke University Press, 2006.

Thompson, Robert Farris. *Face of the Gods: Art and Altars of Africa and the African Americas*. New York: Museum for African Art; Munich: Prestel, 1993.

Thompson, Robert Farris. *Flash of the Spirit: African and Afro-American Art and Philosophy*. New York: Vintage Books, 1984.

Tobin, Beth Fowkes. *Picturing Imperial Power: Colonial Subjects in Eighteenth-Century British Painting*. Durham, NC: Duke University Press, 1999.

Trippi, Laura. "Untitled Artists' Projects by Janine Antoni, Ben Kinmont, and Rirkrit Tiravanija." In *Eating Culture*, edited by Ron Scapp and Brian Seitz, 132–60. New York: State University of New York Press, 1999.

Trouillot, Michel-Rolph. *Silencing the Past: Power and the Production of History*. Boston: Beacon, 1995.

Tseëlon, Efrat. "Introduction: Masquerade and Identities." In *Masquerade and Identities: Essays on Gender, Sexuality and Marginality*, edited by Efrat Tseëlon, 1–17. New York: Routledge, 2001.

Tulloch, Carol, ed. *Black Style*. London: V & A Publications, 2004.

Tunnard, Christopher, and John C. Pollaco. *Jamaica: Conservation and Development of Sites and Monuments*. Paris: UNESCO, 1969.

Turri, Scott. "Janine Antoni." *Bomb* 125 (2013): 13–15.

Ulysse, Gina. "Uptown Ladies and Downtown Women: Female Representations of Class and Color in Jamaica." In *Representations of Blackness and the Performance of Identities*, edited by Jean Muteba Rahier, 147–72. Westport, CT: Bergin and Garvey, 1999.

Varnedoe, Kirk. "Minimalism and After." *MoMA* 4, no. 1 (2001): 2–5.

Vastey, Baron de. *The Colonial System Unveiled*. New ed. Liverpool: Liverpool University Press, 2014.

Vergès, Françoise. *Resolutely Black: Conversations with Françoise Vergès.* Interview by Aimé Césaire. Translated by Matthew B. Smith. Cambridge: Polity, 2020.

Véron, Kora. "Césaire at the Crossroads in Haiti: Correspondence with Henri Seyrig." *Comparative Literature Studies* 50, no. 3 (2013): 430–44.

Véron, Kora, and Thomas A. Hale. *Les écrits d'Aimé Césaire: Biobibliographie commentée (1913–2008).* Paris: Honoré Champion, Coll. Poétiques et Esthétiques Xxe–Xxie Siècles, No. 14, 2013.

Vives, Cristina. "Belkis Ayón: Su propia voz" / "Belkis Ayón in Her Own Voice." In *Nkame: Belkis Ayón*, edited by Katia Ayón and Cristina Vives, 15|260–33|265. Madrid: Turner, 2010.

Vogel, Wendy. "Turning Inside Out: Janine Antoni's New Perspective on Sculpture and Dance." *Modern Painters* 27, no. 3 (2015): 42–45.

Wainwright, Leon. "Americocentrism and Art of the Caribbean: Contours of a Time-Space Logic." *Journal of American Studies* 47, no. 2 (2013): 417–38.

Wainwright, Leon. *Timed Out: Art and the Transnational Caribbean.* Manchester: Manchester University Press, 2011.

Walcott, Derek. "The Antilles Fragments in Epic Memory." Nobel Lecture, December 7, 1992. Nobel Prize. https://www.nobelprize.org/prizes/literature/1992/walcott/lecture/.

Walsh, John Patrick. "Césaire Reads Toussaint Louverture: The Haitian Revolution and the Problem of Departmentalization." *Small Axe: A Caribbean Journal of Criticism* 15, no. 1 (2011): 110–24.

Webster, Mary. *Johan Zoffany, 1733–1810.* New Haven, CT: Yale University Press, 2011.

Weintraub, Linda. *Art on the Edge and Over.* Litchfield, CT: Art Insights, 1996.

Weiss, Rachel. *To and from Utopia in the New Cuban Art.* Minneapolis: University of Minnesota Press, 2011.

Weppler-Grogan, Doreen. "Cultural Policy, the Visual Arts, and the Advance of the Cuban Revolution in the Aftermath of the Gray Years." *Cuban Studies* 41 (2010): 143–65.

Wiesenthal, Christine, and Brad Bucknell. "Essays into the Imagetext: An Interview with W. J. T. Mitchell." *Mosaic: A Journal for the Interdisciplinary Study of Literature* 33, no. 2 (2000): 1–23.

Wilder, Gary. *Freedom Time: Negritude, Decolonization, and the Future of the World.* Durham, NC: Duke University Press, 2015.

Wilder, Gary. "Here/Hear Now Aimé Césaire!" *South Atlantic Quarterly* 115, no. 3 (2016): 585–604.

Wilder, Gary. "Race, Reason, Impasse: Césaire, Fanon, and the Legacy of Emancipation." *Radical History Review* 90 (2004): 31–61.

Williams, Eric. "Massa Day Done (Public Lecture at Woodford Square, 22 March 1961)." *Callaloo* 20, no. 4 (1997): 725–30.

Willis, Deborah. "Shakespeare's *Tempest* and the Discourse of Colonialism." *Studies in English Literature, 1500–1900* 29, no. 2 (1989): 277–89.

Winer, Lise, ed. *Dictionary of the English/Creole of Trinidad and Tobago: On Historical Principles.* Montreal: McGill-Queen's University Press, 2009.

Wood, David. "Tomás Gutiérrez Alea and the Art of Revolutionary Cinema." *Bulletin of Latin American Research* 28, no. 4 (2009): 512–26.

Wood, Yolanda, ed. *Siempre Vuelvo: Colografías de Belkis Ayón—Exposición Homenaje.* Havana: La Galeria Habana, 2000.

Yancy, George. "Colonial Gazing: The Production of the Body as 'Other.'" *Western Journal of Black Studies* 32, no. 1 (2008): 1–15.

Zaya, Octavio. "Trading Plots: The Work of Marc Latamie." *Nka: Journal of Contemporary African Art* 4 (1996): 60–63.

Zoidis, Evangelos. "My Body Is Your Vehicle: Materialität als Reflexionsbegriff in den Werken von Janine Antoni." *Konsthistorisk tidskrift* 88, no. 4 (2019): 173–84.

INDEX

....

Note: Page numbers in italics refer to figures.

Abakuá, 34, 79–89, 93, 95–97, 103–13, 116, 119–20, 152

Abramović, Marina, 62

Abstract Expressionism, 44, 51, 52, 57

Acevedo-Muñoz, Ernesto R., 79

African swine fever, 149–50

Afrocentrism, 141

Afro-Cuban, use of the term, 105

Albers, Josef, 71, 182

Alea, Tomás Gutiérrez, 33–34, 78–80, 97–102, 106–8, 113; *Cumbite*, 100; *Death of a Bureaucrat*, 99; early years and education, 238n44; *Hasta cierto punto*, 243–44n96; *La última cena*, 78–79, 97–102, 110, 117–18; *Los Sobrevivientes*, 243–44n96; *This Is Our Land*, 99; *The Twelve Chairs*, 99

Allen, Jafari, 105

Altunaga, Eliseo, 105

Amenhotep IV (Akhenaten), 130, *131*

Angola, 99, 118

Antoni, Janine, 5, 30, 33–34, 37, 207; award and honors, 70; Ayón and, 78, 80, 106, 110, 117; breast cancer treatment, 70; Cattelan and, 165, 175, 176; common themes of, 61–63; decolonization and, 40, 45–46, 52, 57, 58, 62, 78; desire and, 63–71; Duval-Carrié and, 124, 161, 162; early years and education, 40–41, 219–20, 228n2; feminism and, 40, 42–45, 47–54, 57–58; identity and, 58–60; Minimalism and, 44, 45, 51, 52–53, 57; production process, 42–43; relationship with audience, 42–45; Schor and, 48–51; on "superstructures of civil society," 188

Antoni, Janine, works: *Eureka*, 54; *The Girl Made of Butter*, 55, 70–72; *Gnaw*, 42, *43*, 50–55, 70, 74; *Ingrown*, 55, *56*; *Lick and Lather*, 47–48, *51*, 63–65, 230n35; *Loving Care*, *38–39*, 40, 42, 44–47, 51, 54, 55–56, 58, 74; *Moor*, 72, 73, 74; *The Paper Dance*, 73–74; Sandra Gering Gallery exhibition (1992), 41–42, 45; *Slumber*, 73; *taught, tether, teeter* (retrospective), 72–73; *Tender Buttons*, 70, *71*; *Touch*, 72, 219–20, *221*, 233–34n82; *Wean*, 54, *55*

Antze, Paul, 151–53

Aristide, Jean-Bertrand, 126–28, 135

Arrepetida (Ayón), 96–97

Art and Nation: Things We Must Learn from Day 1 (Cozier), 208, *210*

Association Internationale des Critiques d'Art (AICA), 212–13

Attack of the Sandwich Man (Cozier), 215

autohistoriography, 4–5, 12, 16, 21, 27, 85, 117, 189

Ayón, Belkis, 5, 30, 33–34, 76, 207; Abakuá and, 79–81, 85–90, 93, 95–97, 103–13, 116, 119–20, 152; Antoni and, 78, 80, 106, 110, 117; on artistic process, 93–94; awards and honors, 109; Black history and, 104, 106–7; Black imaginary and, 78–80; Cattelan and, 175–76; on complicity of viewers, 114; decolonization and, 78–79, 110, 120; Duval-Carrié and, 124, 125, 148, 161–62; early years and

Ayón, Belkis (*continued*)
education, 81; exhibition access and, 107–10; feminism and, 114–16; gender and, 80, 85–88, 110–17; suicide of, 77–78, 244n97
Ayón, Belkis, works: *Arrepetida*, 96–97; *Huracán*, 97; *Intolerancia*, 118; *La cena*, 79–80, 81, *82*, 85–93, 102, 110–14, 117–18; *La familia*, 94–96, *95*, 118; *La Jungla*, 97; San Alejandro Academy of Fine Arts and, 104; *Siempre hay algo*, 118; *Tu amor me condena*, 118–19

Bacon, Charles, 198
Bagneris, Mia, 67
Bahamas, The, 31, 33; Burma Road Riots, 198; folktales, 71; National Art Gallery of The Bahamas, 214, 215; Prince Alfred's visit to, 198; tourism, 178, 182, *183*, 184–87. *See also* Antoni, Janine
Bahamas Association of Cultural Studies (BACUS), 58–59, 231n44
Bahktin, Mikhail, 156
Bandera, Quintín, 240n60
Barbados, 14, 212, 217
Barber, Karin, 114
Barbot, Clément, 145–46
Barthes, Roland, 181
Bass Museum (Miami Beach), 133, 161
Bastien, Rémy, 136, 141–42, 246–47n27
Bearden, Romare, 81
Beckles, Guy, 212
Beckles, Hilary, 9
Bedía Valdés, José, 80, 107–8
Beecroft, Vanessa, 168
Békés, 9, 224n14
Bellegarde-Smith, Patrick, 135, 138–39
Benítez-Rojo, Antonio, 25, 26, 79
Bennett, Jill, 153, 157
Benson, Devyn Spence, 106, 235n4
Best, Lloyd, 207
Bettelheim, Judith, 107
Beuys, Joseph, 50
Bey, April, 220, 221
Birch, Geoffrey, 185
Bissainthe, Toto, 14
Biswas, Sutapa, 57
Black Girl (Sembène), 77–78, 79, 234n2
Black Jacobins, The (James), 14, 137
Black Skin, White Masks (Fanon), 13, 44, 174
Blue Soap (Cozier), 208, 209, *211*
Bogle, Paul, 192, 195
Bonilla, Yarimar, 10, 225n33
Boukman, Dutty, 135–36
Bowerbank, Lewis Quier, 192, *194*, 195–96
Bowling, Frank, 29, 175
Branch, Winston, 215
Branson-Gill, Rosemary, 82, 86
Brathwaite, Kamau, 59, 190–92, 197, 217–18
Brecht, Bertolt, 62
Brey, Ricardo, 241n75, 242n82
Brown, David H., 82, 83, 86, 114, 240n57
Brunias, Agostino, 67–68
bulimia, 44–45, 50–51
Buskirk, Martha, 52, 53
Butcher, Joanne, 156
Butcher, Pablo, 149, 153–54, *155*, 159
Butcher, Ras Ishi, 215

Cabral, Francisco, 207, 212
Cabrera, Lydia, 106
Cahier d'un Retour au Pays Natal (Césaire), 6
Cameron, Dan, 45–46, 67, 75
Camnitzer, Luis, 115
Campos Pons, Magdalena, 2, 115, 116
capitalism, 4, 32, 46, 102, 118, 181
Caribbean Artist Movement, 14
Caribbean Biennial, 6th, 30, 34–35, 163–65, 168–69, 174–77, 292–94; advertisements for, *166–67*; catalogue, *172–73*; colonizing imagination and, 199, 202–4; tourism and, 177–88, 197
Caribbean Festival of the Arts (CARIFESTA), 13, 215–17
"Caribbean Man in Space and Time" (Brathwaite), 217–18
carnival, 46–47, 58, 96, 147, 156–59, 209, *213*

carnivalesque, 65, 118, 128, 154, 156–57, 159
Carson, Juli, 46
Castro, Fidel, 91–92, 97, 103, 230n31, 235n4
Castro, Raul, 116
Castro Díaz-Balart, Fidel, 91–92
Catholicism: Antoni and, 4, 66, 71; Cuba and, 83–84, 102; Haiti and, 102, 128, 140–42, 145
Cattelan, Maurizio, 5, 30, 34–36, 162–69, *170*, 174–81, 202–5, 219; *Choose Your Destination: How to Get a Museum-Paid Vacation*, 169; Guggenheim Museum retrospective, 227n70. *See also* Caribbean Biennial, 6th
Césaire, Aimé, 2–17, 163, 164, 216–20, 221–22; Antoni and, 33; on "Caribbean genius, a Caribbean style," 16; decolonizing vision of, 6–12, 21–25, 27, 30–31, 32, 34, 78, 110; divorce from Suzanne, 14; in Haiti, 8–9; on Lumumba, 224n30; Paris Colonial Exhibition (1931) and, 12; political career, 6–7, 197; resignation from French Communist Party, 13
Césaire, Aimé, works: *Cahier d'un Retour au Pays Natal*, 6; "Culture et colonisation," 13; *Discourse on Colonialism*, 23; *La Tragédie du Roi Christophe*, 7, 14; "The Man of Culture and His Responsibilities," 12, 13; *A Tempest*, 1–13, 15–16, 23–24, 59, 120, 217, 225n35; *Toussaint Louverture*, 6, 7; *Une Saison au Congo*, 7, 14
Césaire, Suzanne, 8, 11–14, 21, 23; death of, 14; divorce from Aimé, 14; *Youma, aurore de la liberté*, 11–12, 13, 102, 197
Chard, Chloe, 255n60
Charles, Normil, *139*
Chicago, Judy, 49, 55, 229n22
Christophe, Henri, 8, 12, 124, 137, 138, 141, 157
Clark, T. J., 206
Clarke, Austin, 215
Clarke, LeRoy, 215
Cleaver, Carole, 144
Cliff, Michelle, 75
Code Noir, 125, 157
collagraphy, 80–82, *92*, 95, 109, 110, 112
Color of the Sun (Strachan), 220
Columbus, Christopher, 126, 190, 202
Conner, Randy, 154
Connor, Maureen, 50–51
consumerism and consumption, 2, 17, 25, 45, 46, 66, 68
Conversation with a Shirt Jac (Cozier), 207–8
Cooper, Carolyn, 68–69, 232–33n72
Cosentino, Donald, 154
Courlander, Harold, 141–42, 245n8
Cox, John, 215
Cozier, Christopher, 5, 30, 207–16, 220; *Art and Nation: Things We Must Learn from Day 1*, 208, *210*; *Attack of the Sandwich Man*, 215; *Blue Soap*, 208, 209, *211*; *Conversation with a Shirt Jac*, 207–8; Cultural Autopsy Series, 207–8; "Searching for a Way Out," 207, 209, 212
creolization, 23–26, 34, 75, 82–83, 209, 214, 219
cross-dressing. *See* drag
Cuba: Abakuá, 34, 79–90, 93, 95–97, 103–13, 116, 119–20, 152; Association of Women Communicators (MAGIN), 115–16, 243n90; *blanqueamiento*, 103, 239–40n56; cabildo, 81–83, 86, 235n11; cabildos, 81–83, 86; Èfík Buton, 81–82, 235n12; Federation of Cuban Women (FMC), 116; Grupo Antillano, 105, 107–9, 239n45; Havana Biennial, 109–10, 164, 213, 215; Havana Cultural Congress (1968), 14; National Union of Writers and Artists of Cuba (UNEAC), 111; New Cuban Art, 80, 107–9, 115; Origen, 105, 107; San Alejandro Academy of Fine Arts, 104; Special Period, 78, 80, 116, 235n5, 235n8; Varadero Beach, 241n66; Volumen Uno, 80, 107–8, 241–42n75, 242n82. *See also* Alea, Tomás Gutiérrez; Ayón, Belkis
Cuban Institute of Cinematographic Art and Industry (ICAIC), 97, 106
Cuban Missile Crisis, 14, 79, 99

Cuban Revolution, 13, 34, 81, 99, 110
"Culture et colonisation" (Césaire), 13
Curaçao, 31, 216
Curry, Blue, 2, 198–201, 215, 216; *Repairwork*, 199, *200*, *201*

Dabydeen, David, 215
Dacres, Petrina, 189
Dalmas, Antoine, 135
Damas, Léon, 12
Danner, Mark, 121, 154
da Vinci, Leonardo, 110, *111*, 113
Davis, Angela, 105
Davis, Annalee, 215
Davis, Natalie Zemon, 99–100
Dayan, Colin, 135, 138, 153, 157, 158
De cierta manera (Gómez), 106
decolonization, 2–6, 163, 164, 205, 218–19; Antoni and, 40, 45–46, 52, 57, 58, 62, 78; Ayón and, 78–79, 110, 120; Césaire and, 6–12, 21–25, 27, 30–31, 32, 34, 78, 110; Duval-Carrié and, 34, 124–25, 161–62; feminist art histories and, 33, 40, 45–46, 52, 57, 58, 62, 78; monuments and, 35, 188–99; nature and, 206; rhizome theory and, 27, 28
de la Fuente, Alejandro, 107
Deleuze, Gilles, 25–26
Delva, Zacharie, 145
Democratic Republic of the Congo, 7, 99
Derrida, Jacques, 3, 42, 79, 133, 176
Descourtilz, Michel Étienne, 136–37
Dessalines, Jean-Jacques, 8, 12, 102–3, 124, 135–42, 144, 147, 157
Diawara, Manthia, 23
Diegue, Carlos, 98
Diop, Alioune, 13
Discourse on Colonialism (Césaire), 23
Dit-Cosaque, Gilles Elie, 221
Doig, Peter, 216
Dominique, Max, 128, 245n9
drag, 134, 154–57
Drouin, Louis, 146
Drysdale, William, 184–85
Dubois, Laurent, 135, 158
Duchamp, Marcel, 18, 50
Duval-Carrié, Edouard, 5, 30, 34, 120, 175, 207; decolonization and, 34, 124–25, 161–62; early years, 146; *Mardigras at Fort Dimanche*, *123*, 124–35, 147–48, 151–54, 158–61; *Milocan, ou la migration des esprits*, 142, *143*; post–Middle Passage imagery and, 148; postmodern baroque style of, 34, 125, 147; Vodoun and, 140, 151–54, 157–59, 161
Duvalier, François, 13, 126, 128, 135–36, 140–48, 154, 156–60; as Bawon Samedi, 128, 134, 141, 142, 158; death of, 249n54; *Gradual Elevation of Voodoo, 1944*, 140; "I have chosen him" iconography, 148, *149*, 159
Duvalier, Jean-Claude, 128, 134, 148–50, 153–54, 156, 158–60; deposition and exile of, 153, 249n54; "I have chosen him" iconography, 148, *149*, 159; marriage, 150
Duvalier, Marie-Denise, 128
Duvalier, Michèle Bennett, 128, 150
Duvalier, Nicole-Simone, 128
Duvalier, Simone, 128
Duvalierism, 126, 153–54, 159
Dyal, Susie, 207

Edmondson, Belinda, 59
Èfik people, 83–84, 90, 96
Ejagham (Efo) people, 83–86, 90, 111–12
Eke, Bright, 216
Elias, Charlotte, 216
Eliasson, Olafur, 168, *204*
Elso, Juan Francisco, 80, 107–8
emasculation, 64, 112
Emerald Beach Plantation and Hotel (Bahamas), 182, *183*, 184
Eshu, 115, 133, 134
Espín, Vilma, 116
Esson, Tomás, 91–92, *93*
Eureka (Antoni), 54
Euripides, 87
Eyre, Edward John, 195

Facey, Laura, 189
Family of Sir William Young, The (Zoffany), 130, *131*, 132

Fanon, Frantz, 13, 14, 59, 217; *Black Skin, White Masks*, 13, 44, 174; *Wretched of the Earth*, 14
Fatima, Cécile, 135
First International Conference of Black Writers and Artists, 13
First World Festival of the Arts, 14
Fisher, Jennifer, 62
Floyd, George, 197
Foucault, Michel, 174
Fourcand, Jacque, 145
Fourcand, Jean M., 134
Frazier, Susan, 54
Freud, Sigmund, 62, 64–65
Friedan, Betty, 72
Front Antillo-Guyanais, 14
Frost, Jackqueline, 10
futurism, 12–13

Garber, Marjorie, 156
Gauguin, Paul, 20, 96; *Annah the Javanese Woman*, 94, *95*; *Spirit of the Dead Watching*, 88, *90*, 112
gaze, the, 128–29, 179–81, 189, 192, 218
Geggus, David, 135
Gilroy, Paul, 60
Gingeras, Alison M., 165, 174
Girl Made of Butter, The (Antoni), 55, 70–72
Glissant, Édouard, 14, 23–27, 29, 33, 43–45, 54, 59, 60, 176
global Caribbean art history, 27–32
global Caribbean artist, definition of, 3
Gnaw (Antoni), 42, *43*, 50–55, 70, 74
Golden, Thelma, 45
Golub, Leon, 207
Gómez, Sara, 97, 106–8; *De cierta manera*, 106; *Mi aporte*, 116
González Mandri, Flora, 116–17
Good Hope Plantation (Jamaica), 184, *185*
Gordon, Douglas, 168
Gordon, George William, 192, 195–96
Gramsci, Antonio, 188, 192
Gregory, Joy, 117
Guattari, Félix, 25–26
Guevara, Che, 91, 92, 238n34
Guinea, 103, 136, 141

Haiti: Bois Caïman, 135–36, 150; Centre d'Art, 141; corvée, 141, 248n43; *deshoukaj* (uprooting), 153; destruction of black pigs, 150; Fort Dimanche, 126, *127*, 129, 145, 146, 245n5; Indigenist Movement, 140; Jeune Haiti (Young Haiti), 146; Le Centre d'Art, 216; Les Griots, 141; memory in, 152; National Palace, 134, 150, 161; Pope John Paul II's visit to, 150, 249n69; Rara performances, 67, 157, 159, 250n87; Selassie's visit to, 249n60; Tonton Macoutes, 126, 128, 144–45, 150; United States occupation of, 126, 140–41, 147; "Vespers of Jérémie," 146. *See also under* Duval-Carrié, Edouard; Duvalier, François; Duvalier, Jean-Claude; Vodoun
Haitian Revolution, 8, 102–3, 117–18, 125, 135–36, 150, 237n26
Haiti libre poster (Butcher), 149, 153–54, *155*, 159
Haley, Alex, 98–99
Hall, Marion. *See* Lady Saw
Hall, Stuart, 3, 65–66, 176, 203
Hall of Mirrors (Versailles), 125, 161
Hamilton, Ann, 50–51
Hardouin-Mansart, Jules, 125
Harris, Wilson, 34, 82, 139–40, 227–28n69
Hartman, Saidiya, 130
Havana Biennial, 109–10, 164, 213, 215
Havana Cultural Congress (1968), 14
Hearn, Lafcadio, 11–12
Hearne, John, 217
Heroes Park (Jamaica), 189
Herrera, Georgina, 115–16
Heureuse, Claire, 136
Himid, Lubaina, 57
Hodgett, Vicki, 54
Hoffmann, Jens, 35, 163–65, 168, 199
Holder, Geoffrey, 1, 4, 5, 17, 28, 29, 119
Huggan, Graham, 233n80
Hulme, Peter, 6, 16
Huracán (Ayón), 97

Hurricane Gilbert, 217
Hurricane Lenny, 205–6
Hurston, Zora Neale, 158

Ibarra, Mirtha, 99–100, 241n63
II Salón de Arte Contemporáneo, 109
Ingrown (Antoni), 54, *56*
International Congress of Black Artists and Writers, 13
Intolerancia (Ayón), 118
Iphigenia in Aulis (Euripides), 87

Jamaica: beauty and desire in, 68–69; statuary and national monuments in, 189–92, *193–94*, 195–97, 199; tourism, 182, *183*, *185*
James, C. L. R., 14, 34, 43–44, 53, 69, 137
James, William R., 182
John Paul II, Pope, 150, 249n69
Johnson, Paul, 142
Judd, Donald, 52
Junkanoo, 58, 231n41

Kafka, Franz, 118, 241n63
Kapur, Geeta, 46
Kartel, Vybz, 69
Kennedy, John F., 14, 144, 147
Kennedy, Robert F., 14
Kirshenblatt-Gimblett, Barbara, 177
Klein, Yves, 51, 58
Kwanju Biennial, 110

Lacan, Jacques, 177–80, 182, 184, 189
La cena (Ayón), 79–80, 81, *82*, 85–93, 102, 110–14, 117–18
Lacy, Suzanne, 62
Laderman Ukeles, Mierle, 37, 40, 42; *Maintenance Art*, 54; *Washing Tracks, Maintenance: Maintenance Art Activity III*, 37, 40, 74
Lady Saw (Marion Hall), 68–69, 233nn73–74, 233n79
La familia (Ayón), 94–96, *95*, 118
Laguerre, Michel S., 135, 140, 142
Lahr, John, 1, 28
Lajer-Burcharth, Ewa, 63–64
La Jungla (Ayón), 97
Lam, Wifredo, 29, 97, 104, 109, 115
Lambek, Michael, 151–53
Lamming, George, 14, 35, 119–20
Laracque, Yvan, 146
Las Meninas (Velázquez), 122, 124, 126, 128–30, 132–33
Latamie, Marc, 1–4, 5, 6, 13, 28–29, 189, 207; Americas Society exhibition, 17–23; Antoni and, 40; Ayón and, 80; *Caldera*, 17, *18*; Duval-Carrié and, 133, 161–62
La Tragédie du Roi Christophe (Césaire), 7, 14
Laughlin, Nicholas, 216
La última cena (Alea), 78–79, 97–102, 110, 117–18
Lee, Sandra, 69
Lefevre Tavárez, Jorge E., 10
Leonard, Sean, 216
Lett, James, 188
Lick and Lather (Antoni), 47–48, *51*, 63–65, 230n35
Linebaugh, Peter, 4
Linke, Armin, 168
Liu, Jenny, 169, 174
Long, Richard J., 248n44
López, Rigoberto, 247n30
Lott, Eric, 92
Louis XIV, 125
Louverture, Toussaint, 8, 12, 124, 136, 137, 138, 147
Lovelace, Earl, 215
Loving Care (Antoni), *38–39*, 40, 42, 44–47, 51, 54, 55–56, 58, 74
Lumina Sophie (Marie-Philomena Roptus), 3, 20–22, 189
Lumumba, Patrice, 12, 14

Magloire, Paul, 156
Makandal, François, 135–36, 246n20
Makeba, Miriam, 105
Maldoror, Sarah, 14
Malevich, Kazimir, 71
"Man of Culture and His Responsibilities, The" (Césaire), 12, 13

March on Washington, 14
Mardigras at Fort Dimanche (Duval-Carrié), *123*, 124–135, 147–48, 151–54, 158–61
Marinetti, Filippo, 243n84
Marrero, Norberto, 110
Martí, Jose, 118
Martinez Furé, Rogelio, 105
Martinique, 8–9, 14, 17, 22, 197, 225–26n45
Marxism, 7, 8, 80, 102–4, 113, 115
Masters of the Dew (Roumain), 100
Mateo, David, 115
McAlister, Elizabeth, 157, 158
McCarthy Brown, Karen, 152
McClintock, Anne, 65–66, 232n65
McNish, Althea, 29
Melancholia (Dürer), 88, 112
Menendez, Juan Carlos, 110
Mercer, Kobena, 60
metapicture, 126, 129–30, 132–33, 135, 153, 159
Middle Passage, 23, 82–83, 85, 95, 148, 151–53
Mignolo, Walter, 23, 206, 217
Mi homenaje al Che (Esson), 91–92, *93*
Miller, Ivor L., 82, 236n16
Minimalism, 44, 45, 51, 52–53, 57
Minow, Martha, 161
Minshall, Peter, 46, 209, 212–13, 215
Mintz, Sidney, 134–35, 151
Mitchell, W. J. T., 129, 184, 254n44
Mohammed, Patricia, 67
Moody, Ronald, 29, 191, *193*
Moor (Antoni), 72, 73, 74
Moreno Fraginals, Manuel R., 100, 102, 110, 118, 239n52
Mori, Mariko, 168
Morrison, Toni, 161
Mosquera, Gerardo, 109
multiculturalism, 28–29
Muñoz, José Esteban, 33, 74–75
Munroe, Kishan, 215
Murdoch, Adlai, 12–13, 224n31

Naan, Wendy, 207
Naipaul, V. S., 185, 254n53
Nefertiti, 130, *131*
Négritude, 10, 12, 140, 148
Nichols, Stephen, 65
nongovernmental organizations, 216
Numa, Marcel, 146

Ofili, Chris, 216
Organization of American States (OAS), 147
Orozco, Gabriel, 168
Other, 24, 26–27, 32, 58, 60, 65, 67, 75, 110, 174, 176, 179, 181, 185, 203

Pan-Africanism, 7, 10–11, 14
Paper Dance, The (Antoni), 73–74
Paravisini-Gebert, Lizabeth, 158
Paris Colonial Exhibition (1931), 12
Parti Progressiste Martiniquais, 13
passing, racial, 58–60, 66, 232n53
Patterson, Ebony G., 2
Pattullo, Polly, 165
Pérez Bravo, Marta María, 115
Pérez Sarduy, Pedro, 104
Peyton, Elizabeth, 169
Picasso, Pablo, 57, 207
Piper, Adrian, 62, 63
"play mas," 40, 154, 228n3
Pleasures of Exile, The (Lamming), 14, 35
Pollaco, John, 190
Pollock, Jackson, 51
Poupeye, Veerle, 212, 215
Prado Museum (Madrid), 124
Price-Mars, Jean, 140–41
prismatic forms and relationships, 3, 27, 31, 78–79, 118, 129, 227n63
problem spaces, 5, 26, 28, 30, 75, 78, 110, 163, 176, 206, 219
Prussian, Claire, 55, *56*
Puri, Shalini, 176–77
Pusey, Mavis, 29, 175

Rabbitt, Kara M., 11
racial passing, 58–60, 66, 232n53
Ramos Cruz, Guillermina, 104, 105, 108
Ramsay, Ras Akyem, 215
Rauschenberg, Robert, 18, 20

Rawson, William, 198
Redemption Song Emancipation Monument (Jamaica), 189
Rediker, Marcus, 4
Rehberger, Tobias, 169, *204*
Retamar, Roberto Fernández, 34, 119–20
rhizome theory, 25–26, 63, 66, 72, 74, 75, 176
Richards Marie Joseph, Myrtha, 20, *21*
Riggio, Milla C., 233n81
right to return, 124
Rist, Pipilotti, 169
River, The (Minshall), 46–47, 209, *213*
Robert, Jean, 145
Rodman, Selden, 144
Rogers, Paul, 206
Roptus, Marie-Philomena (Lumina Sophie), 3, 20–22, 189
Rosenberg, Alex and Carole, 237–38n27
Rot, Dieter, 50
Roumain, Jacques, 100
Rubenstein, Sanford A., 133
Rush, Chris, 54

Saar, Alison, 117
Said, Edward, 58
Santería, 80, 107
Sarusky, Jaime, 93–94, 106
Schapiro, Miriam, 49, 55
Schiff, Robin, 54
Schmid, Heino, 216
Schor, Mira, 48–52, 62, 230n30
Schroeder, Paul, 98
Scott, David, 4–5, 26, 41, 212, 218
Scott, James C., 189
Sembène, Ousmane, 77–78, 234n2
Semmel, Joan, 207
Senghor, Léopold, 12
Sese Seko, Mobutu, 99
sex tourism, 254n50
sexuality, 115, 153–54, 184
Seyrig, Henry, 8, 16
Sharpe, Samuel, 190–91
Shaw, Irénée, 205, 207
Sheller, Mimi, 165
Siempre hay algo (Ayón), 118
Sikán, 82, 85–89, 94–96, 106–7, 111–13, 117–20
Simpson, Lorna, 117
situational aesthetics, 21, 164, 225n42
Slumber (Antoni), 73
Small Axe (journal), 212–13
Sosa, Enrique, 106
Spivak, Gayatri, 177, 185, 189
statuary and public monuments, 188–99
Stein, Gertrude, 70
Stella, Frank, 52
Stewart, Susan, 187–88
St. Kitts, 35, 162, 168, 174–75, 178, 203, *204*, 205
Stollmeyer, Hugh, 212
Stollmeyer, John, 207
Stout, Renée, 117
Strachan, Ian, 165, 182
Strachan, Tavares, 220–21
Sugarmill, The (Moreno Fraginals), 100, 102, 110, 118

Tawadros, Gilane, 57
Tempest, A (Césaire), 1–13, 15–16, 23–24, 59, 120, 217, 225n35
Tempest, The (Shakespeare), 1–3, 5–6, 10–11, 14–15, 22, 206, 217, 223n3
Tender Buttons (Antoni), 70, *71*
Thompson, Krista, 165
Thompson, Robert Farris, 82, 111–12, 159–60, 236n17
Tiravanija, Rirkrit, 169
Tobin, Beth Fowkes, 67, 132, 246n15
Touch (Antoni), 72, 219–20, *221*, 233–34n82
Touré, Ahmed Sékou, 103
tourism, 177–88; sex tourism, 254n50
Toussaint Louverture (Césaire), 6, 7
trickster figures, 70, 233n81
Trinidad, 14, 31; Alice Yard, 216; Big River Workshop, 212; Caribbean Contemporary Art Space 7 (CCA7), 212, 216; Granderson Labs, 216; *The River* (Minshall), 46–47, 209, *213*

Trouillot, Michel-Rolph, 134–35, 151
Tu amor me condena (Ayón), 118–19
Tunnard, Christopher, 190

Une Saison au Congo (Césaire), 7, 14

Vastey, Baron de, 137
Velázquez, Diego, 122, 124, 126, 128–30, 132–33
Venice Biennale, 41, 47, 64, 78
Vergès, Françoise, 6, 7, 9
Vives, Cristina, 109
Vodoun, 80, 82–83, 124, 134–36, 138–48, 151–59; Abakuá and, 82, 83; Bawon Samedi, 128, 134, 142, 146, 156, 158; Dessalines and, 138–40; Duval-Carrié and, 124, 134, 135, 140, 151–54, 157–59, 161; Ogun, 124, 136, 154, 159; Pétro, 136, 246–47n27

Walcott, Derek, 175, 215
Wallace, Alan, 215
Wean (Antoni), 54, *55*
Webster, Mary, 245–46n13
Weltsch, Robin, 54
West Indian Federation, 13, 14
Wilder, Gary, 10, 16
Wilding, Faith, 54
Williams, Aubrey, 29, 175
Williams, Eric, 226n56
Wood, Yolanda, 96–97
Woolf, Virginia, 71
World War II, 13, 178, 182
Wretched of the Earth (Fanon), 14
Wynter, Sylvia, 25

Yancy, George, 174, 175, 181
Yoruba people and religion, 16, 115, 191
Youma: The Story of a West Indian Slave (Hearn), 11–12

Zétwal (Dit-Cosaque), 221
Zoffany, Johann, 130, *131*
zombification, 157–59, 253n28
Zonbi, Jean, 157–58